DATE DUE			

Dr. Ida

Books by Dorothy Clarke Wilson

THE BROTHER

THE HERDSMAN

PRINCE OF EGYPT

HOUSE OF EARTH

JEZEBEL

THE GIFTS

DR. IDA

Dr. Ida

The Story of Dr. Ida Scudder of Vellore

DOROTHY CLARKE WILSON

McGraw-Hill
Book Company, Inc.
New York
Toronto
London

DR. IDA

ACKNOWLEDGMENTS

The author wishes to make grateful acknowledgment to the following:

Dr. Ida B. Scudder, niece of Dr. Ida, without whose invaluable assistance, criticism, and inspiration this book could not have been written

Dr. M. Pauline Jeffery, author of *Dr. Ida: India* (Revell, 1939) and of *Dr. Ida S. Scudder of Vellore, India* (Jubilee Edition published in India, 1950), for permission to use these two previous biographies as source material

Mrs. John Scudder III for data gathered from her extensive research on the Scudder family

Mary Taber Sebastian for the details of her own life story

Dr. Ebenezer Gnanamuthu Thomas, Dr. Kamala Vythilingam, Dr. Miriam Manuel, Dr. Helen Ebenezer, Dr. Aely Koruthu John, and others, for details of the early years of the Medical School

Mrs. Reeve H. Betts and the Publicity Department of the Vellore Christian Medical College and Hospital for source materials, maps, and pictures

Mrs. V. T. Rangaswamy Iyengar for permission to include intimate details of family associations with Dr. Ida

Innumerable relatives, friends, and colleagues of Dr. Ida, including the following, for details, anecdotes, and personal recollections: Miss Treva Marshall, Dr. Carol Jameson, Miss Vera Pitman, R. N., Mrs. Lavina Honegger, Mrs. Cornelius, Mr. Arulappam, Mr. Kanakaroyan, Miss Charlotte Wyckoff, Dr. Hilda Lazarus, Dr. and Mrs. John Piet, Dr. and Mrs. John Carman, Dr. Joy Paul, Drs. Edward and Edna Gault, Dr. D. L. Graham, Dr. M. D. Graham, Mrs. Marie Buck, Dr. Reeve H. Betts, Dr. Ruth Myers, Dr. Bernadine Siebers DeValois, Miss Marjorie Van Vrancken, Dr. Blaise Levai, Dr. Rose Chacko, Dr. Kutumbiah, Dr. Florence Nichols, Dr. Paul Brand, Dr. Roy Ebenezer, Mrs. Helen Scudder Bouchier, Mrs. Kathleen Scudder Reed, Miss Alice Van Doren

1

In the heart of a teeming city in South India there is a gate. A Gate Beautiful it might be called, conceived in a flowing pattern of lotus leaves and opening buds and wrought in silvered iron. From dawn to dark it is never closed and seldom empty. Each day at least a thousand persons pass through its portals, a cross section of four hundred million people.

Finding a place on the crowded bench just inside the gate, I watched them come and go. Young Indian doctors in crisp uniforms, moving with the same brisk efficiency as their counterparts in Johns Hopkins or the Mayo Clinic. Patriarchs in long skirts and flowing shirts topped by skullcap or fez or turban. Holy men with Vishnu's trident or the three bars of Shiva scored in sandalwood paste on their foreheads. Student nurses in blue-and-white saris. Officials looking equally impressive in Western suit or Gandhi cap and *vaishti*. Villagers wearing only a strip of cloth about head and loins, yet possessing the peculiar dignity that is endowed by centuries of burden bearing. Women with smooth braids and silken saris, glowing with the excitement of a newly discovered independence. Women still peering timidly from the ancient folds of purdah veils. Women with patient eyes and hard bare feet. Children clean and dirty, dressed and undressed, laughing, whimpering, crying, faces bright with health and pinched with misery.

A car drove up to the gate, and an old woman, leaning heavily on a cane, moved awkwardly out of it. Her face was crinkled with lines and her shoulders were stooped, but her eyes were a clear bright blue, and the mass of soft white hair above them was still faintly aglow with its youthful sheen of gold.

Instantly a dozen hands were outstretched to help her.

"Thank you, thank you." She smiled gratefully even while muttering rebelliously, "Oh, dear, terrible having to be helped like this. How I hate it!"

As she moved through the crowded waiting room of the out-patient dispensary and on into the corridors of the great and busy hospital, crouching figures straightened. Sad eyes brightened. Hands sprang palm to palm in the graceful welcoming gesture of *namaskar*. Lips tensed with pain or futility or impersonal detachment burst into smiles. Unnoticed, a brown hand reached out to touch the hem of her blue-sprigged cotton dress. To her dismay a villager in dingy white *vaishti* sank to his knees, eyes aglow with unmistakable worship, and prostrated himself full length at her feet.

India has a word for it, the sudden radiance of well-being elicited by the appearance of such a woman: *darshan*, the blessing or benediction imparted by the mere sight or physical presence of a mahatma, great soul.

Pausing for a moment on one of the long high open corridors, she and I looked out over the hospital area: courtyards, sprawling wings, crowded verandahs, a vast network of veins and arteries pulsing with ceaseless activity. As far as the eye could see, buildings mounted tier on tier, with more in process of erection, their pulse beats already set in rhythm to the pound of hammers. Where once there had been two stories, now there were three or four. Gardens and courtyards had been buried beneath new wards and laboratories, verandahs and halls compressed into doctors' cubicles and waiting rooms. Only the white dome of the chapel remained as it had been in the beginning, the heart through which all the energy of this vast organism was poured.

But its vigor was not contained within the walls of a hospital compound. A mile from where we stood, beyond crowded streets and bazaars, was a modest red-brick building, now an eye hospital, that was the core from which all these multiplying cells had sprung. Four miles to the south was the green valley housing a great medical college, a rural hospital, a leprosy rehabilitation unit, a mental health center. On and outward flowed the healing energy into a fifty-mile radius of towns and villages where some two hundred thousand persons were ministered to each year in branch hospitals, roadside dispensaries, rural health centers, eye camps, research sanatoria; on and on, to where a thousand graduate doctors, surgeons, nurses, pharmacists, midwives, public health workers were bringing new life to the farthest extremities of this huge subcontinent.

And it was this smiling white-haired woman who had created this greatest medical center in all Asia, supported by forty Protestant denominations in more than ten different countries. Of her remarkable family, forty-two members of which through four generations had given a sum total of nearly eleven hundred years to missionary service in India, she by reason of her achievement was the most remarkable of them all.

I looked at her in wonder. "Don't you feel a great satisfaction," I asked, "seeing all this and remembering how it started?"

"Oh, yes, yes," she replied fervently. "God has been very good to me."

The wonder sharpened. What? Only this to sum up one of the most extraordinary successes of the century? *God has been very good to me.* No pride, only gratitude.

She reached for my arm with one hand, for her cane with the other. "What are we doing, standing here? Don't we still have places to go, things to do?" The voice was animated. "Come, let's hurry!"

And suddenly I too was excited. For I knew that this quest, which had brought me halfway around the world, was no routine assignment. It was high adventure, a journey of discovery past the frontiers of a great soul.

This is the story of the old woman with the blue eyes and gold-white hair, whose very presence means *darshan*—blessing, benediction—to countless thousands in this land of a fast-awakening people.

3

2

Again the train jerked and ground and grated to a stop. And again there was no escape from the world outside. Even though she shut her eyes tight, she could feel the swirls of red dust sifting through her lashes, heat waves quivering against her forehead.

"Look, Idee!" In his eagerness to see, her brother Harry was leaning halfway out the window. "We've left all of the West behind us. Here's the real India. We're home again, where we started. See those wonderful long white skirts and pink turbans? Hear those peddlers jabbering Tamil? I say, doesn't it all look and sound familiar?"

The girl mumbled something in reply. Familiar? Yes, like the sights and sounds of a nightmare from some far distant past! Only it was no longer past, it was present. And it was not really a dream, it was reality. She was no longer Little Missy, a frightened child of eight. She was *Miss* Ida Scudder, a young woman of nearly twenty, newly graduated from a young ladies' seminary in Northfield, Massachusetts. It was not 1878. It was September 20, 1890, and a few weeks ago she had sailed from New York with her brother Harry on a steamship called *The City of Berlin*. A few hours ago they had landed in Madras.

4

Father had met them at the dock, and was now sitting here in the train on the long hard green seat facing hers.

To her dismay he looked no more familiar now than when she had first seen him at the dock. He was much too tall and thin, and the long black beard which she had braided, sitting on his lap as a child, was almost white. Only the bright dark eyes, deep-set beneath bushy brows and framed by the square steel rims of his spectacles, were just as she remembered them.

Those eyes twinkled at her now. "My little maid," he exclaimed, "actually turned into a lady! And such a beautiful one! I'd forgotten her eyes were so blue and her hair such a lovely gold." His voice turned wistful. "How your mother and I have missed your growing up! Eight years, my dear! Such a long, long time!"

Ida turned away her face, confused by a sudden flood of resentment. Whose fault was it that they had missed her growing up? Had she wanted to be left with her mother and brothers on the Nebraska farm eight years ago when he had chosen to return to his missionary post in India? Or with her Uncle Henry in Chicago that night two years later when her mother left her?

The memory of that night could still bring a stabbing pain. The rain outside had been as wild as her own fourteen-year-old helpless grief. She had not even been allowed to go to the station to see her mother off for India. When her clinging arms had been finally, regretfully, unloosed, she had rushed upstairs and sobbed all night into her mother's empty pillow. Uncle Henry had been kind, Aunt Fanny well-meaning. But they had not understood. They had thought her rebellious for shutting herself into her room and refusing to eat; punished her for throwing a plate of good food out the window. With the passing weeks and months the aching loneliness had never ceased, merely subsided.

"Indian people can't understand how I could come to India and leave six children behind in America," her mother had written once. "They would not do it. And *I don't think I could again.*"

It was her father, this strange man sitting opposite, who had separated their family. All these years, Ida realized suddenly, she had been blaming him.

Proudly Harry exhibited a bunch of stunted bananas. "Look! I made the fellow understand my Tamil! *Varaiparam*—plantains! *Arru*—six! And four annas for the bunch. Not bad, what, after twelve years?"

His father laughed. "Your Tamil is better than your bargain, son. They're worth about two." But he looked pleased. "You should feel at home here, both of you. It's your country, where you were born and lived much of your childhood."

Ida compressed her lips. Her country? She was here, yes, and must stay for a while. Her mother was ill and needed her. But—her country! Never. America was her country, with its clean air and uncluttered streets and comfortable houses. Not this—this inferno! Again the world outside the tiny train compartment thrust itself against her senses, its heat choking her throat, its sharp colors burning her eyes. She was suddenly conscious of the station platform, with its raucous vendors, its bustling errand boys, its half-naked idlers, its coolies with their mountainous burdens, its beggars.

One of them was standing now outside her window.

"Ammal, ammal! Pasi, pasi!"

Pasi! It was the sound she had been dreading. Though most of her Tamil had long since been forgotten, she could never forget that word. *Pasi* . . . hungry! She was back in the nightmare again, a child of seven or eight. The hands thrust insistently toward her window were a hundred hands, all belonging to children like herself and all outstretched like tiny claws. She was breaking bread into little pieces and putting them into the hands, except sometimes when the hands were too weak to be lifted and she had to thrust the bread into a small mouth. All around her, as far as she could see, there were the tiny claws, and no matter how small she broke it or how fast she hurried, there was never enough bread in her basket to fill them! *"Pasi . . . pasi. . . ."*

"What's the matter, Idee?" Harry paused in his consumption of a banana to regard her with concern. "You look sick."

She stared at him: the red crew cut and lean features above the high wing collar. Was it possible that he had forgotten, that the beggar and the word *pasi* and the strange world outside aroused in him only pleasant memories?

6

Harry had been part of the nightmare. A famine, people had called it, the Great Famine of 1875. Later she had read accounts of it. One of them, written by her father, had been full of statistics. To her young eyes the zeros had looked like rows of round empty mouths.

"The famine affected Madras and other sections of South India for nearly three years. The total area affected was 257,000 square miles and the population 58,500,000. Mortality due to this famine was said to be 5,250,000."

Dr. John and his wife were asked to distribute money and supplies. Cartloads of rice and clothing were sent from Madras nearly a hundred miles away. A relief camp was opened at his mission station in Vellore, and on the first day he and the regiment doctor examined and admitted over 1,200 people.

"Daily great crowds came to us for help," her father's account went on. "My wife took charge of feeding and clothing the starving children. In our compound at Vellore enclosures were constructed of bamboo into which the children were herded and made to sit in rows while being fed with porridge, milk, and bread. In the dispensing of food my own children helped. . . ."

No need to recall more words. For here words had suddenly become people. Herself, Ida, and her five older brothers, John and Lew and Harry and Charlie and Walt.

Remember, Harry, how we used to watch them to keep them from hiding their conjee and bread in their rags, to take to their parents? How when the doors were opened and the children let out, their starving mothers and fathers would pounce on them to see if they had brought them any food?

"It's the heat, Younker." Using his old pet name for her, Harry interrupted her disturbed thoughts. "You'll get used to it. But meanwhile, if you'll pardon my saying so, you look like one perfect fright!"

The nightmare was shattered. Seizing one of the three remaining overripe bananas, Ida flung it vigorously at the crew cut. Harry dodged just in time, and the missile went whizzing out the opposite window, where it was pounced on and battled over by two half-naked urchins.

Dr. John Scudder tipped back his head and laughed until

the tears ran down his tanned cheeks and disappeared in his curling gray beard. "Now," he exclaimed delightedly, "I know I have my children back again."

Unclasping her new patent-leather handbag, Ida burrowed into it, past the long silk gloves and steamer ticket, the pink ribbon from the bouquet of roses sent to the pier by her Northfield classmates, and the copy of "Daily Strength for Daily Needs" with its flyleaf inscription: "To dear Ida, with love from Auntie. July 30th, '90. *The City of Berlin*" ... and pulled out a tiny mirror. Looking into it, she gasped in dismay. Smooth cheeks and high forehead were streaked with sweat and grime, red dust ground into every pore. And her hair looked as if it had had a henna rinse!

She looked down at her dress. The beautiful blue muslin, which she and Aunt Anna had picked out in the New York store because it so exactly matched the color of her eyes, had turned a sickly purple in places, and its lovely puffed sleeves, wilted by the heat, looked like pricked balloons. Oh, this horrible country, with its heat, dust, noise, and smells! She was ready to cry, until the idea of sticking a pin into the balloons of her sleeves and deflating them with a bang made her giggle instead of crying.

After that her spirits mounted. Suppose she did hate this country and everything about it. She would not be here long, only until her mother was restored to health and she could return, her conscience clear, to pursue the future she had planned, going to college, preparing for a career just in case romance failed to put in an appearance (which didn't seem likely, the girls had scoffed, considering the way Mount Hermon boys had crowded around her at the interschool parties). Anyway, it would be life as she dreamed it, with fun and friends and beauty and wealth and adventure.

"Oh, you'll go to India, pussy willow, and be a missionary like all the rest of your precious Scudders," her best friend "Spook" had accused her tearfully the day her father's cable came. "We'll never see you again."

"I *will not!*" In her fury Ida had stamped her foot and glared about the circle of intimate friends gathered in her room at East Hall. Their faces had revealed sympathy, distress,

8

skepticism; all but little Annie Hancock's, shy and sensitive, which showed a sort of wistful envy.

"Don't you dare say I will," Ida had said fiercely, "because I won't. Never, never, *never!*"

It wasn't fair, everybody jumping to the conclusion that she was going to be another of "those missionary Scudders!" Even her mother and father were always taking it for granted in their letters. *I bought a little organ in New York. It will be here for you to use, Ida, when you come.... Do keep up your piano practice, darling. Music is such a help on the mission field....*

The night after the cable came she had lain awake and tossed, the words pounding against her consciousness.

"COME IMMEDIATELY. YOUR MOTHER ILL AND NEEDS YOU."

See her mother again? Joy unspeakable! But—*go to India to do it?* Heaven forbid! Wide-eyed, she had watched the gray dawn creep through the huge rectangle of her dormitory window, so long and high that the curtains had always looked like a frightened scrap of lace which had blown up to the top. And with daylight had come also the light of decision.

She would go to India. If necessary, she would even enlist as a short-term missionary to get there. She would stay until her mother was well, and she would be a good sport about it. And then— *she would come back home and live.*

Now, on the train riding through India, she became quite light-hearted, remembering that resolution. She even allowed herself to see the beauty outside the train window ... patchwork squares of rice fields embroidered in every shade of green from pale lime to dazzling emerald ... splashes of flaring oleanders and bougainvilleas ... palms so delicately fronded they made your throat ache ... once, limned against the somber undertones of a fresh-plowed field, the single lyric note of a crimson sari.

Resentment quite vanished, Ida regarded her father with a rush of tender emotion. She wanted suddenly to weep because of eight lost years and the deep lines in his thin face and the whiteness of his long, neatly trimmed beard. The memory of its silkiness brought an ache to her fingers.

Tindivanam! For five years it had been nothing but a name

9

in her parents' letters, a black pin point on a map of South India, some sixty miles south of Madras. Now suddenly it became clusters of tile roofs, palms and temple towers, a blare of voices, and a confusion of dark faces. Heart beating with a suffocating excitement, she stepped down into the throbbing heat and color of the station platform. Her mother—? No. In all the crowd there was not a familiar figure, not even a white face. Disappointment gave place to anxiety. Was her mother more ill than she had been given to believe? Was her father hiding—?

"Weren't expecting us so early," said Dr. John cheerfully, setting her fears at rest. "Even Souri isn't here with the pony. We'll have to take a bandy."

Ida was given her choice of the little two-wheeled bullock-drawn conveyances lined up outside the station, some gaily painted and decked with garlands, all looking like a miniature caravan of covered wagons. She finally chose the worst-looking of the lot, because she felt so sorry for the pathetic-looking animal that drew it.

"You and your tender heart!" groaned Harry, telescoping his long frame into the narrow space under the canopy of woven reed. "I suppose the poor *mardu*'s mournful eyes reminded you of your pet cow back in Nebraska."

"Well, as a matter of fact they did," confessed Ida meekly, wrinkling her fastidious nose at the dusty straw with its faded and ragged covering.

She regretted her choice even more when the bandy containing their baggage clattered past them at a smart clip. Their own conveyance seemed to crawl.

"*Juldi, juldi!*" Almost without volition the word sprang from her limited Indian vocabulary, gleaned from common Scudder household phrases.

"That isn't Tamil," teased Harry. "It's Hindi."

"I don't care what it is," she retorted. "I know it means *hurry!*"

"*Hinh! Hinh!*" The driver's shrill nasals, while encouraging, were as ineffective as his sharp proddings into the bullock's bony posterior.

"He'll never make that *mardu* hurry," chuckled Dr. John, "in Tamil or any other language."

"I don't wonder." Harry turned suddenly serious. that raw patch on his neck under the wooden crosspi voice became warm with fervor. "By Jiminy, what topic! 'Take my yoke upon you....' I never knew verse meant before. I vow that's the first sermon I shall pi⌣⌣⌣ in India!"

Ida refused to look at the animal. Her sympathies had caused enough trouble already. Besides, she could see more than she wanted to without turning her head. Seated on the back edge of the bandy, daintily shod feet resting on the sliver of metal step, she clutched the protecting iron bar and watched the half-strange, half-familiar tapestry of Indian life unfold behind the cart.

People! She had never seen so many. Walking, standing, leaning, riding, sitting, squatting, lying. And did they all have nothing better to do than to turn and stare at her? She stared back at them, fascinated, yet fearful of something, without knowing what. The clatter of wheels, the beating hoofs, the cawing crows, the faces, the sharp smells of incense and cow-dung smoke and spices, the throbbing of heat and noise and color.... Surely she had taken this ride before, along this same dusty road, or one just like it! If not, then why did she keep watching with such dread for something she was sure lay just around the edge of the arching hood? *What was she waiting for?*

And then suddenly she saw them, two tiny urchins so tired out that they had stretched themselves prone under a tree close to the road. This nightmare she did not simply remember. She relived it.

She was riding along a street in a bullock bandy much like this one. On one side of her was her mother, on the other her nurse, Mary Ayah, who had taken care of her ever since she could remember. She was wearing her best white starched muslin dress, because she had been to church. Her mother and Mary Ayah were wearing their best clothes, too, a dress of stiff gray poplin and a bright-red cotton sari.

Usually she hated riding in the bandy because it was so slow, and teased to be allowed to walk home from church with her brothers. But not today. She wanted it to be slow, because when she got home there would be the children with their outstretched claws of hands.

"*Ayoh!*" exclaimed Mary Ayah suddenly. "Look at those children!"

Always curious, Ida started up and leaned over the ayah's lap to see what she was pointing at. "Where? You mean those two lying at the side of the road? What makes them lie there, right in the hot sun?" Her voice quavered. "Why—why don't they move? What—"

"They're dead," replied Mary Ayah simply.

It had happened over a dozen years ago, but she could still see the starved little bodies, hear her mother's shocked rebuke to the ayah, feel the chill that had passed through her slowly, from her stomach to the tips of her fingers and toes. Her hands felt cold now on the iron bar, even with the afternoon sun hot upon them.

"*Hinh! Hinh!*"

With a screeching of the loose wheels, the cart grated slowly sideways and passed through a narrow gate.

"We're here!" shouted Dr. John exuberantly. "We're home!"

Ida swung about so sharply that the crown of her new blue hat bumped the curved wall of reed and knocked dust in her eyes. Rubbing them clean and peering through a small triangle between her father's shoulders and Harry's upreared knees, she glimpsed the billowing foliage of a huge tamarind tree, a whitewashed building with a steep thatched roof, and, standing between two square pillars of the porch, a figure. She was out of the cart in one bound, brushing past the plodding bullock, running up the drive.

"Marmee!" she cried. "Marmee!"

Just before reaching her she stopped, haste having become suddenly inappropriate. Six years are a long time, hard to bridge at a single bound. Now that the moment had come, she felt strange and shy. Her mother—this little frail dark-clothed figure with the lined face and graying hair? Her mother had always seemed so young, so strong! But there were the same bright blue eyes and curved bow of mouth, the same smooth wings of hair drawn back from the center part and looped neatly over the high, serene forehead—yes, even the same silver brooch with its three flowers and three long dangles which she had used to finger, sitting on her mother's lap in church!

With a little cry she sprang forward.

Then, with the familiar arms about her, all the bitter loneliness of the six long years was washed away in a healing flood of tears.

3

Ida's father, Dr. John II, though youngest of the seven Scudder brothers, was neither weak nor submissive. When in 1861 he returned to India to join the Arcot Mission founded by three of his brothers, some of the spirit of rebellion then activating his homeland came with him. Finding what he considered injustice on the mission field, he wrote a letter to the mission board of his denomination in bold and sharp protest of low mission salaries. Soundly censured by the board, he was about to resign when, all the other members of the mission threatening to resign with him, the board withdrew its censure and managed through a convenient donation to raise the salaries. However, the incident affected Dr. John's entire career. His reports to the board were terse and infrequent. He moved often, and by his own choice was given the hardest posts.

Tindivanam was no exception. A small town about a hundred miles down the east coast from Madras, not far from the French colony of Pondicherry, it was the southernmost post of the Arcot Mission and was centered in its poorest, most neglected area. Famine-ridden when the monsoons failed, which was often, riddled with cholera, malaria, plague, and other tropical

14

diseases, it offered boundless opportunity to a spirit dedicated to healing both the bodies and the souls of men.

Though on the main railroad line from Madras to Trivandrum, the town was scarcely more than a large village. Cuddalore, colonial headquarters of the South Arcot District, with its remains of Fort St. David and its British mansions overlooking the sea, was far more impressive; Gingee, twelve miles west, ancient stronghold of the Vijayanagar era, more picturesque. Tindivanam, Forest of Tamarinds, was little more than a long bazaar street with the railroad station at one end and the mission compound at the other, the latter's walls still struggling to keep out the tamarind thicket of which it had once been a part.

Its population, like that of most towns and villages of the area, was about 90 per cent Hindu, less than 10 per cent Mohammedan. Since the Moslems of South India were largely descendants of converts from Hinduism, with the same fundamental culture, normally there was little antagonism between the two communities. In Vellore, sixty miles to the northwest, where the Mohammedan minority was much larger, there had been occasional riots through the years, incited usually by some small gesture of defiance when religious emotions were running high. But the Hindus were a tolerant people, and there was little trouble. There were only four Christian families in the town, most of them servants on the mission compound.

Part of Dr. John's responsibility was a boarding school for nearly a hundred boys, about half of them Hindu, the other half Christians from surrounding villages where converts had been made. He was also pastor of the sturdy brick-and-tile church, which he had built with his usual zeal and optimism, large enough to accommodate several hundred. As a doctor he was called to visit many homes in the town. But much of his time was spent in touring a wide circuit of villages where Christian work had been established. It took him sixteen days to tour them all, including three Sundays. For it was in the villages, with their desperate poverty, their large communities of untouchables, that most converts had been made.

Christianity had little appeal for high-caste Hindus, especially Brahmins, who recognized in the doctrine of universal brotherhood a grave threat to their vested privileges. And Mohammedans, already worshipers of one God, found little in the new religion to commend it. Converts were made most often from the low castes or untouchables, who had everything to gain from the new doctrine and nothing to lose. It gave them not only release from fear and superstition, but new social status, education for their children, influential friends to plead their cause against injustice in the colonial courts. Converts from the high castes, on the other hand, were subjected to social ostracism, persecution, even threats to their lives from angry relatives.

This was a new bewildering world in which Ida found herself, its human details as contrasting as its huge piles of boulders rising in fantastic shapes from a land of table-top flatness. Soon after her arrival she sat at her desk in a room of the mission bungalow and tried to assemble some of the confusing details in her diary.

It was not really a diary at all, only a little red notebook which her Aunt Anna had given her last Christmas with the suggestion that she keep her accounts in better order. But the neat lined pages had invited warm confidences, not cold figures. So familiar did it look, lying on the desk in the circle of yellow lamplight, that she snatched it up and immediately began to write.

"September 22, 1890. Tindivanam. I have been in India now for two whole days. Our house—a vigorous black line through the words—*My parents' house is on a big mission compound near a school. It is made of sun-baked bricks plastered with mud, then whitewashed. It has three rooms in a row. You can't go from one to the other, but each has a door opening off the porch. My room*—*the room where I am sleeping is next to the living room with a low partition between. Its floor is of packed mud, with a layer of crumbled lime on top. The thatched roof is full of white ants, and every now and then drops down dust on your head. But we*—very firm black line—*My parents are going to move into a new bungalow soon. It's being built across the road, a real pukka house with two stories and*—"

No use. She could tell the little red book none of the things she was really feeling. With a burst of homesickness she snatched it up again and thumbed back through the pages to its beginning.

DIARY OF IDA SOPHIA SCUDDER

PRIVATE!!!

"Jan. 1, 1890. Poughkeepsie. A very poor day for the beginning of a new year, rainy and warm. In the evening I arrayed myself in my new green dress and started with Walter and two Taylor boys for a party. . . .

"Jan. 4. Tried to get my clothes looking nicely so I can look well on Monday but oh I am so blue over it, for all my things look so badly. Wish I had lots of money. . . .

"Jan. 6. Again at Northfield after a very enjoyable journey. At Hartford I met Spookie. Miss Ford was so nice, and I again want to try to like her. . . .

"Jan. 8. In chapel tonight during silent time we had a great time laughing and carrying on. All day Mittie and I have been eating lots of stuff and Spookie came in and we had coffee. My lessons are not well prepared.

"Jan. 9. Tonight Lottie and I were laughing during study hour when Miss Ford knocked on our door. Oh, me, I must be good again.

"Jan. 10. It's Miss Ford's birthday and I do so want to wish her happy returns but fear I shall not dare. Such a goose as I am.

"Jan. 11. This evening Spook, Annie, Bessie, Mittie and I were going to have a big time having cream, coffee and lobster but as we had prayer meeting in chapel ending the week of prayer we only had fifteen minutes and so couldn't have our fun.

Spook and I went into the attic and smoked cubebs and had a great time over them. Mittie and I had lots of fun in music but on reaching our room Mittie was taken with the pain in her liver and has suffered greatly ever since. She howled over the medicine as it was so very bitter. Much fun.

"Jan. 12. Oh, dear, dear I am so blue tonight, my endeavors so often fail. The girls seem to feel so differently toward me. . . .

"Jan. 13. Miss Ford went for me for whistling again. This morning in Spook's room we had lobster and coffee.

Received a letter from Father and Mother today and they both spoke of Mother's cough. So worried but am going to try to lay my burden on the Lord. . . .

"Jan. 18. Yesterday was an illustration of Longfellow's poem, 'My life is cold and dark and dreary,' but today I have resigned myself. This evening Annie Hancock, Lottie Smith and I went skating and I enjoyed it very much and feel encouraged.

"Jan. 25. Miss Ford called me into the office and talked to me about having coffee and cocoa and said that I had done wrong to take that oil stove and then ended by saying she had seen a great improvement since the first of the school year and that in overcoming some of these things I had strengthened my character.

"Jan. 29, 1890. Had a fine time this afternoon because Annie Hancock and I went sleigh riding with the Fishers' horse. We were to do an errand for him and went to what we supposed was a hotel and I jumped out and knocked at the door and an old woman came and I asked for Mrs. Fisher's bridle and she looked at me as if she thought I were crazy, and when I asked her if that was a hotel she gave me another look and told me that it was not. Therefore I started out again and after having a *good* fine sleigh ride we returned.

"Jan. 30. The Day of Prayer and I spent it in bed. Lottie and I got up and took our turn getting breakfast which was a tremendous one which consisted of coffee, cocoa, muffins, beans, oatmeal, and cream toast. Oh how we did have to work, I seldom see, and after we finished I came in here and "yeeped" for I was so tired. Miss Ford came in and was very nice and oh, how I wish she would like me.

"March 3. Over a month since I last took my pen to write, and much has happened. One day about the 20th of Feb. Edna Skinner and I got to laughing in chapel and oh how I was squelched by Miss Hall. She very kindly told me I had been a stumbling block to some and would still be if I did not do differently."

Ida sat staring at this last entry.

Could she really have written it—and not much more than six months ago? What a frightened, silly little egotist she had been! Was this girl whose words she read really herself? Ida the gay, the irrepressible, voted the most popular girl in her class! Ida the ringleader of pranks, whether an impromptu joy ride with the "borrowed" horse and carriage of the German professor from Mount Hermon or an excursion to the old cider mill near the cobbler's shop!

... *got to laughing in chapel and oh how I was squelched* ...

It sounded like the babbling of a child, and she was not a child any longer. Whatever she might find worth recording in the future, it would not belong in the little red book.

Drawing another black line under the word PRIVATE, making three in all, she closed the book with finality, and tucked it away under a box of childhood souvenirs in her bottom bureau drawer.

The following weeks were not easy. Partly to help her mother and partly as an expiation for the disappointment she must eventually cause her parents, Ida plunged into the activity of the mission compound with a zeal exceeded only by her determination that its duration should be as brief as possible.

Merely her daughter's presence was enough to bring fresh bloom to Sophia Scudder's pale cheeks. With her husband away on village tours much of the time and the only other Western inhabitant of the town an official whose visits were infrequent, Tindivanam had been for the last five years a lonely place.

"It's so good to have someone to *talk* to," she confessed gaily. "When I hadn't seen anybody for three months that I could really talk to in English, I used to talk so much that I had to spend the next three months repenting!"

Assuming many of her mother's duties as household manager and teacher, Ida found both to be full-time jobs. For the household consisted not only of their own family and servants but also of the school of nearly a hundred boys. She ordered food for the house, doled it out to the servants each morning from the storehouse at the rear of the bungalow, directed its cooking, issued money for supplies in the bazaar, saw that the rice for the schoolboys was purchased and administered, their

19

clothes kept in repair and sent each week to the *dhobi* (washerman), new ones occasionally issued.

Certain household tasks she liked, such as planning and helping to care for the shrubs and flower beds; she even found time for planting mango seedlings and bamboo in the cactus jungle across the road where the new house was being built. Others she approached grimly, like cleaning out the godown and battling the army of insects and rodents that populated the old thatched, unscreened bungalow. The coming of the monsoons in October brought not only leaking thatch but, after a few days, deep green mold on leather shoes, bags, and suitcases. Even the pans of water in which the legs of furniture were set became insufficient protection against insects.

But she had little time to worry about such minor problems. Besides helping her mother care for the boys' school and visiting with her in the zenanas, those high-walled inner apartments where Mohammedan and high-caste Hindu women lived in seclusion, Ida had complete charge of a Hindu Girls' School of sixty-eight pupils conducted in the village. Here, working with Mrs. Isaac, a capable Indian woman, she took great enjoyment in teaching gymnastics and far less in teaching English.

This work with little girls was of all her new activities the one she liked best; it absorbed all her best energy and enthusiasm. But there were bad moments, like the time a rival school was opened so close to hers that its motive of competition was obvious. It started one day with a great fanfare of drums and pink and yellow streamers and free sweets for pupils. Ida approached school the next day with trepidation, expecting her enrollment to be depleted by at least half, but to her surprise and delight only two or three were missing.

"Like better here," one smooth-haired, dusky little beauty told her shyly. "Like Missy's pretty hair and eyes."

The children were a source of constant delight with their long full skirts and tinkling anklets, their neat braids intertwined with jasmine or marigolds. On the day of prize distribution the skirts were even brighter, the flowers augmented by many jewels twinkling on small ears and wrists and noses. They looked like so many larger editions of the dolls her mother had dressed for the prizes.

"Watch out for yourself, Ida Scudder," she admonished herself severely. "Don't you dare get too fond of those little minxes! Remember, you're *not* going to be a missionary. Never, never, *never!*"

Most of the time she found little enough to tempt her. Playing the organ in her father's church across the compound was an unpleasant chore. Fond though she was of music, she still associated her own performances with the years in Chicago when Aunt Fanny had interrupted her monotonous piano practice with the tart comment, "What! Those awful noises again?"

Her one trip with her doctor-preacher father on his village circuit was a galling experience.

Uncle Jared and his daughter Dixie came from their mission station in Vellore, ten hours away by train, to accompany them on this special evangelistic mission. Ida's childhood fear of Uncle Jared, a stern unsmiling man, had been reinforced through the years by family gossip she had heard. Once, when her mother had asked Mrs. Jared why she didn't buy herself something she wanted very much, Uncle Jared's wife had answered her significantly: "My dear, we didn't all marry *John* Scudder."

But Dixie, six years her senior, had always been her idol. Dixie was small and dainty with soft hands and an infectious laugh, and remarkably beautiful features. It was rumored that she had had more proposals of marriage than any other foreign woman in South India. It was because Dixie was going on this trip that Ida had teased her father to let her try to fill her mother's place.

The day before the journey a servant was sent ahead with the pony and buggy, accompanied by a bullock cart containing supplies. After traveling sixteen hot, dusty miles by rail the next morning, Dr. John and his party met the conveyance and drove five miles along a shady road through banyan arches to a village, where tents had been pitched for them under a tamarind tree.

The camping might have been fun for Ida if she and Dixie had been given time to enjoy it. But each day there were trips into villages, hours of preaching, baptizing, catechizing, doctoring. Even Sunday was no day of rest. When church services were over at ten, the two men would tie up their beards, Jared his shorter one, John his longer one, and kneel on a sheet to operate, incising boils, extracting teeth, removing cataracts and tumors, setting fractures. And Uncle Jared insisted on having Dixie by his side every minute.

At night, heartsick with the misery and poverty she had seen, Ida would twist and shrug herself out of clinging dress and stays and petticoats, bathe with a meager *parnee* of water behind the thin reed shelter, and crawl onto the cot beside Dixie's to lie, weary but wakeful, listening to her cousin's peaceful breathing. In one village, close to the place for holding evening prayers, there was an immense cactus hedge infested with cobras, which had recently caused the death of seven people, and that night Ida lay tense, seeing in every lamp flicker a deadly gliding shape.

There were pleasant features about the expedition. In one village there was a feast under a shady tamarind, with long trench fires and steaming black pots from which mountains of white rice were piled on big plantain leaves, then drenched with savory curries, all to be washed down with cooling curds and scalding pepper water. But the feast was followed by a service three hours long in the sweltering little mud church, from which Dr. John, the preacher, emerged staggering with weariness and wet as a pail of water.

Ida was kept busy following her mother's instructions. The most important of her chores was helping at baptisms. Since the babies were always oiled with coconut oil, their slippery bodies were hard to hold. Fearful lest her husband would drop one in the process, Mrs. Scudder had made a white garment which could be slipped on each baptismal candidate before the service. It was Ida's duty to see that the transfer of the garment was properly effected.

But she found herself quite unable to take her mother's place. In every village she was confronted with dismayed faces, aggrieved questions.

"Where *dorai sani?*" "No Mrs. John?" "Then how name our babies?"

Ida exhausted her knowledge of Biblical nomenclature from

Adam to Peter, but her suggestions met with disapproving mumbles. Without Mrs. John decisions seemed impossible. One pastor insisted on naming his son Melchizedek.

Ida and Dixie managed one day to escape long enough to go walking along a country road. Finding a gorgeous oleander bush, they filled their arms with great sprays; then, in holiday mood, each fastened one of the deep-rose blossoms in the band of her topee. When they entered the tent, Uncle Jared frowned disapprovingly. "Take it off," he told his daughter with firm kindliness. "We're here to inspire holiness in these new Christians, not frivolity."

"Yes, Father," said Dixie meekly.

Furious, Ida suddenly lost her fear of Uncle Jared. Leaving the tent, she began pulling blossoms from her bouquet and sticking them in the band of her topee, more and more of them, until both rim and crown were barely visible. Then, jamming it on her head, she entered the tent defiantly. Dr. John looked up at her, lips twitching, but he said nothing. Uncle Jared stared, his face growing redder and redder until he looked ready to explode with anger. Instead, he leaned back his head and laughed till the tears came.

"That's what comes," he chuckled, "of having five sons and then one lone daughter. I don't envy you, my dear brother."

That night, lying on their cots side by side in the tent, Ida reared herself on her elbows and looked hard into Dixie's tranquil face.

"Do you really *like* doing what he says all the time?" she whispered. "Aren't there things you'd like to do all by yourself?"

There was a sudden flaring in the tranquil eyes. "Yes," breathed Dixie.

Ida's heart pounded. She had stumbled on a secret. Dixie, her childhood idol, was not happy. She too had dreams. Her head began buzzing with plans. Dixie should go back to America with her. Together they would make her cousin's dreams come true. With her beauty nothing was impossible. A rich husband, adventure, a career ...?

"What?" she pursued, amazed at her own boldness. "What

would you like to do, Dixie, more than anything in the world?"

The flaring subsided to a steady glow. "If I were free—" Dixie began in a tremulous whisper.

"Yes?" prompted Ida. "Please tell me."

"I—I'd like to go into one of these villages, the poorest and dirtiest I could find. And live there. In a tent, maybe, like this. Or in a mud-brick house, the way other villagers live. I'd work mostly with the women, teaching them how to be clean and how to sew and take good care of their children. And after I'd lived in one village a while, I'd move on to another and start over again. That's what I'd like to do, more than anything in the world."

Ida stared at her, speechless.

The real goal of their journey was a large town to the west where a great Hindu festival was taking place. As they drew nearer, the crowds increased. Progress became slower and slower. The buggy was caught in a churning flood of bullock bandies, handcarts, rickshas, bicycles, pedestrians. The air, already burdened with heat and the close co-mingling of animal and human life, grew heavier with odors of burning ghee and crushed flowers and incense. A noisy procession dragging the resplendent image of a god on a towering gilded cart passed so close that Ida caught the acrid smell of ash and sweat from the devotees' half-naked bodies.

Her excited curiosity changed to foreboding. There was something sinister in the sounds of the lumbering cart, the drums, the chanting voices. The huge solid wheels, centuries old, could so easily crush and grind any luckless stranger in their way!

In the center of town, in the very shadow of the stark stone hillock with its impressive temple, her father and uncle made their preparations. The rear of the bullock cart was turned into a bookstand, its wheel hub into an improvised pulpit. Uncle Jared was the first to mount it. He became a different person when he preached, benign, prophetic. One could understand why, when in the lean Civil War years the mission board had been unable to return him to India, his faithful converts had contributed nearly three hundred dollars to bring back their beloved "father in God," though their laborers' wages had averaged less than six cents a day.

A crowd soon gathered. But it was not like the usual crowds that drifted around their outdoor pulpits, curious, tolerant, as willing to be entertained by stories about a foreign God as by the wiles of a magician or snake charmer. These were pilgrims, fiercely intent on their salvation. Many had traveled hundreds of miles on foot, and since dawn had been wearily treading the seven-mile circuit of the sacred hill. The chanting of nearly a hundred thousand devotees, the wailing of conches, the whirling dances of frenzied devadasis had quickened their blood. Like the offerings of ghee and camphor slowly filling the huge copper cauldron in the temple court just above, their emotion was an ever-mounting fuel, ready at the touch of a spark to burst into flame.

From the first moment Ida sensed a murmuring undercurrent of hostility. Uneasily she watched a tightening knot of Shiva devotees, heads shaved, bodies smeared with red powders and sandalwood paste, mumbling together and moving closer to the edge of the circle.

"Govinda! Govinda!" one of them cried suddenly in a loud voice.

The invocation to the gods was the necessary spark. The murmuring swelled to a concerted chant.

"Govinda! Govinda! Govinda!"

Uncle Jared calmly kept on preaching. Dixie continued to pass serenely through the crowd, distributing tracts, talking to the women in her fluent Tamil, wiping small runny noses with her handkerchief, dispensing simple remedies for itching skins and sore eyes, while Ida leaned rigidly against the side of the cart, expecting any moment to feel the impact of a hostile mob.

The next hour was a nightmare. When Uncle Jared finished, her father took his place. The heckling continued, rose to louder and louder crescendos, but Dr. John appeared as unruffled as if he were preaching from his own safe pulpit in his fine new church in Tindivanam. Boldly and without interruption his resonant voice proclaimed the good news he had come to this place to deliver.

25

It was over at last, and they were in the tent outside of town, blessedly secluded except for the usual ring of onlookers, curiously but unobtrusively watching their every move. Humiliated by the day's happenings, Ida felt more conscious than usual of the prying eyes. She bathed, dressed, ate her supper in silence. But when evening prayers were over and the lamps lighted, she could keep silent no longer.

"Surely we don't have to stay here!" she exclaimed. "We don't belong, and they don't want us. Can't we go home the first thing in the morning?"

Uncle Jared looked at her. "What is your name, child?" he demanded sternly.

"You know what my name is," she answered. "Ida."

"Ida what?"

"Ida Scudder."

"And what does the name Scudder signify?"

Ida gave him a cool smile.

"The name Scudder," she replied glibly, "may be derived from the Latin word *scutari*, which means 'shield bearers,' or it may come from the Anglo-Saxon *'scudari,'* meaning 'to scud along before the wind.' In either case—"

"In either case," interrupted Uncle Jared bluntly, "it is not a name for cowards. The shield bearer does not wear his implement of defense on his back. He who scuds before the wind runs ahead of the obstacle, not away from it." He turned to his brother. "I assume the granddaughter of Dr. John Scudder the First has been told the story of her forebears."

"You assume correctly, brother," replied Dr. John II promptly. Though there was a twinkle in his eyes, his voice was sober. "But it would do no harm to tell her again."

"Then listen," ordered Uncle Jared sternly.

Ida listened. Uncle Jared had a way with words. Falling from his lips, shaped into images by his long fingers, they became people . . . the first Dr. John, her grandfather, a successful New York City physician, picking up a pamphlet in the drawing room of a wealthy patient back in 1819, reading about "The Claims of Six Hundred Millions," determining in spite of his father's horrified protests to offer himself as the first medical

26

missionary ever to go out from America to a foreign country.
... Harriet Scudder, his beautiful young wife, sailing cheerfully with her husband and two-year-old child on a six-month
voyage to faraway Ceylon, burying that child on a stopover in
Calcutta, bearing and burying two others within the next
eighteen months; then, as the years passed, not only working
dauntlessly beside her husband but raising ten more children,
eight sons and two daughters.

As her uncle talked, Ida saw them all afresh, those eight
sons of her grandfather. All but one of them (who had died
while a student in theological school) returned to India after
their education in America to follow in their father's footsteps
... Henry, William, Joseph, Ezekiel, Jared, Silas, John.

"Our father had no horse and carriage," Uncle Jared said.
"He went sometimes by palanquin, usually on foot. He traveled
constantly. On one tour he went to the Nilgiris and over them
and down into the Mysore forests on the other side. He had
narrow escapes from wild animals. He was taken sick with
jungle fever. Someone brought word to our mother, and she
felt she must go to him. She hired bearers with a tent and
provisions and, taking her small son, set off, traveling day and
night through the jungle. Her bearers ran off and left her.
Alone that night she heard the tread of wild elephants, the
growls of tigers drawing near, then receding. In the morning
the bearers returned, and she went on. She found our father
there in the forest and brought him back. Did you ever hear
that story, Ida Scudder?"

"Yes," Ida replied, gazing steadily up at her uncle.

He turned on her with fierce intensity. "And do you think
the sons of John Scudder—or his *granddaughters*—should turn
tail and run because a few hecklers take it into their heads to
shout, 'Govinda'?"

The tent was stiflingly hot. Ida felt all at once imprisoned.
Uttering an impatient exclamation, she jumped up and ran out
into the cooler dusk and drew long deep breaths. The sun had
set, but it was not yet fully dark. The sky edging the sharp,
stark outlines of the hills was a deep mauve. In the east appeared a faint glow, then a pale yellow arc changing swiftly

into a half sphere, finally budding into a huge blood-red disk.

Suddenly Ida caught her breath in delight. "What is it?" she wondered aloud, conscious of Dixie's presence beside her.

"*Kathihai Teepam*," replied the other softly. "The Festival of Lights."

The miracle for which tens of thousands of devout pilgrims had journeyed to this holy town was taking place. In the temple courtyard the huge copper cauldron, now brimful with the offerings of ghee and camphor which all day had been pouring into it, was in this first moment of darkness ignited by a torch lit from the sacred fire inside the holy place. At the same instant, as if kindled by the identical torch, light flashed on the hill above the temple, turning its stark outline into a blazing crown of fire. Far away though they were, the girls could hear clearly the mighty shouting of nearly a hundred thousand worshipers.

"They believe," whispered Dixie, "that the gods light the fire on the hilltop. That's why they come here, every year, on the full-moon day when Krithigai is the ascendant star. They think that just to see the light kindled means salvation."

Ida watched breathlessly as all about them on every horizon, like torches kindled one from the other, the surrounding hilltops burst into flame. She caught her cousin's hand and found it cold.

"It's—beautiful," she whispered.

Dixie shivered. "It's—terrifying!"

Ida felt suddenly as if she were encircled by a ring of fire. Yes, it *was* both beautiful and terrifying, like India itself. It was the pagan zeal of a shouted "Govinda! Govinda!" and the ominous rumble of cart wheels. It was karma, inexorably deciding a human fate. Yes, and it was the power of grandfathers, parents, uncles, cousins, all trying to force you into their mold!

She would not be forced into a mold. She was a Scudder, yes, but she would choose for herself what shield to bear and what winds to run before. And they would not be laden with the dusts and rains and fires of India!

4

Kathihai Teepam, the ceremony of fire lighting which the girls had witnessed, was only one of the colorful religious pageants continually being played against the ancient backdrop of South Indian Hinduism.

Feast days abounded. There was *Deepavali* in the fall, when hundreds of little clay lamps were lighted; *Holi* in the spring, royal festival of mischief and frivolity, when the exploits of Krishna were sung and even the most dignified indulged in the pastime of spraying colored water on one another. There was *Pongam,* celebrating the return of the sun after the unlucky days of Margali (December-January), with its lavish procession of gods and goddesses, its nights hideous with discord to drive out evil spirits, its huge mounds of cow-dung fuel cakes, each crowned with a pumpkin flower, its collection of old clay pots, brooms, and baskets, followed by a mighty smashing and burning, with new pots and clothes for every household. And there were a dozen others.

Yet the purpose of such festivals, at least in their origins, was neither praise nor thanksgiving, but the propitiation of angry deities. Their roots burrowed deep into many prehistoric cultures.

For Hinduism, oldest of the world's living religions, included within its tolerant framework not only the pure nature worship of the Vedas, brought into India by Aryan conquerors, and the intricate systems of philosophy developed through subsequent centuries, but also the religious beliefs and customs of the Dravidian peoples who had occupied the country before the Aryan invasion. The Tamil-speaking Hindus of South India were Dravidian in origin, and, while an educated minority understood and followed some school of philosophy, the unlettered majority of village people still clung to the old concepts indigenous to the area.

They subscribed to the great tenets of Hinduism, yes: to karma, the inexorable justice by which a man's action in one life determines his fate in the next; dharma, the obligation of every man to follow the prescribed rules, customs, and traditions of his caste; transmigration. They worshiped the great trinity, Brahma the creator, Vishnu the preserver, Shiva the destroyer. But far closer to their daily experience were the old Dravidian goddesses, the *grama-devatas,* or village deities, responsible for such individual and collective misfortunes as cholera, smallpox, fever, plague, cattle diseases, crop failures, childlessness, fires. While once in a lifetime a villager might journey to the huge temple at Madura or Conjeeveram, every day he paid homage at a little wayside niche, a small brick shrine, or merely a heap of stones in a small walled plot outside his village. Along the dusty roads he traveled were enclosures filled with huge clay horses on which Iyengar, the village watchman and its one male deity, might ride out around the village to protect it at night.

Hindu worship, like the Mohammedan's prayers five times each day, was an individual act, including the offering of ghee, boiled rice, fruit, sugar, incense, camphor, flowers, and spices; circuits of the shrines; incantations by a priest and prayers. While members of the Brahmin priestly caste presided over the main temples, the *pujaris,* or priests, of village shrines were often members of lower castes. These *pujaris,* most of them sincerely devout but a few undoubtedly charlatans, were men of extreme power, since to the Hindu, as to the ancient Hebrew, religion governed every fact and act of daily existence: weather, food, sickness, birth, death, the way one ate, washed, drank, cut his hair, greeted his neighbor, the very breath he drew.

Ida did not have to leave Tindivanam to see popular Hinduism in action. Not far from the compound was a shrine containing images of the seven Dravidian demon-goddesses, all aspects of the terrible and holy Kali, each the goddess of some dreaded disease or misfortune. Whenever she walked there in the evening, she saw them engulfed in offerings and garlands. Going to her school in the morning, she often saw the high-caste Hindus of the town—lawyers, teachers, officers, merchants—going with deep devotion, after their ritual bathing in one of the big square tanks, to the shrine of their favorite lesser god in the Hindu pantheon, Hanuman the monkey king, ancient servant of the great god Rama. And in the inner courtyards of Hindu houses in the town she had often seen the sacred tulsi plant on its pedestal facing the entrance to the "god room," where, before pictures and images of the family gods and goddesses, lights in brass or silver lampstands were kept perpetually burning.

She had a fair knowledge of both philosophic and popular Hinduism. She was bewildered by its philosophy, shocked by its superstition, intrigued by its color and pageantry. But in the short time she planned to remain in India, she wanted as little to do with it as possible. When a letter arrived from her friend Annie Hancock, asking eager questions, envying her the opportunity of bringing "light and truth to places of darkness and ignorance," Ida could hardly wait to let her know how she felt.

"Dear Annie," she wrote. "I am sitting in my room with your letter in front of me. It is late at night, and the compound is so quiet I can almost hear a *palli* (that's a lizard) darting up the wall to catch a bug. My father is working in his bedroom-study next door, and my mother, I hope, is asleep. She is much better and should be quite well by the time my short term is finished."

Ida glanced up sharply. She was always imagining things

here in India, whispers of ghostly footsteps, disembodied eyes peering at her out of the darkness. Resolutely she summoned a vision of Annie Hancock's eager, sensitive features.

"You say you wish you could be a missionary like me. *Don't say that!* I'm not a missionary and never will be. But you're not like me. You always were more—more spiritual, Annie darling. You might really like it here. I can see you going into the zenanas (women's quarters in Indian homes) and visiting the little wives and mothers. Some of them have to live all their lives within four walls, and they're so young, Annie, not near as old as you and I—"

Ida heard a discreet cough from the verandah outside. She was not alarmed. A cough was a substantial thing, with a human body behind it. People were always coming to the bungalow, at any hour of the day or night, to ask help of her father. Lifting the lamp by its long spiraled stem, she went to the door and opened it.

A young Indian stood there, tall and grave and dignified. Even if she had not recognized him as one of the town's leading Brahmins, she would have known he belonged to this highest priestly caste by his dress. Above the spotless white *vaishti* and beneath the finely pleated gold-bordered *angavasthram* over his shoulders she could see the three-stranded white thread that was the badge of the Hindu "twice born." The dark, clean-cut features beneath the neatly bound turban were tense with urgency.

"What is it?" asked Ida. "Can I do anything for you?"

So agitated was the young man that when he lifted his hands in a gesture of greeting she could see that they were trembling.

"Oh, yes, *ammal!*" The voice too, well modulated and speaking in cultured English, was unsteady. "I desperately need your help. My wife, a young girl of only fourteen, is dying in childbirth. The barber woman can do nothing for her and says she must die. And, *ammal,* she is such a lovely girl! I heard that you had come to India from America and thought you might help her."

"Oh!" exclaimed Ida in swift sympathy. "I'm so sorry. But it's my father you want, not I. He's the doctor. He's right next door in his study. Come, I'll take you to him."

About to lead the way, she found passage to the verandah blocked by a shape as unyielding as one of its square white posts. The anxious young husband had vanished. In his place stood a haughty and outraged Brahmin.

"What! Take a man into my house to care for my wife? No man other than those of her own family have ever looked upon her. You don't know what you say!"

"B-but," stammered Ida, "surely, to—to save her life—"

"It is better that she should die," returned the young man, "than that another man should look on her face."

Ida stared at him. "You—you can't mean that." But she could see that he did. She tried again. "I'll go with my father," she promised. "He'll tell me just what to do, and I'll do it. He wouldn't even have to touch her."

The young man turned without answering and started away.

"Wait!" cried Ida. "Don't go yet—please!" She had to find some way to stop him. "You—you said she was young and beautiful. And she's suffering, maybe even dying. You said so yourself. Don't you—don't you *care?*"

The young Brahmin turned. He made no reply, and in the ring of lamplight his fine features looked hard as a stone mask. But—he had turned. The flame of the lamp streaming, Ida ran along the L-shaped verandah and around the corner to her father's bedroom-study. Hastily, but in a whisper so as not to awaken her mother, she poured out the story, brought him back with her to where the young man was waiting, and together they reasoned with him. But it was no use.

"Then—you will not come, *ammal?*" His eyes looked out at her through the mask, tortured and, somehow, accusing.

She shook her head miserably. "It would do no good. I—I don't know anything. I'd be no better than—than the barber's wife."

Nor as good, she added to herself silently. For, crude and unsanitary though they might be, the barber woman, traditional midwife, had her instruments and her techniques. She had nothing.

She watched him turn away and go down the steps, into the darkness. "Why?" she demanded fiercely, turning to her father. *"Why?"*

He patted her shoulder. "Because," he said gently, "it's the rule, the custom. It would violate his caste law."

"Custom—law—" She choked on the words.

"Why, yes." His tone revealed some surprise. "Surely you've known about these things before, my child."

It was true. Since her return to India Ida had become well acquainted with the caste system, that ancient institution separating Hindus by reason of birth into rigid social groups. Though once an undoubted aid to economic security, insuring to every person some occupation, however menial, it had acquired grave evils through the centuries. The original four castes—priests, warriors, merchants, laborers—had been divided and subdivided ad infinitum, each group maintaining its own rigid exclusiveness. Then, below all the castes and subcastes, was the vast army of untouchables who, born to the so-called unclean occupations, like leather working, washing, sweeping, filth removal, were doomed to complete segregation.

Members of castes or even subcastes were forbidden by their own laws to intermarry, hold social intercourse, share food or water with those of lower groups. Especially was this true of the Brahmins, originally the priestly caste. And, while not directly responsible for the inferior position traditionally accorded to Hindu women, the caste system had contributed to its survival.

It was the women Ida had always pitied most, the Brahmins almost more than the untouchables. Visiting with her mother or a Bible woman in the zenanas, she had ached in sympathy for the sheltered wives and mothers and daughters, cringing into subservience behind their veils whenever a man of the household appeared, some of them never in a lifetime emerging from their courtyards except to change one set of high walls for another.

She had gone too with her father to more than one high-caste home, seen him take the pulse of a delicate female wrist thrust through a small hole in a curtain, heard him patiently diagnose and prescribe as best he could with nothing more to guide him than the fluttering of a pulse and the timid muffled answers to his insistent questions.

"Yes," she admitted to him now. "I—I suppose I have known. But—"

34

But always before, she understood suddenly, these had seemed quaint and at times amusing customs, not—*not matters of life and death.*

"Our friend," comforted her father, "is a deeply religious man. We must respect him for it."

"Respect!" She backed away from him, eyes flashing. "When he's letting her suffer, maybe die, a—a girl not much more than a child!"

"Perhaps," said Dr. John gently, "he's sacrificing more for his convictions than we are for ours. He looked to me as if he really loves his little wife. Go back to your room now, child, and forget it."

"Forget—"

"Yes. It's a lesson I learned long ago. If I hadn't, I couldn't have borne it to live in a country where there's so much suffering and despair. If there's nothing you can do to remedy a bad matter, it's the part of wisdom to forget it."

Ida went back to her room. She set the lamp down on the desk. Her father was right, of course. If there was nothing you could do, it was better to forget. The yellow light spread its warm comforting circle as she picked up her pen.

"...and they're so young, Annie, not near as old as you and I—"

She began writing furiously, telling Annie Hancock all the reasons she could think of for not wanting to live in India and not wanting to be a missionary. Her pen fairly flew over the pages.

When the sound of footsteps came again, she sprang up so quickly that the *palli,* poised motionless on the whitewashed wall above her desk, flashed away at lightning speed, not stopping until it reached the narrow shelf under the overhanging eaves of thatch.

Relief lent wings to her feet. The young Brahmin had changed his mind. He had come back for her father, and she would go with them. She had been foolish to feel upset. To save time, on her way to the door she snatched a light wrap from its hook, in case the night should turn cold. If the young man had brought no conveyance, she would run and waken a servant while her father was packing his bag, or, better yet, harness the pony herself.

"I thought you'd come back," she began eagerly, before the figure in the shadows had a chance to speak. "I was sure you really cared—"

She stopped abruptly. Even without the lamp she could tell it was not the young Brahmin. Even before he spoke.

"Salaam, Madam. May Allah give you peace. If you could help me—"

The voice was hesitant, diffident, the face a dark blur between the long tightly buttoned coat and the white brocaded cap.

"Of course," said Ida automatically. "What can I do for you, sir?"

"It's my wife," said the man gently. "She has had other children, but this time the little one does not come. There is no one to help her but an ignorant, untrained woman. I am afraid she is dying. Please forgive me for troubling you."

Ida could not believe her ears. It was just in stories that such coincidences occurred, not in real life. The man moved nearer the door, into the lamplight. She could see his features now, thin and anxious above a gray triangle of beard.

"I have heard there is a doctor here," he continued hesitantly, "one not long since come from America."

"Oh, yes!" Ida's dismay evaporated. God was being good. He was giving them a chance to make up for failing the little fourteen-year-old girl. If one must die, another should live. This man was a Moslem. He would be bound by no laws of caste. "Wait!" she told him impetuously, brushing past him and running along the verandah.

"Here's my father," she explained breathlessly, returning a moment later with Dr. John. "He's the doctor you're looking for. But if you like, I'll be glad to go with him and try to help."

"Madam,"—the voice was apologetic but firm—"you do not understand our ways. Only the men of her immediate family ever enter a Moslem woman's apartment. It is you, a woman, whose help I came seeking, not a man."

Ida stared at him incredulously.

"But I can't help you," she replied. "It's you who don't understand. I'm not even a nurse. I know nothing about midwifery, absolutely nothing. I'd be glad to help you if I could."

36

"Then my wife must die," returned the Moslem with stolid resignation. "It is the will of Allah."

The girl watched him go down the steps and along the path until his white coat was lost in the blur of dust which marked the curving driveway. She heard the faint click of the metal as he passed through the gate and closed it carefully behind him. Then, without even glancing at her father, she fled into her room and shut the door.

Going straight to her desk, she dipped her pen so vigorously that its point jabbed the glass bottom of the inkwell.

"You can see now, Annie, why you wouldn't like being a missionary, especially in India. You'd simply hate it, and I ought to know. Believe me, I'm going to get back home just as quickly as I possibly can. Why, the people here don't even want you to help them. They'd rather let their wives and children die, even if they're beautiful and they say they love them and some of them are no more than fourteen...."

No use trying to write when you got so angry and homesick that the tears kept dropping on your paper and blurring the ink! But she had to do something. Jumping up, she ran across the room to the almirah, opened its doors, and began taking down her dresses, shaking them out, laying them on the bed, until the closet space was empty. Then, wringing a cloth in the wash basin of her cement bathing cubicle, she wiped the closet vigorously from top to bottom, digging her nails into the corners. You couldn't be too careful about clothes in this country, especially if you wanted to keep them looking good for two years, until you could go back home and enjoy them again. She shook the dresses once more as she hung them up: the green silk she had worn to the New Year's party with the Taylor boys, her white graduation dress wrapped in an old sheet, the brown cashmere that was her favorite because her mother had chosen the cloth and made it for her away back when she was only fourteen....

Fourteen. Suddenly she swept up all the remaining dresses and bundled them into the almirah, then stood very still trying to remember what it was like to be fourteen. She had been fourteen when her mother left her, when she had rushed upstairs and cried all night into her pillow. Things hurt so ter-

ribly when you were only fourteen, and life seemed so un-
bearably sweet!

It was then that the third call came.

"*Ammal?*" a diffident voice murmured.

She moved mechanically toward the door, not daring to hope.
*But if it should be one of them, let it be the tall young Brahmin,
with the tortured eyes and the little wife who was just fourteen
and so very beautiful.* She lifted the lamp from the desk as she
passed.

It was neither the tall young Brahmin nor the grave Moslem.
She recognized this man as the father of one of her pupils in
the Hindu Girls' School, a respected member of the Mudaliar
caste. She had gone to his house one day with Mrs. Isaac to
visit his wife, a lovely young woman no older than herself with
a shy smile and big shining eyes.

"Kamla?" The child's name sprang to her lips in response to
the urgency in the man's face. "Is she sick? Has anything
happened?"

"*Illai*, no. Not Kamla, Missy *Ammal*." The man spoke in
stilted, halting English. "But I have trouble. Much trouble."
He lifted his hands palm to palm as his eyes implored her. "I
beg Missy, come to my house. I need much help."

Her eyes widened in horror. Her lips felt dry. "Not—not
your wife—"

"*Amma*, yes." He returned her look with wonder. "How did
Missy know? She is sick, much sick." Suddenly he was prostrating himself before her on the verandah floor, his hands
touching her feet. "I beg Missy *Ammal* to come. If she come
not, my wife dies."

"Please—don't kneel to me!" Ida drew back so swiftly that
the lamp flared.

"The Missy *Ammal* will come?"

"But—it would do no good for me to come!" She repeated
the words tonelessly. "I'm not a doctor. It's my father who is
the doctor. Let me call him. He will go with you. He's a very
good doctor. I'm sure he can do something for your wife. If—
if you'll just let him—"

She knew the answer even before he lifted himself to his
feet, revealing the outraged dignity, the bitterness of disap-

pointment. No need even to listen to his words of shocked protest. She had heard them all twice before. But she did listen. There was no way to help it without covering her ears. And she couldn't do that, with the stem of the lamp clutched tightly in one hand.

"The Missy *Ammal* will come?" he pleaded again finally.

"I'm sorry." She heard her own voice, thin and remote, as if coming from a long distance. "I'd go with you if it would do any good. But it wouldn't. Can't you understand?" The voice rose to a higher pitch, held suddenly a hint of hysteria. "There's nothing—*nothing at all*—that I could do!"

This time she did not tell her father. After the man had turned and gone away, she shut the door tightly and bolted it, set the lamp down on the desk. Then with swift motions, not once pausing to give herself time to think, she made ready for bed. Brushed her hair a hundred times with long fierce strokes. Entered the little bathing cubicle, checking automatically to make sure the open drains had not invited a stray snake or scorpion. Bathed. Pulled on her high-necked, long-sleeved, ruffled nightgown. Turned back the top sheet, lifting it high to make sure the tentlike space beneath was not occupied by an insect, caterpillar, or lizard. Blew out the lamp. Groped her way back to the bed and lay down upon it. But not to sleep.

"Forget," Dr. John had told her. "If there's nothing you can do to remedy a bad matter, it's the part of wisdom to forget it."

If there's nothing you can do. . . .

At first, as she lay tense and wakeful, nothing but darkness and silence. Then, slowly, the night became shape and scent and sound . . . the dim rectangle of a window, a sighing in the dusty thatch, the delicate fragrance of cork tree blossoms mingled with the faintly bitter tang of tamarinds. Somewhere in the distance a nightjar began his restless hawking.

Chuk-chuk-chuk-r-r-r! Chuk-chuk-chuk-r-r-r! Chuk-chuk-chuk-r-r-r!

Funny how often things seemed to come in threes, even the calls of birds! Temptations. The crowing of cocks. A voice speaking to a young boy as he lay wakeful, like this, on his bed. Samuel had known just what to do when he heard his name called three times. The priest Eli had told him. And he

39

had not only known just what to do. *He had wanted to do it.*

There had been only one Samuel lying on his bed, waiting, listening. But here there were two Idas, one tremulously aware, the other rebelling with every fiber of her taut body. As the night wore on they struggled, one with the other.

"It's nonsense! God doesn't speak to people in these days."

No? You have eyes to see things, haven't you, like children lying by the roadside? Ears to hear people coming to your door?

"But—it's not my fault if they're foolish enough to let their wives die! It's nothing to me!"

Isn't it? Women like yourself, loving life, one of them only fourteen—

"Stop! Didn't my father tell me it's better to forget a bad matter?"

If there is nothing you can do to remedy it.

"But there *is* nothing."

Nothing? With three women dying less than a mile away for want of a woman doctor? With millions more—

"No, no, I couldn't do that! Not if God himself were to ask me!"

Can't you understand, Ida Scudder? It's God himself who is asking.

When she heard a coppersmith bird begin his loud metallic "tuk . . . tuk" outside the window, she knew the night was over. Next came the crows, and, even before it began to get light, human sounds: creaking of cart wheels, the *"hinh, hinh"* of a bullock driver, the padding of bare feet, and the gentle sloshing of pails of water. Then, faint at first but growing steadily louder, the insistent beating of tom-toms.

Rising with sudden urgency, she slipped her feet into sandals, pulled a long wrapper over her nightgown, and, unbolting the door, stepped out on the verandah. The sound came from the left, where a road passed the compound beyond the thick clusters of tamarinds. Without hesitation she sped toward it.

Crouched behind the stone wall surrounding the compound, heart accelerating in pace with the insistent drumbeats, she watched the procession come. It was not an unusual sight, for

40

Hindu funeral corteges were always passing along this road on their way to the burning place beside the river. Yet she stared as if she had never seen one before. The white blur in front would be the drummers; the swath of green just behind, another group carrying plantain trees. Her eyes clung to the single bright focus of color, a cloth of crimson wound about the wicker bier. The groups following were blurs also, the chanting relatives and friends, the swaying, wailing women mourners. Nothing remained after the procession's brief passing but the faint beat of drums, the echo of wailing cries, the memory of a bright bit of cloth, crimson like a bridal dress.

When Ida went back through the tamarinds, she caught sight of a servant and called his name.

"Souri, I want you to do something for me."

He peered at her through the gray dawn, blinking a little at her appearance, but only a little, having learned long since that the ways of this youngest Scudder were unpredictable. As she gave him instructions, he wagged his head with that peculiar motion which to a Westerner looks like "no" but invariably means "yes." *Amma,* he knew the house she meant in the street of the Brahmins. *Amma,* he was acquainted with the dwelling place of the Sri Mudaliar who was father of the little Kamla. As for the other, *amma,* yes, there were ways of discovering. He would go. He would inquire. He understood.

She went back to her room. Soon, with the coming of sunrise, the compound was fully astir, schoolboys chattering and darting from one building to another, servants bustling. Ida dressed, combed her hair, waited. It was less than an hour before Souri returned, but it seemed an eternity. Hearing the shuffle of sandals, she ran to the door. The servant's face was, as usual, noncommittal.

"You did what I asked you, Souri?"

"*Amma.* I did so, Missy."

"You were able to find all the places?"

"I found them, Missy."

"And the three women who were sick?"

"Dead," replied Souri.

She gasped. "You—you don't mean—all three of them?"

"*Amma.* All three of them, Missy."

She shut the door and fled back into her room. Throwing herself on the bed, heedless of the carefully puffed and twisted hair, she buried her head deep in a pillow. Not since she was fourteen, crying into that other pillow, had she endured such torture of body and spirit.

A door opened. She heard whispers of footsteps, swift, light. Salomi, Souri's daughter. "Your chota, Missy."

"Put it down, Salomi. On the table. Anywhere."

"Missy not feel well?"

"It's—nothing. Just a headache. Please don't tell Mother."

"Can Salomi help?" The young voice was concerned.

"No. Just tell your father I—I won't be going to school this morning."

"Yes, Missy."

Minutes . . . hours . . . they meant nothing. It was a life she was living. It swept her up, clothed her in silks and velvets and bright colors. It poured music into her ears—a lover's endearments, the voices of children; set her whirling to the tunes of gay polkas.

"See!" it called above the music. "Here they are—all the things you have dreamed about and wanted. Surely you wouldn't give them up for—"

"No, no!" she cried aloud into the pillow. "I wouldn't—couldn't!"

It wasn't fair. Life wasn't supposed to be like this. And death. She had thought it was necessary to die only once. But already today she had died three times. Must it be so every day to the end of life, not just three times but as many times as there were dying women within the possible reach of one's hands?

"No, no!" This time the cry was too deep within her to be spoken aloud. "I—I *can't*, I tell You! How—how can You ask it of me?"

Minutes . . . hours . . . years. . . .

She rose finally from the bed, crossed the room to the mirror, straightened her hair. She went into the washroom, poured water, patted it into her burning face. Salomi had put the tray on the table. She stooped over it, felt the coffee cup and found it stone-cold, lifted the overturned bowl and inspected the soggy toast, waved the cloud of fruit flies from the stubby little plantain.

The letter to Annie Hancock still lay, unfinished, on her desk. She picked it up, read it, tore it slowly into small pieces, and watched them flutter where they would, to the top of the desk, to the chair, to the floor.

Like snow, she thought, *falling white and clean on Massachusetts hills.*

Then she heard again the sound of tom-toms, faint at first, growing insistently louder.

No, not like snow. Like white pollen. Torn that it might be scattered. Dying that it might bring new life into being.

Stooping, she gathered up the bits of paper, careful to retrieve every one, and dropped them in the wastebasket. Then she crossed the room, opened the door, leaving it flung wide to the sunshine, and walked briskly along the verandah. She found her father and mother together in the bedroom-study.

"I'm going to America and study to be a doctor," she announced steadily, "so I can come back here and help the women of India."

The decision made, with her parents' joyful concurrence, Ida would gladly have taken the first ship back home and plunged immediately into the arduous training. But that was impossible. Her mother was not yet able to assume her full duties, and there was still her own short term of missionary service to be completed. Unable to apply her eager faculties to the mastery of anatomy and medicine, she set them to learning an even harder lesson, patience.

In 1892, when Uncle Jared and his family went on furlough, Dr. John moved his household to Vellore, a town of about 40,000 some eighty miles west of Madras. It was an ancient and picturesque town set in the midst of bare rocky hills, its central feature a huge stone fort constructed in the thirteenth century by a Hindu rajah named Bommai Reddy and in subsequent years made famous by the exploits of such military leaders as Clive, Gillespie, and the Mohammedan tyrant Tipu. The towering stone temple at its center, abandoned by the Hindus when the Mohammedan invaders had desecrated it by killing a cow within its walls, contained some of the most exquisite stone carvings in all South India.

Life here was infinitely more varied than at Tindivanam. Being the colonial government center of North Arcot District, Vellore had a good-sized English population, including a district Collector, a judge, and a police superintendent. There was even an English Club, which promoted considerable social activity. The mission maintained not only a boarding school for boys, attended largely by children of Christian families from the surrounding villages, but also day schools for Hindu girls and a splendid boys' high school, which was later to become Voorhees College. The narrow streets and lanes, coiled at the base of the lofty, fort-crowned hill, were as teeming with picturesque life as with dirt, disease, and poverty; and in the crowded bazaars the open-front shops and canvas-roofed stalls displayed among humbler wares treasures of gleaming brass, spices, ropes of marigolds and jasmine, flamboyant textiles, and hand-wrought silver.

But, though Ida appreciated the increased social life and excitement, all such interests had now become secondary to her dominating purpose. Here, back in the mission compound with its high-ceilinged bungalow where she had run and romped and hurled pillows with her five brothers, she managed through furious activity to leash her impatience. There was enough to do. Each day she or her mother must buy and dispense rice for the school boys, sixty full measures; grain for the ponies, bran for the bullocks. The huge bungalow was constantly in need of repairs which must be supervised: walls to be whitewashed, mats woven for the stone floors, new frills for the great ceiling-high punkah fans, new tiles for the roof.

Here, as at Tindivanam, she assumed direction of the day schools for Hindu girls, formerly run by her cousin Dixie. There were two of them, with enrollments of 93 and 108, an indication of the increasing desire of more progressive Hindus to give not only their sons, but also their daughters, the benefits of the best possible education, in spite of the risks incurred by exposing them to a foreign religion. These schools were the source of Ida's greatest joy during these years in Vellore. They were also the occasion of an experience so heartrending that Friday,

September 9, 1892, would always be engraved on her memory.

When Lakshmi, one of her favorite Brahmin pupils, failed that afternoon to appear at school, Ida felt no real concern. However, since the little girl had not looked well that morning, she sent a servant around the corner to the child's home to see why she was absent. Lakshmi, he reported, had left for school as usual. As the afternoon advanced and no trace of the child was found, both Ida and the girl's parents became frantic.

Days passed, while Ida endured sleepless anxiety. It was their punishment from the gods, the parents accused themselves, first for permitting their girl child to acquire wisdom like her brothers, second for sending her to a Christian school. Finally, when Ida was sure she could not bear the strain another day, the family of Lakshmi received a postal card.

"You will find her in a well," it announced, and gave its location.

A group of men, it developed, was trying to find a hidden treasure. They believed that the success of their project would be insured by the offering of a human sacrifice. What better candidate for this office than a child named Lakshmi, after the goddess of prosperity?

The body was found, and three men were convicted of the crime. For some time afterward, Ida noted without surprise, attendance at her school was poor.

There were times when she felt close kinship with the lone bullock that spent his days drawing water from the compound well. (People came from far and near to see him because, instead of the usual two bullocks moving first straight ahead, then straight back, there was only one of him, moving in a circle, round and round.) She also moved in a small wearisome orbit, leaving it only on short tangents. To the hill town of Coonoor for a few weeks in the hot months; to one of the other Reformed Church mission stations for midwinter meeting; to Ranipet, her birthplace, a dozen miles away, where Dr. Lew Scudder, a cousin, was stationed.

Lew was young, like herself. Summers at Shelter Island, the family vacation spot on Long Island Sound, she had endured his teasing along with her brothers'. He had come to India as a full-fledged doctor just two years before she and Harry had arrived. Now in the old Ranipet barracks converted by Dr. John into a makeshift hospital, she stood beside her cousin at the crude operating table, scrubbed and tremulous, handing him instruments, watching with both fright and fascination.

"Do you suppose I'll ever learn?" she whispered on one occasion.

The keen eyes under the beetling Scudder brows appraised her. Suddenly Dr. Lew thrust toward her the needle holder and needle with which he was sewing an incision. "Here," he ordered bluntly. "Take these and finish the job."

"Oh—no, Lew!" Ida stared at him, aghast.

Then, amazingly, her fingers were moving, awkwardly at first, but with increasing confidence. The tools ceased to feel strange, became like parts of her own hands, sensitive as fingertips. She worked painstakingly, absorbed in her task.

Dr. Lew watched her in silence. Then— "You'll learn," he commented quietly.

The years of marking time were over at last. Ida sailed on furlough with her father in 1894. The next summer she took her Regents' examinations in New York, and the fall of 1895 found her name on the roll of the entering class of the Woman's Medical College in Philadelphia.

Though fifty years had passed since Elizabeth Blackwell had sought in vain for a medical school in Philadelphia that would receive her, it still took courage for a woman to study medicine. Public sentiment was strongly opposed. Even the Women's Auxiliary of Ida's church mission board revealed a sharp difference of opinion as to the propriety of sending an unmarried woman doctor to the mission field. The scales were finally tipped by one intrepid member.

"If Ida Scudder feels called to this work," declared Miss Kate Frelinghuysen, "then I move we give her an education and send her. Here is the first ten dollars." Which was not such a small contribution as it might seem, considering that the annual tuition and school expense amounted in the first and most expensive year to $141.50.

The Woman's Medical College was the pioneer institution in the country for training women doctors. Founded by a

Quaker, it was opened in rented back rooms of a building on Arch Street in 1850 with forty women students, eight of them working toward a degree in medicine. In the beginning it had encountered fierce opposition. In 1858 the Philadelphia County Medical Society had gone so far as to recommend to members of the profession that they withhold from both faculty and graduates of the college all countenance and support.

But the school had survived and grown. Clara Swain, first woman doctor to become a missionary, had graduated in 1869, and ten years later another of its graduates, Anna S. Kugler, had followed Dr. Swain to India. A Brahmin woman, Mrs. Anandibai Joshee, coming in the early 1880s, had become the first Hindu woman in the world to receive a medical degree. When Ida arrived in 1896, the college was a full-fledged and accredited institution giving a four-year course leading to the M.D. degree, and of the fifty-five members of its staff, forty of them were women.

Ida arrived at a good time. The new science of bacteriology was coming into prominence. Public health, sanitation, and preventive medicine were looming into sudden importance. A new type of medical college was evolving, teaching a standardized body of medical knowledge. And Dr. Clara Marshall, the gifted and progressive dean, was fully aware of the needs of expansion in science, faculty, and clinical specialties.

But the college had its limitations. Though in 1880 a Woman's Hospital had been established in connection with the school, now treating 7,000 patients annually, and in 1892 a small dispensary had been opened in the slum area of the city, clinical opportunities were limited. According to the requirements of the new American Medical Association, a medical college to have Class A accreditation must be associated with a general hospital used for teaching, and, while students of the Woman's Medical College were admitted for clinical lectures to three of the Philadelphia hospitals, the college was in pressing need of a general hospital of its own.

Despite her eagerness, Ida found the studies difficult. Northfield had nourished its sheltered young females on Latin and English literature, not chemistry and physiology. But there was company to share her problems, a close-knit sorority called

Eta Chi. New names—Nell, Rachel, Jeanette, Elizabeth, Rosalie—slipped into special friendship niches.

Ida's family, too, was in nearby New Brunswick, New Jersey, where Dr. John and his wife were making a home for their three younger sons, Charles, Harry, and Walter, all studying for the ministry. That first Christmas in America was especially gay, with Walter and Harry both starry-eyed over girls named Margaret, and Charlie speechless with his passion for Millie Janeways, daughter of a New Brunswick family long intimate with the Scudders. Speechless in Millie's presence only, however, not in Ida's.

"Tell me the truth, Bones," he implored, addressing her by the new nickname which had superseded Bon and Younker. "If you were a beautiful angel like Millie, would you look at me?"

Ida made an affectionate pass at the faultless sweep of wave crowning his dapper slenderness, missed it, but managed to wreak havoc on the bow tie and one of the long upturned mustache tips. "Not if I could help it, Big Ears!"

She was able to give Harry more practical assistance, helping him stretch his meager dollars to cover the purchase of a ring, and was almost as thrilled as he by the announcement of his engagement to Margaret Booraem on Christmas Eve. Yet, sensing beneath the girl's reserve a slight bewilderment at the unmannerly frolics of herself and her brothers, Ida could not help feeling a little sorry for her. For Harry's bride would be accompanying him and his parents to the mission field in a few months, and if she found the mad Scudders full of surprises demanding difficult adjustments, what would she think of India!

The last summer before her father and mother returned to India in the fall of 1897 was the fulfillment of a dream. The family was all together in its summer cottage on Shelter Island, a few miles off the Connecticut shore of Long Island Sound. Even her oldest brother John came from his business in California and Lewis from his work on the Nebraska farm, bringing their wives and children.

Ida loved Shelter Island. She reveled in the gold-blue-whiteness of it. It blew the dust of dry skeletons from her mind, satisfied the hungry young vigor of her body. It was the one place in the world which signified the unity of the family. Even the commonest things bore childhood nicknames beginning with "s" like Scudder. "Scudhurst" was the house, "Scud" the little motor boat, "Skiddoo" and "Skoot" the rowboats. She swam a mile each day, played tennis furiously, went on clambakes, sang sea chanteys on the water with her brothers until it became too dark to see the landing, then sang with them for hours longer around the roaring fireplace.

Not the least of her pleasures that summer was the new clothes she had just bought in New York. She wore them one day when they sailed up the sound to see the races, for there was to be a big party in the settlement a mile up the coast from the cottage. Never content to remain in the cockpit, she perched herself on the after deck, back to the combing, feet outthrust under her billowing pink skirt to show the new shoes which were her special pride, patent leather, cut low, with high heels.

Ida fell to musing. Her training was only half over. She wished she were sailing this September with her parents. Already at the appeal of her cousin Dr. Lew Scudder, another doctor, a Canadian woman named Louisa Hart, had gone out to be at Ranipet. Ida had seen her in New York before she sailed, a woman young like herself, with smiling lips and strong straight brows and eyes that looked at life squarely. She longed to be there in India with her, working.

Suddenly the sailboat yawed. "Boom!" somebody yelled. "Heads down up there! *Boom!*"

Ida woke from her musing just in time to see the boom come sweeping toward her. Too late to duck, she raised both hands and grabbed it, felt herself lifted bodily and swung into the air. Looking down, she saw a pair of dainty black patent leathers fluttering wildly above the deck.

"Somebody save my shoes! They're new!" she yelled at the top of her voice before plunging headfirst into the sound.

In spite of such unladylike lapses, John wrote from California that he had noted a great improvement in little Bon during the last two years.

The gloom of the following Christmas was due only partially to the emptiness left by Dr. and Mrs. John and Harry and his bride Margaret after their departure for India. A far more depressing factor was the breaking of Walter's engagement to *his* Margaret. For in some ways Ida felt closer to Walter than to any of her other brothers. There was only a year's difference in their ages, and from appearance they might have been twins. To prove it, they had once had a picture taken together, Walter wearing a wig with long curls. Now, it seemed, Ida could scarcely bear the look of hurt bewilderment in her brother's eyes.

When in 1898 Cornell Medical College received an endowment of a million and a half dollars with the proviso that women be admitted on an equality with men, the news was received by the intimate little group in Eta Chi with both jubilation and dismay. The dreams of Elizabeth Blackwell, valiant pioneer woman doctor, were at last fulfilled. Women were to be accepted for medical training in a great university on equal terms with male students. But it meant a breaking of their own ranks. Ida, with her close friend Nell Bartholomew and two other classmates at Philadelphia Woman's Medical College, recognized the superior clinical advantages offered in the city of New York, and decided that they must transfer to Cornell for their fourth and final year.

There were others besides her classmates to whom Ida's decision obviously brought dismay. One was Burchfield Milliken, student at a neighboring men's medical college in Philadelphia. To her confusion and distress her divulging of the news brought to his eyes that same look of hurt bewilderment which she had seen in Walter's.

"But—we've hardly begun to get acquainted," he stammered. "I had hoped—"

"New York isn't far." Ida pretended a gaiety she did not feel. "No doubt you'll be coming there sometimes."

She liked Burchfield Milliken, admired his poised and gentle manner, his sensitivity, his dream of helping people, his ability to draw magic from the strings of a violin or the keys of a piano. She had accorded to him the same warm and unstinted comradeship she gave to all her friends, but she was no more in love with him than with the dozen or so other admirers who had followed in the wake of the Taylor boys. That is, she did not think she was. In the confusion of moments like this, flushing under his gentle but intense scrutiny, she was not certain.

But in the rush of changes taking place she had little time to worry about her own romances. Charles and Millie were married that June with all the excitement of a big wedding, and Walter, magnetized by the sight of Nell Bartholomew in a bridesmaid's dress of pink organdy which set off her fair skin and rich, waving dark hair, showed his first signs of recovery from his unhappy love affair.

"She's lovely, Bones!" he whispered, so excited that he spattered punch on Ida's new foulard silk. "Like a piece of Dresden china! Where have you been keeping her?"

Ida looked at him wonderingly. "But—you've seen Nell before, Walter!"

"Not looking like that, I haven't!"

Two people at least were overjoyed when Ida moved to New York. Myra Moffatt and Katharine Van Nest, two "maiden ladies" who were old friends of the family, invited her to share their luxurious home on West 56th Street. Katharine, secretary for India of their denominational Women's Auxiliary, had long considered Ida her "little sister," and Myra lavished on her that idolatrous affection of a naïve and sentimental spinster for a youthful charm she herself had never possessed. Ida settled contentedly into the odd household, consisting of the two women, a servant Bridget who waited on her hand and foot, a carriage driver named Richardson who was prone to accidents, a curly-haired black dog called Peter, Sambo the cat, a maid named Maggie whose sole accomplishment was "cleaning silver really well," and two canaries.

It was not easy being one of the first women to study medicine at Cornell. Ida and her three classmates from Philadelphia, Nell, Sylvia, and Margaret, together with a few brave females from other colleges, were subjected to some criticism and ridicule. "It was the custom in those days," reported a *Cornell Quarterly* of later years, "for men students to stamp their feet and throw kisses when women entered the classroom or operating theater!" However, most of the badgering was in fun, and Ida herself reported in that same *Quarterly* that she had found the majority of that pioneer class to be "perfect gentlemen."

Criticism and ridicule were the least of her worries. For the first time since starting her medical course she felt the torturing fear of failure. Competition here was far more rigorous. She had to fulfill clinical requirements of preceding years and at the same time keep pace with the steady march of classes.

She was worried also because her clinical work in the United States gave her no chance to specialize in tropical diseases. Leprosy, malaria, cholera, plague, even less deadly afflictions like scabies, Guinea worm, and dysentery, were maladies scarcely mentioned by name in either classroom or textbook. Yet during these very months of her training the virulent form of plague known as the Black Death was sweeping southern India, and new techniques of treatment were being developed which were to change the course of medical history.

A scientist named Haffkine had come to Bombay from Paris to develop cholera inoculations, but, with the sudden eruption of plague in 1896, had turned his attention to the development of plague prophylaxis. By 1897 it had been demonstrated that the *Bacillus pestis*, discovered in 1894, when made into a vaccine, was helpful in immunizing animals. Now Haffkine, through experiments on himself and others, had succeeded in developing a vaccine that was proving effective in immunizing human beings. Anticipating the natural Hindu prejudice against serum made from animal tissues, involving the taking of life, he had even devised a culture medium which employed ghee, or clarified butter.

Ida read of these developments with enthralled interest, knew when the epidemic spread to Vellore and her father and other missionaries were among those who dared accept the new inoculations. Impatient to get back where she could have a part in such pioneering, she decided not to take her year of internship in America but to return to India as soon as her academic course was finished. For what doctors could give her more expert instruction in tropical disease than her own father?

However, some of her clinical assignments at Cornell were supplying invaluable preparation for her work in India. One of the most arduous yet rewarding was the two weeks spent in the downtown Maternity Hospital.

She arrived with her three closest friends on a Friday morning, and they were at once briefed on rules, procedure, and the contents of their medical bags. Then each one was given six names, and they started out. The sight of seven student doctors, three men and four women, all waiting on a corner for a streetcar with seven huge unwieldy bags, all identical, struck Ida and Nell as so funny that they burst out laughing.

But it was the last time either of them laughed that day. Squalid slum apartments, flight after flight of dark, dizzying stairways, cases hopelessly complicated by poverty and neglect, exhausted both energy and optimism. After eight calls Ida returned and dropped wearily on her bed, only to be summoned again immediately. Two more calls, one a delivery, and numerous examinations of patients for pregnancy consumed the rest of the day. She went to bed early, prepared for a long night's sleep, for the other three girls were scheduled for call ahead of her. Soon the office whistle blew for Nell. Ten minutes later it blew again, and Sylvia left. Another five minutes, and it blew for Margaret. Presently Ida herself was fumbling into her clothes, seizing her huge bag, and racing downstairs, weariness dissipated by excitement when she found that she had to start out on a case *alone*. She was prepared for the delivery, a difficult one, when to her disappointment the doctor arrived. But she was glad enough of his presence before the long hard labor was successfully over.

She made a good record during the two weeks, having made seventy-one calls, attended twenty-three maternity cases, and delivered seventeen of them herself, though to her regret the clinical training had offered no practice with abnormal births. She had hoped to apply forceps at least once. But there was assurance in the reminder that when she first faced such emergencies in India, it would be under her father's skillful tutelage. She returned to the house in West 56th Street wearied more by the poverty and misery she had seen than by the long hours of exertion, and impatient with herself for such weakness. If she let her energies become dissipated in tears by the slums of New York, how could she expect to cope with the villages of India?

The loss of precious lecture hours because of such clinical work made the last months at Cornell an increasingly desperate struggle. But Ida tried not to let the looming cloud of examinations dim her enjoyment of this last spring she would spend in America for many years. On the first day of May, when Burchfield Milliken made one of his frequent trips from Philadelphia to New York, she managed to cast aside all worries for a few gay hours, only to find herself confronted when they were over with a greater one.

In the morning they went to Bay Ridge, and heard Charles preach an excellent sermon in his own church, with the long lock of his hair dancing earnestly to emphasize his points. They had dinner with the "turtle doves," as Myra Moffatt liked to call the newlywed Charles and Millie, took a pleasant walk in the afternoon, and after supper started back to the house on 56th Street. The only discordant note in the day thus far was the faint irritation she always felt because of her escort's slightly careless table manners and occasional lapses in grammar—and still sharper irritation toward herself for feeling it. When Burchfield Milliken suggested a last stroll in the park, Ida gladly consented. She loved Central Park in any season, but in May, with the new leaves a tender green and the lilacs just bursting into bloom, she found it irresistible.

As they wandered aimlessly, he told her about spring in his native Tuscarora Valley in Pennsylvania, about his mother's cottage built on a hill among shade trees, about the storms that swept over the valley and its blazing sunsets. He talked like a poet, and Ida was enthralled. Then suddenly the gay mood was shattered. Burchfield Milliken was telling her in a swift outpouring of emotion that he loved her, that, having known her inspiration, he could not, simply could not take up the work of his life alone.

Ida was at first speechless. It was not the first time she had had a proposal, but always before she had known how and what to answer. "I—I think we ought to know each other better," she stammered finally, "before we—decide anything."

He replied with desperation. *When* could they know each

other better? It couldn't be through letters. Every day now she was making further plans to go to India in the fall, and he still had another year of medicine. He could not possibly go to the mission field yet.

"I almost wish," he confessed with a tinge of bitterness, "you might fail your exams so you would have to stay another year. I know I shouldn't, but I can't help it."

Ida remembered with relief the conference they were both planning to attend that summer at Northfield. Perhaps then they could become better acquainted. Yes, he agreed gratefully, then wondered aloud how long it should take two people to become acquainted. Already they had had a year and a half. He had known for many months how he felt toward her and always would.

Back in her room, alone, Ida tried to study, but the words swam before her eyes. Finally she laid down her book and took up pen and paper.

"My dearest Muzzie," she wrote swiftly, "I want you so, oh Marmee, for I can't tell anyone here, not a soul." Then she poured out to her mother all of the day's happenings to the smallest detail.

On Tuesday she added a postscript to her letter: "I am simply overcome this evening. I had a letter from Mr. M. He has taken entirely too much for granted. I tried to make him feel that I did not care for him as he did for me, but from his letter I think he does not understand it at all. And, Marmee, I do like him so much, but I don't know, I really don't know what my feelings are, and what can I do? I must not let it go on if I find out still that I don't care for him. But, Marmee, I *do* want to marry some day. I do want children who will love me as I love you!"

To make her quandary worse, Charles wrote her that same day, May 3, urging her not to decide against her new suitor too hastily. He liked Burchfield Milliken, and he longed for his "dearest Bon" the same happiness that was his and Millie's.

The uncertainty of examinations, one of which she feared she had failed, put the problem in no smaller perspective. Indeed, everything that happened the first of that summer seemed a reminder of the decision she must make: the an-

56

nouncement of Nell's and Walter's engagement, the flurry of plans for their wedding, choosing her own dress as maid of honor. Yes, even the chance question of a sweet little seventy-seven-year-old Quaker lady she met attending a "yearly meeting."

"Ah, so thee is returning to thy India, my dear? And is thee going to take a husband with thee?"

"No," she replied almost curtly.

Dismayed, she found that none of her close friends were attending the mission conference at Northfield except Burchfield Milliken. Nell was too busy with plans for her wedding. Annie Hancock, hoping to go to India that fall with Ida if the board could find money to send her, had decided she must spend all the time possible with her family. But Ida need not have worried. Burchfield was a delightful and impersonal companion. Only once, when they had climbed up the old path through the glen, did he give her a moment's uneasiness. He picked a yellow flower and gave it to her. When she stuck it carelessly into her hair, he stood looking at her, his heart in his eyes.

"You ought always to wear a flower in your hair," he told her gently. "You look like a queen standing there like that— *my* queen."

She laughed and ran on ahead, afraid the spell of pleasant comradeship was to be broken, but when he caught up with her, it was to talk lightly of the speaker they were to hear that evening.

But the day came later in the summer when Ida had to make her decision.

The young Scudders had organized a yachting trip, with Burchfield Milliken as one of the guests. It had been a hilarious jaunt of several days, with trips up and down the sound, attendance at the Larchmont races, a sail through Hell Gate and up the East River. On the final day they started for Gravesend Bay, where the yacht was to be put out of commission for the season. Suddenly conscious of the unspoken question in Burchfield Milliken's eyes, Ida became more than ever troubled and confused.

While Millie and the boys were in the galley preparing

lunch, she took the wheel, glad of something solid to cling to. Her head whirled in tempo with churning motors and throbbing sunshine. How could she possibly analyze her emotions in the few hours she had left? And yet she must do so. Suddenly she heard a step behind her, felt a hand tweak one of the loose strands of her hair. She whirled. Such teasing gestures were one of her suitor's small habits which she found most irritating. "Don't!" she flashed. "Can't you ever understand? Don't touch me! I—I don't like that kind of teasing!"

His face whitened, and he drew away as if she had struck him. He was sorry, he assured her quietly, and he would not bother her again.

Conscience-stricken, she tried to make amends. It was she who should be sorry. She had been guilty of unpardonable rudeness. He must know she did not really mean it. But they both knew that she *had* meant it. And from that moment there was no longer any question in his eyes.

Leaving the yacht at Gravesend, they all went back to Charlie's at Bay Ridge to spend the night. After supper Burchfield Milliken came out and found her on the porch, so weary and miserable she was almost weeping. Sitting beside her in the dusk, he began quietly to talk of his plans. For the moment there seemed nothing but a great wall between him and the bright dreams he had once had, but somehow he would find courage to surmount it. His mother would help.

Ida choked. "How she will condemn me!"

No, no, he assured her, he would never permit that. In all their acquaintance, he had found no fault in her. Or—yes, perhaps just one, that she was too lovable.

The next morning they met as usual, and he went with her to the streetcar which was to take her back to New York. They talked of commonplace things. He put her on the car and shook her hand. They might have been any good friends parting after a pleasant outing together. Turning once, she saw him standing, looking after the car. Then the car rounded a corner, and he was lost to sight.

Dr. Ida S. Scudder. Ida stared at the inscription in her mother's fine slanting handwriting. For the first time com-

58

prehension swept over her. No more of preparations. Her work had begun. She tore open the letter.

Mrs. Scudder was sure Ida would pass her exams, but was overjoyed with the cable telling the good news. If she could only have been there for the graduation! She and Papa are back in the bungalow at Vellore. They have a new pony named Robin. Papa has a bicycle and uses it to travel to his stations. She is training a new boy named Moses, who will be useful to Ida later. The same pleasant tailor, Vankobarai, is working on the upstairs verandah mending ceiling cloths.

They are having cholera in the nearby town of Arni, caused by a woman's washing a sick child's clothes in the tank where the school boys get their drinking water.

She has been making tamarind preserves and chutney.

She wishes Ida would bring a carriage, packed in one box, with the shafts separate. There should be a rack behind strong enough for a man to ride on.

It is wonderful news that dear little Annie Hancock may be coming to India with Ida. If only the board can get enough money to send her!

Has Ida heard about Dr. Louisa Hart's terrible experience? She started to see a patient in a town fifteen miles away with her Mohammedan driver and a Brahmin youth who had come after her. It was dark and raining. Halfway to their destination they were attacked by robbers. The driver and boy explained to the robbers who she was and why she was there. The robbers stripped the other two but did no harm to her, even returned her umbrella! The three were left in the darkness and rain with no lantern. When dawn came, they went on. Louisa treated her patient and returned, having lost nothing but gained a bad cold.

And has Ida heard about the other time when Dr. Hart had to operate on a Mohammedan woman in a house so dark she couldn't see, so what did she do but get the men of the family to go up on the roof and take off the tiles!

Ida was tense with waiting. Though the blaze of a New York autumn was in her eyes and the tang of Atlantic fogs in her nostrils, her senses were already attuned to heat and dust and the bittersweet scent of tamarinds.

59

Fortunately there were things to do: visits to make, clothes to get ready, medical supplies to purchase. With the permission of Katharine Van Nest, who was the Women's Auxiliary secretary for India, she wrote Annie Hancock at her home in Massachusetts assuring her that the money would somehow be found to send her to the mission field. She made her own plans to sail in the middle of November with Walter and Nell and another young missionary and his wife who were to be stationed at Vellore. But she would go straight on to India instead of traveling through Europe with the honeymooners.

Then she found that there was work to be done right here and now.

"We have a letter from Dr. Louisa Hart," said Dr. Cobb, secretary of her denominational mission board. "She thinks there should be a hospital for women in Vellore."

"Oh, yes!" Ida's blue eyes shone. "Of course there should be. There are thousands of women there, needing it, just waiting!"

Dr. Cobb's keen eyes appraised the glowing features. "And she wants you to raise the money for it," he told her bluntly.

Ida gasped. "*Me!* Raise money for—for a hospital!"

"And the board has already voted its permission."

Ida gulped. She felt a little dizzy. Then slowly the spinning in her head steadied. "How much?" she demanded.

"Well—" The secretary's glance wavered. He was not used to dealing with people who came straight to the point—and such a sharp point! "The board thought—"

"Fifty thousand?" suggested Ida.

It was the man's turn to gasp. "Fifty—"

"It would take that much, wouldn't it, to build a good one?"

Regaining his composure, Dr. Cobb regarded her with benign amusement. "My dear child! Fifty thousand!" He chuckled. "The board decided," he told her kindly, "that in accordance with Dr. Hart's request, you might be permitted to ask for eight thousand. And it would be amazed and delighted if you raised half that amount. If you care to try, you will receive help also, of course, from the Women's Auxiliary."

If she cared to try! As she left the board office, Ida's head was already buzzing with plans. Before the day was over, she had discussed the matter with members of the Women's

Auxiliary, drawn up lists, started to interview prospects. A hospital for women in Vellore? Of course they must have one! Why hadn't she herself thought of it before?

As days passed, her first buoyant confidence turned to uneasy optimism, then to dogged determination. People listened with tolerance, even sympathy, but few seemed to realize that it was a life-and-death matter. The ones who did unfortunately had the least to give. The date of her sailing came closer and closer, and still she had collected only promises of a few hundred dollars. She returned to the house on 56th Street one Saturday night, close to despair.

"My poor Bonny!" Framed by its halo of unbecoming but stylishly frizzed hair, Myra Moffat's round face looked puckered and anxious. "If there were only something I could do! But you know I've done all I can with the taxes so high and all, sixty-five hundred on that building of mine, I just heard today!"

Ida patted her plump shoulder. "You've already done more than your part, Myra dear, you and Katharine."

"I do have one idea," suggested Katharine Van Nest. "Our missionary society at Collegiate Church is meeting on Monday morning, and our president, Miss Taber, lives just down the street. Maybe if you were to ask her to let you talk to the group on Monday—"

Ida stopped only long enough to put on a fresh shirtwaist.

"Miss Taber?" she asked the pleasant elderly woman into whose presence she was ushered by a maid. "I'm Dr. Scudder. And I wonder if I could talk with you about something terribly important."

"Of course, my dear." The woman introduced her to an elderly man reading in the corner of the sitting room. "This is my brother-in-law, Mr. Schell. I'm sure he will excuse us."

She led the girl into an adjoining library, leaving the door ajar. Ida was desperately determined to make this woman understand. Unless she could, it would do little good to talk to the other women on Monday morning.

She told of the three calls in the night and the young wives who had died because there had been no woman doctor; of visits to the zenanas, those stifling inner courtyards from which

Mohammedan and high-caste Hindu women never emerged except behind the curtain of a *gosha* cart; of Louisa Hart's performing an operation in a dark inner room because there was no hospital where a woman could go and be treated in seclusion; of babies being brought into the world with the crude tools of an untrained midwife. And she put all her heart into the telling.

Miss Taber was a kind and sympathetic listener, though somehow, perhaps because of her reserved manner, she did not give the impression that she considered Ida's subject a matter of supreme importance. She would be glad to let Ida speak to the society on Monday, but she could make no promises. The women of Collegiate Church had already assumed large obligations. But possibly they could manage a few hundred dollars more.

The elderly gentleman was still sitting in the next room when Ida left the library, and he looked up from his book long enough to toss her a pleasant "Good evening, Doctor. Good to have met you."

Possibly a few hundred! Ida remembered an old Indian proverb: "An ounce of water to quench an elephant's thirst!" She let herself into the house quietly and tiptoed upstairs to her room, so that Myra and Katharine might not see her disappointment.

She was at breakfast the next morning, trying to look rested and hopeful, when Maggie brought a note on a tray. She tore it open and read it, then, frowning, read it again.

"Miss Taber?" queried Myra, hands hovering anxiously over the silver coffeepot.

"No," said Ida. "It—it's from her brother-in-law, Mr. Schell. He wants to see me before I go to the meeting on Monday."

"A donation!" exclaimed Myra happily, so excited she spilled coffee on her Sunday Madeira tablecloth. "He might give as much as—" Her imagination soared optimistically. "—five hundred or a thousand dollars! He's very rich."

"And cautious," added Katharine with her usual outspoken common sense. "It was his wife who used to give money to

62

charity. And now she's dead, I wouldn't count on getting a penny."

"Just the same," insisted Myra stoutly, "it could mean something. And if I were Ida, I'd wear my blue cashmere!"

Ida took Katharine's advice and dared not hope. She also took Myra's and wore the new blue cashmere.

The same maid ushered her into the same upstairs sitting room, where Mr. Schell sat alone, not reading this time, but figuring at a desk with pad and pencil. Ida's heart sank. Katharine was right. This man would want to know exactly what value he was getting for every penny. Even the figures on the pad were small and neat, with not an inch of the paper wasted.

"I was interested," he began abruptly, "in the facts which you gave Miss Taber. I couldn't help overhearing. I would like to ask you more about the situation."

Ida answered his many questions, accurately but without emotion, sensing that this man received dictation from the head rather than from the heart. Vellore was a small city 85 miles west of Madras, its population about 40,000. Yes, it was on a main line of railroad, with a new station about three miles to the north. Building in South India was usually of brick or cement, though crushed stone was also available from the many rocky hills circling Vellore. Labor, of course, was cheap. Yes, there was a government hospital in Velore, but—here for the first time her reply to his question was colored with emotion—they would need another hospital just for women, because the wives of good Hindus and Mohammedans couldn't go where there were men doctors or patients.

"Yes, yes." Mr. Schell nodded impatiently. "You said that before." And now what about her own qualifications? Did she really consider herself, an inexperienced student just out of medical school, competent to run a hospital?

Ida responded to this challenge with dignity. No, of course not. But she expected to become so. Her father was a skilled physician, with years of experience in India. She had chosen to work with him for a year instead of taking her internship in America. By the time the hospital was built, even if the money were now available, she would be ready. And as to her record in medical school, anyone who wished was at liberty to make inquiries.

"I have already done so," Mr. Schell informed her quietly.

Suddenly he was smiling at her warmly across the desk. Drawing a checkbook toward him, he opened it, flattened its pages with his thumb, and began writing in small neat script. Ida's heart almost stopped beating.

"I have decided to make a contribution to your hospital in memory of my beloved wife, Mary Taber Schell. She would have understood and liked this thing you are trying to do. You're asking, I understand, for eight thousand. I want it to be a good hospital, worthy of the memory of a good woman."

Tearing out the check, he pushed it toward her. She took it with stiff fingers. For a moment she had difficulty focusing her eyes on the figures. Then there came a throbbing in her temples like the beating of drums.

The check was for ten thousand dollars.

Though she had her hospital, Ida was not satisfied. One goal attained, she set her sights immediately on another.

There was great rejoicing at the meeting of the women at Collegiate Church that Monday morning. But when called upon to make her speech, Ida did not confine herself to giving thanks. She made an impassioned plea for money to pay for an evangelistic worker to visit in the zenanas of Vellore.

"It isn't enough just to go to these women when they are sick. Hundreds, thousands of them live day after day, month after month, year after year, within the high walls of their courtyards, hungering for love and friendship. I have a friend who graduated in my class at Northfield. She is ready and anxious to go out to India and do this work. If only there were enough of us here in this room this morning who *cared...*."

As she spoke, Ida noticed a fairly young black-haired, black-gowned woman sitting in the front row. Her features were unimpressive, her clothes, though expensive, unbecoming. A rather drab, mousy little person, except for the intense brightness of her eyes. Ida found her own eyes returning to them again and again, as if to rekindle their fervor. Never once, it seemed, while she was speaking did the dark eyes leave her face. Ida finished her speech, sat down, and, no longer in need of their encouragement, forgot about them.

The women discussed the proposition, promised to consider it as soon as it became financially possible, and disbanded. Thereupon Ida found herself surrounded by one small group after another, congratulating, admiring, promising future support, pressing small steamer gifts into her hands. When all of them had gone, she felt a timid touch on her arm. It was the little black-haired, black-clad woman.

"I'm Gertrude Dodd," she said almost apologetically. "My two sisters and I have been talking, and we think it would be such a pity for your friend not to sail with you just because some overfed, overdressed women are either too selfish or too lazy to make up their minds. There's no need of her waiting, my dear. We'll see that the expense is taken care of. Tell your friend she is going with you to India."

Ida was speechless. While trying to find her voice, she reached out and took the little figure in her arms.

"I—I can't tell you—" she choked, half weeping. "If I could only find some way to thank you, to—make it up to you—"

Miss Dodd straightened her modest black hat. There were two spots of color in her cheeks, matching the brightness of her eyes. She seemed suddenly to have absorbed a little of the youthful vigor and beauty which had enfolded her.

"You already have," she said.

Mr. Schell was not a man to leave tasks begun unfinished. To be worthy of his wife's memory the hospital which would bear her name must be not only well built but well equipped. That very day he drove Ida downtown in his luxurious carriage, complete with coachman and two horses, and together they chose the instruments and fittings which would make his gift complete. Boxed and labeled, they were sent promptly to the pier, there, in company with the big crate containing the new carriage, to await the sailing of Ida's ship on November 22.

6

When Ida and Annie Hancock arrived in Vellore, the cannon in the ancient stone fort was booming its welcome to a new day in a new year in a new century. Removing the new woolen suits, cut in the pink of fashion, which Annie's family had presented to them just before the boat sailed, they regretfully packed them away in sealed trunks, secure from moths and white ants.

"Heavenly!" sighed Annie, sniffing the warm, blossom-laden sunshine. "Imagine! Cotton dresses and not even a sweater, in January!"

"Wait till April," advised Ida caustically, "when that nice cool high-necked ruching will begin to feel like a steam compress. But"—she regarded the sensitive eager features with satisfaction—"I'm so glad you're not disappointed, Annie darling."

"I'd be happy in any place where I was needed," returned Annie, "especially if you were there."

That very day she insisted on accompanying Mary Isaac Henry, the evangelist, on her visits to the zenanas, eliciting even more amused curiosity than the Indian woman's usual companion—a doll which could open and shut its eyes. But in response to Annie's concerned friendliness the curiosity quickly changed to smiles and salaams. Before a week had passed she was as much at home under the reed canopy of a jutka as in a horse-drawn carriage. She had picked up a few words of Tamil and paid a call in every one of the thirteen Hindu and Mohammedan homes open to Christian visitors, as well as in the women's quarter of the town jail. So Annie began her work at Vellore—teaching, counseling, witnessing to her faith through a loving spirit and an exceptionally sweet soprano voice—a ministry which was to consume all of Annie Hancock's frail energy and strong devotion for the next quarter of a century.

Dr. John was not well. Ida saw with dismay the aging stoop of the powerful shoulders, the thin drawn features. She dressed the painful boils which were the most recent symptom of his malady—"Job's comforters," her father called them— and speculated anxiously with her cousin Dr. Lew as to their cause. Was it possible that the inoculation with Haffkine's new plague vaccine might be responsible for the infection?

"It's nothing," insisted Dr. John. Gritting his teeth to hide the pain, he would rise before daylight each morning, spend the usual hours in his study, and be ready by eight o'clock to give medical treatment, counsel, or consolation to the waiting queues on the front verandah. Even with Ida's help this ministry often lasted until noon. Then he would grudgingly take a couple of hours' siesta before mounting his bicycle for the rest of the day's activities—visiting patients or parishioners in their homes, directing his schools, meeting with village pastors, distributing literature in the bazaars.

Ida would gladly have relieved him of the morning queues of patients, most of them with minor ailments, but to her vexation even the humblest suppliant eyed her new professional ability askance.

"Not Missy. Doctor," a case of simple abscess would insist gently.

"But I am a doctor too," Ida would patiently explain.

"Not Missy." Withdrawing himself politely but firmly from the reach of her hands, the patient would sit down stubbornly to wait.

"It takes time," her father assured her sympathetically. "Don't worry. You'll soon have enough to do. And it's the women you came to help, remember."

"What women?" Ida fumed. "How do I get to them? Go knocking on their doors? Spread out my medicines like a charm maker in the bazaar?"

Her chance came at last.

"Doctor *Ammal?* The old mother in my house is sick. Could you come?"

Could she! While the stable boy was harnessing the pony to the carriage, she checked the contents of her shiny new satchel with trembling fingers. With the servant perched on the rack behind and the sick woman's son on the seat beside her, Ida herself drove. Never had the two miles between the compound and the center of town seemed longer.

The house was in a narrow street between the bazaar and Fort Hill. When she started to turn into it, her Hindu companion burst into violent objections. Puzzled, Ida reined in the pony. Finally, by a combination of Tamil and English and descriptive gestures, he made her understand. Her stable boy was of low caste. It was not fitting for him to enter this high-caste street. He must remain outside with the carriage. Ida opened her lips in hot protest, then, remembering all that was at stake, meekly agreed.

She followed her guide along a winding street, no wider than a lane, bordered on each side by an open drain and a row of neat houses crowded end to end. Entering one of them through a massive carved doorway, they passed through a narrow court-yard with doors opening into small dark rooms on either side, coming finally to a large open court surrounded by a roofed verandah.

There was a flurry of bare feet as women and children caught sight of her and fled, leaving toys, partly sifted rice, grinding stone and roller dripping with half-mashed spices. A freshly washed orange sari trailed by one end from the veran-dah roof. Only one woman remained, crouching timidly behind one of the pillars, the end of her sari drawn across her face. The man gave her a brusque command in Tamil, and she crept forward, hands raised palm to palm in a shy *namaskar.*

Ida followed the woman along the verandah to a dark, airless inner room, and was shocked anew by the ignorance and superstition which gave people the idea light and air must be kept as far from the sick as possible. Becoming conscious of sound—hoarse breathing, an occasional moan—she was across the room, kneeling beside the dim figure on the mat. Her hands groped along hollowed cheeks to bony forehead, found it cold; moved swiftly down a withered arm to the wrist. When finally she felt a faint flutter at the tips of her fingers, she herself gave a little moan. The woman was dying.

She felt trapped. Her client must have known the case was hopeless. Was that why he had called her, to discredit her before she could have a chance to prove herself? There were Hindu physicians, priests, charm vendors, who would like nothing better. If the woman died, scarcely a person in Vellore would fail to know by nightfall that the American woman doctor had lost her first patient!

Her first instinct was to leave the house at once. Then at least she could say that she had had nothing to do with the case. She had reached the door of the stagnant little room when she came to her senses. Run away? What kind of doctor was she? Leaving an old woman to die all alone in the dark!

She found the man who had summoned her, told him his mother was dying. There was nothing she or any other doctor could do to save her, but she could make the last hours happier and more comfortable if he would tell his wife to help her and follow her directions.

The man's face revealed grief, concern, nothing more. He had summoned her for one reason only, because he loved his mother. *Amma*, yes, he would do anything which the Doctor *Ammal* wished. He would tell the women.

To the shocked amazement of the three daughters-in-law, the old woman was moved out of the small dark room and laid on a mat in a shady end of the verandah. Cool water was brought in a *kuja*, an earthen jar, and—unheard-of procedure in time of illness—urged between the parched lips. Ida gently bathed the wasted body, using her own handkerchief wrung out in a basin.

The old woman opened her eyes and followed her every

movement, the fright in them changing slowly to acceptance. The other women also forgot some of their fear. One of them reached curious fingers to touch the doctor's strange gold hair. The shy children stopped peering from the shelter of the pillars and crept close enough to feel her dress, even daring to finger the white wrist protruding from her long sleeve. She smiled at them, admiring the silver chains and anklets which were their sole attire.

Hours passed. Crouched beside the mat, doing what she could to ease the agonized struggle with death, Ida felt her limbs grow numb. Finally she could stand it no longer and stumbled to her feet. Suddenly she felt a tug on her skirt which almost upset her balance. Looking down, she saw the old woman pulling herself up with a nearly superhuman effort, turning on her side, crawling inch by inch along the mat until her face was close to the hem of the full white skirt.

"Oh, no!" exclaimed Ida in horror. "*Illai!*"

But before she could stop her, the old woman had kissed her feet.

The effort had been too great, and the end came almost immediately. Ida closed the eyes gently, wishing she had the ability to give them more of hope for what lay beyond the dimness. If only Mary Henry could have been here to tell them in her fluent Tamil the story of Infinite Love!

The other three women were no longer strangers. Crowding after her through the narrow passage, they begged her to return. But as she made her way along the winding street, followed by the first shrill wailings and somber drumbeats, she was conscious of blank walls and hastily retreating footsteps. The news of her failure had preceded her.

Mercifully she was soon given another chance to prove her skill. Her father was away on his village circuit when an urgent call came. The man seeking help reluctantly permitted her to return with him to his house in the town. Ida found the patient, his father, so swollen with edema that his eyes would not open.

Again she experienced panic. She wished her father were here to help with the diagnosis. Edema could be due to so many causes, differing perhaps in India from those in the West! Then common sense came to her rescue. Her first duty, at least, was to relieve his suffering. Placing both thumbs on the swollen eyelids, she began pressing and massaging, gently at first, presently with harder and harder pressure, in an attempt to push back the edema. In a few moments the patient was able to open his eyes.

His son stared unbelievingly, then rushed out to proclaim the news to the other members of the joint family.

"Ayoh! A miracle! The Doctor *Ammal* has performed a miracle! She has opened the eyes that were closed! A worker of magic is the Doctor *Ammal!"*

After diagnosing and treating the patient, Ida returned home in a daze. This time the news of success had preceded her. She saw faces upturned in wonder, hands raised in reverent *namaskars.* Her lips twisted ironically. Which was worse, to be dubbed failure or magician?

Her father's health did not improve. With the increase of heat in February came a visible decrease in his strength. The family decided to go earlier than usual to Kodaikanal, the summer resort in the Palani Hills where members of the mission stations of South India usually spent much of the two hottest months of the year. Being treasurer of the mission, Dr. John could take some of his arduous duties with him.

Even anxiety could not dull Ida's enjoyment of the familiar trip. They boarded the crowded Madras-Ceylon Boat Mail train at ten o'clock one night, sharing a small hot compartment with two Indian families and all their baggage, and arrived at Kodai Road Station at ten the next morning. From there they traveled in the two-wheeled bullock carts called transits to the foot of the mountain. For the last part of the trip the women rode in the small roofed and curtained palanquins called dhoolies, while the men either rode horseback or were carried in chairs, which were borne, like the palanquins, by coolies. For the first time in his life Dr. John rode in a chair instead of on a horse, and hated it.

Ida could never ride for long. She was too sorry for the four coolies bearing her weight. Besides, she reveled in the exhilaration of climbing.

As they mounted the steep slope, the coolies chanted rhythmically.

"Ah hungaykum!" those in front would call.

"Ah ho!" those in the rear would reply.

"She is not heavy, *patterum* (take care)," sang Mrs. John's bearers.

> "Carry her softly, *patterum,*
> Nice little lady, *patterum,*
> Here's a bridge, *patterum,*
> Carry her gently, *patterum,*
> Carry her carefully, *patterum,*
> Sing along cheerily, *patterum!*"

Sometimes the improvised lines were not so complimentary. "Oh! What a heavy bag! Ho, ho!" they sang of Dr. John, believing him ignorant of Tamil.

> "Sure it is an elephant. Ho, ho!
> He is an ample weight. Ho, ho!
> Let's let his palkee down. Ho, ho!
> Let's set him in the mud. Ho, ho!
> Let's leave him to his fate. Ho, ho!
> No, but he'll be angry then. Ho, ho!
> Aye, and he'll beat us then. Ho, ho!
> Then let us hasten on. Ho, ho!
> Jump along, jump along. Ho, ho!"

Halfway up they stopped to rest before assaulting the steeper zigzag path leading to Shembaganur.

"So I'm heavy as an elephant, am I?" rumbled Dr. John to his coolies in good village Tamil. "You'd like to set me down in the mud?"

They regarded him first fearfully, then sheepishly as they caught the twinkle in his eyes.

As they climbed up and up, the air became blessedly cool and cooler, and the vegetation changed from tropic palms and jungle growth to wood violets, ferns, and purple orchids. A thousand feet higher they caught the mingled fragrance of roses and eucalyptus, and bundled up in sweaters.

"Ah—*san thosham,* happiness!" sang the coolies in anticipation of the baksheesh which would be their reward. "Ah—ha ho!" came the answer.

Surely Kodai, thought Ida, with its blue lake and high green horizons, was as close to heaven as any place on earth! Dr. John thought so too, and almost miraculously his strength revived. The painful boils healed. By the time Cushing, the big mission cottage, was filled with other vacationers and the summer season of the colony was at its height, he was almost his old self.

Then Ida's happiness was complete. There were the usual long horseback rides, the tennis tournaments, picnics at Pillar Rocks and Silver Cascade, evening strolls along the path called Coaker's Walk, which circled the edge of the sheer seven-thousand-foot slope. With Harry and Walt both there to share the fun, it was almost like Shelter Island.

One day in May the front wheel of the bicycle Dr. John was riding hit a stone and flung him to the ground. Ida, who had witnessed the accident, rushed to help him, but he was unable to lift himself.

"Sorry—spoil fun—" he mumbled, trying to smile up at her.

Some of the young men at Cushing quickly improvised a stretcher and took him to the bungalow, laying him on his own bed in the front room with the bow window. There, clearing the room of all but the immediate family and another competent doctor who was summering in the colony, Dr. Lew examined him. After he had removed the coat, easing it gently over the big shoulders, and unbuttoned the white shirt with its stiff wing collar, a grim look came over his face. Seeing it, Ida leaned forward, her eyes following his, and she uttered a sharp horrified exclamation.

Dr. John opened his eyes. "Glands—axilla," he murmured thickly. "Been so—some time. Started with those—underarm boils. Thought swelling—go down—lately getting worse—fast—"

"Why"—Ida mouthed the word through dry lips—"*why* didn't you tell us?" But she knew the answer. He had always been too busy thinking of others to bother about himself.

His eyes gleamed up at her through the square-rimmed spectacles which had somehow remained intact. "Sorry—" The congestion in his throat made it hard for him to speak. "Hard enough—little Bon—getting started—cause her—more trouble and worry—probably not serious—"

Making him as comfortable as possible, the doctors went into hurried consultation.

"We must operate," said Dr. Lew abruptly.

Ida gasped. "Where? How? We're miles from the nearest hospital in Madura. He'd never stand—"

"Here," replied her cousin tersely. "And as soon as possible. It's his only chance."

It took five days to secure the necessary implements from the plains. No need of summoning other doctors, for two of the best surgeons in India were already in Kodaikanal. Meanwhile Dr. John, rallying from his accident, carried on his treasurer's work with even more diligence than usual, came to his meals in the common dining room, took part in the life of the community as if nothing had happened. If there were pain and trepidation beneath the calm exterior, he gave no sign. Was he remembering, perhaps, the time when his father, the first Dr. John, discovering a growth of cancer in his foot, had shut himself up in a room and, with only a servant to help, had cut it out with his own hand, nearly fainting several times in the process?

Ida wished she had inherited more of this Scudder courage. Somehow she lived through those five days and the even more agonizing one that followed. There seemed to be two parts of her, one that functioned calmly, efficiently, like a doctor, another than panicked and rebelled and tried to run away like a child. One part comforted her mother, spoke words of quiet assurance, laughed and joked with her father as usual, while the other clamored loudly to fling itself, weeping, into their familiar arms.

The doctors arranged an improvised operating table on the front verandah of Cushing, and chose the noon hour, to employ all the light possible. Dr. Lew performed the operation, assisted by his competent colleague. Ida and Nell and Walter did the sterilizing, using the wood cookstove in the bungalow kitchen and a small kerosene stove on the porch. Large kettles were used to boil sheets and dressings, which were then dried in the oven. Ida stood by Lew's side, obeying his orders like an automaton, lifting an instrument from the bubbling water, laying it in a sterile napkin, handing it to him, taking it from him when he had finished, laying it down again....

This wasn't really happening. It was one of those nightmares in which you dream and know that you are dreaming. Presently she would awaken, laughing and crying with relief because the torment was ended. She would run to her father, who would be sitting with his books in the bow window, and she would beg him to go down with her to Coaker's Walk and wait for the sunset. They would walk together, and she would hear his rumbling laugh.

But it was not a dream. And she was never to hear his laugh again.

In spite of the skillfulness of the operation, it had come too late. The malignancy was extensive. It was impossible to eradicate it completely because the patient was sinking too rapidly. Hastily the incision was closed.

"It's finished," said Dr. Lew grimly.

Briefly Dr. John returned to consciousness, but in such pain that he could only murmur, "Oh, Master, let the light go out." He did not regain consciousness again. They took him into the room with the bow window and laid him on his bed, and his wife and sons and daughter kept watch beside him. A day later they found a quiet spot in the old cemetery at Kodaikanal and left him resting there in the high hills beside a green shola.

There were many eulogies. "His heart had a fitting frame, for both were large" .... "Cheerfulness and perseverance, broad sympathies, and strong convictions, self-forgetfulness and unbounded faith" .... "He did the work of three, sometimes five."

"His greatest fault, if it can be called such," wrote Dr. John Wyckoff, one of his great colleagues in mission work, "was self-depreciation."

But it was his son John who gave him the best tribute. "I love papa, yes," he wrote on May 31, 1900, the day he received the cable. "I love him now. It isn't wrong, is it, to love two fathers in heaven? I know and understand my Heavenly Father because I knew and understood and loved my father in the flesh so well. It is proudly that I sign myself John Scudder, Jr., because I loved him so. I and my life will always be Junior because it can never become worthy of the Senior."

7

Ida was like a watch that has lost its
mainspring. The driving purpose within
her had come to a dead stop. Back in the
bungalow at Vellore with her mother and Annie Hancock, she
faced the future with a heavy heart and a sense of vast in-
adequacy. How could she possibly continue her medical work
without her father to help her? Her American training had
included almost no experience with tropical disease. She had
purposely foregone a year of internship under eminent doctors
at home to spend it here under her father's tutelage. Dr. John's
death had come as a double bereavement. She had lost not only
her father but her sole guide and counselor as well. With Dr.
Lew twelve miles away at Ranipet, Nell on a distant mission
field with Walter, and Louisa Hart unable to join her in Vellore
until the new hospital should be built, Ida felt helpless to cope
with the appalling medical problems she saw all about her.

For days she evaded the issue, put off making any vital
decisions, and Mrs. John, wise in her own grief, said nothing,
merely waited. Then one day Ida entered the small ten-by-
twelve-foot room off the downstairs verandah, opened wide the
shuttered window, and began to move furniture about vigorously.

"My dispensary," she announced briefly.

"Are you sure it isn't too small, dear?" inquired Mrs. John mildly. "With that table and cabinet and all your instruments and medicines, where can you put your patients?"

"You may have my room," offered Annie, who would gladly have wrapped herself in a sheet and slept on the bare stones of the verandah like the night watchman if it would have furthered Ida's mission.

The room was quite big enough, Ida assured them with a briskness that attempted gaiety. There was the verandah where her patients could wait, a window on the shady side where she could give out medicines. Besides, it was only for a few months while she was here alone—her voice broke—just until her hospital was built. That very day she sent a servant into town to spread the news that the sick and ailing were again welcome at the mission bungalow.

At first the little room was ample. No patients came! Ida went each morning at eight o'clock to the window, opened the shutters, checked her shelves of medicines and salves and bandages, spread a clean white cloth on the table, laid out the instruments she was most likely to need—and waited. Presently she was pacing the little room, then the length of the verandah, ready to cry with impatience and frustration. Where were the queues that had always been lined up this time of day to see Dr. John? In the two months she had worked with him Ida had helped her father treat dozens of patients. Hadn't she convinced *any* of them of her skill as a physician?

She called the family butler and the stable boy.

"What's the matter? Don't people know I'm here?"

Each of them wagged his head gravely. "They know, Missy."

"Then why—?"

Their silence was answer enough. Besides, had she really needed to ask? When female doctors were still stigmatized in the United States, a country where men and women were supposed to be equal, what could one expect in a land like India?

Then one morning there rolled up the driveway a brightly painted jutka, the mane of its sleek pony braided with marigolds. Flinging the reins to one of the houseboys, the driver alighted, went around to the rear of the conveyance, and lifted the *gosha* curtain. Watching through the window with bated breath, Ida saw a woman emerge. She wore an orange silk sari, much jewelry, and a bandage about her eyes. Ida flew to meet her, praying silently. *Please let it be something I can cure, not that needs an operation, like cataracts!*

"Salaam, *ammal.* I am the doctor. You have come to see me?" Thanks to her daily lesson with the munshi, her language teacher, Ida's Tamil was getting almost intelligible. "Come, let me help you inside."

It was not cataracts. It was a critical case of conjunctivitis. She gave the woman a thorough examination to determine the cause, then treated the inflammation with drops of a silver nitrate solution, followed by irrigation with a boric lotion.

"You must come tomorrow," she told her earnestly. "You must come for many days, *ammal,* or let me come to you. Otherwise I can't promise that you will not lose your eye. You understand?"

To make sure, she called Salomi, the cook's wife, and asked her to repeat the directions. The woman agreed to come, but all that day Ida endured torment wondering if she would and berating herself for neglecting to find out where she lived. The next morning she was up at dawn, and by eight was pacing the floor of her dispensary. By nine, in spite of the scorching heat, she was down watching by the gate.

The woman came. She came faithfully, day after day, until all danger of her losing the eye was past. On the third visit she brought with her another woman with a simple case of sore eyes, which was easy to treat. By the time a fortnight had passed, there were patients squatting in little groups on the verandah when Ida opened the dispensary each morning. By the end of the summer she had all the patients she could treat, men as well as women.

They came with all sorts of ailments: abscesses, sore eyes, scabies, ringworm, roundworm, broken bones, deep cuts, burns, as well as less curable maladies. She was soon performing simple operations in the little room, opening abscesses, setting broken bones, removing small tumors, and the like. One day the mother of a baby with a huge abscess was so frightened that it was impossible to persuade her to hold the child, and Ida called Salomi to help. The girl came from the kitchen, a smile of unmistakable eagerness on her face. She held up a pair of spotless hands.

"See, Missy? Scrubbed with soap. You don't have to tell Salomi this time."

Her long strong fingers held the little body firmly yet gently enough to inspire confidence. While the abscess was being dressed and the howls were diminishing, she held the child close to her breast, patting its head.

"What a pity," thought Ida, "that she has no children of her own!"

While Ida was attending to the mother, who had screamed even louder than the child, Salomi talked with the patients lined up outside the window.

"Parvati is here with a bottle," she called to Ida. "She wishes some more medicine for her baby's sore eyes. Shall I give her some out of this?"

Turning, Ida saw the girl's hand move to the big bottle of boric acid solution. "Why—yes," she said. "But—how did you know which one?"

"I know," returned Salomi. "I have watched Missy."

Ida's eyes suddenly sparkled. An idea had come to her. "How would you like to give up working in the kitchen," she asked the girl a little later, "and work here with me instead?"

"Work with Missy here? All the time?" The dark young face was radiant.

Ida found Salomi Benjamin an apt and willing pupil. Though lacking formal education, she could read and write Tamil and speak fair English, and her interest in the work and her native intelligence made her quick to learn. She was soon handing out medicines through the window, cleaning sores and changing dressings, washing infected eyes and applying ointments for ringworm and scabies.

When the little room was outgrown, the adjoining guest room was pressed into service, and, as its single bed became inadequate for the cases needing prolonged care, another bed and still another were crowded into its limited space. Going to the dispensary at eight each morning, Ida was often kept busy with patients until noon or after; then there were calls to make in the town, an increasing responsibility as her fame spread, for she was the only woman doctor in a congested area of towns and villages containing a half-million Indian women. During one month alone, in 1901, she made visits in 177 Hindu and Mohammedan homes.

Many of the diseases she treated were the common ones she had become familiar with in medical school. Tuberculosis, always prevalent in conditions of undernourishment, overcrowding, and lack of sanitation, was rampant in India. It was said that one person died of the disease every minute. With no sanatoria available, and cases remaining undetected until they had reached an advanced stage, little could be done to check its violence. Cancer was also prevalent, especially cancer of the mouth, often due to the constant chewing of *pan,* a mixture of tobacco, spices, lime, and betel nut. Lodged in the cheek sometimes for days or even weeks on end, this popular savory became a harmful irritant, often leading to malignancy. Typhoid was an ever-present danger. Venereal diseases were rife.

Yet in this land of extremes even familiar ailments became strange and magnified. Cases of leg ulcer were often major problems of surgery. Due to chronic malnutrition and poor hygiene the skin resistance was poor. Soap was an undreamed-of luxury in most village homes. Injuries were not given the proper attention, and the resulting infection might become a chronic ulcer involving, perhaps, the whole leg from knee to ankle. Some so-called "tropical ulcers," due to an infection of mixed bacteria, were even more stubborn and painful, and could be cured only by excision of the whole area.

Eye infections also, while bearing familiar names, were encountered in such magnitude and variation as to seem almost like new diseases. Here cataracts bore little relation to aging. Due probably to diet deficiencies, the gradual opacity of the eye lens, leading to blindness, affected young and old alike. The *poo-padera,* "spreading of the flower," was one of the major causes of India's high rate of blindness, there being at conservative estimate half a million of her people blind from cataracts.

But there were other causes. Severe conjunctivitis, commonly called "country sore eyes," was constantly encountered. A highly infectious ailment caused by a number of different bacteria, it was easily transmitted by direct contact with fingers, clothes, and, especially during the "eye fly" season when the first rains began in June, by flies. Then, victims of the desperately annoying tiny midges which clung to the lids, every child in a village might have sore eyes. With some it would become a chronic ailment, destroying the tissues and finally the sight. Trachoma was also common, especially among Mohammedan women of South India. A chronic and infectious disease resulting in painful irritation and dimmed vision in these days before sulfa drugs and antibiotics, it could be treated in its earlier stages by solutions of silver nitrate and saline irrigations, but in its advanced stage only by surgery. Severe malnutrition was often in itself the cause of blindness. Lack of certain food elements would cause the eye to soften. Small silvery scales would gather over the white, the eye would lose its luster, disintegrate; and finally the whole eyeball would collapse.

It was the tropical diseases, of course, that the Western doctor found most baffling. Like leprosy. One of the oldest diseases on record, associated in Biblical days with an idea of sin and guilt, it was one of the greatest scourges in India, with at least a million sufferers. Some lepers roamed the streets and roads, or haunted train windows and railroad stations with their begging bowls. Others, fearing ostracism and social stigma, attempted to hide the telltale signs of light skin patches, thickened areas, or insensitive hands and feet as they went about their normal life. Only a handful were segregated in the few leprosariums scattered over the country. Little could be done for them except treat and bind ulcerated feet, amputate diseased fingers and toes, and give medicine for the subsidiary ailments which often accompanied the disease.

For cholera there was more hope of eradication. It was now known that the spirella type of bacterium causing the disease was transmitted through contamination of water and food supplies, frequently by the washing of soiled clothing in village tanks which were also the sources of drinking supply, or the eating of vegetables grown in land fertilized by night soil. The vaccine developed by Haffkine in 1893, used as a preventive measure, had reduced susceptibility eight to one. True, the vaccine had no therapeutic value, and once the dread symptoms appeared, there were still no curative measures that could give the patient more than an even chance of survival. When one considered the sure breeding grounds of religious pilgrimages and festivals, the difficulties of mass inoculations, and the popular belief that all such epidemics were the visitation of an angry goddess, eradication of the disease seemed hopeless.

Fortunately some of the tropical diseases were easier to treat. Malaria, curse of at least fifty million of the population, could usually be relieved by quinine. Scabies, one of the most prevalent of the bacterial skin infections, becoming epidemic in the rainy season, responded fairly well to three days' application of sulphur salve, followed by complete bathing and boiling of clothes. The dysenteries, amoebic and bacillary, could be relieved by ipecac and calomel.

Yet all these measures were mere palliatives, failing to resolve the fundamental causes of ill health. And, however hard one labored, there was always the distressing knowledge that the average life expectancy of the country was less than twenty-seven years; that one out of every four babies born failed to survive its first year of life.

Disease was frequently the least powerful enemy Ida had to combat. Ancient superstitions and quack remedies took their toll again and again. There were certain feast days, she discovered, when not a drop of medicine could be given. More than once she returned to a house only to find that her patient had been dragged to another place to escape the evil spirit which, the family was convinced, must be haunting their house. The more critical the illness, the more evil the spirit. This peregrination from house to house might continue indefinitely —or until the patient died.

In one home she found a young girl with facial paralysis, whose daily treatment had consisted in the killing of a dove and allowing the blood to fall drop by drop on the top of her head. In another Ida had just finished cleaning a wound, which it was most important to keep aseptic. Averting her head for the few moments necessary to prepare some dressings, she turned back to find the wound covered with holy ashes. The septic fever resulting nearly cost the sick girl her life.

On the other hand, many of the native remedies Ida encountered were sound and derived from medical experience far older than even the origins of Western medicine. Charaka the physician and Susruta the surgeon, living about 1000 B.C., propounded theories which agreed amazingly with modern scientific findings. The basis of their work, in fact of all Indian medicine, was to be found in the Ayur Veda (Science of Life), a collection of hymns compiled from two of the ancient Vedic scriptures.

Charaka's voluminous book on medicine, with chapters on diet, drugs, antidotes for poisons, medical instruments and appliances, emphasized cleanliness, purity, and professional integrity to a remarkable degree, while the surgeon Susruta was not only familiar with such delicate instruments as scalpels, lancets, saws, scissors, and needles, but used them skillfully, amputating limbs, performing abdominal sections, reducing hernias, and even mending torn ear lobes by skin grafting. He also employed medicinal wines for anesthetics, and in his labor rooms used clean hands and boiled water.

Though all surgery and dissection were discontinued with the rise of Buddhism about 600 B.C., when killing of animals was prohibited, the practice of medicine rose to new levels with the establishment of free hospitals, state pharmacies, and medical universities, control of pestilence by the extermination of insects and rodents, registers of births and deaths, and the wide cultivation of medicinal herbs. And, though the Mohammedan invasions had thrust Hindu medicine into a sharp decline, many of the sound ancient remedies were still in use, along with many more that were rooted in sheer superstition.

Ida commended these native remedies whenever possible: the use of the milky sap of the pagoda tree, combined with sandalwood oil and camphor, as a cure for itch; tamarind leaves used as a poultice for boils; the juice of pongam roots applied to sores, or used for cleaning teeth. Others, such as treating leprosy with the bite of a cobra, or fever with a mixture of ground glass, cayenne pepper, and gingelli oil, pounded in a mortar and put in the patient's eyes, shocked and angered her.

It was in wrestling with such problems that Ida missed her father most. He could have warned her of them, told her from his own experience how to cope with them. Now she must blunder along as best she could, learning strange customs and a new language, treating diseases she had never studied and often failed even to recognize, facing situations which no amount of knowledge and skill could possibly resolve, only quick wits and a sense of humor.

One of them came on a day in summer when the temperature was 112 in the shade.

"A gentleman outside," reported Salomi gently, thrusting her smooth dark head into the room where Ida panted under the swaying punkah, stretched full length on the floor because the bed sheet was too hot. "Most urgent, he says," she added apologetically.

"Oh, no!" Ida groaned. "Tell him I can't—" Surely just once she could refuse, after a long morning in the dispensary and a half-dozen house calls! "Tell him I'll come," she finished meekly.

Stumbling to her feet, she squirmed her perspiring body into stays and underwear and petticoat, made a wry face as she harnessed her throat into the high collar of boned mesh prescribed by Western style, and donned a freshly starched long-sleeved, ankle-length white dress. It was soggily damp before she reached the door.

The man on the verandah might have been one of the three who had come to her door that long-ago night in Tindivanam.

"Doctor *Ammal?*" He spoke with dignity and confidence. "I need your help. My wife, a young girl, is in childbirth. Will you come?"

"Oh—*yes!*" Fervently Ida thanked the providence which had kept her from refusing. Learning the man's name, she recognized him as belonging to a family of well-educated high-caste Hindus, many of them lawyers and all citizens of high rank in the community. As she followed his conveyance with her own carriage and pony, not even the shriveling oven through which she drove could quell her exuberance. What were heat and weariness beside an opportunity to atone for the

84

failure of that distant night? And this was an educated household, where she would be permitted to use all her skill!

Ushered into the inner courtyard of the spacious house, she was met by an old grandmother, and her heart sank. This woman was at least seven hundred years old! With her white widow's garb, her shaved head, her little leather pouch of betel, her stained teeth, she might have stepped bodily from that thirteenth century of Bommai Reddy. She greeted Ida with politeness but without pleasure. "Come, *ammal*," she said briefly in Tamil.

Ida followed her through the courtyard, an inner room, and a smaller court, then on into that windowless, dirty back room of the house where birth, considered to be an unclean thing, was so often consummated. The heat of it was like the blast of a furnace. Brushing past the grandmother, she went swiftly to the woman on the mat, knelt beside her.

"*Ammal*," she called gently. No answer. "*Ammal!*" She spoke again, more urgently, but the figure remained motionless. Her heart gave a sickening lurch. Was her patient already dead? Were the funeral drums to beat again, before she could even try to prevent them?

While her fingers were still groping for a pulse, the girl reached out a feeble hand, grasped hers, and lifted it to thick hot lips. Gently Ida pressed the lips apart to reveal a terribly swollen tongue. She uttered a horrified exclamation. Her patient was literally dying of thirst! She rose to her feet, head throbbing, wanting suddenly to stamp her foot and shout reproach against a society so bound by superstition that it refused to give a sick person a drop of water. Instead she turned to the old grandmother with a smile.

"My medicine is somewhat different from yours," she said politely in the best Tamil she could muster. "It will not work without water. "*Tunni*—water." She repeated the word again and again to the blank features. "Understand?"

To her relief the old woman finally wagged her head in acquiescence, turned, and went away. She had not only understood but had agreed to defy superstition! Presently she was back with a small brass cup, containing a mere thimbleful of

85

liquid. *"Illai,* no! More," explained Ida patiently. "Much more."

The woman again disappeared. This time when she returned there was perhaps half an ounce in the cup. "More," pleaded Ida. "I must have more, all the water I need. Understand?"

The eyes that looked into hers were older even than seven hundred years, as old as the fear of spirits lurking in sticks and stones. Ida knew that not another drop of water would be forthcoming. Without a word she walked out of the room, through the two courtyards, into the front entrance chamber, where several of the men of the family were sitting, the woman's husband among them. He sprang to his feet. "Doctor *Ammal!* Is my wife—her child—"

"Your wife is dying," Ida told him bluntly, "because the women of your household are afraid to give her a drink of water." Her blue eyes flashed about the circle of surprised male faces. She could talk to these men in her own language, and she did so, mincing no words. "Are you men afraid too? And of what? An old superstition that dates back to the days when all our ancestors thought the earth was flat? No. You're educated men. You know better than that. Then it must be your women you're afraid of." She faced the girl's husband squarely. "Which shall it be? A dead superstition or a dead wife?"

There was shocked silence while Ida held her breath and quivered. She had intended to ask politely, beg if necessary, but certainly not to *tell* them! "What do you want us to do?" asked the young husband quietly.

"Tell them—tell them to give me all the water I want," she demanded.

She got it. The young woman's life was saved. The child was born, fortunately a boy, for the misfortune of a girl, even a healthy one, could have been ascribed to the flouting of tradition. Ida drove home in the cool of the evening, with the day's temperature down close to a hundred.

"Water!" She gritted the word through her teeth as she pried herself out of her wet grimy garments and literally wrung them out over a washbasin. But there was triumph in her voice as she uttered it.

At last, after what seemed interminable months, plans for the new hospital were completed, and in a dreadful rainstorm on September 7, 1901, with impressive pomp the cornerstone was laid. But for Ida there was little time to rejoice, for that day of rain was the last of the season. Famine spread swiftly, covering an area of at least 200,000 square miles. Even the wells on the mission compound almost dried up.

Each morning Ida found the lines of patients outside her dispensary window a little longer, faces more haggard, already thin bodies more bony and gaunt. Some, once they had squatted, had insufficient energy to get to their feet and crawl to the window. Feeding stations were set up again on the compound, with doles of ragi gruel for the most destitute. Only the bamboo shelters with the hungry children were lacking to make the horror of her childhood complete. But she had merely to step out of the gate and down the road to see little outstretched claws and rows of empty mouths.

There was no time for brooding, little enough for pity. For famine was disease as well as hunger. During these desperate months the dispensary was forced into larger quarters. Since it would be many months before the new hospital was completed, Ida had a small mud-brick building made ready for her use on the compound, with room for six more beds to house her necessary inpatients. Her days during these months were so full that there was scarcely time to live them, much less record their happenings.

Yet for the sake of friends far away, she did find time to write about one of them. The day she chose was a Thursday, late in November, and the title she picked for the hastily scrawled paragraphs was

"ONE DAY'S WORK"

"While it is still dark I am aroused by the noise of wheels, telling me that day is at hand and I must be on the wing. Dressing in the dark I am nearly ready when a knock tells me that my chota (coffee and toast) is ready, and as I finish this and am ready to start, the first rays of morning are lighting the sky. My Indian assistant, Salomi, is always ready and waiting at the steps.

"The morning is resplendent with beauty, the western sky a beautiful pink and the east like molten gold. Feeling the new life which I need creep into my veins, I thank God for his wonderful handiwork.

"By the time the beauty is fading we are well on our way to the town, a long hard drive when one is in a hurry. We meet picturesque groups of women laden with brass or earthen pots, little girls bending under loads far greater than they ought to bear. Cattle and sheep in great herds are being driven to the grazing lots. Crows by the hundreds flock about picking up their breakfast. The grain bazaar is a regular Venice, with thousands of pigeons gathering up the sweepings. Beggars crowd the streets, poor puny babies without a rag on, crying with the cold (for at this time of year it can be uncomfortably cold at six in the morning). Here is a little group huddled about a blaze started from a pile of rubbish, and there is a woman making *opams,* cakes cooked from rice flour.

"The bazaars are being swept and the doors opened, which means a number of boards taken down one by one and placed at one side until nightfall. The wares are brought out and placed in order. Here we pass a mosque and listen to the morning worship going on. Now we have reached our destination, a spacious house but dark and gloomy, the only light coming in through a small opening in the roof, which is covered with bands of iron. The rooms are dark where the women live, but the men have their apartments upstairs where it is cooler and more airy.

"My patient here is a sweet young girl, suffering for the past two years with an abscess between her shoulders, one of those slow processes coming from a tubercular spine. A crowd always follows me in and watches, commenting or asking questions. As soon as I have completed the treatment, there are five or six women waiting to have me feel their pulse and at once tell them just what their trouble is. A woman's trouble must always be diagnosed from her left hand, a man's from his right. If by mistake I feel a woman's right pulse and don't ask for her left hand, they think me exceedingly ignorant.

"From this house we return part way on the bazaar street and turn into a narrower one, then into a mere alley. We have to leave the carriage and walk. Heads fill the doorways, for in some mysterious way they know that 'Doctor Ammal' is coming. Some smile back at me. Others draw their heads indoors. It is a Mohammedan house to which we are bound, and my patient is a young girl, the mother of two children. Such a nice family, so neat and clean and grateful!

"On to three other houses in a different part of town. Now we must hurry home, for the dispensary opens before eight. I give the reins into Salomi's hands and take this opportunity to read my medical journals. On reaching home, I first run out to my small hospital room to see that all is well.

"A crowd is waiting, and I am soon in the whirl of a dispensary, taking names, diagnosing (or trying to), and then doing all the treatment with Salomi's help. It is hard work, and I sorely need a trained assistant.

"First comes a dear old lady whose finger I had to amputate. I almost took her hand off as the case was desperate, but her son pleaded with me to give it one more try. I did, and am so thankful. Then comes a baby with a frightful burn. A man now comes whom I am treating out of pity. He swallowed a thorn, which was removed by a native doctor, but he has stricture of the throat and when he first came could not even swallow a drop of water and had not eaten for four days. Now he is able to swallow the white of an egg and a little milk. The only objection I have to his gratitude is that he insists on throwing himself at my feet and touching the toes of my shoes with his fingers, which he then kisses. I have learned now to get out of his way.

"Sore eyes, earache, skin diseases, and fevers are always plenty, but each day I have new and interesting cases. My one room is very crowded, and it is often hard to be patient. I always have to repeat my directions as to how and when to take the medicine, how much, and whether to take special diet.

"Now comes a poor village woman with her only little child with a fearful incurable disease. She says she has heard my name and people say I can cure her child, and then, placing the little one in another's arms while she bows before me, calls me first her 'mother', then her 'god.' Oh, it is so hard to tell her that nothing can be done!

"Next comes a child totally blind, on account of having sore eyes neglected. Oh, these poor dependent, helpless people, I do pity them so! The hardest thing I have to do is to tell them they have come too late.

"Morning wears on and the breakfast bell rings, but I cannot go. Someone comes to the door and says that breakfast is nearly over. 'Won't Missy come?' It is nearly one o'clock when I am ready to eat, and everybody has left the table, but Miss Hancock comes and sits with me while I tell her about the patients. After eating I return to my office to make some tests and find that one girl has tuberculosis. I had hoped against hope, but the microscope reveals the fact, and I have to tell her husband, who is waiting, that she will not live very long. All he says is 'Oh, how can I let her die? We have four little children.'

"I go again to the hospital room, where I have three patients. It is a pretty room, bright and airy. All the women say they have only to come to this room to get well, for here the air is fresh and everything clean. After treating them I return to the house and rest a little.

"Soon a call comes from town and I again hurry into another quarter where the streets are narrow and I have a long distance to walk. I find a young girl dying of tuberculosis. A severe hemorrhage frightened her people into coming for me as a 'last resort.' Some day they will understand and will have confidence. Now I must pray for patience.

"I reach home just in time to dress for dinner, for this is Thanksgiving Day, and some friends have come in to help us celebrate. We talk of the dear homeland and wish that we might see our loved ones there. Do we give thanks? Oh, yes! I especially thank God for leading me to India to work among these women whom I love.

"P.S. Two weeks have passed since writing the first part of this. The mother of the baby with the frightful burn brought him a few times, and he was doing beautifully; then because I suggested skin grafting she did not come again but is going to a native doctor. The woman with tuberculosis has died, and I cured the old man with the bad throat so efficiently that he ate an enormous dinner of rice and then drank a large quantity of water and tumbled over dead. I am so sorry, for he was a nice old man."

The letter from Burchfield Milliken came in April, 1902. She opened it as she had opened all his letters in the past months, expectantly but without much emotion, knowing it would be friendly, undemanding, hopeful. In fact, she had come to depend on his letters as a source of strength and courage.

"My very dear friend," he wrote. "With this letter I have some bad news, but I hope you will not find it too disturbing. You have enough to concern you with all your sick friends in India. But since you are always my best of friends, perhaps I ought to tell you."

As Ida read on, her interest changed to apprehension. He had unwisely neglected an attack of grippe, let it develop into a chronic infection. In fact, he was now fighting tuberculosis of the lungs, and he was afraid he did not have long to live.

Without stopping to analyze her emotions, Ida sat down and hastily wrote a reply, fearing that already it might be too late to reach him; then, rereading what she had written, found she had said little, merely a few words of comfort and encouragement, nothing of what she really felt. But—what did she feel? Sympathy and deep concern, of course, as for any of her close friends, as she felt a dozen times a day for people with similar problems who needed the healing strength she could give. Nothing more? Guilt, perhaps, at the thought that if she had known her own heart better, this might never have happened? Love? She did not know. Even in his present need, Burchfield Milliken seemed far away, much farther than the little Indian mother who in addition to the same affliction had had four little children to leave! Hastily Ida slipped the scrawled sheets into an envelope, sealed it, and gave it to a servant to mail.

Weeks passed, so full of heat and toil and worry that she had little time to think. She took the Tamil examination required of all missionaries after the months of language study and—wonder of wonders—passed it, even receiving a note of commendation from Uncle Jared, one of the examiners!

He wrote: "I congratulate you most heartily on the very excellent and happy issue of the ordeal. Your examination was exceedingly creditable to yourself. You must have studied hard indeed to get all that grammar and the rest of it stored up in your brain and memory." Rare praise from stern Uncle Jared!

And then in July came another letter. Ida stood staring at the envelope with its foreign stamp and familiar handwriting. It was as if Burchfield Milliken had returned from the dead. As she tore it open and read, she could actually hear his voice, gentle, tender, a bit whimsical, arousing within her an unexpected tumult of emotion.

"My dearest Friend: I am still alive to receive and enjoy your letter which I received May 27, and that unwelcome thing death seems not so near as when I wrote you two months ago. I think I am a little improved since then. But I'm glad you can't see me now—or hear me. It's a harsh ugly cough to inflict on friends. . . .

"Please don't let this letter make you unhappy. I'm not discouraged, and you must not be, if your thoughts have time to turn to me. Mine are always with you, desiring for you all you wish to attain."

All you wish to attain. And what was that? Love for a good man who loved and needed her? A new hospital to make people well so they could die of famine? Days like these so full of toil and backbreak that she scarcely had energy to bathe away the sweat and crawl into her bed at night? It was almost a relief that she was too busy to decide.

Two years had passed since she had opened the dispensary in the little ten-by-twelve room. And she had treated over five thousand patients.

8

YOU ARE CORDIALLY INVITED TO
THE OPENING
OF THE
MARY TABER SCHELL MEMORIAL HOSPITAL

which will take place on Tuesday afternoon
September the Sixteenth at four o'clock
Mr. and Mrs. Vaughn have kindly consented to be present
and open the building

Vellore   I. S. Scudder, M.D.
No. Arcot District

It was an occasion of such pomp and gaiety that fifty years later Vellore residents still living were to remember its smallest detail.

People poured through the gate by hundreds, their bright saris and turbans twining living garlands about grounds and porches. They loudly approved of the new red brick building with its novel architecture, admired the spacious inner courtyard and sunken garden, marveled at the rows of neat white iron beds, stared with speechless wonder into the gleaming white operating room with its glass table, its sterilizers, its wonderful rolling stretchers.

93

Long streamers extended from the hospital doors to the flag-decked table beneath the festive canopy, and at the appropriate time the wife of the district Collector who was officiating pulled on the ribboned ends. Ida wore a braided and ruffled gown which overspread much of the platform, and a huge platter of hat supporting a garden of flowers. Indian officials did honor to the occasion. There were the Diwan Bahadur Subramaniam, administrator of the high court of Madras, and Mr. V. Subramanian Bantalu, the District Munsiff. The Mohammedan community of Vellore was represented by the secretary of the Municipal Council, the Khan Bahadur Mohammed Habbibullah Sahib, impressive in festive dress and turban.

"The Mohammedan *gosha* ladies will benefit greatly by this hospital," he proclaimed in beautiful English, its one defect the inability to pronounce "s" as the initial letter of a word. "Dr. Escudder is indeed a worthy friend of our beloved Vellore."

The day of triumph passed, leaving Ida with a great heap of wilting garlands, a garden of trampled flowers, and a brand-new women's hospital with its long jutting portico facing the street, its main structure a rectangle of warm red brick built about a sunken garden and completely surrounded by shady verandahs. The two large wards, one for poor patients admitted free of charge, the other for caste people who could afford to pay a little, plus one or two smaller rooms which could be used for wealthier patients, furnished ample space, together with the broad verandahs, for the forty beds included in the hospital plan. At present there were fewer than thirty.

No time, however, to admire the newly completed structure, or to enjoy with her mother the spacious two-storied bungalow close by on the hospital compound; not even to miss the daily intimacy with Annie Hancock, who had remained in the old mission bungalow a mile away! For on the following morning, September 17, she was holding her first dispensary in the small consulting room at the front of the new building, with a long queue of patients squatted beneath the portico of the adjoining verandah, and by the twenty-second she was receiving inpatients into the wards.

The new white iron beds, each with its wire spring and mattress and its accompanying locker covered with a clean white cloth, were objects of terror as well as wonder to these first patients. Accustomed to sleeping on mats at floor level, the frightened occupants felt as if they were being placed on dangerous high shelves, and more than once Ida returned to the wards to find a patient, wrapped carefully in her sheet, lying under the bed instead of on it. But worse problems soon followed, with patients swarming in such numbers that many beds had to harbor two women, one on the mattress and one on the floor underneath!

To Ida's extreme dismay she had to face the increased responsibility of the new hospital alone, for young Dr. Louisa Hart, who had first dreamed of the project and planned to join her from Ranipet, had departed abruptly for America on account of illness. For months Ida had only the willing but untrained Salomi to help her.

Not many days after Louisa's departure, Ida came running along the path from the hospital to the rear verandah of the bungalow where Mrs. John was giving out the morning food supplies to the servants.

"I—can't!" she gasped. "Mother, I—I just can't!"

"Can't what, dear?" asked Mrs. Scudder calmly, continuing to measure rice into a round reed basket.

"It's a tumor," explained Ida, slowly regaining her breath. "A bad one. Abdominal. I—I should operate!"

"Five," counted Mrs. John carefully, dipping her measure into the big earthen jar and leveling it off with her fingers. "Well—and why not? If the woman needs an operation, she's come to the right place."

"But—mother, you don't understand! It's not like the things I've been doing. It—it's a major operation!"

"Well?" The older woman's gaze was steady. "Suppose it is."

"I—I haven't done one for years, not since I was in school, and—and then only a few, with other doctors. Suppose"—the blue eyes were dark with panic—"suppose I do something wrong and—and she dies!"

"And suppose," responded Mrs. John, interrupting herself

to count six, "she dies because there was no woman doctor who had the gumption to operate on her? Wouldn't that be worse?"

"Yes," replied Ida.

She walked back along the path by the asoka tree where the pony was tied, past the big palmyra tree, and, entering the hospital through the door beside S-Ward, followed the long verandah about the rectangular court. She walked with her usual brisk confidence. Going to the little operating room at the far end, she lighted the kerosene lamp under the shining new sterilizer. With methodical swiftness she assembled instruments, pads of cotton, medications, chloroform. She moved the beautiful new glass-topped table a few inches in order to get the full benefit of daylight. Then, summoning Salomi, she calmly returned to the ward and prepped her patient.

She performed the operation, a difficult hysterectomy, with an anesthetist who had given chloroform only twice, an assistant who did not know one instrument from another. Mercifully it was a success. Had it not been, she might never have dared to take a scalpel in her hand again.

Before the year was over she had performed 21 major operations, all of them successful, in addition to 428 minor ones performed in both hospital and dispensary. During the entire year of 1902 she treated 12,359 patients.

Usually it was the operations not performed which were the unsuccessful ones. On one occasion a little woman was brought by her husband and other members of her family from a great distance. Immediate operation for ectopic pregnancy could possibly save her. She wanted it done, begged Ida to do it, but her husband and family refused.

"Oh, *ammal*, save me, save me," begged the woman over and over with tears in her eyes. "I have five little children at home, five little children. Can't you please save me and send me back to them?"

But the family was adamant. Helpless, fuming against an ignorance that could make use of an unclean trowel in childbirth yet fearfully reject a healing scalpel, Ida watched the lumbering bullock cart carry the poor little patient through the hospital gate and to her certain death.

Yet there were compensating satisfactions when fears were

conquered. There was the little lad who came into the dispensary naked as he had been born, complaining of a stone in his ear. It was a large stone, pushed deep into the canal by one of his playmates.

"It will hurt when I take it out," Ida told him frankly, patting his bony little shoulder. "But you're a strong boy. You will be brave."

He was. Keeping his huge eyes fixed on her face, he suffered the painful ordeal without wincing. The next day she felt a gentle tug on her dress. Looking down, she saw the same boy holding another child by the hand.

"Here is another boy with a stone in his ear," he said.

The new patient, a tiny fellow, was speechless with terror, but while the operation was being performed his friend stood close beside him and kept saying, "Don't be afraid. She won't hurt you any more than she can help."

After the stone was removed, the two little chaps, dressed only in nature's clothing, marched out of the room, asked the servant in attendance for the charity box, and, when each one had dropped in a *pie* (about a sixth of a cent), scampered away.

Then there was the young woman from a distant village who came with fears even bigger than the huge abscess which swelled her leg from knee to ankle. Whenever Ida or Salomi approached her, she would shrink into a corner and scream. Finally they succeeded in getting her on the operating table, putting her under chloroform, and opening the abscess. Her joy and relief were unbounded. Some days later a Mohammedan woman came with almost as big an abscess and equally gigantic fears. The two were put in the same ward.

"Do not fear, *ammal*," said the first patient soothingly. "The Doctor *Ammal* is our mother. She will not harm her child."

Because of her gentle persuasion and assurance Ida was able easily to treat the second patient.

The famine was over. Rains such as had not fallen in ten years blessed the land during that fall of 1902. The coronation of King Edward VII apparently cast its beneficent aura even to this far outpost of empire. Festivity ran riot as invited rajahs and native regiments departed for England in a panoply of splendor. Delhi celebrated both the event and the coming of a new year with a magnificent pageant and an assembling of native princes with 37,000 troops.

But the festivity was short-lived in Vellore. For on the heels of famine followed the even more dreadful Black Death. In January of 1903 bubonic plague swept over South India with a fury surpassing all previous epidemics. Within a month the record of the last attack, in 1899, was equaled and exceeded. Arriving finally in North Arcot District, the terrible scourge followed its usual pattern. Rats, bitten by the plague-bearing flea, were found dead. People seeming in perfect health were seen suddenly to sway and stagger. Their speech became slurred. Glandular swellings would appear. A day or two later the victims would develop high fever and prostration, which resulted in almost certain death.

Ten years before, the plague would have taken its deadly toll unchallenged save for ineffective gestures, such as quarantine, isolation in camps, burning of pest-ridden houses, the eradication of infected rats. But since the isolation of the *Bacillus pestis* in 1894 by a pupil of Pasteur, Haffkine's vaccine formula had been perfected. Now, armed with this new weapon, government and medical workers set forth to grapple with the epidemic.

But their efforts only spread new panic. In Arni, Ranipet, Tindivanam, Vellore, people fled their homes, their fear of health officers and their strange inoculations worse even than that of plague. For the Black Death, despite its horror, was familiar. Like smallpox and cholera, they knew it as the visitation of Mari Ammal, incarnation of Kali and Goddess of Death, to be accepted with outward reverence but inward terror, and to be averted only by flocking to her shrines with prayers and gifts. Not so the inoculations! Rumors became rife that the government was using them as a pretext for killing the Indian people and that doctors were paid so much a head for disposing of them.

Overnight the hospital emptied itself, and the daily stream of outpatients shrank to a mere dribble. Fearful of inoculations, even beggars and hucksters shunned the gate as if it were the entrance to a cobra den.

But for Ida work was not lessened. With another young missionary who was chairman of the Vellore Municipal Board, she worked day and night going into the homes of the town, enforcing sanitary measures and administering vaccine. It was a grueling and thankless task. People refused either to be inoculated or to permit the health officers to dismantle and disinfect their homes. They hid stricken members of their families, maneuvering them from one house to another; refused to evacuate and go to the sheds and huts constructed for them outside of town. One day Ida and her co-worker entered the home of the Municipal Chairman, an educated Indian who had worked with them untiringly to enforce the regulations, only to find it deserted.

"Gone!" exclaimed Ida's companion in amazement.

"But—where? Why?" despaired Ida. "He was the first to insist that everybody be inoculated!"

"Everybody but his own family," replied her colleague bitterly. "And now plague has come, he's moved them out of Vellore bag and baggage."

Day after day they moved through a death-stricken city, its streets empty save for a few sullen men who muttered curses and flung them dark looks. Occasionally they would find one brave enough to accept inoculation or to invite them into his home to treat a patient. Entering one house where inoculations had been refused, they found the father and mother on the floor, the mother dead, the father dying, two sons already exhibiting the deadly symptoms of slurred speech, staggering walk, high fever. They did what they could, then summoned the plague officers, who followed their usual routine. Wearing masks and high rubber boots to protect them against the four-inch jump of the plague-carrying flea, these men removed the dead, transported the living to a segregation camp, emptied the house of everything portable, dug up the floor and burned it, removed tiles from the roof, and, by means of huge tubs of disinfectant and a portable pump, drenched both walls and ceiling.

Ida had no fear of plague. Even when two rats were found dead on the hospital compound and the servants' quarters in the rear had to be evacuated, she herself made no change in the day's routine. She moved through both days and nights mechanically, steps geared to the monotonous rhythm of funeral bands and to the clash and din of tom-toms beaten to drive away demons.

For three weeks the plague raged at its height in Vellore, with an average of 17 deaths a day, 400 before the epidemic had run its course. By April it had passed on to other parts of India, increasing in fury all that year and part of the next, claiming in all over a million victims.

Ida did not write Burchfield Milliken about the epidemic. His own white plague was sufficient burden for one man, even one of great courage. He was in the Southwest now—Texas and New Mexico—fighting his battle not only for survival but for purpose to keep on living. He wrote her in March, wondering why she had not written. He was living in a tent in the hills, had done his own cooking at first, until another setback came. Now he employed an Indian woman to clean and cook for him. He had bought a pony and taken a long trip into the desert. And he was worried because she was not going to the mountains and was working too hard.

Self-reproachful because of her neglect, Ida wrote him at length, telling him about everything she could think of except the plague and her own utter weariness; about her little dog Gyp and his clever tricks and the new enclosed swimming pool on the compound, with a bathhouse inside its enclosure, and water drawn by bullocks; about the tennis matches she had played and won at the English Club; about the funny letter which had come addressed to "Empty Shell (M. T. Schell) Hospital;" and especially about the new helpers who had arrived to make her work easier.

She could not be thankful enough for them. Mrs. Gnanammal, her new trained compounder, or pharmacist, was a widow of about thirty-five, well educated, a third-generation Christian. A versatile woman of great energy and intelligence, she not only presided efficiently over the little compounding room at the front of the hospital but also proceeded to make herself useful in a variety of capacities, from midwife to hospital matron to Bible woman. She was to be Ida's loyal friend and dependable co-worker for the next half-century.

Ida also had a good trained nurse, Gnanasundram, who was learning quickly to adjust herself to Ida's exacting standards. With the half-blind evangelist, Mary Isaac Henry, as her hospital matron, some capable young girls whom she was training in simple nursing, and her mother as a constant helper, Ida was slowly assembling a more adequate staff.

Yet so great was the pressure of work that she seemed busier than ever. The two hot months in the summer of 1903, when she should have gone to the hills with her mother, were the most active since the hospital's opening. More patients came from distant villages. Numbers in the dispensary constantly increased. Many days she treated over 150 patients before making the rounds of the hospital, performing operations, paying visits to homes in the town. Heavenly in the broiling heat were the brief moments she and Annie Hancock, who had insisted on remaining in Vellore with her, were able to snatch for bathing in the new pool, which was long enough and deep enough for real swimming.

But often her working hours stretched around the clock. When there were to be operations the next morning, cottons must be sterilized all night, and, dependable though her helpers were, Ida got up several times to see that they were keeping the kerosene stoves pumped up and getting the sterilization done properly. From the beginning she trained her nurses and attendants to consider her on constant call, and night after night they would come to her door with their little smoking lamps.

"Doctor *Ammal?*"

At the sound of the gentle knocking Ida would instantly waken and, pulling on her wrapper, would invariably follow them.

Many patients insisted on her applying dressings and giving treatments which her helpers could have done as well, believing that the Doctor *Ammal* had a "good hand." They would wait an hour for her to treat them, and she had not the heart to refuse.

Her pride received a jolting, however, when after her brief vacation in August, with Nell and her mother taking over her work, a woman came into the small consulting room and, giving

Ida a disdainful glance, asked for the *Peria Ammal* (older lady).

"She's not here just now," said Ida, smiling, "but she will be coming soon. Is there anything I can do for you?"

The patient gave her another scornful look. "I will wait for the *Peria Ammal,*" she replied with dignity. "She treated me yesterday, and I am better. I will wait for her." And, squatting stubbornly on the floor outside the consulting room, she flatly refused treatment.

When the *Peria Ammal* finally arrived and, smiling with amusement, explained that the *Chinna Ammal* was the doctor, the woman nodded and looked on Ida with greater favor. But when Ida gave her a prescription, she still insisted on taking it to Mrs. John to be filled.

It was on one of these arduous days in 1903—September 21 —that Ida delivered a wealthy young Mohammedan girl of a beautifully formed but delicate baby girl. She worked over the child day and night until she was sure her life was out of danger. As usual, members of the family, in this case the mother and sister, had accompanied the patient to the hospital and remained to cook her food and attend to her personal needs. All but the baby's mother regarded the mite with glum disfavor, not only because of her sex but because her birth had occurred on an inauspicious day. Ida was confident, however, that, given a little time, the child would win their hearts.

One day soon after the child's birth she was sitting in her dispensary surrounded by patients when suddenly she felt, as plainly as if the words had been uttered, "I must go this minute and take a look at that baby!"

"What nonsense!" her common sense retorted in a voice equally audible. "If anything were wrong, one of the girls would call me."

But she felt impelled to go. Jumping up abruptly, she hurried out of the consulting room, past the queues of patients, down the passage and along the verandah leading to S-Ward, where paying patients were accommodated. Arrived at the door, she felt absurdly foolish, for there was Salomi bending over one of the beds, faithfully making her rounds. There was the screen in the far corner, partially concealing the bed of the little Mohammedan mother in *gosha* privacy, and all was quiet behind it. *Too quiet.* With sudden inexplicable urgency Ida flew across the room.

"No! No!" she screamed. Pushing the two figures roughly aside, she snatched at the object one of them was holding, a pillow pressed hard against the surface of the bed, and flung it aside. The baby was already blue in the face. Another few moments, and it would have been strangled. She worked over it desperately and in silence, was rewarded finally by the sound of short choking gasps. Soon it was crying lustily.

Cradling the soft bundle fiercely against her breast, Ida glared across the sobbing mother at the two older women. "You—you murderers!" She gave vent to her anger in English which they could not understand. "Oh, what couldn't I do to you!" She choked. "How—how *could* you!" she finished furiously in Tamil. "That darling baby!"

The sister returned her gaze with defensive sullenness. *"Chi!"* she muttered disgustedly. "Better dead. Born on an unlucky day. It was the will of Allah that she die."

"No!" protested Ida hotly. "You can't mean that!"

A look of cunning came into the grandmother's eyes. "You don't want her to die?" she asked craftily. *"Nalla thu!* It is good! You take her."

Ida gasped. *"I!* But—you can't mean—"

The sister smiled with sudden magnanimity. "You like the baby? You don't want her to die? *Nalla thu!* She is yours."

"Please!" The eyes of the little mother implored from the bed. "Please take her, *ammal!*"

Ida's lips compressed. Her eyes sharpened to an icy brightness. "All right," she said abruptly. "I will."

Crossing the yard swiftly to the bungalow, she found her mother sitting on the rear verandah. With a few terse words of explanation she placed the small bundle in the outspread lap.

"There! She's ours," she concluded succinctly, courage suddenly waning as she realized what she had done. "What—what are we going to do with her?"

Sophia Scudder contemplated the unexpected bundle with her usual equanimity. Her life had contained many surprises, and she had approached them all with realistic calmness and prompt decision.

"What are we going to do with her?" she repeated, dandling the bundle with the practiced efficiency of a mother of six. "Feed her, I would say, about the first thing, and give her a name. Have you decided what you're going to call her?"

"Well—hardly!" Ida's quick laughter sprang from both amusement and relief. "That's up to you, I guess. You've named most of the Christian babies within a fifty-mile radius."

Mrs. John considered. "Hmm! Her own mother doesn't want her—or can't have her. So the hospital is in a sense her mother," she mused. "We'll call her Mary Taber!"

And Mary Taber she was christened in the church a few months later, wearing the Scudder baptismal dress and with most of the India Scudders in attendance. A sober mite heretofore, the moment the ceremony was completed she began to laugh, long and heartily. She continued to be a happy baby and thrived, whether fed on Mellen's food or nursed by accommodating mothers in the hospital.

When she was old enough, Ida often carried her around on her hip, like an Indian mother, saying to all she met, *"Yanudiaya pillai!* (This is my child!)" Once somebody snapped a picture of her with Mary Taber, still a mere infant, in her arms, and on an impulse she sent it with some others to Burchfield Milliken.

It was a day late in 1904 when his last letter came. Ida was about to enter the operating room when a servant brought it. She stood staring at the familiar handwriting, eyes wide and incredulous. It was weeks ago that she had received a cable telling her of Burchfield Milliken's death, yet here were words written by his hand. If she opened the letter, she would hear his voice speaking.

She did not open it. Slipping it into the pocket of her white dress, she went on into the theater, where Salomi and two nurses were waiting. She performed an operation, a long and difficult one, with her usual absorption and punctilious attention to detail, then went immediately to the dispensary. She was later than usual in arriving.

The lines of waiting patients were never so long in the after-noon because a small fee of eight annas (about sixteen cents) was charged in contrast with the three-*pie* bit (about half a cent) which each morning outpatient was asked to put into the box to pay for his chit, or small sheet of paper, on which were written his name and number and the date. Today the queues were even shorter than usual because of the recent activities of a pariah leper "swami" who had persuaded the more ignorant citizens of Vellore that he had miraculous heal-ing powers.

Among the new patients today was a young woman with a worn and anxious face. Ida found herself hurrying with the other cases in order to get to her; hurrying also because of the unopened letter in her pocket.

"*Yenna 'mal?*" she was able to ask finally when the young woman knelt beside her chair. "*Yenna sungathi?* What's the matter?"

The woman unwrapped a ragged covering to reveal an in-fant about a year old with such a huge abscess on his tiny leg that Ida recoiled in horror.

"*Ayoh! Pavum!* What a pity! But why, *ammal, why* did you not bring him to me before? He must have been suffering like this for days!"

"*Amma,* yes," said the woman sadly. "But—I could not bring him, Doctor *Ammal.* I—I didn't dare—"

"And why not?" demanded Ida almost angrily. For if she had spoken gently, she would surely have burst into tears.

The dark eyes were piteously pleading. "Because, *ammal,* they all told me it was the image of my god growing on his leg and I must not touch it or let any one else do anything for him."

Without a word Ida took the child to the operating room and proceeded to open the abscess. But when the lance was applied she found, as she had expected, that the bone was so diseased there was no possibility that the child would live. The god had indeed inscribed his image on the leg of the child. And the name of the god was ignorance, and his image was death.

It was after five when she finished in the dispensary, and there was still no time for the letter. There were patients to

105

be visited again in the wards. An old lady with cataracts was on the floor under her bed, her daughter lying asleep on the mattress above. The nurse came running, both concerned and exasperated. *"Chi!* There she is again! I told her—"

"Never mind," said Ida, smiling. "Let her be. If I'd slept on the floor all my life, I'd probably be as frightened as she to be put on a high shelf."

She stopped to congratulate Jeevamonie, an enteric fever patient, who after a milk diet of three weeks had just had her first meal of rice and curry. The small round face with its big brown eyes was radiant. In the next bed was a wee mite of four years suffering from congenital heart disease. Ida stopped to massage the withered legs and to inquire gently how the little patient felt. Smiling feebly, the child raised a thin hand to her head. *"Thalai novoo,"* came the usual reply. "Head aching."

The husband of Armonie, a patient most dangerously ill with heart disease and severe dropsy, was waiting outside the door of S-Ward, his kind face beaming. The Doctor *Ammal* would be glad to know that he had consulted astrologers as to his wife's fate, and she was to live another twenty-eight years, outliving himself by at least ten. This was news, he was sure, which would cheer the Doctor *Ammal.*

"Yes," said Ida. "It is news indeed. Thanks for telling me." She turned away. It was a little after six. She would have time now, perhaps an hour, for the unopened letter in her pocket. But one needed more than an hour to keep one's last tryst with a valued friend.

She went into the sunken garden and, summoning a servant to fill an earthen tub, began for the second time that day to water the pots of roses and glory lilies and hibiscus, conscious of anxious eyes upon her. For, though the year had opened with rivers in full flood, the summer rains had failed, causing the "dry" crops to wither, and the northeast monsoon, though starting well, had soon ceased. Now rivers were dry, tanks empty, crops blighted.

"Flowers," she could sense the servants thinking reproachfully, "with the crops withering?"

But she did not care. Because of the letter in her pocket,

she had somehow to create beauty out of ugliness, life out of death.

Since morning the Changeable Rose hibiscus had turned from pure white to crimson pink. Exclaiming in dismay to find the most perfect bloom hanging by a broken stem, she plucked it, took it to the bungalow, placed it in a dish of water, and carried it to her room.

Dinner was finished at last, and evening prayers, and the final visit to the hospital. She went up to her room, lighted the lamp, closed the door. Taking the letter from her pocket, she placed it within the circle of lamplight, close to the blooming hibiscus. Still she did not open it. Instead she took a packet of other letters from a small locked box, shuffled through them until she found one thicker than the rest, and began reading. It was dated over a year ago.

"June 8, 1903. My dearest Bonny, I loved your three letters. As I have ridden day after day behind the caravan with no one to disturb me and my thoughts always of Bonny, a few ideas have crystallized. One is that I love Bonny as much as ever, and I always shall. Yet everything except my heart tells me that Bonny is out of the question for me even though she has written me things which four years ago I should almost have sold my soul to hear. For I see it this way. If I could not awaken love when I was perhaps at my best, why should I hope to do so now?

"Bonny has unconsciously been forming in her mind a concept of her ideal man. She has used me as a nucleus, but the attributes are of her ideal, and when she wrote in her letter, 'My heart has gone out to you in love' (sweet words), she was writing to this ideal man, and if Bonny were to come to me and know me as I am, she would find me so far from this ideal that she would be, oh, so disappointed!

"So my Bonny dreamed of me! Was it a pleasant dream? In my mind I have had Bonny in my arms many times, but never once in reality. In my mind I have kissed her too, but never once in reality .... She asks, do I remember our climb in the glen, our afternoon by the brook among the ferns, our walk home, our last day together on the yacht, our last evening together? I have seen cattle branded here in the West. Well,

Bonny has her brand on me, and all the little incidents are interwoven to make a complete pattern. Even the cruel incident at the wheel of the yacht, long since forgiven, is there. And like other brands, it will last while life lasts."

Ida laid the letter aside and opened others. In July 1903 Burchfield Milliken is living in a hotel in New Mexico. He is stronger. But he is still losing weight.

In August he tells of a dream he had. Bonny was at his home and all the family were together. He was happy. But he looked into her eyes and saw there negation. He knows he would see it there if he were really to look in her eyes. He urges her to keep well. "Some day some man will claim you for his own, and you must be well, my Bonny."

In October he is on top of a high mountain. He has received a letter from Bonny in which is a violet. As he holds it now in his hand, it gives him its message: "Tell him that I love him with a *sister's* love."

In January he has been gaining steadily for three months.

Only two letters left now in the pile, one thick, one very thin.

"March 1, 1904. So Bonny is getting frivolous and wearing low-necked dresses! I think I would not like her in black. With her golden hair, fair skin, and blue eyes, black would surely be incongruous.

"I like the pictures you sent the best I have ever seen of you. You have in them the look that I have always felt you ought to have. Yet in the years of our association I never saw it. Are your little brown babies responsible for it? If so, bless the babies. If I could have once seen that look on your face when we were together, I should have defied the powers of hell to take you away from me!

"I have had the grippe again. Even if I get well, I sometimes wonder what there is left for me. I could not pass my exams in this state to practice medicine. I might marry an Indian squaw who has an income from the government!

"Last night after I read your letter I went for a walk all alone. My mind went forward three years, and I met Bonny when she came home. Will I meet her when she does come home? I walked toward the full moon, which was rising. Did you look at the same old moon last night? Good-by, Bonny. May God keep you from fretting over things you should not fret over."

One more in the pile, very thin. She picked it up reluctantly. "I have been looking you up on the map and am surprised to see how far south you are. It must be so hot! You must take a good vacation this year to make up for the one you did not have last year . . . . I have not been so well since that attack of grippe. There is no one to examine me . . . . Tell Dr. Hart I said she was to stay there and help you."

Ida sat staring at the two objects remaining on the desk, the flower and the unopened letter. Life and death, both of them, and who could tell where one left off and the other began? For the flower was alive, yet in the act of dying. And Burchfield Milliken was dead, yet in the act of coming alive. She tore open the letter.

It is late August, 1904. He has just been examined. The doctors have found his condition much worse. He is getting very tired of being sick. The love of life does not seem nearly so strong in him as it has been.

"I hope by this time you have been out of Vellore for a vacation. How I wish I could have you here in a tent and you could ride over the plains with me and of an evening stand in the moonlight! I would keep you out of doors all the time until you were brown as a berry and your eyes sparkled with life and vigor. Then I would say funny things to make you laugh, and when you were utterly weary you should sleep on a blanket under a tree, only to begin the same laughter when you awoke. But, ah! What vain imaginings!

"Take time from your little detail work to contemplate the vast, world-wide, centuries-long things. Your little troubles will vanish in comparison with God and his vastness and doings. . . . Now good-by, little girl. God bless you and keep you strong and courageous, broad-minded and true. With love, Burchfield."

Now at last, for the first time since the coming of the cable, Ida wept.

9

In the next two years the hospital grew from precarious infancy to lusty childhood. Eighteen more beds were added, making a total of forty-two. Though Dr. Louisa Hart returned from furlough with her sister Lillian, a trained nurse, in 1904, and both were assigned to Schell, the constantly increasing numbers of patients required more than the additional resources. There was enough work to tax the strength of five doctors. As the fame of the hospital spread, women began coming from more and more distant villages, five, ten, even up to fifty miles away. In 1906 there were 152 more inpatients than in the preceding year, 189 more operations, 36 more maternity cases. By autumn of that year the annual number of inpatients had already reached 800, the outpatient treatments given nearly 30,000.

The nursing staff had been slowly increased to include eleven nurses, such as they were, and two compounders. With the young Indian women whom Ida had gathered about her and tried to teach, a few trained nurses had been added from time to time from other hospitals, government or mission, though some of these had proved so ineffective that they had been sent away. Though Lillian Hart attempted to add a full schedule of classes to her exhausting duties as head nurse, she found herself fighting a losing battle not only with tropical fever but with those nursing problems peculiar to the environment.

It was hard enough merely being a nurse in India without attempting to train inexperienced girls, most of them from sheltered homes, in the exacting duties of the profession. Hospital discipline, as known in the West, was impossible. A patient would spit betel juice on floor and walls, wipe her dirty hands on wall or sheet. She would wear her sheet when she got out of bed, walk around in her bare feet, get back into bed without a thought of wiping them. The floor was the easiest place to throw skins or rubbish. Members of the family, permitted of necessity to accompany the patients to the hospital in order to satisfy the numerous caste dietary requirements, were constantly getting underfoot with their sleeping mats, their cooking equipment; the single attendant allowed to remain being often augmented, while the harassed nurse's back was turned, by a whole army of relatives.

To complicate the teaching problem, students reared with no concept of sanitation were hard to train. One might prepare a sterile douche, only to see a hand put in to test its warmth. Conditioned to use only the right hand for most activities, the girls took months learning to pass things with both hands in the operating room. Even direction of the smallest details of hospital management consumed a vast amount of time—like teaching the seamstress not to mend a hole in a table cover by buttonholing it neatly all around to keep it from tearing!

Ida found the small problems of a doctor even more disconcerting, especially in the morning dispensary, where, after making her rounds of the hospital and sometimes several calls in the town, she often treated up to 150 patients. Hurrying to her small consulting room at the front of the hospital as close as possible to seven o'clock in the morning, she always had difficulty in entering it unseen. Patients crowded around her, pulling at her dress, all talking at once.

"Oh, for the quiet order of a good well-run insane asylum!" she would often long fervently.

Patients were given numbers, but often they bore no relation to order. While she attempted to diagnose Number 76, Numbers

82 and 95 would manage to rush past the attendant, each accompanied by four or five members of her family. It was even more frustrating to have to leave her consulting room at the arrival of a *gosha* cart whose Mohammedan occupants refused to enter. Then she must go outside and wait behind the cart until the male relatives had shooed away any man within spying distance, thrust her head under the cloth which served for a curtain, and attempt to diagnose and treat one or more females crowded into a dark space barely large enough to squat in. There was a time in the morning when large numbers arrived at once, and after fifty or so had been seen, Ida's nerves were like tingling wires. Many were not content to be seen only once but must come back to tell of things forgotten, ask more questions, or have directions repeated.

"We are only women," they would say. "How can we remember and understand? You must come and talk to the men."

Their gratitude, though touching, was equally time-consuming. When leaving, these wealthier Mohammedan women would load her with garlands of jasmine and marigolds, fill her hands with sweets and limes. She would order the garlands cut up in small nosegays and distributed, with the sweets and fruits, among nurses and patients. Little Mary Taber, often in the compounding room with Mrs. Gnanammal, absorbed in her task of cutting waste paper into bits for "Gnanamanti" to use in wrapping powders, was always eager to help distribute them. It was almost as much fun as dipping into the two bags hanging from Aunt Ida's chair—one containing picture cards, the other dolls with china heads and hands—and carrying presents to the children in the wards.

But these small annoyances were nothing beside the deep-seated social problems Ida daily encountered: child marriage and motherhood, the well-meaning but appalling techniques of ignorant midwives, the Devadasi System of temple prostitution which in those early years of the century had not yet become the target of such ardent and intelligent Hindu reformers as Dr. Muthu Lakshmi Reddy.

There was the case of Lakshmi, a thirteen-year-old girl dedicated in childhood by devout parents to the life of a temple dancing girl, who at the age of fifteen was brought into the

112

hospital repulsive with infection, yet possessing a certain dignity and sweetness of spirit that endeared her to both doctors and nurses. Thrilled with the message of a God whose only demands were those of love, she accepted Christianity, becoming increasingly winsome and beautiful. Ida went to Madras and consulted firms of lawyers about the possibility of keeping her, but they were unable to give her any satisfaction, since the girl was underage.

One morning when she was visiting in the hospital with Lakshmi, a look of horror came into the girl's face, and she clutched Ida's arm with a painful grip.

"Oh, doctor!" she whispered. "There she is, the woman from the temple. She's come to take me back again. Don't let her— please!"

Looking up, Ida saw an old woman, face hard and sinister. It was the guardian of the temple dancers, and she had come to take Lakshmi away. In spite of all Ida's offers and pleas, the woman was adamant. Lakshmi was legally bound to the temple until she became of age. Her renewed health and beauty made her even more valuable. One of the saddest days of Ida's life was when she clasped the girl in her arms and said good-by.

Months passed, and Ida tried in vain to get in touch with Lakshmi. Finally a woman from the temple town where Lakshmi lived came to the hospital. Yes, she knew the girl. One day during a festival the woman had gone to the temple to worship. Lakshmi had come to her and asked her to bring Ida a message. She was still a Christian. She could bear her evil existence no longer. She bade them all good-by and hoped to meet them in God's house. That very night she had thrown herself into a well.

Almost as tragic were some of Ida's experiences with young wives and mothers. The position of womanhood in India, as defined by Hinduism in the ancient Code of Manu and by subsequent laws in the puranas, was one of complete subservience to the male members of her family. A woman's husband was her god, and her salvation in any future life depended on her fulfillment of her wifely duties. From early childhood she was reared on the popular stories of Sita and Savitri, ideal wives who had found holy joy in utter subjugation to their god-husbands. She was taught to have no desires, no thoughts, apart

113

from those of her husband. She was not even permitted to refer to him by name. Her one purpose in existence was to bear him sons, who would perform the necessary rites to insure his salvation in an afterlife, and failure to do this was sufficient reason for being cast aside. Once she bore sons, she was as much a slave to their wishes as to her husband's, often spoiling them beyond all reason. If her husband died, she was not permitted to remarry but usually occupied a degraded position under the dominance of her mother-in-law. Only at one stage of her existence did she become an individual in her own right: when, outliving elder females, she became mistress of the women's quarters in the joint family household. Then at long last she came into her own, often ruling, as she had been ruled, with an iron hand.

It was natural that in this type of society early marriage should be considered a religious obligation. Still many years before Gandhi's bitter denunciation of child marriage and its attendant evils, and before the child-marriage restraint law of 1930 known as the Sarda Act, nearly half the Hindu girls and over one-third of the Mohammedan girls were being married under the age of fifteen, many in very early childhood. For Mohammedanism also, like most other Eastern religions including Judaism, emphasized the value of producing sons. And in a country where the average life span was less than twenty-seven years, marriage before the age of fifteen seemed by no means unreasonable. While many of these child marriages were only betrothals, they were arrangements as legally binding as the marriage ceremony itself, and if the male member of the contract—sometimes a boy, often a mature or elderly man—died, his child bride was reduced to the degraded status of a widow. Although early marriage was not always followed by consummation, it generally was as soon as puberty was reached.

Understanding its reasons, Ida could not condemn the ancient practice. Yet, working tirelessly in wards and operating room, going out on calls at all hours of the night whenever she was given a chance to ease the suffering or save the life of one of these child mothers, she deplored it with vigorous intensity.

Often, however, she was called only as a last resort, when the ignorant midwife had failed at her task and the patient, racked with fever and her body hopelessly mutilated, was beyond saving.

Although she realized they were used with the best of intentions, Ida found some of the techniques of these untrained midwives hard to believe. One little girl in labor, having suffered for five or six days, was placed on a table, a board laid across her abdomen, and in order to hasten the delivery two midwives teetered upon it, one on either end. Another woman was about to bring her child into the world in normal fashion when India's "dark hour" was about to begin. "It must not be," the midwives insisted. "Those born in the dark hour are unlucky. We must stop it somehow." They did. Placing ropes around the mother's ankles, they strung her feet up to a beam and kept her there for the hour. And the child was born neither in the "dark hour" nor any other time. Both it and its mother were dead.

Yet all these practices were the result of ignorance, not cruelty, and many of the barbers' wives, schooled to their work as midwives by the experience of long generations, were remarkably skillful. It was ignorance also, coupled with superstition, which brought the mother to bed in a corner of the darkest, most neglected room, probed into her body with unclean hands, kept her without water for three days after the child was born, wrapped her baby in soiled rags, cauterized its severed cord with a rolled leaf dipped in oil and lighted at the wick of a tiny clay lamp. The values of sanitation, Ida often reminded herself, were but a recent discovery among Western peoples. The Indian surgeon Susruta had advocated cleanliness in operating procedure when her own ancestors were living in a state of jungle savagery. And until the findings of Pasteur, about the time her own father had begun his medical work in India, germs had never been heard of! Yet it was a costly and tragic ignorance.

It was one day in October, 1906, that all Ida's seething frustration over such problems came suddenly to the bursting point.

The day started pleasantly enough. Though she had been up half the night with a patient, she arose as usual at five, dressed quickly, and with her dog Gyp chasing after, hurried immediately to the bungalow garden to water her pots of roses.

This time she could spend water with a clearer conscience, for last season's rains had been abundant, and already the fall monsoon had brought several good downpours. Mary Taber, now a chattering happy child of three, ran after her with her small watering pot.

It was the hour of the day Ida loved best. With the sun not yet risen and the air cool as a New England spring, she felt so alive with energy that swift motion became necessity. Taking Mary Taber by the hand and calling Gyp to follow, she ran to the gate at the far end of the compound. Before returning, they had helped Gyp chase a bandicoot into the cactus hedge, discovered the hiding place of a coppersmith bird, stopped to admire the fanned crest of a strutting hoopoe. Still in a gay mood, Ida took Mary Taber up to her room and tied a bright ribbon in her hair. "There!" She placed her before the mirror. "Now how do you look?"

The child preened and cocked her head like the hoopoe. "Nice!" she cooed.

"Spoiled!" thought Ida wryly. But it was not her mother's fault. In spite of her mildness, Mrs. John could be a stern disciplinarian. Her punishments had always been suited to the offense. There was the time, for instance, when her son Lew had engaged in the intriguing pastime of baptizing a chicken by immersion in the rain barrel. Firmly requesting the pursuit to be discontinued, with no results, Mrs. John had appeared suddenly around the corner of the bungalow, picked him up, and, holding him by the heels, had without uttering a word given her son an abrupt and thorough immersion.

After chota and morning prayers, Ida took the child with her to the hospital. The pony was tied to the asoka tree by the path, a bag of bran about her neck, but it whinnied excitedly for the plantain Mary Taber brought her each morning. Ida took time to pet her and hoist the child to her back, saying gaily, "Dolly, this is Mary. You know—Mary Taber?"

She went immediately to the patient with whom she had spent many hours in the night. "Still living," reported the nurse in charge, "but very weak."

The patient was a gentle little woman who had been brought in with a baby three days old and a case of raging fever. The

116

family, though living but a stone's throw from the hospital, had employed the usual barber-woman midwife for her confinement, but as her fever increased they had become frightened. Ida had worked desperately to save her, but yesterday she had sent word to the family that if they wished they could take her home to die. The woman had called Ida to her bedside and begged to be allowed to stay. Consent had gladly been given. Last night she had rallied, and Ida had gone home long after midnight hoping she might still have a chance.

"Salaam, little mother," she said gently, touching the fevered forehead.

The woman groped for her hand. "You—thought I would die—last night," she said faintly. "But I felt—would live until today. If I do die"—her eyes pleaded—"please let me die here! Don't send me home—please!"

Ida pressed the hot hand reassuringly. "You shall stay here, little mother."

The voice persisted. "I—want you—close by me, if I must die. Before little one came—was in such agony—begged them to bring me here—would not. Now I want—stay until the end. Promise—"

"I promise," said Ida, smiling. But she was not smiling when she turned from the bed. So easy it would have been to save her! Just around the corner!

After making the rounds of the wards and private rooms, she was later than usual in entering her dispensary, but she had finished with her work by twelve, for there were never so many outpatients in the rainy season. No time yet, however, for breakfast, which was usually eaten about noon. Ida was called immediately to the delivery room. At sight of her patient, a little Brahmin girl of not more than twelve or thirteen, the helpless frustration she had felt earlier in the day welled into hot indignation. For three hours she worked grimly over the tortured, immature body. She was able finally to save the young mother's life but not her child's.

Having no appetite for the breakfast which Mrs. John had sent over from the bungalow, Ida went straight to her afternoon dispensary. A group of Brahmin women was gathered in a tight knot on the verandah, well removed from low-caste pollution, and, obeying a sudden impulse too overpowering to resist, Ida went toward them. At sight of her blazing eyes and crimson cheeks, the chattering group lapsed into silence.

"Sisters!" Unpremeditated words poured from her lips. "Please listen to me!"

For once her Tamil was pungently eloquent. They listened, wide-eyed, to the story of the twelve-year-old girl, of the small racked body and the dead baby.

"These are your daughters," Ida told them with desperate earnestness. "Can't you see what wrongs are being inflicted on them? How can you let them suffer so!"

She stopped, aghast at her own temerity. But the women were not angry. Instead they nodded in sober agreement. *Amma,* yes, it was all wrong. *Pavum,* a pity! But, *cha!* What to do? The laws of their caste required child marriage, and were not those laws as unshakable as the heaps of stone all around Vellore which Hanuman the monkey king had piled up for stepping stones on his way to kill the terrible demon Ravan in Ceylon? *Ayoh!* So it had always been, and so, they supposed, it must ever be.

How? *How!* The words beat like drums against Ida's consciousness as she jabbed needles, washed eyes, swabbed sores, dusted burns, smeared scabies, opened abscesses. Somehow India's women must be awakened. Foreign doctors and nurses could not save them. Their men would not save them. They must save themselves. But how? *How!* Drum beats. Wedding drums, dooming little children. Ritual drums, frightening away the goddesses of smallpox, plague, and cholera. And then, funeral drums.

"The mother with the bad case of fever," said Salomi breathlessly.

Ida sat beside her, as she had promised, and held her hand. It did not take long. Ignorance and neglect had done their work well. When it was over, she closed the gentle eyes and folded the still hands.

But as she turned from the bed, there was neither frustration nor rebellion in her blue eyes, only determination. She had thought it was enough to visit a few homes, to build a hospital to which women could come, to train a few nurses to meet the

118

needs of that hospital. It was not enough. She must help the women of India to help themselves. She must start a school of nursing, train young Indian women to go out into the villages, live with the people, show them better ways of living. Yes, and she must go into them herself. That year she had made two long village trips. When she returned from furlough, she must make dozens of trips—hundreds.

Impossible, common sense told her. A school of nursing? It would mean more facilities, a full-time instructor, more funds, a program of intense promotion in a country where nursing was considered a degrading profession. Trips into the villages? A motor car, another doctor, the one prerequisite which was always lacking—time! She simply could not do it.

But it wasn't a question of whether she could or not. She *must*.

Like the furloughs of all missionaries, Ida's year in America was no vacation. She was expected to do much traveling and speaking, acquainting people with her work and stimulating them to make contributions. Since the achievement of her two new goals depended on the success of her campaign, she availed herself of every opportunity to present her cause. Every minute not thus engaged she planned to use in increasing her knowledge and medical skill: visiting hospitals, attending lectures, doing library research, taking some of the many postgraduate courses offered in New York.

But that summer of 1907 she managed to get a short vacation when the family gathered for a month with her brother Lew and his wife Cora on the Nebraska farm. Charles and Millie came from their pastorate in the East. John's wife was there from California with her two young daughters. Harry and Margaret, also on furlough, were accompanied by their four children. Together they constituted such a crowd that tents were set up to house them in the farmyard. Everybody had a wonderful time, except possibly Cora, who bore the responsibility of keeping the small army fed, bathed, and laundered. The mere item of providing hot water for their baths was no small task, especially for visitors accustomed to Indian servants and the luxury of a bath at least once a day.

Ida reveled in this reliving of her childhood. In her noisy, frolicking nieces and nephews she saw herself and her five brothers, racing through the fields, riding bareback across the prairies. There was even another small Ida to ride the tail end of the horse, her brother Lew's small daughter, Ida Belle. Her delight in this seven-year-old namesake, a shy but happy little blonde, was almost as keen as a mother's in her first child. They became close companions, and Ida B., as she soon came to be called to distinguish their names, was an adoring shadow of her Aunt Ida.

But the vacation was short. The hectic round of speeches, luncheons, interviews began again. And on Wednesday, February 12, Ida started a three months postgraduate course in medicine in a New York hospital.

While she lived in New York, she stayed with the black-haired, bright-eyed little woman who, years before, had financed Annie Hancock's trip to India. Gertrude Dodd's interest in both Ida and India had been fueled through the years by a regular and intimate correspondence, and despite the distance between them they had become more than casual friends. It was obvious just from seeing them together that in the strength and youth and beauty of Ida Scudder, Gertrude, twelve years her senior, had found fulfillment. She was like a little brown wren basking in the presence of a gorgeous bird of paradise, perfectly happy, both then and to the end of her life, to become a foil enhancing, if necessary by her own lack of them, the charms of her beloved Idee.

Two assets Gertrude Dodd had, however, which Ida did not possess, and she put both at the service of her idol. One was her administrative ability, dedicated for many years to her duties as treasurer of the New York City Mission and of the Woman's Board of Missions of her denomination. The other was her money. For she was the youngest daughter of a wealthy New York contractor.

"If only I could *see* your work in India!" Gertrude said one day.

"Well—why not?" Ida leaped at the idea with her usual impulsiveness. "Why not go back with us, you and Katharine? You can afford it. And in your jobs you both need to see what missions are doing around the world."

120

Gertrude needed only the spark of suggestion. Before the day was over she had sold the proposition to her friend and Ida's former hostess Katharine Van Nest, who was the Women's Auxiliary secretary for India; paid visits to her dressmaker and travel agent; and secured innumerable folders on points of interest in Europe which she would like to show her idol. And on the way home she remembered to pick up two tickets for a concert by a new and much talked-of violinist, Fritz Kreisler.

Gertrude Dodd was not the only person who fell captive to Ida's spell during these months of furlough. As she traveled about the country speaking, in Eastern cities, at Northfield, in Canada, people flocked to hear her. They were fascinated by her beauty, her vivid easy style, her intense earnestness. They were startled and intrigued by the fact that, since 1819, when her grandfather had become the first medical missionary from the United States to India, over thirty members of the Scudder family had given a total of nearly a thousand years to missionary service. And they were moved by the story she had to tell.

She told them about the little Brahmin mother who had died and about the boy with a stone in his ear and about Mary Taber. She told them of the woman with a severe case of tetanus, whose life might have been saved if they could have afforded to give her all the serum she needed. She told of Lakshmi the temple girl, and the woman who had almost died from thirst, and the midwives practicing their profession in the little dark rooms. And she told of her two dreams—a school to train nurses and a program of village medical work —which could not and yet *must* be fulfilled.

Her audience responded. Money was contributed to make possible a small nurses' training school. In New York Ida met Delia Houghton, R.N., secured by the mission board to be the school's first instructor as well as head nurse for the hospital, efficient, scrupulously neat in appearance, and solidly dependable.

"It seems strange when I think of it," wrote one woman who had heard Ida speak, "that I feel such a deep interest in one whom I never saw but once (and then without exchanging more

121

than a few words) on that afternoon when you talked in our chapel and carried our hearts away with you, but so it is. I have heard of people falling in love with a voice. That must be largely my case, as when you spoke that afternoon you stood against the lights from a window."

So attracted to Ida was this woman that she pledged a thousand dollars for the purchase of a motor car.

They sailed in November, 1908, on the *S. S. Cedric*—Mrs. Scudder, Ida, Annie, Gertrude Dodd, Katharine Van Nest, and Delia Houghton. Gertrude faithfully studied Tamil on the ship and realized her dream of showing her beloved Europe to Ida. They visited London, Paris, Lucerne, Milan, Venice, Florence, Rome, Naples.

But Ida viewed all these wonders with secret impatience. The stones of Venice seemed but poor substitutes for those of Vellore, whose huge fort walls were built of stones hand-hewn to fit perfectly without mortar. The spires of cathedrals, gray against wintry skies, could not compare with the savage beauty of Vellore's towering temple gopuram, carved with strange gods yet cleaving bright blue heavens. And her Arc de Triomphe, still half a world away, was the gate leading to a low brick hospital. Walking the ancient Appian Way, already her skin tingled with the red dust of unpaved roads. Her ears were attuned to drums and temple bells. And the tang of cow-dung fires was in her nostrils.

As soon as she arrived back in Vellore, she began putting her two new plans into action. Though the formal opening of the school of nursing could not take place until later in the year, she wrote numerous letters to mission schools of the area, and arranged visits to some of them in an attempt to locate possible candidates for students. She planned a more rigorous schedule of classes for the hospital helpers already receiving some practical training. Since Louisa Hart was leaving on her furlough in March, Ida filled the intervening weeks with a teaching program which she would not be able to find time for later. Dell Houghton, once her language study was completed, promised to become a bulwark of strength and efficiency.

The problem of securing students for a school of nursing proved even more difficult than she had expected. Most girls of

122

intelligence and education either married young or chose teaching as a career. In these pioneer days, long before the birth of an All-India Association of Registered Nurses, with its efficient organization, alert leadership, progressive publications, and high standards, the profession of nursing was considered unsuitable for well-bred intelligent young women.

"My daughter has failed three times in second standard," wrote the father of one applicant to Ida. "I am sure she would make a very good nurse."

But applications came. Two fine girls from Methodist schools, another from an Episcopalian institution, together with two Anglo-Indians, joined the students already in residence to form the first class.

Though unable to accelerate her program of village visitation until the arrival of a motor car, Ida soon added to her busy schedule regular trips to two new dispensaries opened by Dr. Louisa Hart during her absence, one at Gudiyattam twenty-three miles away, the other at Punganur, her brother Harry's distant station. She started on her first trip one Wednesday morning, soon after her return to India, hopes high, for Gudiyattam was a city teeming with thousands of Hindus and Mohammedans, and only last month a small new church with a dispensary room in the rear had been dedicated.

Roused by a nurse at five, she had barely time to take chota, gather her equipment together, and drive the pony cart the four miles to the Katpadi railroad station. But by six-thirty she was in the small train compartment with all her paraphernalia: roll containing bedding, mattress, and pillow, box of medicines and dressings, traveling bag, lunch basket, a container of bottles, and water jar—enough for an Indian family bound on a thousand-mile pilgrimage!

As at Vellore, the station at Gudiyattam was several miles from town, and she had to hire a jutka. In the tiny dispensary behind the church she treated fifty-six persons, the cases, many of them hopeless cancers, arousing her deep interest and pity. Some of the women were so frightened they cringed when she approached them; others came forward eagerly and knelt beside her chair.

After a hasty lunch she set out again in the jutka on the

long hot pull up the ghats to Palmaner, where Uncle Jared was stationed and where she planned to spend the night on her trip to Punganur. Wedged with all her luggage into the narrow space beneath the arching reed top, she could scarcely sit upright. Shins and shoulder blades were soon sore, and once she was flung about so abruptly that her nose was flattened hard against her medicine box. As the road climbed into the hills, growing steeper and steeper, dust thickened, blinding her eyes and choking her throat. She was so sorry for the toiling pony that she got out and walked up the steepest slopes.

Arriving finally in Palmaner, she was shocked to see Uncle Jared looking so weak and old. Startled, she remembered that it was nearly fifty-five years since he and Aunt Julia had begun their work in India. Dixie, his beautiful daughter, was still his dutiful helper, her dream of doing village work still unrealized. When the two cousins had finished exchanging confidences, Ida slept long and deeply in the delightful upland coolness. The twenty-mile ride to Punganur the next day was almost comfortable.

An Indian nurse whom Ida herself had trained was in charge of the little dispensary, and Ida was delighted with the progress made. After she had treated the host of waiting patients, her brother Harry came and drove her to his bungalow. Before starting home the next day, she was called to the rajah's palace to treat a woman in the royal household. Ida gave the family no hope, though after a minor operation the woman seemed a little better. Soon she grew steadily worse. Knowing that there was a remote chance of saving the woman's life by a more radical operation, Ida boldly decided to take the chance, and performed the operation. Her worst fears were realized, for the patient died that same afternoon. Miserable, frustrated, Ida surrendered the tortured body to the wailing women of the household and watched them prepare it for the funeral pyre. Fortunately they did not seem to blame her for the woman's death. It was her karma, destiny. Perhaps, too, they felt that there were already enough women in the rajah's household.

As she was leaving Punganur in her jutka, Ida saw a strange sight: hundreds of people and at least a thousand sheep and goats, all gathered about a small shrine in a field beside the road. Instantly curious, she stopped the jutka, descended, and hunted through the crowd until she found an old man who, though living in this Telegu language area, could speak Tamil.

"*Yenna?*" she inquired. "What is it?"

The old man was friendly and garrulous. The animals had been brought, he explained, to be sacrificed to the smallpox goddess. Every household must bring at least one sheep, which was taken before the image of the goddess and with a single stroke of the knife beheaded. Its head was then placed in front of the shrine, and if the nose turned one way it meant good luck; if the other, bad.

Ida returned to the jutka sick at heart. She knew suddenly how the young boy Jesus must have felt on his first visit to the temple in Jerusalem.

Another night in Palmaner, then down the ghat to Gudiyattam. It was like moving from an airy kitchen into a brick oven. But the hours at the dispensary seemed short this time, for Gertrude Dodd had come by train from Vellore to help. The next night Ida slept in her own bed, but in her dreams she still lurched and rolled, and whichever way she turned, her bones felt sore against the sheet. No wonder! For in her few days absence she had traveled over a hundred miles in a jutka.

After Louisa Hart left on furlough in March, Ida raced to keep pace with the days, only occasionally catching one long enough to pin it in her diary.

"March 27. Bought a new horse, Lassie, for $275. Lovely to drive.

"April 1. Had seven operations, four chloroform. Cancer rectum. Removal of eye. Curetting.

"April 9. Oh, such a day full of trials and discouragements! Some operation cases had pus, showing things had not been properly sterilized. Dispensary largest yet. 166 cases. Called to bad case in town. Jaw. Tooth had been extracted. Man dying.

"April 10. Forceps case at 1:00 A.M. Went to Gudiyattam. Only two hours sleep. Pretty tired.

"April 17. Rose at 3:30. Went to Gudiyattam, Gertrude with me. Had 83 patients. Drove Lassie to station. Brought back sick woman all the way in jutka.

"May 15. My time is so full. Sometimes I wonder why the patients are willing to wait so long. Today I heard one say to another, 'Can you not see how busy the Doctor *Ammal* is? She will see us all as soon as she can.' One time I heard another say, 'If our Doctor had a thousand eyes and a thousand hands, she could even then be kept busy, but she has only two eyes and two hands, so let us be patient and wait for her.'

"July 30. Went to Punganur again and did operations. Making raid on bedbugs in the hospital.

"September 15. Said good-by to Gertrude and Katharine. Annie and I went with them to Villupuram. It broke my heart to see my dearest friend Gertrude go. I don't think I have ever felt quite so lonely."

10

"September 23, 1909. THE NEW MOTOR CAME TODAY!"

No wonder she wrote it in capitals. It was one of the great events of the decade. The first motor car to arrive in Vellore, it attracted far more attention than had the King's coronation.

When it was uncrated, Ida stared at the confusion in hopeless bewilderment. A mechanic was called immediately from Madras to assemble the machine and, after a cursory examination, he disclosed the somber fact that it had but one cylinder. This meant little to Ida until she took her first ride in it. It was a small French car, a Peugeot, high and open with a folding top, wire-spoked wheels, and two seats. Its steering wheel rose straight up from the footboard, and the vibrations from the engine were so violent that the driver's hands seemed at times to shiver with ague.

It was a great moment when they made their first trip to a village. The day was a lovely one. Though the car was so small that only a few drugs could be taken, powders of all kinds were put in bags and hung along the windshield. Small bottles of iodine and other medicines were arranged in long boxes. White uniform swathed in a duster, topee securely anchored by a long veil, Ida sat in front with the driver, Salomi and a religious teacher behind. They set forth gleefully, even the little car seeming to sense its responsibility and chugging gaily, if noisily, through the town, horn honking incessantly, bicycles, pushcarts, cows, bullock bandies, pedestrians, all scrambling madly to get out of the way. And wisely, for Hussain, the driver, had little more knowledge of the car's workings than the woman at his side, and slightly less of common sense.

As they turned into the country road leading to the village, a group of coolies on the road ahead saw them coming, stood staring dumfounded, then rushed off shrieking across the fields.

"The devil is coming! The devil is coming!" they yelled.

Stopping the car and running after them, Ida tried to explain. But it was no use. That day she had to walk to the village to treat her patients. After a couple of trips, however, children were swarming over hood, wheels, seats, and top like flies, and it was all she could do to keep curious fingers from dissecting the car inch by inch. Soon somebody did manage to run away with the horn.

"*Chi!*" exclaimed Ida to Hussain in dismay. "We must get another."

"But, Doctor *Ammal*," replied the driver gravely, "we don't need a horn. We make so much noise everybody hears us coming."

Ida was soon driving each Wednesday to Gudiyattam. The Katpadi railway overbridge was the little car's first defeat. It would climb halfway up, then gasp for breath as if with asthma, then utter a prolonged wheeze before coming to a dead stop. Always, however, there was plenty of manpower available, and bullock drivers would leave their carts, farmers their head loads of produce, pedestrians their staring, to throng goodnaturedly and haul the Peugeot over the bridge.

After the first few trips villagers began to line the roadsides instead of running away screaming, and, slowly winning their confidence, Ida was able to treat some of them. Word went abroad that a new animalless bandy was coming each Wednesday to bring medicines and help the sick, and telling about a God who loved them all. People were told that if medicine was wanted, they must stand by the roadside and hold out a bottle.

128

The next few weeks it was laughable—and heartrending—to see the strings of people all along the way holding up a vast assortment of receptacles: coconut shells, inkwells, tin lamps, flower vases, bottles. Some parts of the road were lined with them. Stops had to be made constantly. The notations in Ida's diary were first elated, then anxious, finally desperate.

"Nov. 3, 1909. Started for G. at seven. Motor went beautifully and drew a great crowd. We were very busy. Stopped at several villages on the way. I drove the motor home.

"Nov. 10. Motor went slowly. People in many villages came for medicines. Some people brought a man on a string cot. Home late. 153 cases.

"Nov. 24. Such a full day! 122 patients in Gudiyattam and 108 on the way, and I could have treated many more if there had been time. My heart was made so sad by their need.

"Dec. 1. 269 cases. Reached home 8:30.

"Dec. 8. 305 cases, and I could have treated many more. Were late reaching Gudiyattam and had only 86 there."

Something had to be done. She decided to appoint certain stations where she would stop each week, under a shady tree or in a village. As she approached each one, ten to fifty people might be waiting. Hearing the rattle of the engine and blasts of the horn (a new one fastened on more securely) others would drop their work and come running across the fields. They came with every sort of ailment and disease—dysentery, blindness, scabies, lameness, abscesses, broken bones, foreign objects in ears and noses, elephantiasis, leprosy, tumors. Though all were friendly, many resisted the idea of having abscesses opened or any kind of treatment given.

Difficulties were legion, for the patients were at first as naïve as children. When Ida gave one man some cotton for his ear, he at once asked if he should eat it.

"What are you washing your hands for now? They will get all dirty again," said one woman innocently as Ida scrubbed up to deliver a baby from its half-dead mother.

The black snorting vehicle changed slowly from "devil" to curiosity to friend. Villagers began to accept both it and its occupants as belonging to them. One night as they were passing through a village a long distance from Gudiyattam, some boys threw stones at their car. Deciding that they must make an example of them to avoid future trouble, Ida stopped the car and sent for the police. The inevitable crowd gathered. While they were waiting, a voice spoke suddenly out of the darkness.

"Who threw stones at this motor car?" it inquired with loud boldness. "Do you not know that every Wednesday the doctor goes out in the car taking medicines with her and gives them to any one who is sick and needs help? *Pavum!* A shame it is that anyone should throw stones!"

At some villages along the way fears still persisted. A crowd would gather at the appointed stop, hang about curiously, but persistently refuse to be examined, much less submit to treatment. On one Wednesday when Ida stopped at such a point, a big banyan on the edge of a village, she noticed an especially large number of children with sore eyes, the purulent ophthalmia which was so prevalent and the cause of so much blindness. Finally, with the aid of a bright picture card, she persuaded one little chap to let her put a drop of medicine in each eye. No sooner had she finished, however, than the head man of the village came bearing down upon her, arms waving, dhoti flapping about bony legs, showering upon her a stream of abusive and threatening Tamil. Sorely frustrated, she retreated behind the wheel and chugged off to the next stopping place.

When they returned that night, the space under the banyan was alive with figures. Tiny lamps glinted like fireflies. A man stood in the road in front of the car frantically waving his arms, the same virulent head man of the morning. What now? It had been a grueling day, and she felt as if she could not stand any more abuse.

"*Yenna?*" she inquired with weary resignation.

The head man smiled and bowed, the tail of his turban trailing in the dust. He had good news for the Doctor *Ammal.* The child she had treated that morning was so much better that all the other village children with sore eyes had been brought, and if the Doctor *Ammal* would only be kind enough to give them also of the magic medicine. . . .

Weariness forgotten, Ida lined the children up in queues

and jubilantly treated over thirty patients. The next week an eager crowd was waiting under the banyan tree. Some, too ill to walk, had been brought on string cots. Even the head man had brought his bottle!

More stubborn still in its resistance to her efforts was the village of Lathery, one of the largest and most needy on the road to Gudiyattam. Week after week she would stop the car outside the village and try to make friends with its women, only to find all doors closed in her face. Proud of their high caste, the villagers would not deign to accept assistance from one "polluted." But a day came when, to Ida's delight, she saw a large group of men approaching her car as she made the usual stop at Lathery. Her delight soon changed to consternation. *They were bringing a sick bullock for her to cure!*

Ida's glance darted in horror from the beast's hot baleful eyes to the hopeful pleading ones of his owner. A bullock was in a sense even more important to a villager than a human being. His life or death might well mean life or death, not just to an individual but to an entire family. She could not fail them.

"Amma," she said grimly. "I'll do what I can."

The bullock had other ideas. Each time she approached he stamped and kicked and glared in frightening fashion. Finally some of the villagers threw him to the ground, and the whole group obligingly sat on him while Ida removed an ugly tumor from his ear. She packed up her instruments and went on, leaving the village staring after her with mingled admiration and skepticism. Never had she prayed so hard for an operation to be a success.

The next week she approached the Lathery stop with trepidation. A crowd was waiting. The shaking in her hands was not all from the fierce vibration of the engine. When the Peugeot came to a hiccuping stop and she saw the broad smiles wreathing all the faces, she joined the little car in its long wheezing sigh of relief. The patient had made a complete recovery! Henceforth the village of Lathery would be "open" to her ministrations.

By the middle of 1910 "Roadside"—the peripatetic dispensary—had graduated from an experiment to an institution, with its own crazy pattern. Ida would start out in the morning about 6:30 with the motor car so packed full of boxes of medicines and appliances that there was barely enough room for the driver, herself, and her two assistants. The first stop would be made about six miles out, where a crowd of fifty or sixty would be waiting. After an assistant had recorded the name and number on a prescription blank and in a record book and received a tiny fee from those able to pay, Ida would diagnose the case, fill in the blank, and give necessary treatments. Meanwhile her other assistant would be dispensing medicines, giving out packets of powder, pouring liquid remedies into the motley assortment of containers, patiently giving instructions over and over and over again. Those given powders must be shown how to open the packets, lest they swallow them paper and all. Even the driver was often pressed into duty, keeping patients in line, applying ointments and liniments, putting drops in eyes, holding unwilling bodies steady while abscesses were lanced and dressed.

By this time Ida was making ten stops each Wednesday, visiting all villages within ten miles of Vellore in the morning, spending the noon hours in Gudiyattam, visiting the remaining villages on her way home in the afternoon or evening. Though each day followed the same general pattern, every one was different, as unpredictable as the monsoon, as varied in color and design as a checkerboard of rice fields.

There was the time when she was called aside into a mango grove. There she found a bullock bandy, a woman in childbirth lying beside it on the ground, so maltreated by the village midwife that the swelling would not permit normal birth. There was no time to take her to the hospital. Hastily Ida converted the bandy into an operating table, ordered the woman lifted upon it. Summoning a group of women from the road, she persuaded them to make a curtain of privacy with their outspread saris. The bullocks having been unhitched, the husband was impressed to hold up the bandy in front and keep it steady. While the nurse handed her the instruments and the driver kept water boiling over a small oilstove, Ida worked silently, grimly. And, though the baby was born dead, the mother's life was saved.

132

Then there was that Wednesday in May, with the thermometer still registering 106 when she had finished at the last stop and was returning home at dusk, her aching head swaying with the little car as it zigzagged its course among long lines of oxcarts with their sleeping drivers. It had been a day filled with patients, and she had reached that point of utter fatigue when even a scratched finger would have seemed the last straw. *"No, no!"* she groaned aloud at sight of the man running toward them across a field and beckoning. But they stopped, of course. Even Hussain, who was lazy and not very intelligent, knew better than to take her protest seriously.

The man was a forlorn sight, so weak he could scarcely drag himself along the narrow path topping the irrigation ditch, and up the bank to the road. One hand was fearfully infected and carried in a sling, the arm swollen to the shoulder. His eyes were aglitter with high fever and his mumblings half delirious. Ida had no choice. She must act promptly if the hand was to be saved.

Though night was fast approaching, she set up the little operating table beside the road. There was no one to help but the driver, for she had left her sole assistant of the day at Gudiyattam, and Hussain did not know where to find a pulse. After giving him a short but thorough lecture on how to administer chloroform, Ida carbolized her instruments and proceeded by the light of a lantern to operate on the most fearfully infected hand she had ever seen. When the operation was finished and she had dressed the hand, she watched the man stumble away across the field, his figure barely visible against the parched whiteness of the dry rice field. Would she ever see him again? She gravely doubted it. But she did! The hand made a splendid recovery, and in his gratitude the man donated to the hospital a big bag of rice.

There was never a routine on Roadside. Each day was unpredictable. As unpredictable as what might lie behind the tightly closed eyes of a child.

Completely gummed they were. It must have been days— weeks—since they had been opened. The child's affliction was the highly infectious form of conjunctivitis known in that part of India as "country sore eyes." Ida worked over them patiently, applying all sorts of medications. Finally she managed to pry them open, only to find that *there was nothing there*.

She looked at the child's mother. "Why—*why* didn't you come to me before?" she asked.

The eyes of the woman were dull with an age-old weariness. "We took her on a pilgrimage to the temple," was the answer. "We asked the goddess to cure her eyes. The priest said to us, 'Go home and hire the silversmith to make for you eyes of silver. Bring them and offer them to the goddess. Perhaps then she will grant your prayer.' It was a long journey, but we went back through all the dust and heat and did as he commanded. It took much money, all we had. We offered to the goddess the eyes made of silver. But—the child's eyes did not get better. They got worse. Is there nothing, Doctor *Ammal*— nothing at all that you can do?"

Ida did not reply. For a moment it was all she could do to forgive the doubtless well-intentioned priest for his tragic ignorance. Yet she knew it wasn't his fault that he was still living back in Old Testament times, when men had brought an offering of five golden tumors and five golden mice to placate the Hebrew God who had presumably brought a plague of tumors upon them. No, if there was forgiveness needed, it was for those who, knowing better ways, did not care enough to share the knowledge with their human brothers. And she herself had almost been one of them.

Gently she closed the lids over the ravaged emptiness and applied a soothing lotion.

But just when tears seemed almost too many to be borne, there would come laughter—as in the shape of the young boy with very bushy curly hair, thrusting a half-anna into her hand. "Please, Doctor *Ammal?* You will please to give me medicine to make my hair straight and glossy?"

At last Ida's two dreams were being fulfilled. More and more villages around Vellore, perhaps fifty, were receiving periodic service. And with Delia Houghton's return from language school the new School of Nursing became firmly established. By the end of 1909 fifteen girls were in training. Ida herself maintained constant contact with every student, and spent several hours each week teaching physiology and obstetrics.

In spite of the visible progress made, she was far from satisfied. For there were a thousand villages still unvisited within driving distance of Vellore, and as yet she was training barely enough nurses to service the hospital and the two dispensaries at Punganur and Gudiyattam, much less those she hoped to establish. And doctors! Where were they? The board had promised to send them if sufficient funds could be raised. Yet Louisa Hart was home on furlough, and again Ida was the only doctor in the hospital. Suppose they did send one or two, five or six. There would still not be enough. Never enough.

"Soon," she read in her medical journals, "in the United States there will be one doctor to every 600 people."

In India less than one to every 10,000!

Never enough. The words became a clock beat. Everything moved and echoed to its rhythm—swish and sway of punkahs, pounding of *dhobis'* paddles, creaking of the irrigation wheel in early morning, smashing of tennis balls on rare occasions in the late afternoon, swift headlong marching of her days.

"Monday, October 4. Operation for hydatid cyst. Enormous. All went well. Hard sad maternity case. Little girl 13. She died.

"October 7. Called up in the night. Busy in hospital and did not get into breakfast until two o'clock. Rounds at 4:30.

"November 23. The Governor, Sir Arthur Lawley, was here. What a hurry and scurry!

"December 14. Lutchmi's baby born early. I was called at six. Large dispensary. Made three calls and then to club to finish tennis tournament. We won. Mrs. Formby's to dinner. Dress affair.

"March 15. As soon as I reached hospital, found maternity case. Girl had no vagina. Dilated and delivered. Vaginal fistula on wee girl of 13.

"Sunday, May 15. Hard day. Death of Brahmin girl in hospital. Bad forceps case in town. Baby died. Woman begged for poison. Hot 107 degrees."

To complicate her work, the year 1910 saw the beginning of several years of drought. Always a bare subsistence, the

135

daily diet of the poor sank to a minimum for survival. On an average, villagers ate once in every other day. The poorest ate leaves to satisfy their first hunger, then a little rice or ragi. Week by week Ida saw her Roadside patients grow more starved, watched diseases multiply. That year, still the only doctor in the hospital, she treated 1,048 inpatients, welcomed 14,684 new cases.

The Peugeot, always temperamental, finally had a complete breakdown, and again the weekly trip to Gudiyattam had to be made by train and jutka. It was heartbreaking to think of the ten stops along the way, with the crowds waiting. Sometimes, as the train stopped at a station, a face would appear at the window, anxious, pleading.

"Have you forgotten us?" a voice would ask, gently accusing. "Are you never coming again? Many have died since you stopped coming."

One day a man brought four annas (about ten cents) for medicine for chills and fever, that curse of malaria, which, no matter what other diseases came and went, was the constant companion of at least half the country's population. She did not have it with her on the train, but she promised to bring it back from Gudiyattam.

"I will wait for you, if you will throw it to me," he said hopefully.

That night when the train dashed past the station Ida hurled out a packet of quinine powder to a solitary waiting figure.

But in the hospital the operating work grew larger and more fascinating. Presently there were eighteen nurses and four compounders in training. The courses taught included physiology, anatomy, nursing, bandaging and massage, obstetrics, three of them taught by Ida herself.

Mary Taber Schell Hospital was getting far too small. There were days when the verandahs were full, patients under the beds. The dispensary averaged 100 patients a day, but there were sometimes up to 169. Ida ventured to ask the board for three thousand dollars to make additions to the hospital.

But her dreams were soaring high above the heads of plodding boards. It wasn't an addition they needed. It was a new hospital! And it wasn't three thousand dollars they should be

136

hoping to raise. It was at least fifty thousand! And—most daring and impossible dream of all—it wasn't just a new hospital which she must build. *It was a medical college!*

The startling new idea pursued her even to Kodaikanal, when she was able to escape during the hot season for a few brief weeks of vacation. She remained preoccupied even while joining in the season's sports with her usual zest.

There were thirteen of the missionaries who met three times a week at Cushing, the mission lodginghouse, each with a riding horse. Most of them were members of the younger set, and Ida, now forty years of age, was the most vigorous of them all. She would always manage to have the fastest horse, ride the hardest, climb the highest hills. Now, especially, she could not get enough of swiftness, of high places. They helped satisfy the restlessness caused by her unfulfilled ambitions.

There were plenty of gay activities to divert her mind from the needs of India: tennis and badminton tournaments between the English and American summer colonies, candy pulls, picnics to Silver Cascade and Fairy Falls and the caves beneath Pillar Rocks, an early morning trip to Neutral Saddle, followed by a brisk five-mile climb to Perumal Peak, beautiful cone-shaped queen of mountains visible from the whole Kodai plateau, racing to reach the top before it became bathed in mists after 10 A.M. "He is a fool who has not ascended Perumal," the saying went, "and he is equally a fool who has ascended it twice." Ida was the second kind of fool. She had been to the top many times.

One day she and Lavina Honegger, new bride of one of the missionaries, and other young members of the summer colony went for a long hike down the mountain along Levering Stream. Temperatures at Kodai's seven thousand feet were brisk, and the women of the party wore their red flannel petticoats. As they descended to lower elevations, the weather became hotter and hotter. They itched and steamed and sweltered until the discomfort became unbearable.

"What shall we do?" asked Lavina in her gay birdlike voice.

They did the only possible thing—sent the young men on ahead, removed the redundant articles of clothing, and proceeded on the hike, each with a flamboyant red petticoat draped shamelessly over her arm.

But, though Ida joined heartily in the sports, her thoughts refused to be diverted. As the weeks of vacation passed, her desire for a medical school became more urgent and concrete. Finally, at the Kodaikanal Missionary Medical Conference, held each summer by missionary doctors of all denominations, she could contain her restlessness no longer. She exploded a bombshell.

"I propose," she said boldly after a brief impassioned speech, "that this body approve the founding of a union medical college for women in South India, and that we begin to make plans for it immediately."

The bombshell elicited a startled volley of comment. Even her cousin, Dr. Lew Scudder, was skeptical.

"Impossible!"

"My dear young woman, do you know what such a thing would cost?"

"Train Indian women in medicine? Not in a hundred years!"

"We can't get funds for our own missions, to say nothing of union projects!"

"The denominational boards would never agree."

"There are already seven medical colleges for men in South India!"

"Government would never consent!"

"Wonderful if it could be done! *But—*"

Ida had two ardent supporters, both women. Dr. Anna Kugler, graduate of the Woman's Medical College of Philadelphia, who, landing in Madras with only $200, had built a beautiful hospital at Guntur for the Lutherans, had long entertained such a dream herself. And Dr. McPhail, of the Free Church of Scotland, was an enthusiastic ally. They at least succeeded in getting a committee appointed to study the project.

The committee met at Kodaikanal in the summer of 1912, but Ida was not with them. There was no doctor to carry on her work, so she remained in Vellore while the others went on vacation. She was just as well pleased, for she was nursing an injured knee, and Kodaikanal would have been torture without riding and hiking and tennis. But the spark which she had kindled caught fire, for the committee, inspired by Drs. Kugler and McPhail, reported favorably. Even the men of the Medical Conference admitted that there should be a union medical college for women in South India. All that remained now was to choose the place, obtain permission and financial help from a hard-headed colonial government, sell the idea to at least four hard-pressed denominational mission boards, and raise the money. Though lending their approval, the men of the commission still considered the project impossible, but the women, who had feared it might take years of spadework to secure even a favorable vote from the group, were more hopeful.

Ida was jubilant. Already she had a site in mind which, she believed, would make an ideal spot for a medical college. It lay about four miles south of Vellore's center, close to the Arni Road, in a beautiful rolling valley with perhaps two hundred acres of unused land, enclosed within rocky hills, the highest and most majestic of them, Kailasa, no mean likeness of the Himalayan "abode of the gods" whose name it bore. In her mind's eye, she could see its native rock crushed to bits and fashioned into buildings of stately stone, surrounded by gardens where there was now wild scrub or grazing patch or cactus hedge.

"Why can't you be satisfied with what you have?" chided Mrs. John during the following months. "You have your hospital. You're doing far too much now. Why can't you let well enough alone?"

"Because it's not well enough," Ida would retort with firm finality.

It was a bitter blow when she fell ill in 1913 and the board recommended that she return home on furlough a year early. She *could* not leave India now. The medical school was in its most sensitive prenatal period. Without her constant and patient treatment it might never be born. And other places than Vellore were being mentioned for its possible location: Bangalore, Mysore, Guntur, Nellore, Madura, Madras. Vellore must at least have its ardent spokesman. She compromised by going to Kodai for a three-month rest.

This time she went to Restalrig, a cottage three miles from

139

the town near the top of the outthrust spur forming the high plateau. On this enforced vacation there were no gay crowds and riding parties and tennis tournaments. Almost for the first time in her life she experienced aloneness, inactivity.

She took long walks with her dog through woodland paths, not with her usual briskness, but slowly, savoring every whiff of cool freshness; lay down at night on an unscreened porch, exulting in the luxurious necessity of blankets; fell asleep, not heavily from sheer weariness, but languidly. She usually awoke at dawn and sometimes earlier, in time to see the Southern Cross swing above the horizon, but she awoke with no sense of urgency. Once she sat wrapped in a blanket on the edge of the cliff until all the lamps and fires had winked out on the plain below, until Scorpio appeared to lash the eastern hills with his jeweled tail, and Virgo was bright as a flaming candelabrum.

At last she was heeding Burchfield Milliken's parting wisdom. *Take time from your little detailed work to contemplate the vast world-wide centuries-long things.*

She took time, and the tensions of both body and spirit slackened. A hymn, which had always been her favorite, became the harmony to which she moved.

> "Be thou my vision, O Lord of my heart;
> Naught be all else to me, save that thou art,—
> Thou my best thought, by day or by night,
> Waking or sleeping, thy presence my light."

Yet, just when she believed herself to have subdued all lesser impulses, she felt herself possessed by a new desire, very human and material. Each time she climbed to the bare hilltop forming the jutting pinnacle of the plateau above Restalrig, fuel was added to its fire.

Standing on the crest, she had the world at her hands and feet. On a clear day she could look across the plain seven thousand feet below and see the gopurams of the Madura temple glinting gold forty miles away. Perumal, on her left, was no higher, no lower, than herself. On her right, atop a far mountain range, an old man seemed to be lying—Moses on his Nebo?—beard flowing, hands folded peacefully. All the beauty

140

of creation was within the circle of her arms. *Hill Top*. It became the symbol of all the dreams she had ever dreamed, all the mountains she had climbed. *She had to own it*.

She made inquiries. Mr. Logan, owner of Restalrig, was a government official. The land at the top of the hill, he told her, was owned by the Kodaikanal Municipal Government. Sometime, but not now, it might be for sale. His vagueness was not reassuring. If she wanted it, she would have to wait. But even if it should be posted for sale, he warned, its price would no doubt be prohibitive. It was the most scenic piece of property on the range, and some rich maharajah would probably buy it.

Health restored, Ida returned to Vellore, but with restlessness increased instead of quelled. As the days passed, her desire to own Hill Top only became more acute. She wanted it with almost as keen a passion as she wanted a medical school to train the women of India.

11

Late in 1913 a small party of American tourists, two women and two girls, was traveling through South India. It was three o'clock in the morning when the train jolted into a station and the guard knocked on their locked door.

"Katpadi! Katpadi!" he called shrilly.

Lucy Peabody, the more briskly competent of the two American women, had already assembled the baggage. Sliding the bolt in the door, she surveyed the confusion outside with the composure of a born presiding officer. "Coolie! Coolie!" she called with polite insistence.

The two girls, one a recent Wellesley graduate, the other from Vassar, scrambled down fully dressed from the high narrow shelves hung by supporting chains, and crowded out of the compartment at the bare heels of the scantily clad porters. Less than ten days off the ship and still wide-eyed with wonder, they stood staring at the screaming vendors running alongside the train with trays of fruits, sweets, cold drinks, tea, and coffee; the train officials and policemen in natty shorts and high frilled turbans; the porters with huge trunks and towering baskets balanced on slender necks; the swarm of drab human figures drifting like moths in and out of the teeming third-class com-

142

partments. Then suddenly the train was gone, and the color and confusion vanished. The little party found itself standing in comparative darkness in what looked like the middle of a wilderness.

A tall neatly dressed figure appeared out of the dimness. "Salaam," he said with dignity. "This Dr. Ida Scudder man. You come me."

Gratefully the little party followed the long white skirt and towering turban to the waiting carriage. They drove for miles along an empty silent road, a thin moon casting weird patterns of light across their path. They passed tight-shuttered shops, carved gateways, and, off to the right, walls of gray stone with the waters of a moat gleaming green in moonlight.

"Why did we come here, anyway?" asked one of the girls curiously. "I thought we had a rigid schedule, and this place called Vellore certainly wasn't on it."

"No," returned Mrs. Peabody with a hint of impatience. "But this Dr. Scudder was so insistent in her letters! At least we won't have to stay long. We'll go on to Madras tomorrow early and attend to our business."

The carriage turned into an attractive gateway, clattered up a curving drive. Light streamed toward them from an open door, illuminating bright red poinsettias and the figure of a woman, a lamp held high in her hand. She wore a long soft white dress, and her hair, prematurely white, held a faint sheen of gold. Her blue eyes danced a lively welcome.

"My dears, you must be so tired! Your rooms are ready. Don't try to talk tonight. I'll see that you're called for chota hazri, 'little breakfast.' "

They might have been old friends or relatives instead of strangers.

"I think," whispered Wellesley to Vassar as she tucked the mosquito netting under the mattress of her cot, "that she's the most beautiful woman I've ever seen."

As hostess and guests sat about the table the next morning, Ida Scudder and Lucy Peabody measured one another across their "little breakfast" of coffee, toast, and plantains, each intuitively recognizing the other as true kin. Not only did they resemble each other physically—blue eyes bright with energy, generous proportions, swift motions—but they were the same sort of woman. Both measured progress in miles rather than inches. Neither would have thought of setting her goal on a hilltop if a mountain was in sight, nor of knowing a moment's peace until it was attained.

This woman, Ida sensed with excitement, might well be the key to the fulfillment of her purpose. Yet Mrs. Peabody had no special interest either in Vellore or in medical education for Indian women. The only woman representative from the United States to the recent International Missionary Council in Holland, Mrs. Peabody, accompanied by her friend, Mrs. Helen Barrett Montgomery, and their two daughters, had come to India with one commission: to investigate the suitability of Madras as the possible location for a Union Christian Arts College for women. The idea had originated in England, and was being supported by committees of women in both Great Britain and America. But if there was to be a union college of liberal arts for women in South India, why not also a union medical college? Somehow, Ida reflected swiftly, she must make this woman see her vision. No—her eyes shrewdly evaluated the proud angle of chin, the straight line of lips—she must make this woman conjure her own vision. And she had only a few hours to do it.

Smiling, she leaned across the table. "I suppose you're too tired to do much sightseeing this morning. And, anyway, you wouldn't be interested in watching me work."

"Oh, but we would," interposed Vassar eagerly.

"If we could only see what some of the houses look like inside," yearned Wellesley, "and how the people live in one of those picturesque villages!"

"Well, it just happens that I have to make some house calls this morning," admitted Ida, "also a short trip to a village. If you'd care to come—"

Three faces lighted eagerly. Turning to the other, Ida noted that the blue eyes had chilled, the straight lips tightened. "Probably Mrs. Peabody would prefer to rest. I know she has a busy day tomorrow."

"I believe you do look tired, Lucy," sympathized her friend with concern.

144

The leader of the expedition bristled. "If you three can take it, I can." She turned graciously to Ida. "We shall be glad to go, Dr. Scudder."

It was not a conducted tour. Ida made no change in her usual routine except to leave both driver and nurse at home in order to crowd her four guests into the little car, temporarily in commission. It was her usual day for going to a small village on the edge of Vellore. There were always house calls to be made in the town before hospital rounds and work in the dispensary.

They went to the village.

"I can't believe it!" Climbing back into the car, Wellesley was in tears. "Those mud houses with no windows and just dirt floors and not a stick of furniture except maybe a string cot and a few baskets and cooking pots! Why, those people don't have anything at all!"

"Oh, yes they do," countered Vassar wisely. "They were friendly and cheerful."

"Is it true," asked Wellesley, still distressed, "that almost all of India is made up of villages?"

"Yes," said Ida. "Over seven hundred thousand of them."

"And are they all like that one?"

"No," said Ida. "Most of them have never seen a doctor."

Mrs. Peabody said nothing.

They visited two houses in town, one in a Hindu high-caste street, the other in a comfortable Mohammedan quarter. The latter was one of the homes where Annie Hancock had been admitted regularly as a teacher. The women of the family welcomed them eagerly, insisting on entertaining them with tea and fruits and sweetmeats. Beautifully dressed in their silk trousers, long blouses, scarves, and jewels, they were fascinating hostesses, and the guests were captivated. One of the members of the household, a girl of sixteen, was especially charming.

"Recite your piece to them," urged the mother-in-law proudly in Tamil.

Shyly but with clear diction the girl recited in English the 121st Psalm.

"I will lift up mine eyes unto the hills . . . ."

Mrs. Peabody was enchanted. "Lovely!" she exclaimed. "My dear, doesn't it remind you of these rugged hills encircling your own city of Vellore?"

The girl slowly shook her head. "I have never seen them," she said simply.

Returning to the car, the guests rode for awhile in shocked silence.

"Those poor lovely little women!" choked Vassar finally. "Living all the time in that tiny courtyard, those musty rooms! It's unbelievable."

"That little Hindu girl with the fever," said Vassar in a muffled voice. "You think she's going to live?"

"I hope so," said Ida.

"But—suppose there hadn't been a doctor to go to her, what would they have done? Taken her to the government hospital in town?"

"Oh, no," replied Ida. "There are only men doctors in the government hospitals. No high-caste Hindu or Mohammedan woman would think of going there or of letting a man come to her."

"And such a lot of women there must be in India," continued Vassar thoughtfully. "How many, Dr. Scudder?"

"A hundred and fifty million," Ida replied, praying that the eager young things would continue to ask the right questions.

They did. "And how many women doctors?"

"About a hundred and fifty. With fifty of those perhaps on furlough."

"But—why don't they train Indian women to be doctors?"

Bless the child! Ida chose her words carefully. "There is one mission school in the north, at Ludhiana, where they train women in medicine. But it's a thousand miles from us, and Indian parents, even devoted Christian ones, would be reluctant to send their daughters so far away, entrusting them to another climate, language, and race. Of course, some people have thought of starting such a school here in the south. In fact, there's a union committee of several denominations working on the idea now."

"What a splendid idea!" exclaimed Mrs. Montgomery. "A

146

union college of medicine for women, with all the Christian women of both America and Britain behind it! Don't you think it's a wonderful idea, Lucy?"

"A good idea, yes," replied Mrs. Peabody without enthusiasm.

Ida's heart sank. It was her fault. She should not have broached the plan. Mrs. Peabody was a leader, not a follower, a builder of castles both in the air and on the ground, but never according to another's blueprints.

In the rush of the dispensary Ida almost forgot her visitors. At noontime breakfast Mrs. Peabody's gaze already held a distant look. She had been inquiring about trains and was sorry, but felt they must leave early the next morning. Operations and afternoon dispensary took longer than usual, and Ida went straight from the hospital to tea at the bungalow, having invited some of the leading Hindu and Mohammedan women of Vellore to meet the Americans. Expecting only a few less timorous souls to take advantage of the invitation, she gasped with amazement. Silk saris rippled and glowed in every shade of the rainbow. Jewels worth a small fortune scintillated on slender brown necks, wrists, ankles, brows, and noses. Ida moved among the guests with her usual charm and poise, putting them at their ease, interpreting shy Tamil courtesies into English, making sure that the high-caste ladies were not embarrassed by offerings of food.

"This could never have happened a few years ago," she heard Annie Hancock's gentle voice explain to Mrs. Peabody. "When I came here thirteen years ago, these women would not even have welcomed us into their homes. It just shows what this hospital has done for Vellore."

"Doesn't it?" agreed the American guest politely.

Ida moved on. When the last jutka had trickled through the gate, she felt as if all her energy had drained with it. But there was still one task remaining.

"There's a lovely valley outside the town," she told her guests brightly, "which you really must see."

Again they crowded into the tiny car, the girls eagerly, Mrs. Montgomery politely, Mrs. Peabody with silent resignation. "Already," thought Ida, "she's picking the site for her arts college, cutting its stone, rearing its walls. But she's not going to get away without an eyeful of *my* site."

They rattled southward along the dusty road, through the little village of Torapadi, past the jail with its imposing gate and red earthen walls, into a lonely gravel road winding among huge upflung masses of rocks. Close to one of them, a steep rounded heap topped by three spears of palmyra palms, the car chugged to a stop.

"Would you mind climbing a little way?" asked Ida.

"I'm game," agreed Mrs. Montgomery cheerfully.

Mrs. Peabody emerged choking from a cloud of dust. "We've come this far," she said stoically. "I never plan to start anything I can't finish."

Letting the girls scramble on ahead, Ida led the way. Already her desperately tired body was charged with fresh energy. She envied the girls, already climbing the steeper rocks high above, the brown goatherd scampering with bare foot agility atop a sharp rock to peer warily down at them. Arrived at a flat table of rock a third of the way up, she dared not climb higher. Her guests were wheezing.

"There!" She spread her arms to enfold the valley. "Two hundred acres of it, and belonging to nobody! Nobody, that is, but the goats and crows and paddy birds and a few cows and monkeys—and to God himself!"

"Beautiful," agreed Mrs. Montgomery, gallantly looking beyond the barren wasteland to the patchwork of emerald rice fields fading into purple hills.

"You mean," demanded Mrs. Peabody bluntly, "those bare brown fields just below? Two hundred acres, you say. Hmm! Practically wasteland."

Despite the fact that Ida had really not expected this woman to share her vision, she was bleakly disappointed. Suddenly she knew she could restrain herself no longer. Somehow she must make these two see it as she did—the brown wastes velveted with green, planted with mimosas, *gol mohrs,* pink and yellow cassias; long buildings of stone with encompassing verandahs, arching porticos; paths filled with hurrying students in white saris. She opened her lips.

148

"Water," said Mrs. Peabody with cool precision. "What about it?"

"Water—" Ida stared at her blankly.

"It would be no good, you know, without it. No better than a desert. Could we get water into these two hundred acres?"

"I—I think so. I've talked with some nearby villagers, and they say there's a spring."

"Then I have an idea!" Lucy Peabody came suddenly alive, her blue eyes warmly glowing. She focused their full intensity on Ida's bewildered face. "I've been thinking about the problem all day, but the solution just came to me. It's about that medical college we were talking of this morning."

"Yes?" murmured Ida, scarcely daring to breathe.

"You must be the one to start it, Dr. Scudder. You are going to build the college and—*you are going to build it here, in this valley!*"

"But—" Ida's bewilderment was genuine. Surely this was not the same aloof stranger who had climbed the hill with her not ten minutes ago!

"Don't say no yet, Dr. Scudder. As you say, the difficulties are imposing, but you won't have to do it alone. We'll enlist the help of hundreds of women in America and Britain. *Thousands*. Once we make them realize the need of the women of India as we have seen it today, they won't fail us. Why, you and I together—I believe we can move mountains, Ida Scudder!"

Ida drew a long breath. The barren brown fields, gold in the slanting sun, were already gleaming with white domes and terraces, astir with eager youthful figures. She felt like Moses looking into the Promised Land.

"Yes," she said. "I believe we can." Her gaze moved over the bare expanses, past the emerald haze of rice fields, to the high bold crest of Kailasa upthrust against a crimson sky. "Or, better yet," she added even more confidently, "we can climb them."

But after her guests departed, even though they had kindled bright hopes for the future, Ida was forced to adjust herself to the more sobering realities of the present. The college must remain a dream for a long time to come. The immediate need was for more hospital space, and the problem was desperate. The denominational board was poor. Retrenchment, not expansion, was its order of the day. Often she was given insufficient funds even for running expenses. The difficulty of collecting fees from patients added to the financial problem. To the very poor, of course, she expected to give almost free service. It was the delinquency of the wealthy that galled her.

"Never mind the expense, we will pay anything," the family of a rich patient would announce magnanimously on arrival. But when it came time for payment, it would be a different story. The patient, accompanied by many relatives, would come to the bungalow, smilingly produce a huge rose garland, limes, sweets, bows, profuse thanks, and possibly five rupees. The actual expenditure would have been at least forty. If she remonstrated, the family might grudgingly produce a few more rupees and consider themselves generous. In the course of a year 30,000 free meals would have been served.

There were other discouraging features. The Gudiyattam dispensary had to be closed on account of plague. Opposition to the hospital arose in Vellore, and for weeks the beds were practically empty. Then came a revival of confidence, and wards, verandahs, even spaces under the beds, were full to overflowing, until again there came sudden exodus.

"I can't understand it!" Dr. Lilian Cook, a new skilled, enthusiastic young doctor from Scotland, looked about the empty wards in amazement. "Yesterday they were full. Today—"

Ida laughed. "Just another feast day. It always happens. Even the sickest patients insist on going home. They'll be back when it's over. In worse condition," she added ruefully.

Dr. Cook, new to India, was even more disturbed by her first experiences with patients exposed to treatment by *vaithyans*, untrained Indian doctors. She once showed Ida an indignant letter she was writing home:

"A sweet little married girl of fifteen came to us after treatment by six or seven *vaithyans*. She had fever and was on the

150

verge of death. We tried to save her, only to have her relatives insist on taking her back to the same dark airless little room! We sent a nurse with her, but the *vaithyan* sent her away. And how do you suppose he treated that dying girl? By tying a rag around her arm and muttering prayers!"

Ida smiled when she read it. What would her new colleague say when she encountered some of the more positive remedies, like treating a bleeding wound with a poultice of hard coal and oil? Yet it wasn't so long ago, she reminded herself, that her own ancestors were practicing bloodletting.

In spite of her impatience she could see progress. The dispensary was always full, averaging 100 patients a day. There were now eighteen nurses in the hospital, all but two of them Indians, four of the latter certificated. Three of the seniors, who had successfully passed their second-year nursing examinations, were enrolled in her midwifery class. And during the year 1913, 500 visits were made by her nurses in the town and surrounding villages.

The board finally gave her permission to raise money on her next furlough for four additional wards, and voted $2,000 for enlarging the hospital. Four wards! Two thousand dollars! It would take at least $50,000 to house the 150 beds she would need as a mere start toward a medical college, since the government requirement for university-affiliated colleges was a minimum of three teaching beds per student. With increasing clarity she saw that additions to Schell, no matter how extensive, would never be adequate. The visit of Mrs. Peabody had made her impatient to turn her dream into action. With grim courage she set herself the gigantic task of building a new hospital.

She asked the colonial government of Madras Presidency for a grant. No. Government did not sponsor such activities. Schools, yes, but not hospitals. Ida persisted. Her powers of persuasion were exceeded only by her ability to marshal facts and figures. She listed the hundreds of villages within working radius of Vellore, the thousands of women patients already treated, the million and more in the presidency who needed medical attention. She pleaded eloquently for a philosophy of education that would rate nurses as highly as clerks and lawyers, healthy bodies as essential as trained minds. And she won. Government consented to give one-third of the amount she needed subject to a maximum of $20,000, provided she could guarantee the other two-thirds. This meant that she must raise at least $40,000 while on furlough in America!

"Please," she wrote the secretary of the board, "*please* allow me to raise it. I have about two-thirds of it in view now." (Wishful thinking accounted for the phrase "in view.") "I can surely get the rest, and I hope the board will trust me to do so and that you will cable to India to go ahead and accept the government grant. Oh, *please* do make the board do it!"

The principal of her denomination's Voorhees College in Vellore, who was an old friend, exerted still more pressure on the financially harassed board. Katharine Van Nest, always loyal, used her persuasion as an officer of the Women's Auxiliary. An opportunity like this, they argued, must not be allowed to pass. On March 2, 1914, the board voted to buy new land for a hospital, but, as usual, failed to appropriate as much as Ida wished. This did not mean, they assured her, that her dream was not to be realized ... only postponed. If when she was at home some person were to offer her a large amount, they would gladly permit her to accept.

Only 100 beds instead of 150, and those far in the future! But at least she was permitted to apply for the government grant. And on May 27 at a conference of the South India Missionary Association, representing four denominations, a committee made the following recommendations: that a medical school for women be established in Vellore in connection with the hospital; that Dr. Ida S. Scudder be its principal; and that she represent the committee in a fund-raising campaign both in Great Britain and in the United States.

Ida could hardly contain her joy. If only her friends at home proved as eager to make her dream come true as those in India—Thungammah, for instance, a Hindu servant in the hospital whose monthly wage was only five rupees! For months Thungammah had been living on three of them, saving the other two, as everybody supposed, for an old-age pension. One day she brought to Ida all her savings, sixty-nine rupees, over twenty dollars. "For new hospital," she said in beaming triumph. "I help make for it the pump!"

Ida sailed home in July, 1914, with high hopes. Before she arrived in America a certain archduke had been assassinated in an obscure town in Serbia, and all Europe had burst into flame.

12

Ida's American campaign during 1914 and 1915, when war was raging in Europe, proved a bitter disappointment. From November to April she spoke constantly, to large groups and small, in cities and towns and villages. She spoke eloquently, incisively, telling about conditions in village India, the necessity of building a new hospital, the imperative need of training women doctors. And occasionally, when she told about the sufferings of child wives or the practices of untrained midwives, something she said vied for interest with the horrors allegedly being perpetrated in Europe.

But India seemed far away compared with Belgium, the unintentional atrocities of ignorance less conscience-plaguing than the deliberate ones of war. Eyes focused on European battlefields refused to become more far-sighted. Hands loosed their hold on purse strings chiefly for such urgent demands as war charities and Liberty bonds. Ida contemplated the results of her campaign with dismay. As the months passed, dismay changed to panic. Without the support of loyal friends—Lucy Peabody, Katharine Van Nest, her closest friend Gertrude Dodd—she could hardly have borne the disappointment.

154

One day when her courage was at its lowest ebb, Ida went with her mother to Gertrude's apartment. As they talked, she stood at a window overlooking New York harbor. A great steamer lay in the strong current making not the slightest headway, while a small puffing energetic little tug was trying to get it moving.

"There!" exclaimed Ida with bitter irony. "Look at us! That steamer is our hospital and medical school, and we're that tug, puffing with all our might but getting nowhere."

"Wait," advised Gertrude shrewdly. They watched and watched for what seemed an eternity. "See! It's moving!"

Ida's pulses hammered. Her muscles strained. Sure enough, the steamer was getting slowly under way. Soon it was moving majestically upstream, the little tug puffing triumphantly along.

Ida did not lose courage again. She doubled her activity, speaking often three and four times a day, many days in succession. And slowly, in small amounts, money came. She succeeded in raising no forty thousand dollars, as she had hoped —less than ten—but at least she could go back to India assured of the beginnings of a new hospital.

And this assurance was not her only source of satisfaction. Her friend Dr. William Bancroft Hill, one of the prominent leaders of the Reformed Church, and his wife had given her a new Ford. Best of all, Gertrude Dodd planned to follow her to India in a few months, not for a brief visit, but to stay for the rest of her life. Gertrude had decided that she could make no better use of her wealth and talents than in the service of the missionary enterprise which had long commanded her interest and loyalty, and of the one person whom she had come to admire beyond all others.

Not even the recent sinking of a great American liner called the *Lusitania* deterred Ida in the slightest from sailing back to India through the mine-infested waters of the Atlantic and Mediterranean in the late fall of 1915. She could hardly wait to get back to a little corner of the world where saving life seemed more important than destroying it.

In India again her days became as full and multiform as the crazy quilts of rice fields stretching to the fringed and rocky horizons: plowing, planting, cultivating, reaping, threshing, winnowing, all going on at once and side by side. The pattern of them was like her own struggle to create and build. She was the farmer pushing his wooden plow behind lean oxen, knee-deep in mud; the women bending over pale green shoots, trans-planting, weeding; the toiling figures, both men and women, cutting the ripe stalks with small sickles, strewing them on the hard-packed threshing floors, driving bullocks round and round, tossing the golden grain to the wind for winnowing. Only in one thing she was unlike them. She was not permitted the satisfaction of bearing home triumphantly on her head the results of her labors.

In January of 1916 the building committee appointed by the South India Medical Association, the interdenominational mission group which was promoting the building of a women's medical school, came to Vellore, inspected the 200-acre site four miles south of town, and, to Ida's joy, approved it as the location for the proposed union medical college. A missionary of the Reformed Church, who had shown remarkable talent as a builder, immediately started sketching plans. That same month the Governor of Madras and his wife made a similar visit and gave their full approbation.

"Plans, government approval, an option on the land—we have everything now!" reported Ida jubilantly to her mother.

"Except the million dollars it will take to build it," reminded Mrs. Scudder gently.

"That will come," Ida assured her confidently.

But even her own confidence was little solace to her impatience. It would come, yes, it must come, but *when?* War was still raging. Mrs. Peabody, struggling valiantly to push the campaign in the United States, reported little headway. Work in Britain at present was out of the question. And there were other difficulties.

"Many members of the board object," wrote Katharine Van Nest worriedly, "to making the hospital interdenominational and turning it over to the proposed college. Mrs. Peabody has gone ahead and taken quite a lot for granted. I'm afraid she isn't always as tactful as she might be."

Here in India Dr. Anna Kugler was having the same troubles up at Guntur. The men of her denomination didn't want a *union* medical college for women. It was her job, they were telling her, to stick to her Lutheran work. Dr. Kugler opposed them with spirit. "You mean," she would argue, "you want a Lutheran medical college to train Lutheran doctors to take out a Lutheran appendix?"

"People!" fumed Ida, jabbing needles, disinfecting, white-washing, after a plague scare caused by the discovery of several dead rats and squirrels. "How can they be so small! As if we were fighting Dutch Reformed germs or Methodist Guinea worms or Baptist rats!"

Even children were more enthusiastic than most of the men. One four-year-old son of a missionary, having heard the project much discussed, was heard to pray: "O God, bless my sick pet monkey and make him well, and send a million dollars to build the Medical College for Women. Amen."

Fortunately there were things Ida could do to promote the project without waiting. A lot must be picked for the dispensary, which was to be built in the center of town. In March she made a trip north with Dr. McPhail, visited the mission medical school for women in Ludhiana and the government one in Delhi, and saw the Taj Mahal by moonlight. It was so beautiful it made her bones ache. But what a pity, she thought, that it had to be a tomb!

Though there were now other doctors to assist her in the hospital, Ida's daily schedule often stretched around the clock. Operative work was steadily increasing in spite of the persisting fears of patients who would often plead, "Medicine please to give, plasters please to put on, anything to drive away tumor, but please to not operate!"

Her scalpel flashed constantly through the pages of her diary.

"Jan. 26, 1916. Amputated a finger, opened a breast abscess, burned out a sarcoma . . . .

"April 3. Busy day, but the kind I most enjoy. In A.M. had a D. and C., later an R.V.F. and abdominal tumor. Big dinner at Wyckoffs'. . . .

"May 16. Had operation 63-pound solid abdominal tumor. Woman only lived 6½ hours. I am so disappointed.

"Aug. 21. Well, the die is cast, and we have decided to buy

a piece of land near the jutka stand on Katpadi Road for the dispensary.

"Oct. 28. Undertook to extend David's legs. He took chloroform badly. Nearly died on table. Was low all day. Died.

"Nov. 24. A busy morning, but I wish work were heavier.

"Dec. 12. Went to Villupuram to meet Gertrude and the rest of the delegation coming by way of Colombo. The party consisted of Mrs. Knox, Katharine Olcott, Miss Camp, and—oh, the joy of having her here nearly smothered me!"

Within a week Gertrude Dodd had made herself so essential to the Schell ménage that everybody wondered how they had gotten along without her. Though her furniture did not arrive until the following March, she made herself thoroughly at home immediately and, establishing an office in her room on the second floor of the bungalow, assumed management of both hospital and household accounts. She hired workmen to erect a wonderful high sleeping porch, like a tower, which Ida dubbed "Kailasa," on a corner of the bungalow. She assumed direction of the little family of destitute children, who, since Mary Taber, had been gradually accumulating, Ida never having the heart to turn any small foundling or derelict away. There were fifteen of them now being cared for by the nurses and housed on the hospital verandahs. Under Gertrude's efficient supervision they were provided with both discipline and better sleeping quarters. She helped in kitchen, compounding room, dispensary, wherever needed, and to Ida she became personal secretary as well as a kind mentor and the closest of personal friends.

Each week she went out with Ida on the Gudiyattam Roadside. The new Model-T Ford, though not much bigger than the old Peugeot, was less temperamental. It traveled 7,000 miles during its first year.

The little high-built open car was as loaded on a Wednesday morning as a third-class train compartment on the way to a pilgrimage center: Ida, her driver (often riding on the running board while she sat behind the wheel), Gertrude Dodd with her bag of scissors, bandages, and pencils; a nurse, Mrs. Gnanammal the compounder, Mrs. Cornelius the Indian pastor's wife with a bag of colored picture cards; the big box of medicines, salves, instruments, and sterilized dressings.

Often now they made as many as fourteen stops on the way to and from Gudiyattam. As they approached each one, such a crowd would be waiting that it looked like a *shandy,* one of the village outdoor markets. When Ida blew her horn, other figures came running: cowherds with head cloths flapping, workmen from the fields, children with flowers clutched in brown grubby hands.

"Sir! Sir!" they screamed, the only word of English they knew.

Ida's love of flowers was known from Vellore to Gudiyattam. If the bouquets were clean and unwilted, they were exchanged for picture cards with scripture verses in Tamil pasted on the backs. On the way home the car was often besieged by children coming out all along the road, holding up bunches of flowers. There were so many that Ida regretfully ordered the driver not to stop for them. Only twice did he disobey, once when children had made a long rope of oleander and cassia blossoms and stretched it across the road. The second time it was so dark that at first Ida could see nothing.

"Why—" she began to question sharply. Then she breathed a soft "Oh!" Her eyes could barely distinguish the tot standing by the roadside holding up a single perfect pink rose.

Eagerly, at each medical station, they would scan the group for the very ill treated the week before, relieved to note signs of improvement. At first the rich and high-born would be gathered on one side of the road, the poor and outcastes on the other, but soon high-caste was standing beside untouchable, each awaiting his turn. Besides the five hundred or more cases of the usual ailments treated during the day—sore eyes, ring-worm, roundworm, scabies, chronic ulcers, leprosy—there might be a dozen minor operations to perform: burns to treat, bones to set, abscesses to open and dress. If chloroform was needed, Ida would take the patients to Gudiyattam, operate in the dispensary, and bring them back at night.

"An avatar she must be," said a villager wonderingly. "One of the incarnations of the god Vishnu."

159

"You think so?" questioned Mrs. Cornelius shrewdly. "And did you ever hear of one of the avatars doing any good in this world?"

"*Ayoh!* No," admitted the villager thoughtfully.

"Don't you think, then," persisted the pastor's wife, "that the Doctor *Ammal* does more than the avatars?"

"*Amma*, yes," was the reply. The wonder was even greater. "But—why? *Why* does she do it?"

"It's her God living in her heart," explained Mrs. Cornelius gently. "A God of love he is, who makes her care about people."

The villager was satisfied.

Often people tried to flag them between stops. Once the patient was a woman with a bad tooth. Already very late, Ida could not take the time then to examine her. "Be here when I come back," she told her cheerfully. There were even more delays than usual on the return trip, and it was nine o'clock when they saw the tiny waving lantern. "Oh-oh!" remembered Ida, applying the brake with a jerk. "The woman with the tooth! I'd forgotten all about her."

She took out her forceps. The nurse had been left behind at Gudiyattam, but with her for the day was the young daughter of one of the resident missionaries of Vellore. "Get me a wad of cotton," Ida ordered the girl briskly, "and soak it in iodine."

Eagerly, with unpracticed fingers, the girl obeyed. Still sitting behind the wheel, with her driver holding the lantern at the proper angle, Ida made the necessary diagnosis, yanked out the offending member, swabbed the cavity with cotton, gave the surprised patient some simple directions and a reassuring pat on the jaw, and drove off without having stopped her engine.

There was another occasion when someone tried to flag them between stations and they almost failed to stop. It was in May, the height of the hot season. The sun's rays beat down relentlessly from a grayish-copper sky. Dust filmed the air and ground into every pore. Old leaves hung dead on many of the trees, and the brave little green clusters pushing their way through the buds looked drooping. Not a breath of air stirred. Even the crows were almost silent.

It was after one when they made their last usual stop before

Gudiyattam. Settling wearily into her seat, Ida said to her driver "Now, Selvam, we won't stop again. We are all exhausted, and this heat is simply unbearable."

One and all, even the intrepid Gertrude Dodd, groaned with relief.

They had driven about four miles when they saw a little group standing by the roadside, a man and a woman, the latter holding a baby. As the car drew nearer, the man came out into the road and signaled them to stop.

"No!" exclaimed Ida. "We simply cannot. I'm faint with the heat. Tell them, Selvam, to wait here until evening if they must see us."

The driver shouted the direction as he drove by. But in passing Ida leaned out to take a closer look at the group. "Stop," she said suddenly. "All of them, especially that baby, look so very sick. We must go back."

There were more groans, not expressive of relief, but all knew better than to protest. Selvam reluctantly backed the car to where the man and woman were now squatting, utterly disconsolate.

"*Yenna?*" demanded the driver with weary impatience. "What is it you want?"

The two faces lighted with pitiable eagerness. Words poured from the man's lips.

"Oh, *ammal,* you have come back! So glad we are. We have walked so many miles! We came last week, too, and you had passed by, so we came very early today, are very hungry, for we have had nothing to eat since four o'clock, but we dared not leave the road for fear you would pass. Then you came and went on, and we were so unhappy, but you came back, and your God will bless you."

Tears were rolling down their cheeks. The father was a leper. The mother was blind. As she held up her baby to Ida, the sightless eyes reflected the bright gray-copper of the sky.

"My baby, *ammal,*" she said eagerly. "We have lost many children. Eight have died, and now only this one we have, besides a little girl."

Ida reached down from the car and took the inert little body. It lay hot as fire against her lap, its two tiny fists clenched

161

tightly over its eyes. Gently she removed them and pushed back the lids. She could not speak. For long moments there was not even the caw of a crow to break the stillness. The sightless eyes of the mother, still uplifted, lost the bright glint of copper and turned slowly gray.

"*Ammal*," she pleaded, "why do you not speak to me about my little son?"

Ida wet her lips, dust grating against her tongue. "I'm sorry," she said. Instead of being gentle, as she intended, her voice sounded dry and harsh. She opened her lips to try again, closed them. Would a sword hurt any less, pulled from a velvet sheath?

The woman understood. It was the way of her people to find release in words. "Blind? Hopeless? Can you do nothing, *ammal?* Oh, how can I let my baby be blind, like me!" Hands clutching her hair, she sank down moaning beside the car.

Ida also had her means of release, in action. Unpacking her box, she bathed and treated the baby's eyes, rubbed its hot body with oil. Sterilizing her instruments, she opened an abscess on the man's leprous insensitive foot, then bound both his sorely ravaged feet with clean bandages. Only for the mother, squatting on the ground with the blind baby in her lap and sobbing her heart out, could she do nothing.

Suddenly the woman stopped weeping and lifted her head. "*Ammal,* if we had been in time last week, could you have saved my baby's eyes?"

Ida caught her breath in dismay. How could she tell this mother that if the child had been brought only a week sooner, it might not have become blind? She did not need to. The sightless eyes had penetrated her silence.

Again the woman bent over her baby. "My god is very cruel to me," she murmured with a deep tearless resignation. "I must be a very great sinner."

It was late at night on another occasion when a group of men came into their path and tried to stop them. "Urgent! Urgent!" they shouted, waving their arms.

But Selvam, the driver, stubbornly kept on going. It was monsoon season after a day of heavy rain, and he had no wish to be stranded on a muddy road far from Vellore in the late evening.

162

"We don't stop on the way home!" he yelled back over his shoulder.

But this time also he was forced to yield. In the flare of the headlights Ida had seen the anxiety on the men's faces. "They said 'urgent,'" she reminded him. "Stop, Selvam. We must go back."

Silently the driver backed the car. The men came running up beside them.

"Water has come up over the road ahead," they explained. "Afraid we were that the Doctor *Ammal* and her bandy without bullocks might stick fast in the mud. So waiting here we have been for many hours to help push you through!"

Though Ida's dream of training women doctors to meet India's needs seemed as yet far from fulfillment, she was already helping to create them, for her example stirred many young women to imitate her. One of these, a girl in her mid-twenties named Pauline Jeffery, felt the stirring anew as she sat one summer day at Kodaikanal, watching a tennis match between the British and American teams.

It was the deciding game of the tournament, and the score was deuce. The server, a woman in white, stepped briskly to the back line, tossed the ball, and swung her racquet. A hundred pairs of eyes followed the flash of motion, but only one, Pauline's, clung to the white-clad figure rather than to the ball she served.

It skimmed across the net, was returned in a smashing curve far out over the left alley. The woman's partner, a young man half her age, lunged for it and missed, but in an instant the woman had sent it spinning to the far right-hand corner of the opposite court, yards out of her opponents' reach. Even the loyal rooters of the British team applauded.

"Advantage in!" sang the umpire above the confusion.

Again the woman stepped briskly to the line. The ball smashed over the net, landed in the exact center of the prescribed rectangle, slithered across it without once bouncing. Her opponent reached for it belatedly, stood blinking. It was a moment before even the umpire realized what had happened. "Game, set, tournament, Americans!" he managed to shout before the spectators burst into loud cheering.

"Isn't she wonderful?" Pauline Jeffery continued to gaze after the woman in white as she moved to the net, complimenting her partner, commiserating with her opponents, receiving the accolades of victory with a matter-of-fact pleasure.

"Who is she?" asked a newcomer to the Kodaikanal summer colony.

Pauline looked at the stranger as if she had inquired the identity of the Mona Lisa. "You mean you don't know *Dr. Ida Scudder?*"

"Oh, so that's who it is! Well, she's certainly tops in tennis."

"Not only tennis," came the firm reply.

Pauline Jeffery, daughter of missionaries in Madura and now principal of a mission high school in that South Indian city, had been reared in India, and her eyes had followed the winner of the match with the same rapt intentness when the sun had glinted on gold hair instead of silver, and the white dress had sported puffed sleeves and a ruffled hem that swept the tennis court. Now the very sight of Dr. Ida tantalized the girl with what she had missed. Oh, if only she had listened to her father's advice and stuck to science and a medical course instead of taking her M.A. in education! The regret became intensified for her during the following week when she was helpless to assist intelligently in the home of one of her Madura high-school girls, sick with high fever. Hurrying to the girl's side on the following Sunday evening, she met the Western doctor in charge of the case as he was leaving the house.

"How's Anbu?" she inquired anxiously.

"She won't live until morning," replied the doctor bluntly, swinging himself into his saddle.

"Won't live until morning!" exclaimed Pauline, aghast.

"No." The doctor was emphatic. "They haven't done a thing I told them to."

The girl took note of the directions which had been neglected, and promised to have them carried out at once. "Can we call you in the night if she's worse?" she inquired hopefully.

"No use," he replied abruptly. "The girl hasn't a chance."

Pauline found her pupil in a coma with a temperature of 104, and immediately started applying to the hot but otherwise lifeless figure the cold packs the doctor had prescribed. Finally, unable to bear the anxiety, she rushed over to Cushing to ask Dr. Ida what she could do. Her friend was concerned, but as the girl had expected, felt that she could do nothing on account of professional etiquette.

"Are you sure the doctor doesn't want you to call him?" she asked worriedly.

"He said absolutely *not*," replied Pauline, in tears.

"I can understand," said Ida. "He hasn't been in touch with these critical cases lately. It's easy to lose hope. No doubt he's done everything possible. Do you know if he's tried a Murphy drip?" She began describing a treatment she had sometimes used.

"I—I don't think so. No, I'm sure he hasn't." Something in the blue eyes sent Pauline's hopes soaring. "Would—would you come—"

Her hopes plunged. No, Ida could not come. Surely Pauline could see that. But she would give complete directions. And the patient could not possibly be harmed by the treatment.

Pauline rushed back to her pupil. Clumsily but with desperate pains, she began following the directions. Members of the anxious family had returned with the necessary equipment, and Pauline herself was just about to take the kettle off the earthen stove with its wood fire when Dr. Ida and Miss Dodd walked quietly into the room. "I'll take over," said the former abruptly.

"She just had to come," whispered Miss Dodd to Pauline.

Hours later Pauline lifted her arm to wipe the tears and sweat and weariness from her eyes. As she turned them to Dr. Ida, there was a brightness in them born only partly of triumph. "You've saved her!" she said in awe. "It's as if she were dead, and you've brought her back to life. Oh, how—*how I wish I could be a doctor!*"

"Well, why can't you?" asked Ida calmly, scrubbing her hands.

The brightness in the young eyes grew white-hot, then faded. The girl laughed ironically. Study medicine *now?*

"I was older than you," said Ida quietly, "when I started."

"*You*—yes!" This time the laughter sounded really amused. But Pauline wasn't meant to be a doctor. Plenty of people, including her mother, had told her so. And, anyway, no use dreaming about it! A poor school teacher—!

No more was said, but the desire, long suppressed, pursued the young woman relentlessly. As she sat brooding one day on the slope below Coaker's Walk, the footpath which followed the edge of the high plateau, it kept nagging as incessantly as the shrill drumming of locusts in the huge blue-gum grove in the valley far below.

"Pauline, come on up!" sang a voice from above, and Pauline was delighted as she joined Dr. Ida, who was taking her mother around Coaker's Walk for her Sunday morning constitutional. Back at Cushing they found Miss Dodd.

"Pauline," said Dr. Ida, "if you had the money, could you go home to America and study medicine?"

The girl's pulses pounded. "When?" she asked faintly.

"Now. Right away. My friend Miss Dodd is willing to send you."

"You—you mean—"

"Pay all your expenses. What about it? Will you go?"

Pauline wet her lips. "I—I couldn't. Not now. I've come out on a three-year term. I promised. I—I do hope you understand."

She rushed blindly out of Cushing, walked clear around the little lake before returning home. As the months passed, bitter disappointment changed to resignation, resignation to near contentment. Only occasionally did she stop to wonder what lucky young thing had become the recipient of Miss Dodd's generosity. Some Indian girl, she hoped. At least she could do her part by trying to promote Dr. Ida's plan for a medical school. In order to learn more about it, she paid a visit to Vellore.

She went out on a Wednesday Roadside and, like all of Dr. Ida's visitors, was put to work. "Here, Pauline, cut this baby's hair so I can get at those scalp sores." . . . "Write the name of each new patient on these chits." . . . "Have the swabs ready the minute this awful abscess is lanced." . . . "Here are the forceps, Pauline. How would you like to pull a tooth?"

The girl took the instrument with elation mingled with trepidation, until she looked into the tall villager's mouth and found the tooth hanging by a slender root and ready to tumble out almost by itself.

It was two o'clock before they reached Gudiyattam. Among

the crowd waiting were some Gypsy bird-catchers, poorest of the poor, with their two hopelessly undernourished children. Ida took one look at them and decided they must go to the hospital in Vellore. But how? Finally she left the medicines behind and bundled the two boys with their mother into the little Ford, making nine occupants in all. Pauline sat wedged into the back seat between Mrs. Gnanammal and Miss Dodd, one of the pitiably thin little beggars in her lap and the other crowded between her knees. Never had she been so uncomfortable—nor so happy.

It was on the morning after she had spent an hour in the operating room with Dr. Ida that she went upstairs to find Miss Dodd sitting at her desk. "Oh, dear!" she sighed ecstatically. "Just watching her operate makes my fingers tingle!"

Miss Dodd looked up from her pile of letters, bright eyes resting thoughtfully on the flushed face. "The offer is still yours, Pauline," she said quietly.

The girl stared incredulously. "You—you mean—"

"I mean that the money for your medical education is still yours if you want it. But it's you who have to make the decision."

Pauline made it. As soon as her three-year term of teaching was finished, she sailed for America. Having no educational background for the study of medicine, she compressed a full premedical course into one summer session of intensive study; then, though nearly thirty years of age, she entered Yale Medical School that fall, beginning the long five-year apprenticeship which would prepare her to walk in Dr. Ida's footsteps. Her health was poor, the studies difficult. Once she thought she had failed a course. Her chosen specialty of ophthalmology, vital to the needs of India, was to demand still more grueling and intensive training.

But to Pauline Jeffery no price was too great for the attainment of her goal: to return to Vellore and to become partner of Dr. Ida in that greatest of all her tournaments, the struggle to win new life for the women of a land they both loved.

13

Ida had never believed in waiting for things to happen. The best way to get anything started, she had proved through experience, was to start it herself. Therefore one day early in 1918 found her sitting in the office of Colonel Bryson, head of the British Medical Department of Madras Presidency.

"So,"—the colonel leaned across his desk—"you actually think you're ready to start a medical college for women?"

"Not a college," corrected Ida carefully. "A medical *school*. We know we can't hope for university affiliation yet, though we expect to raise our standards as soon as possible. All we're asking now is the chance to train Indian women for the L.M.P. —Licensed Medical Practitioner—diploma."

Colonel Bryson regarded her with a mingling of admiration, skepticism, and tolerant amusement.

"You have as yet no buildings—"

"We'll get them," Ida assured him confidently. "Meanwhile we are prepared to rent houses near our present hospital."

"—almost no money in hand—"

"It's being raised. Women of four denominations are working constantly in America to raise it. We trust that after the war there will be similar groups working in Britain."

168

"—and as for staff—"

Ida sat very straight in her chair. "I am equipped to teach most of the subjects needed for first-year students. One of my nurses will assist me in teaching anatomy. The girls will receive instruction in physics and chemistry at Voorhees College, our mission institution in Vellore. In another year we shall be prepared to increase our staff."

"No buildings, no money, no staff!" repeated Colonel Bryson with more wonder than impatience. "Yet you're asking permission to start a medical school *now* for Indian women. It would be ridiculous if it weren't so—so heroic!"

"There's nothing heroic," retorted Ida, "about tackling a job that needs desperately to be done, and surely nothing ridiculous. You are one person, Colonel, who should understand the need of India for women doctors!"

The look of amusement was gone from the man's eyes. For a moment they revealed only admiration. "Indeed I do, Doctor, and I commend you for your—courage. I almost said audacity. But"—the look of skepticism returned—"medical education *for Indian women!* You know yourself we can't persuade many of them to become nurses. And, even if you find a few who are willing, do you realize what they'll be up against? Competing against men from seven medical schools when they come up for their examinations!"

"You think women haven't the brains to compete with men?" demanded Ida coolly.

"We're talking about *Indian* women," reminded the Colonel with a deprecating smile.

"And in the manner of an *Indian* man," retorted Ida. Her blue eyes danced. "Have you heard the story, Colonel, about the dinner somebody just gave here in India where there were to be sheep's brains served?"

"No," replied the Colonel. "Afraid I haven't."

"When the meal was served, ordinary mutton came on. Later the mistress went to the kitchen and said to the cook, 'Why didn't you serve the sheep's brains, boy?' 'Oh, madam,' replied the cook, 'this sheep was a female and had no brains.'"

The Colonel laughed goodnaturedly. "All right, Doctor. You win. I'll tell you what we'll do." The tolerant amusement was back in his eyes. "You'll be fortunate if you get three applications. But if you get as many as six, go ahead and start your school. You have government permission."

Ida left the office of the surgeon general in triumph. She could hardly wait to get back to Vellore to set the necessary machinery in motion. Before leaving the train compartment she had a brochure ready for the printer.

MEDICAL SCHOOL FOR WOMEN

A Medical School for Women is to be opened in July 1918 in Vellore, North Arcot, South India, under the auspices of the Union Missionary Medical College Committee.

The first classes are to be for Apothecary and Sub-Assistant Surgeons only. After the war is over and new buildings are erected, it is planned that University classes will be opened.

School Final certificates with good English will be necessary for admission; character certificates essential; age over eighteen.

Some scholarships will be available. The School will be open to all, without respect to Caste or Creed.

As the first class is to be limited to twenty-five in number, applications should be sent without delay to—

Miss Ida S. Scudder, M.D.,
Mary Taber Schell Hospital,
Vellore, North Arcot

Though this prospectus was sent out to all mission and government high schools and colleges for girls in Madras Presidency, Ida was not satisfied. She visited numerous schools herself, wrote innumerable letters, arranged for dozens of personal interviews with possible candidates.

It was after she had made a stirring appeal to a group of students at Sarah Tucker College, an institution of the Methodist Church in Tinnevelly, near the southern tip of India, that she noticed a girl lingering behind the others, staring at her with a shy but bright intentness.

"There's one who would do you credit," said the principal, nodding in her direction. "One of our finest scholars."

The gate
of the Cole
Dispensary.

Ida Sophia Scudder
as a young girl.

Dr. Scudder with two children in the Mission Compound. Before the building of Schell.

Scudder family. Nell and Gertrude are seated behind John, Jr., Sophie and Dr. John, and Lewis. In front are Walter, Ida, Charles, Cora, and Harry.

Roadside in
the early days.

Ida on roadside
in the Pugeot.

Dr. Ida at work
in Schell Hospital
in the early days.

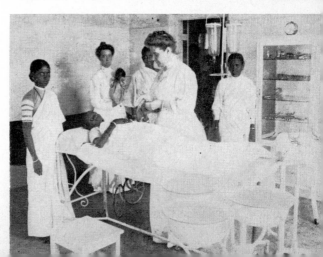

Vellore Hospital.
The mother stays with her sick child.

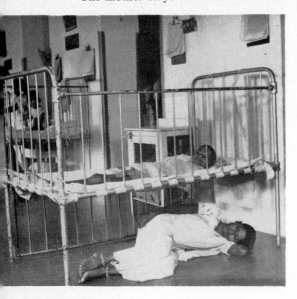

Roadside in recent years.

stian Medical College.

Medical students
at graduation.

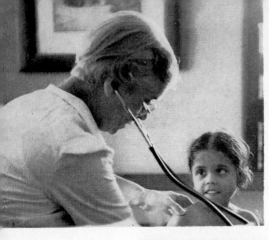

Doctor and child.

Two young patients
in the new hospital.

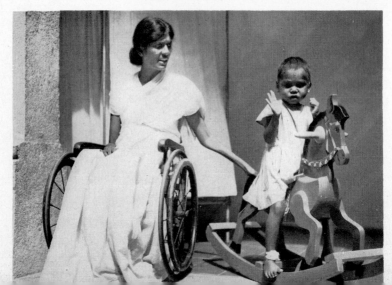

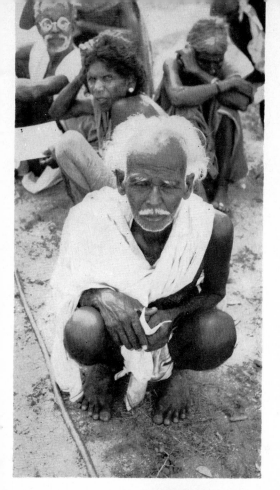

Patients waiting
at eye camp.

crippled Bible woman
siting a blind patient in
e Vellore children's
ard.

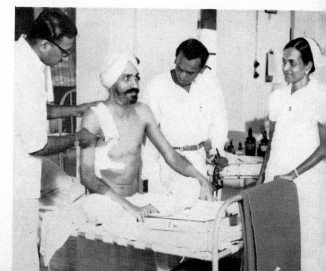

tient and doctors in the
w thoracic surgery
partment.

Dr. Scudder at the hospital on her
eighty-seventh birthday.

While talking with other more forward students, Ida watched the girl covertly. Finally she approached her, smiling. "I've been watching you," she said without preliminaries. "And I think you'd make a wonderful doctor."

"You—you do?" The girl was startled out of her shyness.

Ida took one of the firm brown hands in hers. "Good," she said. "Strong. Long fingers. And you're not nervous. You've been standing for a long time perfectly still. What's your name, my dear?"

"Ebenezer."

"I mean your first name."

The girl flushed, all the shyness back again. "That's it. Ebenezer. Ebenezer Gnanamuthu."

Stupid! Ida chided herself. Whoever decided it was supposed to be a man's name? And even if it was, India abounded in female Krishnas and Ganeshas and Garudas, all male deities. Why not a female Ebenezer?

"It's a lovely name," she said with a warm smile. "A good name for a doctor, because it means something like 'stone of help.' But I'd rather call you Ebbie, if you don't mind. Wouldn't you like to be a doctor, Ebbie?"

"I—I don't know." Fear of the unknown quelled the brightness of the intelligent dark eyes. "I'm not sure I could—"

Ida was sure, so sure that she saw to it that Ebbie Gnanamuthu, whose father was a poor preacher earning only nineteen rupees (less than seven dollars) a month, was offered a scholarship to attend the new medical school. Before she left Sarah Tucker College, Ebbie had been persuaded, somewhat against her will, that the one thing she desired above all others was to become a doctor. "Become like Dr. Ida" would have been the more correct statement. If this involved initiation into the horrors of medicine, Ebbie was dismayed but resigned to fate.

"Don't be discouraged," Colonel Bryson had warned Ida, "if only three or possibly six apply for admission."

There were sixty-nine applications. Since Ida was rigidly high in her standards of choice, only eighteen girls were accepted, one of them being forced to drop out before school opened.

Ebbie Gnanamuthu was among the seventeen remaining. In

fact, she was the first to arrive. Her sister, a student at the Union Woman's Christian College in Madras, brought her to Vellore and left her several days before the school was scheduled to open in July. With the ghastly horrors of medicine become suddenly flesh and blood reality, Ebbie was terrified. Even the radiant and enthusiastic welcome of her idol failed to dispel the gloom of shy homesick fear. Ebbie stood under a coconut palm and wept.

"Come with me," said Ida with the graciousness of a fairy godmother conferring a boon. "I'll take you to see a maternity case."

Ebbie went, trembling but obedient. It was even worse than she had anticipated. She quailed at the sounds of human torment, turned faint at sight of blood.

"I will die," she wrote her sister that night, "if you don't take me away."

Ida gaily persuaded her to go with her to visit another patient. The patient died. Ebbie very nearly died with her, recovering barely sufficient strength to write another frantic appeal for release. This time her sister unwillingly yielded and made the eighty-mile trip to Vellore, prepared to take her home.

"No," said Ida firmly. "She shall not go."

They were almost the same words she was to use years later as, side by side, she and this girl were fighting for the life of a patient desperately ill. "We two bulldogs are here," she was to say to Ebbie. "We'll not let her go."

They fought side by side now in those days before school opened, Ebbie living in the home for nurses at Schell with Mrs. Gnanammal and Salomi, but spending most of her time with Ida and Miss Dodd. So, though possibly the least hopeful and most bewildered of the seventeen young women who composed the first class of the Woman's Medical School when it opened in 1918, at least Ebenezer Gnanamuthu was among them.

It was not an auspicious year to start such a prodigious project. War was still raging in Europe. Prices of food and clothing in India passed the all-time high of the great famine of 1878. The rains of July and August, later those of October, failed altogether. And on the heels of a scourge of cholera followed the strange and awful curse of influenza.

Strange and awful this new disease was, yes. Yet the millions of India's villagers thought they knew whence it came. Like other scourges—smallpox, cholera, plague—must it not also be the visitation of a goddess? A new deity, to be sure, heretofore unknown and even now unnamed, yet to be placated like the more familiar Kaliathal and Mariammal, both manifestations of the goddess of death. Old baskets, dustpans, tattered rags were hung in trees outside of villages, that the goddess, seeing them, might think the village not worth visiting. In some places a little cart was made and, a wooden image placed upon it, was drawn outside the village and left with pots and baskets and other gifts to appease the goddess. Sacred circles were drawn, caste marks painted on the doors of houses.

Christians also, braving the epidemic for a great denominational conference in August, prayed for a cessation of the scourge. Streaming into Katpadi by train, bullock cart, jutka, and on foot, they camped for five days in tents like ancient Jews at the Feast of Tabernacles. Yet neither Hindu charms nor Christian prayers availed. Whether visitation of an unknown goddess or of germs spawned on the battlegrounds of Europe, the epidemic ran its course.

The hospital was not immune. Death stalked its wards, corridors, and verandahs. Sixteen nurses were stricken at one time, six of them gravely. Blind Mary Isaac Henry was one of its victims, also "Wee Mary," one of the most appealing of the orphaned children. The two Marys were buried in one grave on a Saturday morning. That week dozens of patients were brought in, so ill that no treatment availed.

It was a bitter blow to Ida when her beloved Indian head nurse Gnanasundram was fatally stricken. Conscientious, quick, ready at all times with the right medication or instrument, she had worked twelve years with Ida in the operating room, her frail body a dynamo of enthusiasm and energy.

The dying woman comforted Ida.

"There, Doctor," she said, smiling. "My mansion is ready, but I'd much rather stay and help you in the operating room."

With aching hearts they laid her beside the two Marys.

It was in this atmosphere of uncertainty and tension that the child of Ida's fondest dreams was born. The new Union Missionary Medical School for Women was formally opened early on the morning of August 12 by the Governor of Madras. It was a large and imposing gathering. Ida read and then presented to the Governor the most impressive one-paper address ever seen in Vellore, an artistic pictorial document nearly two by three feet in size and entitled:

"TO

His Excellency
THE RIGHT HON'BLE THE LORD PENTLAND,
P. G., G.C.S.I., G.C.I.E."

In her address she outlined the history of the project, spoke eloquently of its need, detailed plans for building and funds already secured, made urgent appeal to government and private interests for the future support necessary to carry the dream to fulfillment.

But it was Colonel Bryson who paid the school and its founder the greatest tribute. "Seeing is believing," he declared fervently. To the seventeen hopeful but slightly bewildered young freshmen he said, "I wonder if you realize what important people you are. Fifty years hence you will remind the students of that generation that you were among those present at the opening of this school. It is an honor that none can ever share with you."

To house her students Ida had rented a bungalow in the Officers' Line, a row of buildings formerly occupied by British government officials. For teaching purposes she employed the facilities of Schell Hospital, rooms in her own bungalow, and a small thatched shed at the rear of the rented building for a dissecting room. For their science courses the students attended classes in Voorhees College, on a compound close by. There were difficulties of adjustment involving personality as well as meager staff, cramped space, and an incredible lack of facilities, for the students came from widely differing language areas, cultures, and creeds, the latter including Catholic, Syrian Christian, Hindu, and Protestant.

From the day the school opened, Ida scarcely breathed apart

from her seventeen young medical students. Like the "ten little Indians," the number was slowly depleted. One girl left on account of sickness, another to get married. A third simply dropped out. But to the fourteen remaining Ida gave the full abundance of her vast energy and concern. Her relationship was like that of a guru with his followers. They were her work, her play, her joy, her despair, her first and last anxiety both sleeping and waking, the very air she breathed.

Rising often at three in the morning, she prepared for the day's teaching. That first year she taught them almost everything but science: histology, physiology, anatomy. Teaching of the latter required the learning of a whole new vocabulary, the 30,000 anatomical terms in use during her own medical training having been radically reduced and changed. Since there was no curtailment of her own hospital work and general practice, there was no time for preparation during the day. She was often forced to study half the night. Classes were held from eight to ten in the morning. At ten or ten-thirty she would take the whole troop to the hospital. They would make the rounds with her, receive briefings on each diagnosis and treatment, assist in the dispensary, observe each operation. Every patient was an object lesson, every surgical triumph an educational adventure.

"Look, my lambs!" The first time they witnessed a cataract operation she held up the clouded lens she had removed from the patient's eye, then took it around for all of them to see. "Many people think it's milk in the eye," she explained. "Others believe it is fluid from the brain washing down into the eye. Our very word 'cataract' may come from that idea. Come! We'd better show everybody we can while we have the chance."

Letting them trail after her, she took the visual aid in question through the wards, showing it to all interested patients, explaining that improvement in diet could often prevent it and that the only cure was an operation performed by a credited doctor. She gave graphic descriptions of the dire consequences when Mohammedan "couchers," who specialized in removing cataracts, attempted to push back the clouded lens with an unclean needle. Though couching had been a wonderful ad-

175

vancement in medical techniques when discovered by the ancient Indian surgeon Susruta, its practice in modern days of sterile surgery was, or should be, a criminal offense. While temporary sight might be restored to the sufferer by the displacement of the clouded lens, the subsequent infection was likely to bring not only extreme pain but permanent blindness.

Sometimes Ida's object lessons took an even more dramatic form. Once the visual aid exhibited to her students after an operation was a seventy-four-pound tumor!

In a day when lecturing was the approved method of teaching, Ida's pupils learned by doing. "Here, Thai, dress this finger." . . . . "I'm turning this child with the bad burns over to you, Dhanamma. Remember each step carefully. First the sterile saline solution—" . . . . "Give this lad the scabies treatment, Kanagam, with sulphur ointment. Tell the mother about applying it for three days, then bathing. You'll have to tell her at least five times." . . . . "Examine this woman, please, Navamani. Tell me if you find signs of tumor." . . . . "Could you ride with me to a village, Ebbie? I need your help."

As Ida had anticipated, Ebbie Gnanamuthu, her horror of blood and cadavers once mastered, was her most promising student. Ebbie's thirst for knowledge was insatiable, her tireless energy equal to Ida's own. Her fear of human bones quite forgotten, she pored with fascination over the few specimens available, hiding them away from her classmates and under her pillow at night for more intensive observation. Expected to win at least 90 per cent on the weekly examinations given the class, Ebbie was never satisfied with anything short of perfection. In the operating room she observed each detail with fierce intentness.

"Here, Ebbie," said Ida one day when about to operate on a simple breast abscess. "Take this knife."

The girl's eyes opened wide with horror. "But—"

"Make a big incision," directed Ida coolly. "A big incision helps the poison to drain out. Don't be afraid. I'm right here."

Her calm confidence was as energizing as a shot of adrenalin. It was with steady fingers that her pupil took the knife and made the deep cut.

An extraordinarily gifted and efficient teacher, Ida was still

176

not above a bit of bluffing if the occasion demanded. One day a child came into the dispensary with a bad skin disease.

"Diagnose it," she told her assisting students promptly.

They confessed that they hadn't the slightest idea what it was.

"You don't!" exclaimed Ida. "Then go this minute and look it up."

After they had gone, she turned to her doctor colleague. "What is it?" she inquired.

Knowledge was acquired by that first class with difficulty. Dissection had to be practiced on an occasional cadaver from the Vellore jail. There were only one or two books, one microscope, and one skeleton. But Ida made full and graphic use of the latter. She equipped it with all appurtenances, using red ribbons for arteries, blue for veins, yellow for nerves; stitched muscles which would flex when strings were pulled; covered it with pale-colored cloth simulating skin. The girls in return did some costuming of their own, dressing the skeleton in fancy clothes and placing it in various staff bedrooms.

Ida encouraged their fun. Though keeping them to a rigid schedule, she followed it with them, usually a few steps ahead. They were always having to run to keep up with her. Her pupils were never, now or later, quite fast enough to suit her. Once when she sent for one of them, a bright pupil named Kamala, it took the girl some time to arrive even though she hurried, for she had to come a long way.

"Did you crawl?" asked Ida tartly. The expression came to be a byword with her students: *Did you crawl?*

Requiring this first class of girls to engage in outdoor sports each day from five to six, Ida played badminton and basketball with them. Then she would bundle them into the Ford, on mudguards, hood, and in double rows inside, and take them on a drive or picnic—a gay party, with Jessie Asirvatham, the class singer, leading them in "Pack up your troubles in your old kit bag." Seldom did Ida attend a party in the town without taking her girls with her. If the whole fourteen were not invited, she would often refuse to go. A group of them went with her to Gudiyattam each Wednesday, sharing her lunch in a mango grove.

Feeding her students was her worst headache. With Christian, Hindu, and, later, Mohammedan students living together, many of them with caste and other religious obligations, it was a herculean task to satisfy all. Finally she had to divide them into three groups: (1) Vegetarians, (2) Meatarians, (3) Eggarians.

There were some disciplinary problems. Coming from villages, many of the girls exhibited poor table manners. If the food did not please them, they were likely to throw it outdoors. They had little sense of time or punctuality. They were careless about dress. Ida dealt with these problems in her own way. Instead of reprimanding them for their poor table manners, she went to their hostel and ate with them, invited them in groups of four to come to dinner at the bungalow. Beset here by an irresistible triple example—their charming hostess, the gracious Mrs. Scudder, the inimitably proper Miss Dodd—they soon learned the correct use of the Western napkin, knife, and fork.

When one of them was late to class, Ida punished her simply by neglecting to say "Good morning." It was enough.

Perhaps it was the Tuesday Bible classes that her pupils were to remember best and longest. That year and every year for the next quarter-century she taught one subject, a course called the Life of Paul, based on her favorite Bible character. It took her four years to go through it, and with each new class she would start at the beginning. It was as much a ritual as the reading at Monday morning chapel of the thirteenth chapter of I Corinthians. These Bible classes were social occasions as well as inspirational. Ida always wore blue, the color of her eyes. And, though the rugged outlines of Paul the Dauntless were undoubtedly blurred to young eyes by a blue-and-silver image of Ida the Dauntless, the hour on Tuesday was productive of genuine spiritual experience.

Ida was more than teacher to her brood. Those who climbed the stairs to "Kailasa" to discuss their personal problems with her on a Sunday morning found her an understanding sister. Ebbie, returning desolately one day after the death of her mother, discovered an even more intimate relationship.

178

"Don't think that you have no mother," Ida comforted her. "From today I am your mother."

Generous as she was with both time and energy, Ida expected as much of that first class as she was willing to give. Only a few times was she disappointed. Once, just as she was about to start a morning lecture, the girls timidly reminded her that it was a national holiday and wondered if they might not have the day off. Ida, who had sat up until two o'clock preparing for the lecture, angrily slammed together the covers of her notebook.

"Holidays!" she blazed. "So that's what you're thinking of! All right. Then we'll have a holiday. Not only today but all other days!"

When the door had banged shut behind her, the girls regarded one another with dismay. They had wanted the holiday merely to catch up on their studying. Picking a big bouquet of the roses they knew she loved best, they followed her with apologies and explanations. Ida, already ashamed of herself, received them with open arms. The class was held that afternoon, whereupon all enjoyed tea and cakes to celebrate the holiday.

Though a comprehensive examination would be given at the end of the four-year course before the conferring of a Licensed Medical Practitioner's diploma, according to the British educational system examinations were held also at the end of each year covering all the work studied. These were formidable tests, conducted by the Madras Medical Department for the whole presidency. As the year ended and examination time approached, Ida grew more and more panicky. What brazen effrontery! Starting a medical school with a few books, a microscope, and a skeleton! Oh, Colonel Bryson was right! How could she possibly expect a group of raw unsophisticates with centuries of female inferiority complex behind them to compete with the products of efficiently run government schools! But she hid her fears under a mask of gay confidence.

"Don't worry," she chattered brightly, bundling them all into a train compartment for the trip to Madras Medical School, where the examinations were conducted. "It's no worse than

179

our weekly quizzes. All anybody can expect of you is to do your best."

The girls were not deceived. "Best" to Dr. Ida meant nothing short of 90 per cent. They huddled on the long hard seats staring at each other in terrified silence. And no wonder! Examinations according to the British system were matters of educational life or death.

Ida, herself one of the examiners, met Colonel Bryson in the hall of the Medical School.

"Ah, Dr. Scudder! So you've brought up your first class for examination?"

"Yes." Ida smiled at him brightly.

His face clouded with sympathetic concern. "My dear doctor, please don't be discouraged if none of your students makes the grade this first time."

"*None* of them?" echoed Ida bleakly.

"It wouldn't be surprising. It's a stiff exam, you know. Only a small percentage of the men pass it. Naturally we couldn't expect too much of such a young project, especially all women. But they can always try again. Promise me you won't give up, whatever happens."

"I promise," said Ida. She went on, head held high but heart sinking to the region of her shoes.

The grim days passed. Huddled in a tight silent group in the mission bungalow in Madras where they were housed, the girls waited to hear the results. Lists from various men's colleges were posted and read with dismay. Only about 20 per cent—one in five—was passing!

"And we're only women!" wailed one of the fourteen in anguish.

In a note from the considerate Colonel Bryson, Ida learned the results before they were posted. The distance from college to mission bungalow seemed interminable. She wished it were a tennis court or a race track so she could run at top speed and still be considered proper. But she reached it finally, stood in the doorway of the room where they were waiting. They read the answer in her radiant face.

"Lambs!" She held out her arms to them. "You did it! Passed. Every single one of you. And four of you in the first class. And—can you believe it?—this places our school at the head of all the medical schools in the presidency!"

Laughing with excitement they rushed toward her and, one after another, received a congratulatory hug:—Ebbie and Krupamma and Jessielet and Lizzie, Navamani, Lucy, Dhanamma, Elizabeth, Cecilia, Sophie, Thai, Kanagam, Anna, and Saramma.

The next time she met Colonel Bryson, he shook his head. "I'm afraid, Doctor," he said sheepishly, "that your girls are setting too high a standard for our men to live up to."

Ida only smiled.

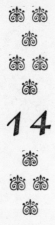

14

1920. Year of all-time-highs.

India seethed with high temperatures, high prices, high emotions. The words "freedom" and "democracy," which were sweeping the world, were on every educated tongue. And a little man named Gandhi was starting a revolutionary movement known as *Satyagraha*, soul force through nonviolence, a simple technique of noncooperation which was destined to rock a great empire's foundations.

Returning to India in 1915 after winning a remarkable victory for the rights of Indians in South Africa, Gandhi had been hailed by the Nationalists as the champion of independence. But his concern was less for national freedom than for social liberation. It was the quality of his country's rulers that interested him most, not their nationality. No country could be really free, he contended, whoever governed it, when over 80 per cent of its people lived in ignorance, disease, and poverty. Therefore village uplift became his primary goal. If the fundamental freedoms of the individual—basic education, economic self-sufficiency, equal status of every human being with every other—could be secured, Gandhi believed, national freedom would soon follow.

In the years immediately following 1915, however, his concept of national freedom, like that of many Nationalists, was dominion status, not complete independence. So loyal was he to the British government that in 1918 he went about recruiting for the British wartime cause, certain that the promise of a more liberal policy would result in dominion status once the war was over. And, though many extreme Nationalists were opposed to his moderate goals and many strict Hindus to his denunciation of the caste system, his popularity had become so great that few voices were raised against him. Both the Moslem League and the predominantly Hindu Congress Party, the two most active Indian political groups, were agreed on his program of moderate reform.

But when the war ended, Gandhi was bitterly disillusioned. The Rowlatt Acts of 1919 not only blasted all hopes of immediate dominion status but failed to restore prewar civil liberties. In protest Gandhi invoked the technique of noncooperation used so successfully in South Africa, calling a hartal, or general strike, against all British agencies. To his distress Indians proved not yet ready for such disciplined action. The violence that followed in a few areas came to swift culmination in a wholesale massacre by British troops at Amritsar, in the Punjab, of Indians gathered in a peaceful demonstration. This massacre, in April, 1919, changed the whole direction of Gandhi's policy. In spite of the British attempt to make amends by the Montague-Chelmsford reforms, which promised Indians more authority in provincial governments, Gandhi regretfully yielded to the anti-British passion that was uniting Hindus and Moslems in a solid front.

"I can retain neither respect nor affection," he wrote, returning his two South African medals to the viceroy, "for a government which has been moving from wrong to wrong to defend its immorality."

In 1920 Gandhi, now a revered mahatma, was trekking about the country preaching his doctrine of nonviolent noncooperation; village peasants, oppressed for centuries by unjust landlords, marched across north India in a great agrarian revolt; and a wealthy young lawyer, Jawaharlal Nehru, who traveled with them, was becoming conscience-stricken at his country's poverty. It was a turning point in the long struggle toward independence.

Ida was little concerned with politics, either British or Indian. She was too busy creating healthier citizens to implement those fundamental freedoms which Gandhi considered of supreme importance. It was a year of highs for her also—high hopes, high adventures, and, incidentally, the highest honor possible for the British colonial government to bestow.

"The Kaisar-i-Hind medal!" she murmured incredulously, opening the heavily embossed envelope bearing the royal seal of the king-emperor of India. "They—they want to give it to *me!*"

Kaisar-i-Hind, "emperor of India," regal title borne by the great Moguls of Delhi and assumed in 1876 by Her Majesty Queen Victoria! Supreme award since 1900 for public service in India!

"And about time," said Gertrude Dodd, her bright eyes snapping. "To my mind you should have gotten it long ago. Why they should have given one to Louisa Hart and not to you, I never could understand."

"She deserved it," Ida replied. "It was for her work helping government with plague in 1907 while I was on furlough."

"Anyway," conceded Gertrude, studying the engraved announcement, "she received only the second-class medal, not the first-class gold one that they're giving you."

It was pouring rain on the night of Ida's investiture, but eight hundred persons attended. The ceremony was conducted in glittering splendor. Arriving in state from Government House in Madras, the Governor, Lord Willingdon, and his Lady entered the Madras state banqueting hall by the south portal and walked through a long line of crimson-clad lancers to the dais. The ceremonies included many awards, both civil and military, but only two beside Ida received the gold medal, first class.

Even after the investiture, with its solemn march to the dais, its flattering citation, its dignified retreat complicated by three formal curtseys, she could scarcely believe that such honor had been paid her. But she had felt more triumph of achievement a few days before when, at a modest ceremony at the new town site in Vellore, they had laid out the ground plan of the doctors' bungalow and nurses' quarters.

It was one day in April, 1920, that Ida made her way, leisurely for once, out of the hospital compound and along the sweltering street toward the bungalow in the Officers' Line used by the first class of her medical school. Two other houses had been rented since and added to it, but the school was still cramped for space.

She could afford to be a little leisurely, for the school year was just over. Two classes had gone up for the annual examination. There had been some failures, but Ida's school still led the presidency. This second year she had received 89 applications, accepted 25 of them, ended the year, including both classes, with 38 pupils.

The hospital was more crowded than ever. Government required three beds for each student, and there often had to be as many as sixty beds on the verandahs! But Schell Hospital was now a definite part of the Union Medical School, the joint project supported by several denominational mission groups. This meant reinforcement in staff from other denominations: Dr. McPhail from the United Free Church, Dr. Kinnaman from the American Baptists. Two sisters, Drs. Jessie and Elizabeth Findlay, representing the Canadian Baptists, were already en route for Vellore.

And in the United States Mrs. Peabody and her valiant cohorts of many Protestant denominations were laboring to raise the necessary money, not for Vellore alone, but for seven proposed colleges for women in the Orient. Her hundreds of committee chairmen were waiting with bated breath to learn the result of their application for a million dollars to the Laura Spelman Rockefeller Memorial Fund. With almost every overseas letter Ida learned of new triumphs and disappointments.

"A church in Providence," Mrs. Peabody had just written, "has appropriated $10,000 for the operating theater." A man named Fillebrown had presented another $10,000 for a nurses' home as a wedding gift to his daughter Rachel. A retiring little woman in Massachusetts, Ellen Cole, had provided enough money to build the dispensary on the town site. Ida could

185

scarcely contain her joy and excitement. She longed to be at home on the battlefront.

Her steps quickened as she turned into the path leading past the students' bungalow to a small outbuilding at the rear of the compound. Hardly had she set foot in its small courtyard when twenty young voices shrieked ecstatic welcome.

"It's Doctor Mother! It's Doctor Mother!"

Breasting the sea of eager wriggling bodies and clinging hands, she finally reached the verandah of the little house and sank down laughing on a bench.

"*Vanthuparungle*, my little ones! Come and see what I've brought you." Slipping the lid off the basket she was carrying, she counted luscious ripe mangoes into their outstretched hands. "One for you, Mana, and for you, Esther ... Padmathi ... Thanabakiam ... Devadesen. ..." She looked up as a motherly Indian woman in spotless white sari appeared in the doorway. "Have they been good today, Mrs. Enoch?"

The matron smiled serenely. "They're no angels. But when they get too fractious, I just have them all sit down and sing."

Sounds not altogether hilarious issued from the stone slabs in the corner where one of the two nurses in charge was administering the nightly baths. Ida sighed with satisfaction. Her "adopted" children at last had a home of their own, this outbuilding behind the students' house, with two rooms, a kitchen, plenty of verandah, trees to play under, and an open courtyard ablaze with marigolds. No more scolding or shushing when they made too much noise and might disturb the patients!

Mana, one of the orphans bequeathed by the influenza epidemic, sidled close, big dark eyes fixed in fascination on the white-gold halo of Ida's hair. "Is it—real?" she asked shyly. "Mana touch?"

Laughing, Ida pulled the child to her lap, leaned over so the small fingers could bury themselves in the soft fluffiness. More than one wide-eyed student had asked her the same question.

Starting with Mary Taber and Keziah, a little Albino girl brought to them years ago by Ida's cousin, Dr. Lew Scudder, the family of children had grown from time to time, until now

186

there were twenty-three, ranging from six months to sixteen years. Ida looked fondly about the group, remembering how many of them had come: the two motherless babies she had found on Roadside, mere scraps of skin and bones; Padmathi, thrown into a thorn bush right after birth, found crying and helpless by a cowherd, reported to the police, and brought to Gudiyattam; Esther Thayamma, handed over by her consumptive mother on her deathbed; children Annie Hancock had brought from the jail when their mothers died. Her gaze rested with special fondness on a slim bright-eyed boy brimming with health and energy. She had been sitting at dinner one night when she had heard a sweet high voice singing. Going to the door, she had found a little naked boy of four clinging to a tall policeman's hand. Of course she had kept the little lad.

"We could keep fifty instead of twenty-three," she thought yearningly, "if we only had a bigger house!"

She mulled over the problem as she walked back to the bungalow, slowly in the April heat. Mary Taber, just home from a mission boarding school in Madras, came to meet her, a lovely girl with laughing eyes and smoothly shining dark braids. They walked to the bungalow together, then Mary left her to go to the nurses' quarters for the evening meal, for in spite of her partly Western upbringing, the girl still preferred rice and curry to mutton and potatoes.

"Mrs. Gnanammal came to me today about a certain matter," said Mrs. Scudder composedly after the pudding had been served. "It seems there's an Indian Christian woman here from Bombay who came to the hospital as a patient. She was in church on Sunday."

"I know the one you mean," said Gertrude Dodd, watching Ida's face to see if she liked the pudding. "Her husband is a Church of England minister. An intelligent, refined-looking woman."

Ida was only half listening. The huge ruffled punkah, instead of cooling the air, seemed to be agitating small gusts from a furnace. Its rhythmic swish, together with the heat, had a stupefying effect. She barely roused herself to lift the spoon to her lips and murmur, "Good pudding, Gertrude. Nice and cool."

Gertrude smiled with pleasure. "It's mango custard. I kept it in the well, Idee. The boy came running with it just before serving."

"This woman saw Mary Taber in church," continued Mrs. Scudder calmly. "She was pleased with her. She wishes Mrs. Gnanammal to act as go-between in arranging a marriage between Mary and her son."

Ida came sharply to full consciousness. "Marriage! Mary Taber!" She choked on both words and pudding. "How—how dare the woman? Doesn't she know we don't believe in child marriage?"

Mrs. Scudder chuckled. "Exactly what my mother said when I announced my engagement! The 'child' you speak of, my dear, is sixteen. She will be seventeen before any arrangements can be completed. Even in the United States marriage at seventeen is quite proper. And this is India, my dear, not America."

Ida was stunned. That night, looking in her mirror, she remembered suddenly that she was almost fifty years old. True, she did not look it, much less act it. Her fair skin was unlined. Her white hair, radiantly lustrous, seemed a badge of youth rather than of age. She could beat teen-agers at climbing mountains and make them look ridiculous on the tennis court. But it was fifteen years since Burchfield Milliken had died. And Mary Taber, her baby, was ready for betrothal.

But not, she thought rebelliously, without romance, to a man she had never seen! She could not let her. And yet—who was she to claim that the ways of the West in this matter were better than those of the East? Had the right to choose for herself brought her love or fulfillment?

The next day she had a long talk with Mrs. Gnanammal. A letter was sent to the parents of the boy requesting an interview; another to a minister in Bombay asking for detailed information about the prospective bridegroom and his family. If Mary Taber must be married Eastern fashion, then, like good Indian parents, Ida and her mother would provide her with the best husband they could find and the finest wedding they could afford.

Months passed, and finally the day of meeting came.

"There! How do you look?"

It was the same question Ida had asked her years before, tying a bright ribbon in the child's hair and lifting her to the mirror. It seemed only yesterday.

Mary Taber regarded her reflection gravely, running her firm brown hand over a glistening wing of hair, smoothing down the crisp folds of her white sari over the left shoulder.

"Nice." She gave the same reply, but this time there was no vanity in the shining dark eyes, only a quiet satisfaction. Mrs. Scudder had done her work well. Mary Taber was no longer spoiled. She had grown at sixteen into a poised and mature woman. It was Ida who felt suddenly young and tongue-tied.

"I—have something to tell you, dear. I really don't know how you will feel about it. But—Mrs. Gnanammal—Gnanamantie—thought it was the right thing to do."

"Yes?" said Mary Taber, her dark eyes steady.

"There's a boy waiting downstairs to meet you. He has come from Bombay with his parents and some of his relatives. We've met him before, Nanna and I, and we like him. He is strong and healthy, too." *Oh, dear!* thought Ida, aghast. *What am I doing! Trying to sell her a bullock?*

"Yes," said the girl calmly. "I understand. Gnanamantie told me."

Ida drew a long breath of relief. Holding out her arms, she drew her young ward close. "You needn't marry him if you don't want to, darling. We just want you to be happy. It seems so strange to us, betrothing you to somebody you've never seen!"

"But I'm going to see him today," objected Mary Taber innocently. "You just said so."

"Yes, dear. So you are. How stupid of me!" Smiling with sudden gay tenderness, Ida plucked a huge double pink hibiscus from a low dish on her table and fastened it just above the smooth dark braid. "He'll like you," she said fondly. "He can't help it. But—promise me, dear, you'll tell me if—if you don't like him."

"I promise," said Mary Taber solemnly.

They went down to the living room where the prospective

189

bridegroom and his parents were having tea with Mrs. Scudder and Miss Dodd. The two young people were introduced, exchanged a few perfunctory words, glanced at each other shyly over the edges of their teacups. Ida observed no such restraint. She stared at the young man with a frank, almost jealous, appraisal, noted with approval the kindness and intelligence in his dark eyes, the gentleness in his sensitive sober young features. Yet she was not quite satisfied. For Mary Taber was a creature of laughter, and not once during the interview did her prospective bridegroom smile.

"Do you like him?" the girl was asked after the guests had departed.

Her reply was untinged with emotion. Yes, she liked him. She thought him very nice. But of course she knew little about men. She would leave the matter to their judgment. They knew what was best for her.

Two days later the families gathered on the verandah beneath the high sleeping porch at six o'clock in the evening. The bridegroom's family presented five trays, one loaded with fruits, one with coconuts, one with betel leaves and nuts, one with garlands of flowers, one bearing an engagement ring and a sari, a blouse, and perfume. According to custom, everything was presented in odd numbers, such as five or seven, but never thirteen. One of the gifts was a necklace hung with seventeen sovereigns.

Rev. Simon Cornelius, the Indian pastor, was there among the many guests. After several hymns had been sung, he rose from his seat.

"We have come for the purpose," he announced with dignity, "of declaring the engagement of Mary Taber to Barnabas Charles Guest Sebastian."

There followed a reading from Genesis about Isaac and Rebekah, then more hymns, then another pronouncement by Mr. Cornelius. "As Isaac brought gifts to Rebekah, so these gifts have been brought."

Mary Taber rose from her chair. The sisters of the bridegroom brought the five trays to the pastor, who blessed them. The sisters took Mary to Mrs. Scudder's bedroom, where they dressed her in the new sari, then brought her back to her chair.

190

There were more prayers, followed by a formal dinner. The betrothal was completed.

The banns were published at church on the three following Sundays. Mrs. Gnanammal had carefully coached the Westerners on the proper procedures for an Indian Christian wedding. A house was rented for the bridegroom's family nearby. After church on the last Sunday Mrs. Scudder—"Nanna"— put Mary Taber in the carriage and took her to the rented house, where she was permitted to spend the rest of the day with the bridegroom and his family. The meeting was hardly a social triumph, for the young man was reserved to the point of taciturnity, and she was too shy even to look at him. Since he knew not a word of Tamil, coming from a different language area, the few words of conversation they exchanged had to be in English, which, fortunately, they both spoke fluently.

The wedding a week later was a grand affair. All the missionaries of the area were in Vellore for the January annual meeting, and the church was full. Long skirts brushed flowing saris. Flowered hats vied in elegance with turbans and gold-embroidered sari borders. And the bride, looking small and frightened as she approached the sober stranger at the altar, seemed the very embodiment of this merging of East and West. From the folds of her heavy, gold-bordered wedding sari, gift of the groom, emerged the stiff outlines of a lined blouse with high boned neck and long sleeves of flowing lace. And over all, crowning the incongruities, a wreath of orange blossoms and a white wedding veil!

"Oh, dear!" thought Ida, stricken with remorse at sight of the unsmiling, downcast face. "What have we done! What *should* we have done?"

At the reception the couple sat side by side on a lavishly decorated settee, half buried in garlands, presents piled on the raised platform at their feet. Mary Taber opened the packages, smiled dutiful appreciation, but without her usual spontaneous gaiety. During the music, prayers, and speeches that followed, the bride and groom exchanged scarcely a word or a glance. Ida watched them with mounting concern.

With the preparations for the wedding feast, the gulf between East and West widened. Tables were set for the Westerners with plates, knives, and forks; mats were placed on the lawn for the Indian guests, with huge plantain leaves for dishes. It was the custom for the bridal couple to help serve the guests. When the time came to make ready for this duty, Mary Taber, looking as meekly subservient as the traditional Hindu wife, followed her new husband into a small room off the courtyard. Still troubled, Ida watched them go. She would have been even more concerned had she known the emotions hidden beneath the meek exterior.

Alone for the first time with her husband, Mary Taber was inarticulate with terror. Bulked beneath the weight of many garlands and his formal garments, he looked huge, forbidding. She dared not even raise her eyes to his face. With trembling fingers she removed her veil, pulled the end of the white silk sari over her head. It was so heavy it kept sliding back, and she had to anchor it with her fingers beneath her chin. She felt like one of the Mohammedan or high-caste Hindu women who sidled timidly into the hospital, half crouched, features hidden behind a burka or protecting veil.

Nothing in all her seventeen years had prepared her for this moment. Nanna had tried. Gnanamantie had tried. But their advice had not agreed. "Just be yourself, darling." . . . . "Whatever these Westerners may tell you, a woman is expected to keep her place behind her husband."

The bridegroom removed his coat, stood for a moment holding it in helpless indecision, then held it out to her.

"Here," he said stiffly. "You will please hang it for me."

It might have been a question or a command. Curiosity getting the better of timidity, Mary Taber briefly raised her eyes to find out which. But the sober dark features gave no sign. She took the coat, stood duplicating his awkward helplessness. It was the first time she had ever held a man's coat. What to do with it? It was not a sari to be folded flat, not a blouse nor a woman's jacket to be smoothed hem to hem, sleeve to sleeve. Finally she crossed the room and, holding it gingerly between thumb and forefinger, dropped it in a heap across the seat of a chair.

"No, no, not like that! It must be done properly. See, I will show you."

192

With tightening lips she watched her husband rescue the garment, carefully smooth out the imaginary wrinkles, and with great care start to drape it over the back of a chair. As her chin lifted, the sari slipped back over her head, leaving it quite uncovered, but her clenched hands did not move to replace it. She was no longer frightened. She was furious.

"*Nalla thu!* All right!" she exclaimed spiritedly. "If you don't like the way I do it, then next time you can just jolly well do it yourself!"

The young man turned with such startled swiftness that the coat slipped to the floor in an untidy heap. He stood staring at her, as if he had never seen her before, and she stared back with unabashed curiosity, familiarizing herself with the strong dark lines of his features, the set of his proud square shoulders. Finally a twinkle appeared in his eyes, and his sober lips curved into a smile.

Meekly then Mary Taber Sebastian stooped, picked up her husband's coat, shook and smoothed and patted it to get out the wrinkles, and draped it with wifely competence over the back of the chair.

As they returned to the courtyard, not one behind the other but side by side, and went about serving the guests, Ida's eyes followed her young ward with a mingling of wonder and relief. The girl's face was no longer downcast. The mischievous sparkle was back in her eyes. As she stood beside her husband, his hand enclosing hers while together, Western fashion, they cut the first slice of the towering wedding cake, the look they exchanged was certainly not that of strangers. It was unmistakably that of husband and wife, full of some secret shared amusement.

15

Colonel Paton, resident surgeon of the Indian Medical Service in the Vellore Government Hospital, was having a difficult day. His hospital was swarming with patients. Finally he was confronted with a case that taxed not only his endurance but his professional skill as well. He dared not diagnose, much less operate, without expert assistance.

"Send for Dr. Ida Scudder," he ordered.

She came promptly and willingly as she always did, looking as fresh and vigorous as if she enjoyed having the thermometer register 107 in the shade.

"Sorry to bother you," he apologized with a good Scotsman's economy of words. "Shorthanded. Bad case. Hospital packed like sardines. Such a beastly day."

"I know." She smiled sympathetically. "I'm having one too."

She confirmed his diagnosis, and they worked together competently, without tension. Colonel Paton always enjoyed operating with Dr. Ida. Though not a brilliant surgeon, she was both swift and painstaking, and she had a way with human tissues.

"An uncanny way," he thought, watching the delicate sure touch of her fingers. "As if she were re-creating them."

Feeling guilty for calling her from her own work on such

194

a busy morning, he was almost glad when, later in the day, she was obliged to call him to Schell to assist with another emergency case. The operation successfully performed, he returned to Government Hospital with a pleasant feeling of cooperative achievement. The day continued to be fearfully grueling. It was ten that night when, satisfied that his patient of the morning was going to live, he wearily finished his rounds.

"Poor Dr. Scudder!" he thought ruefully. "She must be half dead with exhaustion. I wonder how her patient is."

Tired though he was, he called a conveyance and rode out to Schell Compound to condone with her. Arrived at the bungalow entrance, he saw a pinprick of lantern light in the nearby garden, and thought, "Poor woman, she's probably out there on her knees praying. It was the only place she could find to be alone."

Quietly he crossed the grass until he could distinguish the white hair and dress of the kneeling figure. It was Dr. Scudder. But she was not praying. He halted suddenly, staring, to make sure. She was *digging*. Heavens, had her day been that bad? Had it driven her a little—

"Can—can I help you?" he stammered.

"Colonel Paton!" She greeted him with blithe gaiety. "How nice of you to come! When I found out both of our patients were all right, I was so happy that I couldn't contain myself. I invited some friends in to celebrate. Then I remembered this basket of nasturtium plants that had been neglected all day. I was so sorry for them I just had to get them put into the ground. Everybody else had been working hard and was too tired."

She sprang up, shaking the loose dirt from her hands, stooping again to lift the lantern, her blue eyes catching fire from its light. To the colonel's amazement she looked as unwearied as if it were early morning.

"Come into the house, Colonel Paton," she invited gaily. "We'll have some more coffee and music. You've had an exhausting day."

Ida needed all this abundance of energy. She was running a hospital, two weekly dispensaries, and a medical college now three years old and, with this year's entering group, containing four complete classes with 65 students.

True, she had more help than formerly. Among her most valuable staff members were Drs. Jessie and Elizabeth Findlay from Canada, the former tall, dignified, and competent, the latter daintily and prettily feminine, with fluffy hair and blue eyes. Jessie especially was an immediate tower of strength, and before she had been there a month Ida wondered how she had ever managed without her. Another new arrival was a German-born American physician, Dr. Anna Degenring, who brought with her a tart tongue tempered by a twinkling smile, an uncanny ear for dripping water taps, and a German frugality which was to qualify her for a long career as the efficient college bursar.

Ida needed all this extra assistance, for besides her other duties she was experiencing all the headaches of a big building program, to say nothing of the nervous strain of a great financial campaign ten thousand miles away.

The success of the campaign was more urgent than ever. All the government funds donated for hospital expansion had been spent. It was imperative that more be forthcoming. When Lord Willingdon, Governor of Madras Presidency, paid a visit to Vellore, Ida made every effort to obtain an interview with him, but without success. Invited to a tea at the Collector's bungalow, she determined to approach the Governor at all odds. She was greatly surprised when he himself asked that she be brought to his table and seated at his right hand. She made full use of the opportunity. The effect of her enthusiasm and personal charm was still in evidence years later when, as viceroy, Lord Willingdon, being honored by a reception at Government House in Madras, not only asked that Ida be invited, but, when her turn came to greet him, held up the long line for several minutes for personal and animated conversation.

The immediate effect of the interview was more to her taste, for not long after his visit the Madras Government voted her project five lakhs of rupees (about $100,000 at the rate of exchange then current) provided she could raise an equal

196

amount elsewhere. *Provided ... on condition....* Most frustrating of words!

"The Rockefeller Fund will give us a million dollars for our seven women's colleges of the Orient," reported the valiant Mrs. Peabody after a visit to the West Coast of the United States for sixty speaking engagements, "but only *on condition* that we raise two million to go with it. And they will give us just twelve months, the calendar year of 1922, to raise it!"

Oh, to be with her on the battlefront! But there were still long months to the beginning of her furlough. It was patience Ida lacked, not courage. This she proved during the difficult days when the storm of conflict known as the Moplah Rebellion was sweeping from the west coast through South India.

As the struggle for freedom progressed, there were occasional clashes between Hindus and Moslems, fomented, many Indians claimed, by the British in accordance with their principle of "divide and rule." In 1921 a group of peasants among the moplahs, an extremist Moslem sect centered in Malabar on the extreme southwest coast of the Indian peninsula, rose in rebellion against their Hindu landlords and moneylenders. Starting as a local uprising against economic injustice, with little political or religious significance, the incident was played up by newspapers and other agencies, and the tumult spread. Other groups of Moslems rose against Hindus in sympathy with the moplahs, and the wave of religious conflict swept sporadically through various parts of South India.

When the surge of conflict reached Vellore, the city was placed under martial law. Missionaries and hospital staff were permitted to travel only through well guarded streets. Certain areas of the city where the Moslem population was centered became forbidden precincts. During this time Ida was called to the home of a Mohammedan patient, critically ill, who lived in one of these dangerous and forbidden sections. She prepared to go.

"But—you can't!" her friends protested. "You'll be breaking the law!"

"I'll be breaking a higher law if I don't," retorted Ida.

Donning a burka, one of the all-enveloping garments worn

by Mohammedan women in the streets, and traveling in a rough country cart, she entered the forbidden area, treated her patient, and returned home, neglecting to report the incident to the authorities. In the heat of racial tension sweeping the city, the discovery of a Western woman masquerading as a Mohammedan, however sound the reason, might easily have started a riot.

Meanwhile the building program at Thotapalayam, the section of Vellore where the new hospital units were being constructed, was proceeding slowly but steadily. The doctors' bungalow, which was to be Ida's new home, and the nurses' quarters were the first buildings to be constructed. Close by on the same compound and within a stone's throw of the bungalow the walls of the new dispensary were already rising. Near it would be a chapel, a children's ward, a maternity hospital unit. Plans for the latter, having been finally adopted by the building committee, were already in the hands of the draftsman and would then go to Government to be approved by the Medical Department and the Department of Public Works of Madras Presidency. Following that, they must be submitted to another department of Government for the sanctioning of a grant-in-aid. Only then could the building be actually started.

Eventually the twenty-acre site at Thotapalayam would include all the units necessary for an adequate and modern hospital. The college buildings, yet to be planned, Ida still envisioned for the 200-acre site outside the city four miles to the south.

She marked time before her furlough in 1922 to the pounding of the workmen's mallets, patiently beating stone into bits. The walls of the new buildings seemed to mount with the crawling slowness of the laboring women climbing up ladders with heaped baskets of earth or stone or dizzying burdens of bricks on their heads. But at least they mounted, and finally, with the completion of the doctors' bungalow, Ida triumphantly moved her household from the Schell Hospital compound to the new site a mile away at Thotapalayam.

Moving into the new quarters, however, meant that her labors were magnified, not lessened. Half her medical students were in the new nurses' building, half in the last of the three

198

rented bungalows two miles away. Schell Hospital lay midway between the two. Transportation presented difficulties. It would be at least three years before the main buildings on the town site could be completed, ten before her dreams for the 200-acre paradise outside the city could possibly reach fulfillment.

"*Juldi, juldi!* Hurry, hurry!" she cried silently to workmen, draftsmen, carpenters, to the women campaigning in America, to her already swiftly moving feet.

The margosa trees, which she planted in rows behind the new bungalow, taught her patience. So did the big banyan dropping tenuous plumb lines to measure the expanding arches of other decades, another century. "No hurry," they told her. "See how long it takes God to make a little tree trunk."

The serenity of her mother also helped to still her impatience. Now over eighty years of age, Mrs. John was still capably directing the household, naming new babies, remembering the names and needs of the hundreds of visitors with uncanny accuracy. Within a few hours of moving, she was as much at home in the new house as the beaded strings of portieres which she had brought with her from the archways in the bungalow at Schell.

There were hours of achievement when Ida could see her dreams visibly grow. One came with the graduation of her first class of medical students on March 24, 1922. Watching them plant a tree as a symbol that the end was only a beginning, she could almost resign herself to the patient waiting until it could spring into blossom and spread shade.

Principal and staff, followed by the graduates, marched in procession from the nurses' quarters to a large tent. The students of the other classes were a beautiful sight, walking two abreast and carrying jasmine chains, twining the ends among palms and ferns on the platform, forming an aisle of white blossoms for the graduates to pass through. Colonel Bryson, the surgeon general, skeptical four years ago, was now pleased to honor the achievement. His address was as triumphant as the flourishes of the police band which preceded it. He had known from the first that the daring project was destined for success, due to the large proportion of teachers to students, the fact that all students were residents, and—Dr. Ida Scudder.

"A woman not only of vision but of persistence. 'Medical School, Medical School, Medical School,' she kept saying. And,"—he smiled somewhat wryly—"she has not been over-silent, overmodest, in her demands."

Ida had reason to feel satisfied. Ebbie Gnanamuthu, standing first in general proficiency and surgery, had also won a gold medal in anatomy from the Government of India, competing with men from six medical schools. The other prize winners—Kanakam, Navamani, Lucy, Jessie, Thai—were all top-ranking students. And behind these fourteen graduates were fifty-two other students of equal ability and commitment. Each year now she was getting nearly two hundred applications for admission.

But just as one of her fond desires became realized, another seemed suddenly doomed. For that spring at Kodaikanal she learned that at last the long-coveted land where she wanted to build a vacation home for herself—her beloved "Hill Top"—was to be put up for auction. Due to sail on furlough May 5, she remained at Kodai the last minute possible, then appealed to her brother Walter, who was staying longer.

"Watty, you must get it for me! Get it as cheaply as you can, but—get it. You can use the little legacy I got from Auntie."

He regarded her soberly. Like any other of her five brothers, he would have attemped to get her the Koh-i-noor diamond if she had asked for it. "I'll try, Younker. But it's likely to go high, you know. It's the most scenic property on the whole mountain range. If some of these rich Britishers get wind of the sale, or even some maharajah, we're sunk. Don't set your heart on it, Bonny."

But he could see by her face that she already had.

The time came when Walter also must leave Kodai for the season, and still the notice of sale had not been posted. He asked a friend and fellow missionary at Kodaikanal to act as Ida's agent in the transaction. Finally it was announced that the land was to be put up for sale at eight o'clock on the morning of September 15, with a starting price of 330 rupees and 6 annas. The day came, and Ida's representative arrived at the proper time. No one else appeared except Mr. Logan, who was representing the municipality.

The missionary looked at his watch. "It's eight o'clock," he reminded the agent with businesslike brusqueness. "You agreed to put that land up for sale at eight o'clock this morning."

"But—there's nobody here," protested Mr. Logan helplessly.

"I'm here," replied the other man firmly. "I'm a purchaser. I bid 340 rupees for the whole property."

In accordance with the terms of the posted notice, since there were no competitors, Mr. Logan was obliged to accept for the eight-acre tract of land, by far the most desirable lookout point in all of Kodaikanal, the modest sum of a little over one hundred dollars!

After the auction had been closed, some wealthy Indians appeared with the announcement that they were ready to bid up to 2,000 rupees for the land.

"Sorry," Mr. Logan told them curtly. "You're just too late."

"Our friend had a little expense," wrote Watty to Ida, "of one rupee, nine annas, in getting notes up from Madras. So your Naboth's Vineyard has cost you just 341 rupees and 9 annas. Aren't you a happy girl? Congratulations, Younker! Your loving little brother.

"P.S. You sure were born under a lucky star!"

Ida's ship went straight from Bombay to Boston almost without stopping. After putting in at Aden, it steamed past Tunis and Algiers without once giving passengers time to set foot on shore. Though Mrs. John and Gertrude cast longing glances toward the colorful horizons, Ida felt no regrets. Even her promenades on deck caught their martial rhythm from Lucy Peabody's urgent letters.

"The memorial gifts are continuing to come for both hospital and college buildings. Mrs. William Bancroft Hill will give the college chapel in memory of her parents, Mr. and Mrs. Weyerhauser. Miss Cole wants either the children's ward or the dispensary. She will give $6,000. Professor Frank Ewart will give $10,000 for the maternity hospital. But the bulk of the building fund, of course, will come from your share of the Rockefeller money, which is to be divided among the seven colleges for women in the Orient."

And to get the million dollars from the Rockefeller Fund, Ida reminded herself grimly, they must raise two million to go with it—and before the end of that very calendar year!

It was June 5, 1922, when her ship steamed slowly into Boston Harbor. People waved from tiny boats down below and cried out greetings. "Where do you come from?" they shouted curiously.

"India, India...." Ida added her voice to the gay cries of her shipmates. *India.* Looking down, she could see the excitement in their eyes. And no wonder, poor things! What drab, colorless clothes, what washed-out faces! She wished she could give them a *real* greeting—pelt them with marigolds, toss garlands of jasmine and silver-meshed roses on their heads!

Mrs. Peabody was an able general and her captains worthy assistants. Representative women of ten leading denominations, both in the United States and in Canada, composed the Joint Committee for the Women's Union Christian Colleges in the Orient. But they faced a gigantic task. When Ida arrived, with the year half over, the two million still looked as unattainable as the top of Mount Everest. Pausing only long enough to deposit her mother in the arms of adoring sons and daughters-in-law and to buy herself some new clothes, including a black dress with a blue vest and a hat plumed like a knight's helmet, Ida set out on tour.

Mrs. Peabody was the King Arthur assigning the heroic engagements on behalf of needy and defenseless women. Buffalo ... Flint ... New York ... Des Moines ... Cincinnati ... Dayton ... St. Paul ... St. Louis....

Ida's sword blade was sharp, its strokes blue and scintillating.

In India 165 million women and girls ... 33 million widowed, hundreds of thousands of them children.... Only 159 Christian women doctors.... The women of India must come to their own aid! But we must help them!

Boston ... New Haven ... Hartford....

She was on her way to Hartford with Pauline Jeffery, now in medical school in the United States on the scholarship provided by Gertrude Dodd, when she opened the letter that sent her spirits plunging. She read it again, incredulously.

"No!" she moaned aloud. "They can't do it! They just *can't* do it!"

Pauline was as distressed as Ida when she heard the news. The Arcot Mission Assembly at their annual meeting in India had registered disapproval of building the medical college on the 200-acre site south of Vellore which, with the help of the Madras Government, Ida had secured title to in the name of the Union Missionary Medical School. The decision of the assembly had been almost unanimous. Dr. Jessie Findlay was almost the only one who had supported her in this long-time dream for her project.

"People!" Ida lamented bitterly. "No vision at all beyond their noses!"

But there was still Mrs. Peabody, she consoled herself hopefully, who did have vision and who believed in the project. And the matter must be decided by the planning committees in the United States as well as those in India. Mrs. Peabody would help her fight.

It was a crushing blow when on December 22 Lucy Peabody wrote: "I'm really glad it's been decided. I've always had a question on the divided site, as I know you must have had. We won't lose the 200-acre tract entirely. We can keep it for a camp or convalescent place. I think we should have a meeting of our union women's committee immediately to approve the change of site for the college."

Ida entered into a long and furious battle for her dream. She made speeches, wrote letters outlining her arguments. No matter what the women's committee decided, she would not yield until ground for the new college buildings had actually been broken—no, not until their walls were up. Build her beautiful white college on that little plot in the middle of crowded, smelly bazaars when there were two hundred wide free acres with no boundaries but skies and mountains? It would be like crowding the Taj Mahal into a vacant lot off Times Square!

Ida was as determined to draft new recruits as she was to raise money, and as inflexibly persistent. At the Mayo Clinic she found Carol Jameson, promising young graduate of Stanford Medical College presently on fellowship at the Clinic, who had already accepted a missionary assignment in Peking Medical School.

"We just have to have you," Ida told the young woman with finality. "What have you done in the way of teaching?"

"Not much," Dr. Jameson replied. "But I have taught chemistry."

"Fine. Then you must come to Vellore and teach chemistry for us."

And Carol Jameson agreed.

Persistence was not always necessary. Sometimes the mere magnetism of her own person was sufficient to draw volunteers. It was so with Treva Marshall, student of dietetics at Western Reserve Women's College.

"Oh, you should have been at chapel and seen this missionary," a classmate told Treva. "She's perfectly beautiful. The most marvelous white hair! She wore a black dress trimmed with blue and a hat with a gorgeous plume!"

That night Treva plowed through snowdrifts to hear the visitor. She was deeply moved. She stood in line for a long time, but failed to meet her. Encouraged by the advice of the dietician at Lakeside Hospital, on the next Sunday morning she tried again, pursuing the waving plume from church to church where the doctor was speaking, always just missing contact. Fate further thwarted her efforts by burying the city in another huge snowstorm, making further pursuit impossible. But when the storm was over that evening, the girl received a message from Dr. Ida saying that Vellore was in need of a dietician. It was enough. From that moment Treva Marshall set her sights on India. Even the abrupt shock of a cable six months later, saying STUDY X RAY, was not to turn her from her purpose. Very well. If an X-ray technician was needed more than a dietician, then she would study X ray. Fortunately she had had a premedical course. Another year of study was a small price to pay for the long decades of service Treva Marshall was destined to give in the fulfillment of Dr. Ida's dream.

The campaign was a medley of triumph, hope, and frustration. A hundred "college days" were organized, with luncheons and meetings throughout the country. The first, held in

204

Washington on the Saturday preceding the Conference on the Limitation of Armaments, was promoted by such leading women as Mrs. Hughes, Mrs. Coolidge, and Mrs. Lansing. Wellesley, Vassar, Smith, and Mt. Holyoke, besides lending the assistance of their presidents, adopted "sister colleges" in the Orient and raised creditable sums. The project, both interdenominational and international, fired the enthusiasm of a country sick of war and anxious to heal its wounds. Donations came from churches, clubs, service groups, sororities, newsboys, the American Legion, the Jewish Women's League. On one October day in New Haven Mrs. Peabody raised $1,500 in fifteen minutes.

But it was a depression year, and two million dollars were a vast amount of money. As the deadline of December 31 drew near, with the goal still far from attained, the struggle became desperate. December 9—by coincidence Ida's birthday—was designated as "Dollar Day," with a huge nationwide effort to obtain small contributions, especially from college students.

During these crucial weeks Ida's services were in tremendous demand. She was kept busy day and night, traveling, speaking, attending teas and luncheons, visiting colleges in an attempt to rouse students to observe the special day.

Though an unqualified success, Dollar Day was not enough. December 31 found the Laura Spelman Rockefeller Fund far from completion. Mercifully the deadline was postponed for another month. The army of gallant women, Ida and Mrs. Peabody in their forefront, continued to battle furiously, speaking many times a day, taxing their strength to the limits of endurance.

"It's no use," Lucy Peabody was forced to admit at last. "We're at least fifty thousand short. We can't possibly do it." She was making a last desperate effort toward the end of January on a coast-to-coast trip which had brought her to California.

"I've made an appointment for you to see a woman," said a friend without offering much encouragement. "She isn't much interested in missions, but she has agreed to see you for half an hour."

The woman was Miss Ellen Scripps of La Jolla, eighty years

old and in bed with a broken hip. She was cordial but unencouraging. Though the half hour stretched to an hour and a half, Mrs. Peabody left with little hope of a response. The next evening a call came to her from Pasadena.

"I've been trying to reach you all day," her friend reported excitedly. "Miss Scripps has asked that you write down everything you said in a detailed report and send it to her."

Lucy Peabody sat up until three o'clock writing. She sent the report, scarcely daring to hope. And, anyway, the campaign was so far from its goal that even a sizable donation would make little difference. They had obviously forfeited the Rockefeller million.

Returning to her headquarters, she found a letter waiting, brief but to the point. Miss Scripps would send her a check. She would like half of it to be used to help build the new children's hospital in Vellore. And—*the check would be in the amount of fifty thousand dollars*.

The day was January 31, 1923.

The physical and nervous strain had been too great. Mrs. Peabody promptly collapsed and was taken to a hospital.

Headlines in the *New York Times* of February 4 proclaimed the victory:

"$3,000,000 ASSURED TO SCHOOLS IN EAST
Church Women Win $2,000,000 Campaign and
Rockefellers Give the Rest"

After announcing the triumphant completion of the campaign, the *Times* article described the dark outlook for the campaign in the early weeks, mentioned Mrs. Peabody's arduous labors and her collapse, and added that practically all of the two million dollars had been given by women, thousands coming in gifts of one dollar.

"Thank God!" commented Gertrude Dodd when she heard the news.

"San thosham! Happiness!" exclaimed Ida fervently.

16

One night soon after her return to India Ida awoke suddenly to midnight darkness and a sharp sense of urgency. At first she did not know why. Then she remembered. Of course. The telegram! A young American sailor with only twenty-four hours' leave had wired from Madras that he wanted to see her work in Vellore and was arriving on the midnight train for a two-hour stopover. She had told Solomon, her driver, to meet him at the station.

Easing herself noiselessly under the netting, she pulled on her clothes. So used was she to rising in the night that she could sense the time intuitively, knew that the blare of a train whistle and the rumble of car wheels had mingled in her dreams with the rhythmic trillings of a nightjar. Solomon must have met the train and returned. Why had he not called her? Grumbling silently at her slowness, she groped her way out of the sleeping porch and down the stairway.

The stars smote her with their close brightness. Strange how much nearer heaven Vellore was than New York! And pity the poor uninterrupted sleepers who never saw the stars at this hour! She could read the time now like a clock. Taurus and Pleiades overhead, with Aldebaran blazing like a torchlight;

Cassiopeia and Andromeda close to the northern rim of hills; Orion, broadside down, just off of overhead; the Pole Star barely visible. It was close to two on a December morning. If the young sailor had come and gone, she would never forgive herself.

Spying a faint gleam near the huge pipal tree, she rushed toward it. A beam of lantern light, pale compared with the blazing flame of Sirius, picked out of the darkness a high white turban and an agreeable assortment of fresh young American features topped by a jaunty sailor's cap.

"You said you'd call me," Ida reproached her driver swiftly.

Solomon was apologetic. He had thought the Doctor *Ammal* should not be disturbed by a mere—. He coughed discreetly.— And the visitor could stay such a short time—only two hours! He had shown him the new dispensary—the outside of it, that is—and the peanut godown and the *dhobi* place, and after all, what else was there?

Ida seized the lantern. "Come!" Her gay zest jabbed the bored and sleepy young sailor awake like a shot of adrenalin. "You haven't seen anything. Thank goodness there's still more than an hour left!"

The surgeon-general himself could not have been given a more complete tour.

"Our new dispensary—isn't it lovely with its big open court and verandahs? Don't you like the palms and crotons and hanging baskets of ferns? Wouldn't know it was a hospital, would you? That's the way we want it to be. We have no in-patients yet, but how the day patients are flocking! And besides being a dispensary, it's also a clinical training school for students. Each specialist will have a room for examining patients and another adjoining room where students will receive instruction. But this is only the beginning! I *must* make you see it as it's going to be! Over there to the north a big children's block and a maternity hospital with fifty beds each, in that open space to the west a medical and surgical hospital with a capacity of a hundred and fifty beds, here the administration building with a lovely curving drive and garden in front, and in the center of all the beautiful white dome of a chapel. Tell me —*you do see it?*"

"You bet!" The sailor was wide-awake now. "Wait till I tell my mother! She heard you speak and gave ten dollars to your campaign."

"But that's not all!" The woman's blue eyes kindled sparks from the lantern flame. "Four miles out of town, in the most beautiful valley—oh, dear, I wish there were time to show you! I wonder—no, worse luck, there isn't. I'll just have to tell you. . . ."

Solomon chased after them, wagging his head in bewilderment. *Ayoh*, you never could tell! Here he'd thought this midnight visitor was just a nobody, but the way the Doctor *Ammal* was acting he must be at least son to that big American maharajah who had given so many lakhs of rupees! Returning him to the station, the servant treated him with the respect due visiting royalty.

Not many weeks afterward Solomon was despatched to meet another new arrival, one come to spend not two hours but at least two generations.

Young Dr. Carol Jameson had kept her promise. Spending the voyage boning up furiously on the chemistry she had been engaged to teach, she arrived in India just two months after Ida's own triumphant homecoming in October, 1923. If she still entertained doubts as to the wisdom of her decision, they were dispelled by the three-mile trip from the station in the old Model T with Solomon.

It was cool in December, and South India was at its loveliest. The rice fields were a tapestry of green velvet and cloud-flecked silver. Even the Palar River, usually only a broad brown desert of river bed, boasted a meager rivulet from the fall monsoon, its banks festooned with rainbow patches of drying laundry.

Vellore! Breathlessly the young American doctor tried to absorb it all at once: rough-hewn hills and huge carved temple tower; a funeral pyre smoking on the river bank; houses of yellowed stucco drowsing behind walls of flaming poinsettias; a hotel with gaudily painted front and a jolly elephant above its doorway; a funeral procession with a corpse sitting upright on its bier; medley of strange faces, strange costumes, strange conveyances.

Turning sharp left at the jutka stand with its rows of

209

shabby covered wagons and patient ponies, they jolted past a huddled line of dingy teashops; swerved dangerously close to a deep open drain as they wove their way, horn squawking, among bicycles, bullock carts, pedestrians; came finally to a beautiful spreading tamarind beyond which lay a gleaming new white building.

"Cole Dispensary." Solomon gestured with expansive pride. "Only just now it is finished." They swept triumphantly past its front entrance, a gate of carved wrought iron painted silver; bore down presently on a large white building with big pillars supporting a long front verandah.

"Fillebrown Nurses' Home," explained the driver glibly. "Just new also."

Carol Jameson's eager young eyes glowed appreciatively, then widened in disbelief as a cow emerged from the stately portico of the new building and proceeded with dignity down the steps. "Home for—*nurses?*" she said weakly. Thus introduced to India as a land of the unexpected, she was not too much surprised to be welcomed a few moments later by the celebrated Dr. Scudder from the unconventional depths of a washbasin.

"My dear!" The greeting was muffled but enthusiastic. "I'm so glad you've come. We've been shampooing, Michael and I. We're almost finished."

Michael was a small squirming bundle of wooly dog, with hair almost as soft and pure white as his mistress'. Entranced, Carol watched the two of them emerge from the washroom, equally clean, brushed, fluffed, and combed, equally highlighted by the same pale bluing rinse!

She took her first dose of India not in sips, but in big gulps, for the next day she went out with Ida on Roadside. It was a humbling, shattering experience.

During the first two stops she could only stand and stare helplessly—at the swarms of people, the strange dress (or lack of it), the starved bodies, the dark faces with the suffering eyes and smiling lips . . . at the ravages of diseases never encountered at Stanford or the Mayo Clinic: flesh riddled with scabies, hands and feet reduced to stumps by leprosy, eyes blinded by trachoma . . . at the competent second-year students

210

"But—" Carol caught her breath in dismay. "I know nothing about it."

"No matter," was the serene reply. "You'll learn."

And Carol did. She learned in time not only to run the clinical laboratory, but during successive stages of her long service at Vellore, to direct the department of gynecology, the entire hospital, and, for a brief period, the medical college. She was to learn all these duties so well that when twenty years later the signal honor of Kaisar-i-Hind was added to her other distinguished degrees in surgery, Canadian and American, it was to be said of her, "This reward is for long, distinguished, and unostentatious service to India, and we would emphasize that Dr. Carol Jameson's self-effacement embodies the worth of the medal in her own personality."

Carol arrived just in time to see the silvered iron gates of Cole Dispensary officially opened by Their Excellencies, Lord and Lady Willingdon, Governor of Madras Presidency and his wife, on December 19, 1923.

Here for the first time Ida sensed a moment of complete fulfillment. Girls of one class were already carrying healing and new life into scores of outlying towns and distant villages, and others were now ready to follow. The school was no longer dependent on her for existence. It had become a living organism. She could hear the strong beat of its pulse as the girls, a full hundred of them, sang to the rousing accompaniment of the police band their fervent pledge of loyalty in "Three cheers for the silver and blue!"

But her sense of fulfillment did not last long. There was too much to do, too much always left undone. Though never able again to give any class such a monopoly of her time as those first fourteen girls received, she was more than principal of her medical school, more than teacher of the gynecological surgery that became her special province. Every girl in the school was her personal and intimate concern, and never did she permit other duties to interfere with her rigid, self-imposed responsibility to her students. Once when she was examiner for the University of Madras and snowed under with work, she retired to her room, drew a tub of cold water, and sat in it in order to wake herself sufficiently to correct her many papers.

She had students always with her, in the dispensary, making rounds at the hospital, on the weekly trips to Gudiyattam, in the operating room. For Ida an operation was never a success unless it served two purposes: a means of healing and an object lesson; three, if possible, with young hands gaining experience through action. On one occasion she almost failed to meet any of these standards.

A teacher in one of the mission schools was brought to Schell violently ill and terrified. "I don't want an operation," she wailed. "She'll have all her medical students in to see it!"

Ida was chagrined. Sympathy, honesty joined battle with the passion to share knowledge. A ruptured appendix—and not a student eye to see? Impossible! But equally impossible the unnecessary distress of a patient or the telling of a falsehood. What to do?

"Jeevali." With gentle understanding she called the young teacher by name. "I'm so sorry that all our medical students are away. They won't be able to see this."

Ida waited until the patient was fully under the anesthetic. Then she summoned not her medical students, but all the available pupils in the school of nursing to witness the operation.

Her sensitivity to the pain and emotional suffering of her patients was so acute as to be sometimes a source of personal embarrassment. It was so on the occasion when Hilda Lazarus came to Vellore for medical treatment. Dr. Lazarus, one of Christian India's most distinguished daughters, gold-medal graduate of the Madras Government Medical College, with degrees in obstetrics and gynecology from both England and Ireland, was to Ida more than just an admired acquaintance. As superintendent of the Purdah Hospital for Women and Children in Madras and principal of the newly founded Lady Willingdon Medical School for Women, she was committed with Ida to the same task and goal. In this tiny dark-skinned daughter of India, with her fine Brahmin features and brilliant compassionate eyes, Ida saw the Indian counterpart of herself, her very dream made flesh. The discovery that she must cause her pain in order to heal distressed her like an actual physical hurt.

214

Walking through the hospital early on the morning of her impending operation, Dr. Hilda Lazarus found her surgeon sitting on the stone steps weeping.

"My dear, what is it? Is something the matter?"

Half ashamed, Ida wiped her eyes. "I can't help it," she confessed. "I—I'm just so sorry I have to hurt you!"

"You've already healed all the hurt," Dr. Lazarus assured her gently, "with your tears."

17

The new white building with its silver gate and simple but attractive interior, its wide-arched verandahs opening on the garden courtyard, was a delight to both doctors and patients.

"This isn't like a hospital," said a timid little woman who had come for treatment. "I have always been afraid of a hospital, but I have no fear here."

Her sentiment was echoed by a prominent government official who, visiting the dispensary during its busy hours, said wonderingly, "People here all look so happy, even though many of them are so sick!"

The beauty of the place was not the only reason for this spirit of contentment. The Mohammedan woman recovering from a sudden attack of acute malarial mania understood this and wondered. "Why?" she demanded, seizing the hand of her doctor as she appeared on her morning rounds. "Tell me, I want to know! Why didn't you lose your temper with me that time I went out of my mind?"

It was not the doctor who answered but the Hindu woman in the next bed. She sprang up with a glowing face. "Don't you know why?" she returned eagerly. "That's what their God is like, 'long-suffering and slow to anger.'"

216

But with the new building there seemed to be less space, not more. So great was the inpatient work at Schell that the entire surgical department had to be moved to Cole, its space already taxed by the demands of the dispensary and student classes. To Ida's dismay here also patients were soon being crowded into empty corners, sleeping on the floors. If only the new buildings did not take so long in growing! *"Juldi, juldi!* Hurry, hurry!" cried every vibrant nerve of her body.

But India would not be hurried. It had taken Bommai Reddy nine years to build his temple, Shah Jahan twenty-two to build his Taj. What matter a few years more or less when one built to outlast the centuries? The plans for the new buildings had yet to pass through the hands of the council, then through the government offices, where there might be endless delay.

Moreover, Ida was still waging a desperate battle for her beloved site. It was a bitter disappointment that of all her staff only two, Gertrude Dodd and Dr. Jessie Findlay, supported the building of the medical school on the 200-acre tract south of town. So close was the project to her heart that the opposition of her colleagues seemed like personal betrayal.

"A difference of opinion and conviction," young Carol Jameson reminded her gently, "is not disloyalty."

Something in the steady eyes prevented Ida from making a sharp rejoinder. She managed a smile. "Oh, well," she returned lightly, "my shoulders are broad."

Then suddenly, one day in February, something happened that made even the building of a medical college seem for a while unimportant. Ida was in the midst of a Medical School Committee meeting which had been called for 6 P.M. on a Friday when she heard a motor come into the yard, then, immediately afterward, the agitated voice of her cousin Dr. Lew Scudder. She went to him at once.

"It's Annie Hancock," he said. "Can you come? I feel troubled about her. She has a severe bilious attack, which might be—" He did not finish.

Ida's heart gave a lurch. "Oh, Lew! Not—it couldn't be—"

"It looks like it," he said grimly. "Cholera."

In the two-mile drive to the mission compound Ida relived a quarter of a century. Annie! Her adoring classmate at Northfield, loyal friend through the years, quiet, loving, self-effacing little Annie! Going joyfully into the hot dark houses of Vellore, into the ugly jail, day after day, year after year, telling—*showing*—the good news of her God who was a loving Father. Twenty-four years ago there had been only thirteen homes that would accept her presence. Now there was not a house in this city of 60,000 where she would not be welcomed. It was five years now since she had started her Women's Social Service Society in a rented house, teaching her Indian sisters reading, sewing, health, baby care, games like ping-pong, bean bags, musical chairs; gently coaxing, day after day in the zenanas, trying to persuade them to lead normal lives. "No, no, we cannot come." "But so many women do come." "Oh, yes, they may come, but it is not our custom. No, no, our husbands will not allow!" And now Annie's dream was at last coming true. Her Women's Social Service Center was to have a home of its own. Only a few days ago Ida and Gertrude had gone with her to the building site, seen her thin earnest features transfigured with joy.

"There isn't enough money to do it as I would like," she had regretted. "The estimates are so much higher than I had expected."

Ida had comforted her, reminded her that she would soon have a chance to tell her friends in America about the need. For in just another month Annie was going home on furlough. To have something happen now—!

Lew's fears were realized. It was cholera, probably contracted from some infected food or drink which she had politely accepted in one of her zenana visits. Annie would rather die than hurt the feelings of one of her Indian friends by refusing a proffered dainty. And she was always too busy thinking of others to consider precautions for herself of great importance. Even with the recommended periodic injections of vaccine, the utmost caution was necessary in the matter of accepting food and water.

They moved Annie to Schell Hospital, put her in a warm bed, and joined battle with the deadly foe. Dell Houghton, Ida's colleagues Dr. Innes and Dr. Findlay, with two graduate nurses, worked incessantly for fifty-six hours; saw the slender body transformed slowly into an aspect of living death—sodden, shriveled hands, sunken eyes, inelastic clammy skin—yet with its mental faculties still painfully alert. Five times their patient almost slipped away from them, but the intravenous injections of normal saline brought her back. When she felt the severe sinking symptoms coming on, she would say, "Give me the injection, quickly!" It was a long and painful treatment, but she was always patient and sweet, and when they told her she must not move, she would smile and say, "I'll try, yes, I'll try."

Ida took longer turns than the others, sitting beside her, tensed for the slightest change. Little enough to make up for the years she had failed this friend of her girlhood! For she knew now that she had failed her. There was the same look in Annie's eyes as in Gertrude Dodd's—something beyond devotion, almost akin to worship. She should have found more time to share with Annie.

Once, on Saturday, Ida thought the battle had been won, but the enemy only returned with renewed violence. Annie remained conscious to the end.

"Finish—finish the building—" were the last words they heard her say.

It was on Monday, at the midday memorial service in the Tamil church, that Ida felt the first shock of genuine bereavement. It came at the time of singing, when she realized suddenly that the clearest, sweetest voice was missing.

Yet in spite of her grief the routine of her life continued, with its round-the-clock activity, its problems of administration, its anxieties connected with the slowly mounting hospital units. When April came with its intense heat, she was ready for both rest and the blessed coolness of Kodaikanal. The coolness she found, but not the rest, for no sooner had she arrived than plans were set in motion for the building of her new summer home at Hill Top.

The summer colony at Kodaikanal considered Ida and Gertrude extremely foolish when in that spring of 1924 they began building a house four miles from the residential center, with all the materials having to be transported by bullock cart.

But Ida was indifferent to their scoffings. There were no committees this time to thwart her, no denomination boards to shrink and cramp and shrivel. Thanks to Gertrude's generosity, for once she could build as big and as high as she pleased. Mr. Samuel, the builder, came up each day from town, bringing often his bright-eyed six-year-old daughter. Never having built a two-story house before, he encountered difficulties, but Gertrude Dodd was equal to the occasion, giving orders with the same thrifty competence with which she fulfilled her duties as college bursar.

"Did you say a *house*, Bones?" Ida's brother Harry whistled when he saw the plans. "Looks as if you're having your mansion in the sky right here and now!"

Relieved of the responsibility for the details she abhorred, Ida was free to create. She planned not just a garden, but gardens: formal ones at each side of the house, with beds and paths and trellises; rock ones on the bony ridges descending toward the sheer slope in front; terraced ones following the rounded contours of the long spiral driveway. Blue would be the prevailing color—delphiniums, morning glories, lavender blues of wisteria, maybe even lilacs. There would be hollyhocks tall enough to climb to the big circular balcony. And, of course, there would be roses: pink Dorothy Perkins' ramblers, orange and red and gold Talismans, Sunsets, Mermaids, big white Karl Druschkes, apple roses, smelling like a ripe red McIntosh. There would be nasturtiums, dahlias, azaleas, poppies, red cactus, carnations, chrysanthemums, white camellias, sweet peas. Yes, even goldenrod! She was credited with introducing the tomato into South India. Why not goldenrod?

There were soon names for everything, as there had been at Shelter Island. The long curving drive was "Queen's Highway," the flat bare tableland "King Henry's Plateau." The sun went down behind "The Old Man of the Mountain." Ida and Gertrude lived at Restalrig while the house was being built— one season, two—and, rushing up and down the hill with her little dog Michael racing at her heels, Ida could have felt almost young again except for her mother's frailty.

"I don't like to be helped," complained Mrs. John as Ida half lifted her in and out of the little buggy. "How I hate to be treated as if I were old and to be given the best chair and all! If it weren't for this rheumatism, I'd be as young as any of you."

But she was serene even in her complaints. Sophia Scudder's life had contained many abrupt changes, and she had faced them all with realistic calmness. When on a Sunday morning in 1860, sitting in a little Congregational church in Northfield, Massachusetts, she had received from a young man in a neighboring pew a folded bit of paper marked on the outside with the name "Sophia Weld" and inscribed with the simple words: "II John, verse 5" ("And now I beseech thee, lady ... that we love one another"), she had written back without the slightest hesitation: "Ruth 1:16,17" ("Entreat me not to leave thee, or to return from following after thee; for whither thou goest I will go....")

That the "following" was to involve four long months of rough sea voyage, an initial absence of seventeen years from home and country, unbelievable hardships and privations, separation from her children, sixty years spent in a strange and foreign land, would not have altered her decision in the least. Though after that first perilous voyage, when told that land was in sight, she had retorted tartly, "I don't believe it!" and though she had burst into tears at sight of the emerald beauty of Ceylon in June, neither reaction had signified cowardice or regret. Leaving the anchored ship two miles from Madras in monsoon season, then riding the waves in a masulah, a big trough of a boat tied together with thongs, seams stopped with grass so it would give going over the waves, she had surrendered herself without a quiver into the brown arms waiting to carry her and her twenty-six-year-old husband to the sandy shore where his brothers William and Ezekiel had come to meet them.

Years ago the board in New York, while accepting Dr. John II for missionary service, had believed the climate of India too rigorous for the delicate health of his fiancée, Miss Sophia Weld, and had refused to send her.

"I'll take the chance," Dr. John had assured them confidently, "and full responsibility. I know she can live there."

Fifty-eight years later, in June, 1919, a generation after his death, Sophia Weld Scudder had turned the sod for the Scudder Memorial Hospital in Ranipet, donated by the Scudder Memorial Association and honoring Dr. John Scudder I on the hundredth anniversary of his coming to India, first medical missionary ever to go out from America to a foreign country. It was fitting that she, the sole surviving member of her husband's generation, should represent those forty of Dr. John's descendants and their husbands or wives who, in India, Japan, Arabia, Hawaii, and the United States had already given nearly a thousand years to missionary service. Soon afterward she herself had been honored, when on another June day in 1921 three hundred relatives and friends had gathered at Cushing to pay tribute to "Aunt Fida" on the completion of sixty years of missionary work in India. Children and grandchildren, nieces and nephews, one grand-niece and one grand-nephew were present. Members of twelve denominations spoke and sang her praises, piled her arms high with flowers.

Mrs. Scudder was never to see the house at Hill Top completed. On her eighty-sixth birthday, sixty-three years after her arrival in India, the students of the medical school, now eighty in number, set her in a birthday chair twined with ferns and flowers. It was the last birthday she spent on earth. Her return to Vellore from Kodaikanal in July, 1925, was followed by increased weakness and days of pain. When it was realized that the end was not far off, the compound of the bungalow at Thotapalayam became thronged with people, begging to be allowed just to see her. "Everything has stopped," someone in the mission observed. "We cannot do anything. We cannot think of anything but Mrs. John." It was just at sunrise, on the Sabbath morning of August 30, that she died.

The polished teak casket from the Industrial School in Katpadi was soon buried in flowers. Hindus, Mohammedans, Christians, all came bearing gifts according to their customs: a jasmine wreath, a rose, crosses and crowns of blossoms. One Hindu brought a quilt of flowers woven and tied together. A woman came bearing a vial of perfume and poured the contents over the neat black dress. Half of Vellore lined the streets as the flower-laden ambulance moved slowly from church to cemetery, and stood silently saluting the beloved *dorai sani,* honored lady.

At first Ida felt only a numb grief mingled with relief that the long days of pain were over. Then suddenly the years slipped away, and she was a child again. It was night, rain streaming against the windows. She was rushing upstairs to bury her face in a pillow bearing a familiar imprint. Alone, terribly alone she was, and in the dark, for her best beloved had gone away to a far country.

18

The years of the early and middle twenties were as filled with triumphs as with losses and discouragements. One of the more recent developments which gave Ida and her colleagues the greatest satisfaction was the discovery of a possible cure for leprosy.

Chaulmoogra oil was by no means a new remedy for the disease in India. Tradition ascribed its first use to a Burmese prince who, discovering that he had leprosy, was told by the gods to go into the forest and meditate. Sitting under a tree with large fruits containing many seeds, he was directed to eat some of these seeds, and was cured. During the middle of the nineteenth century the oil was used as a therapy by British surgeons. For years a standard treatment for leprosy had been chaulmoogra oil given internally in capsules. In recent years, however, it had been discovered that a mixture of chaulmoogra oil, camphorated oil, and resorcinol, administered by injections in successive and increased doses, proved efficacious in not only reducing the painful manifestations but in apparently arresting the disease.

As in Bible times, leprosy was still shrouded in misconceptions. Few people knew the facts: that it was no mysterious curse, but a disease caused by a bacillus, very much like tuberculosis only less contagious; that it was not hereditary and only mildly infective, being transmitted through the skin or mucous membranes usually to children under eighteen through prolonged and intimate contact with carriers of the bacillus. Contracted in childhood, it might remain latent for years. Conditions of overcrowding, presence of skin abrasions as in scars left by scabies, and a humid climate, all contributing factors, made the village huts of South India a prolific breeding ground.

Compulsory segregation, unless of an intelligent type gaining the cooperation of the patient, was next to impossible, for even had there been sufficient leprosariums, victims would conceal themselves to keep from leaving their families. Nor was it wholly desirable. Often the most obvious cases of the neural type, resulting in mutilation such as the claw hand, blindness, loss of fingers and toes, were the least infectious. Cases of the lepromatous type, where the skin was primarily affected and thickened, though far more serious, often went undetected in their earlier and more contagious stages.

The news of a new remedy spread quickly. One after another of the nurses would stop Ida and ask eagerly, "Is it true that leprosy is now curable? So-and-so has it. When can he come to see you?"

So in twos and threes the first leprosy patients came, starting the long series of injections which gave hope of arresting the disease. But few would come to the hospital. It was in the villages that the need lay, where early cases could be found and cured before they became a source of infection. But where find workers to go into the villages? How find villagers willing to trust themselves to the *oosie* (needle) with its strange new medicine? Where—how—but on Roadside?

The new program became a regular service of the four weekly mobile clinics. Leprosy patients began coming to the stations from villages up to thirty miles away, hobbling, walking, crawling, brought on carts and stretchers. Often as an ambulance team traveled a road, they would find a new group waiting.

"We have heard of the cures of other lepers," the newcomers would announce eagerly, "and we also have come for the *oosie*."

Fortunately the British Mission to Lepers made it possible to give an injection for a price between two and eight annas. But even this was often too much. At one stop Ida had treated a fine fourteen-year-old boy for about three months, but just as he began to get better he stopped coming. Ida urged someone to beg him to return. The following week she saw him on the outskirts of the crowd.

"I cannot afford to pay," he said when she spoke to him. "I was hungry so often I had to stop coming."

The Roadside program was only partially successful. It made possible the treatment of predisposing diseases, such as malaria, hookworm, malnutrition, which must be cleaned up before the injections could be really effective. It approached the problem of leprosy in the best way possible, treating incipient cases on the village level, hospitals and leprosariums to be provided only for those suffering from the acute and complicated stages of the disease. And there were apparently some cures.

But it had its weaknesses. As the doses increased in strength, they became increasingly painful. Often it took the physical robustness of a man to push the needle into the quivering flesh while the patient stood groaning. Children had to be held forcibly while the injections were given. Unless the intramuscular injection was given under sterile conditions there was danger of producing a deep muscular abscess. And it took many months, sometimes years, of treatments, vast patience, endless miles of weary traveling on the part of the patients. Many, expecting an immediate magic cure, became discouraged. And even the four mobile clinics could reach only the few who came.

Ida's satisfaction was mingled with frustration. If they could only employ a full-time superintendent for the work, put three motor cars at work constantly, three Indian doctors!

There were personal triumphs also in these years. In 1925, the year of her mother's death, the people of Vellore rejoiced with Ida as well as wept, for it was her silver jubilee, marking a quarter-century since her return to India as a doctor. They showed their love and appreciation by giving a clock tower to the new hospital. Gertrude Dodd added the clock and the bell, and gave a true Indian-style feast, a tamasha, with a rousing band, lengthy speeches, and a banquet of rice, curry, and sweets served to guests by the thousands.

But the real climax of the quarter-century came on Ida's birthday, December 9, observed since the founding of the school as "College Day," when all the old students who could do so came back to make her "family" again complete. Ida surveyed her graduates, read their letters, with deep gratitude and satisfaction. There were seventy of them now—four classes—sent out like the disciples of old, into the towns and villages, with power to heal.

One wrote: "I have been working in this village since I left school except for five months in a government hospital for freshening up. (She did not mention that a good position had been offered her in the city at that time.) I am the first woman to work here. People thought that only men with wonderful skill of brain could be doctors, not a woman born and brought up like them."

Not all of the seventy had gone into villages. Two, Ebbie Gnanamuthu and Kamala Vytbilingam, were on her own hospital staff. Twenty-eight were in mission hospitals, many having refused posts with higher salaries. One had taken a government post in order to earn money to educate her seven brothers and sisters. Twenty-three were in government or municipal dispensaries, five of them in child welfare centers. Two were in private practice, one in New York doing successful postgraduate work.

"Now, doctor," wrote one high-ranking graduate, "let me make your heart leap with joy. I am so tired I can hardly write anything, yet I should let you know about this, or my joy will not be complete." Then followed the story of how this graduate, a doctor for only one year, had fought against fearful odds, daring to attempt what two of her superior officers would not undertake (a caesarian), and saving a mother and baby in the face of overwhelming difficulties.

Ida was grateful for all that had been accomplished. She

227

was pleased but not satisfied. Her goal was not Licensed Medical Practitioners, but fully accredited Bachelors of Science and Surgery, not seventy graduates, but seventy times seven!

Ida took her new missionary colleague, Treva Marshall, with her when she went to the village of Vaniambadi, several miles from Vellore, to visit a Mohammedan patient. Treva was all Ida had hoped she would be, versatile, energetic, earnestly anxious to serve. The year of study in X ray had not presupposed a substitution of activities, merely an addition. Treva was assigned not only to taking X-ray pictures but to the duties of hospital dietitian as well.

This last was no easy task. Funds for running the hospital were at a minimum. Treva was expected to cut from a three-thousand-rupee diet to a two-thousand. In other words, she was allotted about four annas (less than eight cents) a day per patient. No easy assignment for a dietitian coming from a hospital where orange juice had been a daily essential and a balanced diet the eleventh commandment! In addition to these two full-time occupations she was soon to acquire other duties: coaching basketball, counseling students, teaching hygiene, and acting as warden of the girls' hostel.

The visit to the village was not professional. It was a celebration. Their hostess was a well-to-do Mohammedan woman who had been in the hospital a long time with a serious abdominal operation and had invited them to celebrate her homecoming with a gala dinner. She had a daughter twelve years old, Azeenabee, a bright mischievous child to whom Ida had taken a great fancy.

"If she could only stay young and mischievous!" she sighed to Treva, watching the gay little figure flit about the courtyard. "Another year or two, and she must be a woman."

Treva thought of the long gray-white burkas swathing Mohammedan women like ghosts, and shivered. There were no burkas today, however. The women were at home, shy but poised and gracious, in the fastness of their harem quarters.

The foods were rich and delicious: rice and curries; tender vegetable leaves fried in oil; *laddus,* balls of sweetened gram, with raisins, cardamon, and cashew nuts; a *payasam* (pudding)

228

made of vermicelli, dried grapes, cashews, spices, coconut, and sugar. Ida bit into what looked like a large hard-boiled egg and made a surprised face. The little Azeenabee laughed and laughed, jumping up and down and clapping her hands. It was she who had played the trick, blowing *halwa* into the empty shell, breaking it after the delicious sweet had hardened.

As they rode home after dark, the news of Ida's coming preceded them. All along the way lanterns shone and villagers stopped the car, insisting that she come into their homes and take refreshment.

"But," whispered Treva, carefully schooled in the gastric dangers of the tropics, "how can we be sure everything is peeled or boiled?"

"We can't," returned Ida cheerfully. "We have to be as careful as we can, of course. But—when it comes to a choice between taking a risk and refusing a friend's hospitality—" She sighed, remembering that Annie Hancock had taken such a risk and died.

Subsequently Ida's fears about the little Azeenabee were justified. The child was married at thirteen. Though she had a good husband, she was a great favourite with her father and spent much time in his home, so much that her father-in-law became jealous of her obvious preference for her own parents. When a baby arrived, Ida was invited to the naming ceremony. The mother and father sat together on a couch; the grandmother presented the baby to them, decorated with jasmine garlands, and the solemn moment arrived. The name of the child (a boy, or there would have been no such celebration) was announced with great pomp and ceremony.

Presently little Azeenabee became very ill. Finally her parents brought her to the hospital, the mother touchingly confident that her beloved doctor could cure her. To Ida's horror she found upon reading the X rays that the girl's lungs were riddled with tuberculosis. "Why," she reproached the parents, *"Why* didn't you bring her to me before?"

The father shook his head sadly. It would have done no good, he told her simply, for the sickness was caused by black magic worked by the girl's father-in-law on account of his jealousy.

There had been an incantation, he was sure, for he had found a pot with magic stuff boiled in it, buried outside their house. There was nothing the foreign doctor could have done.

Ida gritted her teeth. Somebody was dying of tuberculosis in India every sixty seconds, and in nine cases out of ten it was unnecessary. Oh, for enough nurses to do a really good job in preventive medicine and public health education! But in spite of all she could do, the work grew so fast that there were never enough nurses even for the hospital alone.

However, she could see progress. In 1924 she had helped organize a Vellore branch of the Madras Maternity and Child Welfare Association at a meeting in the Collector's bungalow, and was elected its president. Sixty-five prominent citizens had lent assistance to the project. Many Indian women had attended the meeting. Following the drafting of a plan prepared by the Ministry of Health of Great Britain in 1914, the organizing committees in various centers raised money by popular subscription to establish maternity and child welfare centers and employ health visitors to go into the homes of the communities and invite women to these centers. In accordance with this plan a center for the Association had been opened in Cole Dispensary.

The hospital was growing, the empty spaces in the land at Thotapalayam filling slowly with beautiful buildings. And as her judgment became vindicated by the needs of the expanding program, Ida finally won her battle for the building of the college on the 200-acre lot outside the town. The hospital compound was proving too small for all the units which would soon be necessary. Objections of distance, while never completely overcome, were surmounted by the development of a practical plan for transportation by private buses. And Ida's arguments for the superior health advantages of a country site were a deciding factor. The council finally agreed that her site should be used for the college buildings if water could be found on it. A diviner was employed to go over the two hundred acres, and a well was dug. Its flow proved to be abundant.

By this time the government of the Missionary Medical School for Women was stabilized in a three-fold organization. Any church, society, or other missionary body contributing

$1,000 a year became a subscriber with a voice in its management. There were two governing boards, one British, one American. Each subscriber was entitled to nominate two persons to one of these boards, which included additional coopted members. The boards had the authority to appoint the principal and all foreign professors and nursing superintendents, determine salaries, pass on the budget, and exercise general control over the college.

In India there was a College Council made up of members designated by the cooperating missionary bodies on the field. This council, which met once a year, though bound by the general instructions of the two governing boards on major issues, was responsible for the actual running of the medical school with its affiliated hospitals.

Now that the matter of site had been cleared with both boards and council, Ida could scarcely wait to get the building project under way at College Hill. But first, of course, the hospital units must be finished.

"The buildings are making real progress," she wrote in her diary one day in 1926. "Electricity such a comfort. Weather getting cool. Feel cheerful."

That year, too, the house at Hill Top was finished. Instead of bricks and mortar, it was now Gertrude Dodd's Italian carved chests and tables that were transported the four miles in a bullock cart, having been brought by lorry up the ten-year-old Law's Ghat Road. So spacious were the rooms and so beautifully appointed that the luxurious furniture looked as much at home as in Gertrude's sumptuous New York apartment.

The house was dedicated with a party and a service of thanksgiving. Guests roamed the rooms and gardens, had tea at tables on the semicircular verandahs. Presents were given everybody —even Mr. Solomon's bright-eyed little daughter, who was presented with a whole tin of biscuits, such a huge fortune that she was to remember the thrill after a quarter of a century.

"Now," thought Ida, surveying the wide sweep of earth and heaven, "there will be time. Time to rest and think."

She was mistaken. The two months of the hot season usually spent at Hill Top were as busy as any of the other ten. She was always inviting people—tired nurses, doctors, patients—

for a "nice restful vacation." Summer residents came constantly and at all hours to look at her famous gardens, and of course she had to show them every plant and shrub and blossom herself. She was especially proud of the rare varieties, like the daffodils that had been smuggled in in the toe of a returning missionary's shoe, and like her celebrated "green rose." Sometimes, to write necessary letters, she rose at three in the morning and went into the bathroom to work in order not to disturb her guests. But there were compensating moments: the sudden sheen of sunlight on the tender green of young eucalyptus; the lights of Periakulam stabbing through a cloud rift seven thousand feet below; a perfect white camellia; the "old man of the mountain" asleep like an ancient rishi in a robe of saffron; mists rolling suddenly away.

"Thank You, thank You!" The cry came a dozen times a day to her lips.

"O God, if this be your footstool,
What must your throne be!"

The summer of 1927 she and Gertrude Dodd considered 143 applications for the medical school. They became accustomed to being told: "I belong to a respectable but poor family and will therefore need a scholarship," and "Though I have not fully passed my High School exams, I feel satisfied I can pass the Medical School examinations." How little these girls knew of the task facing women in medicine!

Finally thirty of the most promising were selected, and when the new class assembled on July 13 Ida knew they had chosen well. From all parts of South India the students came—Travancore, Cochin, Hyderabad, Bombay, Madras—and even from as far north as Central Provinces and Bengal, most of ·them arriving finally in a two-wheeled jutka drawn by a forlorn pony. Out they tumbled with their boxes, tin trunks, food tins, bedding rolls, the old girls exuberant, the new ones shy and frightened but with faces lighting at sight of the big white building with its blue-twined pillars, exclaiming in delight as on entering Fillebrown they glimpsed the inner court with its green grass and pink oleanders framed by graceful palms, its beauty eclipsing the frightening specters of the dissecting room.

232

Treva, the new warden, was ready for them, assigning to the old students "little sisters"; allotting to each girl a corner of a small room with table, chair, cupboard, and bookrack; no closet, for saris could be folded flat in her small trunk; no bed, for mats were rolled down at night on the verandah or in the large hall upstairs. In the morning each girl would roll up her bedding and carry it away, making the hall ready for morning prayers. This year the hall was screened, so the girls need not sleep with their saris over their faces.

Treva still marveled at the smallness of the kitchen. A little room ten by twelve in which to prepare food for seventy hungry girls—no tables, no chairs, no sinks, no iron stoves, just a low open fire, a flat stone in one corner, and some large brass vessels! The curries were ground on the stone, the rice sorted and the vegetables cut on the floor, where the workers sat to do all their work. Early in the morning the milkman brought his cows and milked them outside the kitchen, bringing always a calf for each cow, believing that the cow would not give her milk unless she thought it was taken by her calf. Treva was amazed one morning to see him milking with the stuffed skin of a dead calf propped deceptively against the cow's flank!

Her duties as college dietitian were simplified by the fact that every day's diet was the same: at 6 A.M. coffee and bread; at 9 milk; at 12 rice, vegetable curry, pepper water, curds, and vegetable fry; coffee and cake at 3; at 6:30 rice, meat curry, vegetable and pepper water; at 8:30 milk for those who wished it. The food for the Hindu students was prepared in a separate kitchen and served by a caste cook.

Pauline Jeffery, back from America with her hard-earned M.D., welcomed the new girls to the dissecting room with enthusiasm, soon dispelling their dread and setting them to work . . . all but one. After two weeks Helen, one of the first-year students, came to Pauline and Dr. Ida, trembling and in tears.

"It's no use," she said woefully. "I can't stay any longer. Those awful skeletons frighten me sick. I see them day and night. I have to go home."

Afraid her tears would upset the other students, Ida reluctantly consented, and Helen returned to her mission school in

Madurai. Her grandmother, a matron in the school, was terribly disappointed.

"You ought to be ashamed," said the principal, "for running away."

Helen was ashamed. She wrote Dr. Ida and applied for readmission.

"Very well," Ida wrote back promptly, "you may return. But only if you will promise to behave yourself."

Helen returned, to conquer her oversensitivity and become a shining example to other students; not only to graduate with honors but to remain afterward for eight years to manage Vellore's bacteriological laboratory and serve capably in the children's ward—also, incidentally, to marry one of the handsomest men in South India. When later she was called to a position of even greater responsibility in Madras, Ida was to write her new employer with deep emotion: "It is as if I were sending away my own beloved daughter."

By this year, 1927, the Union Missionary Medical School for Women was becoming well known throughout India, to the Indian as well as the Western population. Even so, Ida was surprised and gratified when the great Mahatma Gandhi accepted her invitation to visit the hospital and school late in the year on one of his tours of South India. At that time it took courage to invite him, for he had been outlawed by influential Hindus in Madras Presidency for his condemnation of child marriage and the observance of untouchability. Perhaps it took even more courage to brave the disapproval of her many British friends, in whose flesh the mahatma was becoming a more and more nettling thorn.

Gandhi's campaign after 1920 for nonviolent noncooperation with the British had created a widespread bloodless revolution. His appeal to all Indians to boycott foreign clothing, to spin and weave their own clothes, to wear nothing but homespun, had won startling response. His campaigns of civil disobedience had resulted in the jailing of hosts of patriotic Indians, ten thousand of them being imprisoned in a single month. Gandhi himself had invited arrest, been tried, and spent twenty-two months of a six-year sentence in prison. In an attempt to persuade Hindus and Moslems to forget their enmities, he had subjected himself to a twenty-one-day fast.

Gandhi's program of civil disobedience was challenging the courage and imagination of thousands of bold young patriots, like Sardar Patel and Rajendra Prasad and Jawaharlal Nehru. For, nonviolent though it was, it was no technique for cowards. No coward would sit unmoving and let a policeman strike him with a lathi, or lie on the ground in the path of galloping police horses. But the building of character was the major part of Gandhi's program. He was creating a free nation by creating free men.

His acceptance of Ida's invitation was all the more gratifying because she had politely refused the great man's request that her staff and student body all wear khadi, the homespun cloth which had become a symbol of the independence movement. Even so, they did not quite escape his gentle potency of persuasion, for on the afternoon before his arrival a bright-red Ford motor car came honking up to the hostel steps, loaded with khadi towels, table cloths, bed spreads, and saris. But Ida also possessed a strong streak of individualism. No one was going to tell her girls what to wear. Besides, her admiration for the Mahatma was tempered with a slight personal grievance. He had refused to make a donation to her hospital.

She arranged a meeting for the distinguished visitor in one of the large newly completed wards of the hospital, with more than four hundred persons in attendance. The two presented a strange contrast as they faced the crowd from the platform: the woman faultlessly dressed and coiffured, firm and vibrant of voice, so straight and buoyant of carriage that she seemed much taller than her five feet four . . . the frail little man squatted crosslegged on a table top, wearing nothing but his khadi loincloth and the sacred string about his neck, ugly and solemn except when his lips burst into a captivating smile, speech so feeble that even those sitting at his feet could hardly hear all he said. Yet their eyes, one pair bright blue, the other twinkling darkly behind steel-rimmed spectacles, regarded each other with more than respect. For they possessed one mutual and single passion—the bringing of new life to India.

The Mahatma spoke in very simple straightforward English,

with no more embellishments than he affected in the way of clothes. Though he urged his listeners to wear khadi, his emphasis was on moral and spiritual, not political, themes. "Pursue a high standard of morals," he urged the nurses and medical students with terse simplicity. "Do not strut around like big *dorai sanis*. Remember at all times your high calling to service."

After the meeting Ida showed him around the hospital. The crowds, following, bowed and kissed his feet. He was gracious and appreciative until Pauline Jeffery asked him to pause for a snapshot outside the hospital building.

"I hope," he told her with caustic bluntness, "it turns out to be a complete failure."

Her next distinguished visitor, Ida anticipated, would be Viscount Goschen, governor of Madras Presidency, whom she had invited to dedicate the new hospital buildings, asking him to give her the latest possible date in March, 1928. Bernard Rottschaefer, the missionary who was superintending the building operations had assured her that by exerting the utmost effort the work might be nearly finished by the end of March.

When the Governor's reply came, Ida tore open the heavy vellum envelope with its embossed seal, and anxiously read its contents. "Oh—*no!*" she exclaimed in horror. His Excellency had chosen *March fifth* for his official visit! It couldn't be done, of course. "We *must* do it!" said Ida grimly.

Bernard Rottschaefer was a person of equal determination. Engaging Indian laborers for both day and night shifts, he set in motion such feverish activity as the unhurried land had seldom seen. On the morning of the fifth the confusion, instead of lessening, was multiplied a thousandfold. The actual process of building, it seemed, went on until the last minute, painting until the last second before Their Excellencies arrived. Ida was everywhere at once, giving orders, sweeping floors, running errands, arranging flowers, sending to the bazaar for garlands, putting the last touches on her speech.

And then suddenly, as one of the nurses put it later, "as if by magic, the confusion all stopped. Everything was cleaned up. Potted plants, bowls of beautiful hill flowers, furniture, even

236

books and a table cover and a tea set on the tea table in the staff library appeared in their places. The lovely airy wards, which an hour before were getting their floor tiles laid, were full of patients in their rows of white beds with flowers on the nurses' tables. And the staff, gowned and gloved and looking as though their entire day's work had consisted of getting a wave and a manicure, were greeting Their Excellencies and the College Council at the hospital bungalow for tea."

The dedication was all Ida had hoped. Vellore did full justice to this biggest event in her history since the invasion of the great Tipu Sultan and the Mutiny of 1805. Bridges were freshly whitewashed, roads cleaned and spanned by leafy arches, natty policemen in shorts and red turbans stationed every few yards, even garlands and streamers decking the railroad station! There was not a child in town who could not point the way proudly to the Vellore Missionary Medical School Hospital, even though he could not pronounce the words.

From the platform where she sat with Their Excellencies, Ida looked out over the crowd of two thousand seated under the spacious canopy adorned with waving mango and plantain leaves: Englishmen, Americans, Europeans, Hindus in gorgeous scarfs and turbans, nationalists in rough khadi wearing the white Gandhi cap, Mohammedans in their long coats and flowing beards; and, best of all, in the section reserved for Indian women, at least a thousand of them sitting, looking like a flower garden in their rainbow saris, holding their heads with a new smiling pride in this institution so peculiarly their own.

Yet somehow, even after the buildings were opened and the crowds were streaming through, gazing at the airy, beautifully tiled rooms and verandahs, peering into the operating room with its great windows and spotless marble floors, lingering to gaze delightedly about the spacious waiting room with its carved stone pillars, its restful palms and ferns, it seemed unreal. Even then Ida saw it only in fragments, like the parts of a jigsaw puzzle laid out on a table but not yet put together. To make it become real, she knew what she must do: climb to a higher level of vision, see it from above in its entirety.

"This morning," the first Dr. John Scudder had written in

his diary on September 25, 1824, "I went out to view the size of Vellore. As it is situated at the base of a mountain, I thought I would ascend it. After half an hour's hard labor I had nearly reached the top of it when I came to a fortification which surrounds the peak of the mountain. The view is most charming. Vellore is an excellent place for missionary labor. It needs a dozen laborers."

Over a hundred years later his granddaughter stood in the same spot, panting from her swift climb, sweat pouring down her face. Lucky he had climbed the hill late in September rather than in March! So ill with malaria that he had been sent by the mission to the cooler climate of Bangalore, he would surely have succumbed before he reached the top. Then the last seven of his fourteen children, including her father, might never have been born, and she would not be keeping her tryst with him now, crying out to him silently across the century that his dream was being fulfilled.

A dozen laborers? There were a dozen dozen! Wiping the sweat from her eyes, she focused them on the cluster of new buildings filling the large walled space close to the foot of the hill, gleaming white, block upon block of them, crowned by their majestic clock tower: the administration building, Cole Dispensary, the children's hospital, Ewart Maternity and Gynecological Block, in the center lovely Northfield Chapel with its white dome and cross. It was to them that the eye turned now, unerringly, instead of to the old gray fort with its crumbling walls, its empty temple, its deep green moat with lotuses floating in its stagnant waters. Centuries ago Bommai Reddy the adventurer and Tipu the tyrant had come, stood here in this very spot, and gone. To show for their coming and going there were only a fort without a garrison and a temple without a god. Dr. John the healer had come also, he and his children—please God, to stay.

"Bravo!" a voice seemed to say in her ears. "Worth waiting a hundred years to see!" So vivid was the impression that Ida could actually feel him there beside her. Not even at the centenary nearly ten years ago, when Scudders from all over the world had come to Ranipet to lay the corner stone for the fine

238

new hospital they planned to build in his memory, had her grandfather seemed so vitally alive, so close.

It was still early in the morning, for she had started up the hill before sunrise. Now at last, seeing the new hospital gathered suddenly into the young sun's embrace, she was convinced of its reality. Watching, she saw a blue-bright spark kindled as a car emerged from the hospital gate far below and swung into the street. That would be the new ambulance starting out on Arni Roadside. She followed it with her mind's eye, through the maze of traffic, past Schell and the mission compound, toward the hills to the south and the Arni Road. As the team of doctors and nurses and pharmacists passed the 200-acre lot four miles from the town's center, they would see workmen pounding up the rocks at College Hill, see the new white walls of the college buildings rising.

Ida laughed aloud. Grandfather John's dream fulfilled?

"Good-by," she said silently, looking back once as she went hurrying downward. "Wait for me. I'll be back. You haven't seen anything yet!"

19

With the hospital finished, Ida could depart on her year of furlough without regret, even take time at its beginning for a leisurely vacation, at Gertrude Dodd's invitation, in Kashmir. But Gertrude's idea of a Kashmir vacation—a quiet sojourn on a houseboat drifting among cool lakes in the lee of purple mountains—was not Ida's. Mountains were not for gazing at but for climbing. Jubilantly Ida planned three months of hiking, climbing, camping, high on the rim of the world. Louisa Hart, who came from her medical station in Madanapalle to spend the first weeks with them in Kashmir, was a willing partner in these expeditions, True, they started in a houseboat, a craft named the *Valley Bell*, returned to it at intervals, ended in it.

They secured the services of the famous guide, Ali Goosani, noted for his colorful personality and picturesque speech. Almost beside himself with joy to discover such an eager accomplice in adventure, he found Ida the highest peaks to climb, the most inaccessible trails. On each new expedition Gertrude, who had an aversion to discomfort and was terrified of high places, grimly accompanied them. Where Idee went, she followed, not on foot—in spite of the immortal blackness of her

240

pompadour, she was now seventy years old—but either on pony back or in one of those fearfully swaying coolie-borne chairs known in that part of the country as dandies.

"Asthi, asthi! Careful, careful!" the coolies would chant shrilly as they approached an especially dangerous hazard, and Gertrude would close her eyes and clench her teeth, drawing her breath again only when she heard the approving "Shabash!" Once, traveling very high on a route which led over a snow bridge, they returned to find part of the bridge gone, leaving only a sliver of path. Looking down, Gertrude turned sick. Finally the coolies blindfolded her, and she went across between them, clutching their shoulders.

They were a curious-looking caravan. Every living necessity was included in the baggage piled on the little ponies' backs: tents, beds, food, cooking pots, bathtubs, hot-water bottles. The chamber vessels were hoisted conspicuously on the tent poles protruding from the packs. There were the inevitable samovars, with frequent stops for tea. Some of the food went along alive, including chickens. There was one hen that laid an egg every day. Ida took a fancy to her, made her a pet, and called her Bo Bo. She rode along with them uncaged, perched on top of the luggage.

There were other minor unpleasantnesses besides teetering on the edge of cliffs. While never complaining of them aloud, Gertrude took solace in confiding them cheerfully to her diary.

"April 28. Started on trip to Srinagar. Rain and hail-stones. . . .

"April 30. Followed towpath and got into mud over shoe.

"May 17. Went camping to Pahlgam. Slept in tents. Much ice and snow. Ida and Louisa walked, I went in *dandy*. Hundreds of flies.

"June 2. Great time getting ponies and coolies. Hot, no shade. Hundreds of flies in ceiling of our tent. Strawberries. Heavy wind, rain and thunder. 1000 flies in the roof of tent.

"June 9. Up early to go up the Valley of the Glaciers. Hard walk, first on stones and then snow. Louisa gave out. There was a half-hollowed trunk of tree fifteen ft. long. Ida laid her there and covered her up, coolies made a fire in the other end.

"June 13. Dandy men gave plenty trouble. . . . Many great

cracks and crevasses in snow and ice. All afternoon in snow, slush, mud, and water.

"July 2. Monday. Started off before 7 A.M. Heavy pull of 4,000 ft. ascent in four miles. I walked most of way. Climbed and climbed. Wonderful lemon-colored columbine, found a blue poppy at the top!

"July 7. Started off very early. Three miles up hill on snow. I took a pony, was so frightened on it. Old pony man, *malidu,* led me. Raining hard when we pitched tents. Rained so hard we shut off our bathroom and let the dandy and pony men sleep there.

"July 8. Started off on pony down snowy ice, crossed streams. Went right from ice to steep zigzags. On top a most beautiful grassy slope with white birches. Descent all zigzags but through lovely columbine. Bearer took us down by river to camp in horrid place. Grapefruit for dinner.

"July 10. Rained in torrents when we got to top of our ascent. Everything wet but our bedclothes, so we got into bed.

"July 13. Climbed all day. Pitched camp for last time."

"The most perfect vacation," pronounced Ida happily. "The most wonderful rest!"

She had traveled 500 miles on foot, much of it at forty-five degree angles. Her eyes shone with the wonders of purple mountains and blue glaciers and the roses of Shalimar and the flashing magic of the silver-white paradise flycatcher.

She kept Bo Bo with her to the end, then reluctantly surrendered her to Ali. "Promise you won't eat her," she begged. "Keep her for me." Ali promised vehemently by Allah and several non-Moslem deities.

"That hen," the wily fellow sent word to her long afterward, "I swear I kept it by me until it died!" Which probably occurred, Ida and Gertrude agreed, the minute their backs were turned.

Since Ida had spent three months of her furlough in Kashmir, this time her trek through Europe was strictly business. She spent a month studying in Vienna, the Mecca for doctors, at-

242

tending lectures in surgery and gynecology, and observing operations; spent some days in Prague, Berlin, Dresden, and Paris, where she was inspired by what was being done for the sick and suffering. The sight of villages provided with well-equipped hospitals, doctors, and nurses all over the Western world ignited her imagination like sparks in tinder. She was glad when October came and it was time to start campaigning. Now that buildings were assured, her sights were on at least a half-million dollars for endowment.

She had intended to spend a month in Britain helping the committee there in its campaign for funds, but a cable summoned her home to America. Signing an answering cable with their usual "Scuddodd," she and Gertrude joyfully set sail.

Mrs. Peabody was as indefatigable as ever, and Ida found a capable new ally in Hilda Olson, treasurer of the Vellore board, short, stoutish, and extremely efficient. In addition to her mathematical genius, Miss Olson possessed another surprising asset. Trained in finances by her father, she was a wizard at investments.

"Raise what you can for endowment," she told Ida, "and I'll at least double it for you." Of course neither of them realized that a long and deep depression was just around the turn of the decade.

Ida prepared for her campaign, as usual, by bringing her wardrobe up to date. Skirts had gone up and waistlines down in the last five years. She had her own technique of buying— not that she thought of it as a technique. It was merely her natural way of doing things. She would go into a store, smile sweetly at a clerk, and say, "I'm looking for a dark dress that I can wear on a platform. I do a great deal of speaking, and I want something nice but not conspicuous, so that what I wear will not distract attention from what I say. Now I'm sure *you* will find me just what I want." Whereupon the clerk, both charmed and flattered, would probably call the head of the department. Other salesgirls would flock around with friendly advice. Then, while trying on dresses, Ida would tell them all about Vellore. She would captivate them as she did her audiences. Where was she going to be speaking? Could they come and hear her? She would leave the store not only with the right dress but with several new friends and an increased audience potential.

The half-million dollars did not come. Main Street was more interested at the moment in providing a radio and a washing machine for every home in America than a doctor or nurse for every village of India. Ida found the most encouraging response among college girls with vision but little money, and among young business women who, having recently been born into independence themselves, were healthily concerned about the birth pangs of their sisters around the world.

It was a relief to get back to India and to the simpler business of building a college.

Her welcome left nothing to be desired. The students had even composed a song to the tune of "Solomon Levi":

"Her name is Dr. Scudder, and she travels far and wide,
And everyone who meets her gladly rallies to her side.
She talks with kings and presidents, and sways the hearts of
    men;
But Vellore sends her evidence that brings her back again.
O Dr. Scudder, joyfully we sing!
Dear Dr. Scudder, loud our praises ring!
We greet you on this gala day, and ask you not to roam,
But stay to chase our blues away and make yourself at home!"

Before leaving on furlough the year before, Ida had performed an operation on an Indian friend, wife of Vellore's Municipal Chairman, in the hope that she might have a child. Scarcely had she got inside the door when the family arrived bearing a big welcoming chair and many garlands. Seating her in the chair, the parents proudly presented to her a pillow cradling the new lord and heir.

"This is your baby," they informed her joyfully. That night, for the first time in years, Ida remembered Burchfield Milliken, and wept.

She arrived home in time for the Diamond Jubilee of the Arcot Mission held in January, 1930. Christians by the thousands came from near and far villages, arrayed in their best clothes. And among them came the whole Scudder clan. Ida enjoyed this reunion to the full. There were Scudders all over the place: Dr. Lew and his son Galen; her brother Harry, red hair a rusty gray, hearing a bit impaired, but still urging people gaily to "Try my cigarettes" as he extended his box of extra strong peppermints; his faithful wife Margaret; Walter and Nell, proud in their son, Dr. John IV and his wife Dorothy, newly come as missionaries. John played the part of his great-grandfather in the big Jubilee pageant.

But it was to her cousin Dixie, Uncle Jared's daughter, that Ida's eyes most often turned, a Dixie old now but happier than in her whole life before. For at last, just two years before her retirement in 1928, she had been given permission and equipment to fulfill her long desire. Accompanied by only one Bible woman and living in a tent, she had gone touring through the villages, staying in each camp three or four weeks, working among the women, teaching them such simple skills as sewing, cleanliness, nutritious feeding of their families. Looking at Dixie, Ida felt a new peace and well-being. For she also knew what it was to be possessed by a dream.

After the Jubilee she plunged abruptly into the familiar but always exciting routine: classes, dispensaries, rounds of the hospital, operations, Roadsides. There were mobile clinics now operating on four roads each week, and soon after Ida's return a fifth was opened.

The first day of a new Roadside was always one of excitement and uncertainty, and this was no exception. Would people come in response to the circulated invitation? Would they accept treatment? How long would it take to arouse trust and confidence? As the ambulance swung along the new dusty road outside Vellore, Ida found herself asking all these questions. But if she could have looked ahead to the first stopping place, she would have seen even more of excitement and uncertainty.

A great banyan, symbol of Mother India herself, stretched its gaunt arms to shelter the unusual crowd, even managing to include within a fringe of shade a little knot of leprosy victims huddled some distance from the rest.

It was the same sort of group that waited, some all night,

many half the day, at a score of similar stations within a radius of fifty miles. They wore the same clothes: the men ragged dhotis or loin cloths, the women faded saris, the children scraps of tunics coming halfway to the knees or, more often, nothing at all but an amulet about the waist. Their bare feet and hands and arms were hardened to the same leatherlike texture, hung with the same cheap jewelry; their teeth stained with the same lime and betel nut. They had the same ailments: abscesses, sore eyes, running ears, cataracts, worms, dysentery, fever, tuberculosis, leprosy, syphilis. Some had three or four. But there was one difference. These patients had less hope in their eyes. Only one, a villager named Abbai, was broadly smiling.

"This way it is said they will come," said one of the men in the little knot sitting apart. "I will believe when I see."

"A stranger came telling it in our village," said a second, a young man with fever in his eyes. "*Onnu, rendu, mundru*—yes, three days ago. 'A white *vaithyan* will come,' he said. 'You are to bring a half-anna and a bottle.' "

"A *female* white *vaithyan*," scoffed a third. "I also believe when I see."

Abbai swaggered confidently among the little group of leprosy victims. "They will come. You will see." The information he had been withholding spilled out triumphantly. He had been going to another tree like this where a white *vaithyan* came. Each week he had been going for as many moons as he could count on both hands. Twenty miles he had walked from his village to get the *oosie,* the magic needle which stung the flesh and drove the sickness from his body. Now he could come each week to this tree, which was only ten miles from his home.

The three pairs of eyes were curious, interested, skeptical. A needle which stung the arm like a snake's bite? He had heard, said the first man, that the sickness would be cured if one let a cobra bite him. He had heard also of a man who had let himself be bitten, had roused the cobra to bite twice, but an hour later he had died.

Ayoh, he would like to try this needle, said the second, the one with the fever in his eyes. If he could only get well enough to cultivate his little plot of land again, to help feed his wife and four children!

The third held up an unshapely hand, fingers stiffened and

curled at the ends into the shape of a claw. *Chi!* Could the needle give a man a new hand, so that once again he could pick up tools, close his fingers about a plow or a sickle? Could it give him a new face, a new nose, so people would no longer look away from him in revulsion? Could it—?

There was a rumbling up the road, a cloud of red dust, then a flashing of sunlight on bright blue and silver. The crowd stared, speechless. They had seen buses before, lorries, but never anything like this. It rolled smoothly into the shade beneath the tree. People poured out of it. At first they did nothing but stand in a half circle with heads down while one of them talked in Tamil.

"They always do that first," whispered Abbai. "They're talking to their God, asking him to help them make us well."

Then many things happened at once. A long flat piece of metal was pulled out of a slot under the car and fastened on at one side like a shelf. Tables appeared under the tree. There was not only one white *vaithyan,* but two—one big and dark, the other shorter with eyes the color of the sky and strange hair like soft cobwebs. All the rest of the people were dark-skinned like themselves. The *vaithyan* with the blue eyes could not speak Tamil very well. When she wanted one woman to stand up, she said *"Utkaringal!* Sit down!" But they did not mind that. It made them laugh among themselves, feeling more at ease. Soon they were standing in long lines, taking their turns at kneeling beside one of the smiling dark-skinned young women in the clean blue-and-white saris, telling her all about their troubles. *Vaithyans* too these young women must be and so much like themselves that they had no fear but did just what they were told to do. Some were given treatment beside the shelf. Others took their small chits to the side of the big vehicle and held up their bottles, many of them cracked and broken, for the magic potions, listened solemnly while the directions were given over and over, wagging their heads.

"Illai! No. Just the powder inside must be eaten, not the paper...."

"One swallow each day, *one only...."*

"Bathe the child first, then rub this on every night for three nights—*mundru,* three—count them so on your fingers. Then on the fourth morning...."

It was the white *vaithyan* with the blue eyes who came to Abbai and his little group. Smiling, Ida told them in her inexpert Tamil about the *oosie,* which would help their sickness, but not all at once. Next week they must come also, and the next, and the next. Patient they must be. Now then—she smiled again, brightly—who would be first?

They remained silent, eying the needle with wariness, if not hostility.

Ida's heart sank. She knew from experience that it might take weeks to win their confidence. Then with immeasurable relief she recognized the familiar figure as it stepped confidently forward. "Abbai!" she greeted him thankfully. *"San thosham,* happiness!"

Abbai had reached the more advanced stage of treatment for leprosy. It took all her strength to push the needle with its heavy dose of chaulmoogra oil finger-deep into the quivering flesh. (If only the whole arm could be for the moment as insensitive as the poor hands and feet!) The pain must be terrific. She could feel him tremble as he suppressed a groan, but he did not flinch.

"See," he told the others with cool disdain. "It is nothing. Look at me."

It was easy then. They all pushed forward begging, *"Oosie! Oosie!"* Only to the one who was most eager, the one with the wife and four children and the fever in his eyes, did she have to refuse it. His sickness had reached the stage where the injection would only have added fuel to the fire.

"I will give you another kind of medicine now," she said gently. "Later you shall have the *oosie*. If you will only come again . . ."

It had been a good day, this one in 1930 when Ida and Jessie Findlay christened the brand-new ambulance and opened the fifth Roadside. The Bronson-Porter Highway they called it, after two of Vellore's most generous donors in New Haven, who had made the ambulance possible. The new car ran so smoothly and was so wonderfully equipped with boxes and cupboard shelves and sliding tables, even with running water to scrub with just by turning a tap beneath the body, that it was hard to remember the old days of the chugging "devil wagon" and its successor, the humble Model T.

But Ida did remember. That night, tossing wakefully from sheer weariness, she traveled the old Roadsides again and again, saw the lines upon lines of waiting crowds, with here and there a familiar figure . . . the woman who wouldn't let the huge tumor be removed from the back of her neck because she used it for a pillow, the shy little girl with the faded crumpled flowers who wanted a card for her sick brother. *Pudum, pudum*—please, *pudum!*

"I lifted and carried him a little way, but he is older than I and I couldn't bring him so many miles. Please give me a card for him, for he may die."

Ida had reached into her bag and pulled out a doll with a flame-colored dress. "See! Would he like this better?"

"Oh, *amma*, yes! Now he will get well, he will get well!"

But he did not get well. Next week the little girl had been there again, this time with a bunch of fresh flowers in one hand, the doll in the other. "Your brother?" "Oh, he died, *ammal*, but the doll he pressed close to his cheek and was so happy!"

Again she saw the little lad suffering from leprosy who had come weekly for a long time from his distant village. So happy he had always been and smiling, until one day he had come with great tears in his eyes, leading a small frightened child by the hand.

"*Etho paru*, look, Dr. *Ammal!* I have brought my little brother. He—he has *it*, too!"

But among all her memories she most often saw the woman leading the three men across the fields. Years ago it had been, in the beginnings of Roadside, yet she saw it as if it had been yesterday, and relived it.

They had finished the work of the day, the car just ready to start home, when she saw them coming. Impatiently she watched, for they came so slowly, picking their way along the hard ridges bordering the brimming rice fields. It was not until they nearly reached the road that she knew the three men were blind.

Reaching it, they sat down exhausted, for they had been walking all night to get there in time. But their faces were radiant.

Someone had come to their village telling of a doctor who came in a motor car and could give them their sight.

"And we're not too late!" they cried joyfully, one of the men breaking into a chuckle. "We're in time!"

Eagerly Ida examined the three pairs of eyes, hoping ... but there was no hope. They were not in time. All three were hopelessly blind. Two had had smallpox, the third fever. To cure it his wife had sought the temple priest, who had sent her home to get an offering for the god. She had returned bringing all she had, her small *chemby*, brass bowl. "Go home." The priest had given well-meaning but ignorant counsel. "Put ground glass, cayenne pepper, and oil into your husband's eyes, and he will become conscious." He *had* become conscious, terribly, painfully so.

Even now, years later, Ida could feel the coldness of her disappointment.

"Are you sure, *ammal*, you can do nothing? We have very little money, we are poor, but we will give all we have. Only restore to us our sight!"

Oh, for the hands which had opened the eyes of one blind Bar Timaeus!

"I'm sorry." She murmured the words now in her half-sleep. "I can do nothing."

"Nothing." Over the hills, over the years, their cry came echoing back. "We came so far, but she can do nothing ... nothing ... nothing...."

She had been feeling happy today, well satisfied, because now they had five Roadsides instead of four. Five? They were not enough. Ten would not be enough. There were still hundreds of villages within reach of Vellore that were untouched by medical help. There was so much to do and so little time to do it! Already she was nearly sixty years old, with a college to build, an endowment to raise, a hundred million women to be provided with nurses and doctors. Heaven forgive her for feeling satisfied!

All night she kept turning restlessly, half wakeful, half dreaming, as again and again she saw them coming, the woman and the three blind men, slowly, across the fields.

20

By 1930 the fires of nationalism, banked by defeat and depression in the late twenties, were sweeping India with new violence. The hope for dominion status, which had followed the accession of a Labor government in Britain, was swiftly quelled when Tories and Liberals united in opposing the Labor premier's liberal India policy. Now for the first time Gandhi declared himself in favor of complete independence. He encouraged the Congress Party to affirm a bold declaration of independence and secession from the empire. War was declared, but it was to be fought on his terms and with his weapons of *Satyagraha*.

He wrote a letter to the viceroy, denouncing British rule yet affirming his good will toward every Englishman. He listed various evils of the colonial regime, especially such abuses as the salt tax, which cost the peasant three days' income a year, and plainly announced what his program would be if these evils were not removed. He received no reply. On March 12, 1930, Gandhi started his famous Salt March, a twenty-four day trek of 241 miles to the sea, where he picked up a handful of salt left by the waves, thus breaking the British law which forbade the possession of salt not purchased from the government—a gesture as dramatic as the Boston Tea Party.

It was the signal for mass civil disobedience. Hundreds began making salt and purposely breaking other laws deemed unjust. Indian legislators resigned in boycott of the government. Hosts of leaders, including Gandhi, were arrested. In one month the viceroy filled the jails with 60,000 offenders. It was an angry but peaceful revolution. Knowing that Gandhi would cancel the movement if violence ensued, most participants remained nonviolent in spite of arrests, blows from steel-shod lathis and rifle butts, and savage beatings.

Returning from furlough in August of 1931, Treva Marshall had visions of scenes of rioting she had seen pictured on the screen in the United States, with cables stretched across railroad tracks and everybody dressed in militant *khadi*. True, there were white Gandhi caps in profusion, and riding in her compartment from Bombay to Madras were two *khadi*-clad nationalists, courteous and educated gentlemen, fresh from a three-month term in prison. But she saw no violence. In the Vellore bazaars there were peaceful picketings of the cloth shops, and the foreigners on the hospital staff, Americans as well as British, were sensitive to a certain reserve in the manner of some of their Indian colleagues.

Deeply sympathetic with the desire of awakening people for independence, yet bound with strong ties to the British constituency of both Vellore and Madras, Dr. Ida might have had a serious problem had she not been too busy to become really concerned about it. In warning her staff to take care that by neither speech nor action they let themselves be misunderstood, she remarked a bit humorously, "I heard lately that even *I* am being watched!" To which her colleague Dr. Jessie Findlay, always an admirer, burst out impulsively, "Who could help it?"

Treva Marshall found other changes in Vellore indicative not only of the awakening of India but of Dr. Ida's influence in bringing it to pass. One of these changes was in the Vellore Ladies' Recreation Club, an organization which Ida had been instrumental in starting in response to a community need that the Social Service Center, ministering to uneducated women, many of them in the underprivileged groups, could not possibly fill.

"When we stopped at the Club," Treva wrote home excitedly,

252

"I gasped at the contrast. Five years ago we worked so hard to get it started! Five or ten women would come once a week but felt they were being criticized by the more orthodox for coming. Now twenty to forty women come three times a week. The spirit of sportsmanship is wonderful and the friendliness between Hindu and Mohammedan and various castes is remarkable."

The story of the Vellore Ladies' Recreation Club is the story of Indian womanhood's awakening; the story, for example, of Mrs. Pankajam Venketachari, wife of a Brahmin lawyer. In a day when it was considered the Indian woman's place to walk behind her husband in the street, she boldly acquired other ideas.

"You don't see me walking behind my husband," she was heard to remark decisively. "I walk right beside him. I'm an emancipated woman."

A generation later, when her country also had become free, this same Brahmin woman, reared to a life of seclusion and forbidden by tradition even to accept a drop of water from one of lower caste, was to become chairman of the Social Welfare Board for all North Arcot District, superintending workers in ten different centers and driving into villages every day in her jeep to promote health and social welfare among women, many of them outcastes!

Ida's concern was always for the complete liberation of India's women, spirit as well as mind and body. She had begun promoting the idea of the Ladies' Recreation Club back in the early twenties.

"These Hindu and Mohammedan women—if we could only get them together to do things with us, like playing games! Think what it would do for them, get them out of their stuffy courtyards, give them healthy exercise, get them acquainted with us and with each other. Who knows? It might work miracles!"

How Annie Hancock's face would have shone at the idea! However, Annie's brave plans for the social betterment of the women of Vellore had found a worthy champion in her successor, Lavina Honegger, long Ida's intimate friend and her companion in the red-flannel petticoat episode. Widowed soon after her arrival in India as a missionary, Lavina had spent some years teaching in Ranipet. Now, transferred to Vellore to continue her teaching and the social service work begun by Annie Hancock, she welcomed the idea of a women's recreation club with all her gay enthusiasm.

They got it started finally, Ida and Lavina and Gertrude and Treva and a few other Christian and Hindu women with social vision.

The games played were badminton, ping-pong, and caroms. The first women who braved tradition to come had never played games before, and their efforts were pitifully childish. At home they had servants to do their housework, tailors their sewing. They cheated at the games and got into all sorts of quarreling. Someone's feelings would inevitably get hurt, and the sessions would end in bickerings and tears. Often one of the women went home in a pet. But Ida and her colleagues persisted. The women learned to fold bandages, knit, even make speeches, at first written by their husbands and delivered in very soft voices, but as time passed with increasing originality and confidence.

It was a time of dramatic change for Indian women. All over the country miracles were taking place. A thousand years of seclusion, ignorance, suppression, inferiority were being bridged in a single decade. In April, 1930, the Sarda Act, prohibiting child marriage, went into force, implementing one of Gandhi's strong principles of reform, first of a long succession of legislative acts designed to effect the emancipation of women. Educated Hindu women were crying out against the system of devadasis—temple dancing girls—and forming organizations for its reform; agitating for juvenile courts; pleading for the relief of women and children in industrial situations. An act of 1922 had raised the minimum age of employment in factories to twelve and prohibited the employment of children under fifteen for more than six hours a day.

And women were becoming increasingly active in politics. An India Women's Association, with over forty branches of more than 2,000 members, had long been working for women's suffrage, and, in the second election for the Legislative Councils and the Legislative Assembly in 1924, women had voted for the first time. Madras Presidency had been first to confer the suffrage on its women. Women were becoming followers of

Mahatma Gandhi by the thousands and participating in the noncooperation movement. Mrs. Gandhi, the poet Mrs. Sarojini Naidu, the wife and sisters of Jawaharlal Nehru—all were prominent in the nationalist movement, inviting arrest by breaking unjust laws, going to prison with their men to help win their country's independence.

Such miracles, thanks to Ida and others like her, were taking place also in Vellore. Take, for example, the story of Mrs. V. T. Rangaswamy Iyengar, who was the wife of a strict Brahmin lawyer and was considered in after years the founder of the Vellore Ladies' Recreation Club. For Treva Marshall, who happened to take part in all the incidents, her story became a drama —a miracle play—in three acts.

The first act of the drama took place in 1923, soon after Treva's arrival in India. She was invited, with Ida and Mrs. Cornelius, the pastor's wife, to Mrs. Rangaswamy's home for a party to celebrate the first birthday of Padmini, the young daughter of the household. There were several Brahmin women present, also Hindus of other castes. As the guests arrived, all in their best afternoon dresses or gay saris, they were ushered into the front room of the house and seated on a beautiful Oriental rug, to be entertained by dancers, a woman playing on the *veena,* and other skilled performers.

Treva was charmed, not only with the baby Padmini but also with her two older brothers, Chamalu, a winsome boy of six, and Krishnamurthi, nicknamed "Blue" because someone, seeing the child shivering on a chilly day, had once remarked, "Poor little fellow, he is blue with cold!" Having delivered all three of the babies, Ida was almost as proud of them as their mother.

When it came time for tea to be served, a delicious meal including *laddus,* coffee, bananas, and *jelebes,* an Indian sweet, the Brahmin women were fed indoors on the rug, the non-Brahmin Hindus were seated on the floor at one side of the porch, and the three Christians were seated in a swing at the other end of the porch, pointedly segregated from both groups.

Treva was hotly indignant. "I say, what do they mean," she protested to her two companions, "putting us away off here by ourselves! Don't they think we're good enough to eat with them?"

255

Ida patted her arm soothingly. "My dear, if you could only know what a wonderful thing this is!" Her voice was warm with enthusiasm. "It's the first time this high-caste woman has ever fed non-Brahmins in her home. This is a wonderful step forward!"

The second act of the drama took place about five years later, when Treva and several others of the college staff, including Ida, were again invited to a tea in the lawyer's home—a finer house this time, since Mr. Rangaswamy was becoming one of the leading townsmen of his profession. There was a butler with white gloves to serve the guests, a beautiful silver tea service.

"Have you noticed?" demanded Ida of Treva in an excited whisper. "Mrs. Rangaswamy has invited not only Christians and other Hindus. See that woman over there? She was a Brahmin once, yes, but now she is married to a Moslem!"

Treva looked doubtful. "But," she objected, "Mr. and Mrs. Rangaswamy are still not eating with us."

"My dear," Ida was jubilant, "what do you expect? Two thousand years of tradition to be overthrown in five? What you're seeing today is revolution!"

The third act took place in the early 1930s. An International Fellowship had been organized in Vellore, meeting in different homes. After inviting the group to meet one day at her house, Mrs. Rangaswamy encountered difficulties. She asked Treva to come and give her advice.

"Miss Marshall," she said in distress, "what shall I do? I have invited the group to come, and it is our Lord Krishna's birthday, one of our Hindu holy days, when we're supposed to fast all day. And I've invited the Fellowship!"

"Well," suggested Treva helpfully, "why not do what you did when you invited some of us before? Serve us but don't eat with us."

Mrs. Rangaswamy nodded thoughtfully. "We will manage."

On the appointed day the guests arrived at the Fellowship meeting, Christians, Hindus, Moslems, men and women, all mingling in the utmost friendliness and equality. When the time came for refreshments, Mr. and Mrs. Rangaswamy sat down with their guests and ate with them.

"But—" Puzzled, Treva approached her hostess after the meal was finished. "I thought you said—"

"Oh," explained Mrs. Rangaswamy serenely, "the horoscope, it seems, was not clear. We discovered that it might not be Krishna's birthday, after all. His birthday we shall celebrate the next day instead."

On the way home Ida was as joyfully triumphant as Treva had ever seen her. "My dear, did you see?" She spoke with more awe than jubilation. "We all sat down together, Brahmins, non-caste Hindus, Moslems, Christians. Mr. and Mrs. Rangaswamy sat down with us, too, and—*they ate with us*. You have seen a miracle take place."

There were other scenes of the drama to be enacted later: when the young son Blue returned from California after studying aeronautics, so Americanized that his mother gave up in good-natured despair ("Oh, go over and see Miss Marshall or Dr. Scudder, they can understand you!"); when on the club's twenty-fifth anniversary Mrs. Rangaswamy returned from Madras where she had become a leader in activities for social uplift, accompanied by her daughter Padmini, now a practicing lawyer of the Madras High Court, to accept the club's homage as its founder and first secretary.

Of course the miracle might have happened without Dr. Ida and the Ladies' Recreation Club. The time was ripe for such miracles in India. So might independence have happened—in time—without Gandhi.

21

They had come to Kodaikanal in the mountains to spend Christmas of 1931 at Hill Top: Gertrude Dodd, Ida, her niece Dr. Ida B. Scudder, newly come from America as a missionary, and Dr. Anna Degenring. Hill Top was heavenly in December, the air cold and clear as frosted wine, the gardens ablaze with poinsettias, all the hills Christmas-trimmed with pine and spruce and flaming red rhododendrons. There was even a plant that looked like holly, with bright yellow berries.

The arrival a few months ago of her niece, Ida B., her brother Lewis's daughter, now a full-fledged doctor, was the realization of one of Ida's fondest hopes. Her namesake, dear to her as a daughter, not only here beside her but dedicated to the same life purpose! The shy child had grown into a poised and mature woman, eyes alert with a lively curiosity and an intense interest in everything around her. They had always had much in common, speaking the same language from the early days at the Nebraska farm and Shelter Island. They felt the same way about flowers and dogs and sunsets and cold spray and stars and being on a high hill with the wind in their faces. Now, after sitting up together all night by the beds of patients, and working side by side all day on Roadside, dressing foul abscesses and soothing dirty itching bodies and leprous flesh, Ida knew to her intense satisfaction that they felt the same way about people.

Ida B. had arrived at Hill Top in May, after a broiling journey that had made her sure she was going to hate India. She would never forget the ride up the ghat, seeing the desert cactus give way to tall savannah grass, to coffee plants and spreading plantains, to tropical jungles with tall trees cranning their necks out of a sheer abyss, finally to the unexpected paradise of wood violets, begonias, ferns, and purple orchids; feeling the scalding heat give way to blessed coolness, so that at five thousand feet she actually had to don a sweater. No wonder Kodaikanal, with its blue lake, its fragrance of roses and eucalyptus, had seemed like heaven!

She had begun her year's study in language school at the hill station only to be recalled in August to take the place of Dr. Pauline Jeffery in the Eye, Ear, Nose, and Throat department, when Pauline was sent home early on furlough because of illness. Later in the year she had been put in charge of medicine while Dr. Flora Innes was away on leave—a frustrating task because of her lack of experience and one which might well have caused her a mental depression had she not once a week enjoyed the diversion of horseback riding. So already, though only seven months in India, she had experienced more of its beauty and ugliness than some foreigners of many years' residence. As a consequence of the language school curtailment, her Tamil, practical rather than academic, was to acquire a colloquial pungency that endeared her to the humble villagers of dispensary and Roadside. The name Ida B. was also a happy coincidence, insuring her popularity with Mohammedan patients, who, knowing the word "Bee" as a suffix denoting respect to a woman, believed it to be an honorary title.

Delighted at the prospect of spending her first Christmas at Hill Top, even though it meant bundling in winter suits and sweaters and huddling about the fireplaces, Ida B. was even more disappointed than the others when a telegram came saying that important guests were arriving on Christmas Day from America.

"No use," sighed Ida. "We have to go back to Vellore."

Crowding the entire holiday party into the Ford, they started back down the mountain in a pouring rain. When they finally arrived at the railroad station at Kodai Road, Ida took a train for Madras to meet her guests, Gertrude another to Vellore to prepare the bungalow household for their entertainment. Deggie, Ida B., the dogs, and Rajamanickam, the driver, continued on their way by car. The rain turned to cloudbursts; the road became impassable. The car was forced to detour by way of Erode, where Deggie and Ida B. decided to spend the night in a travelers' bungalow. Between leaking roofs and a more than normal population of bedbugs, they got little sleep.

At midnight Deggie murmured, "Ida B."

"Eh?" grunted her roommate sleepily.

"Merry Christmas!"

In the morning, with the rain still pouring, they sang Christmas carols to raise their morale as they plowed and skidded to Vellore. Arriving just at dinnertime, they found the distinguished guests waiting, a faultlessly appointed table set for a several-course dinner, and Ida and Gertrude dressed in the height of fashion.

Bernard Rottschaefer looked more amazed than disapproving. "But—that's impossible! The fixtures are in. To change the plans now would cost—"

"No matter what it costs, they must be changed. And nothing, you know, is really impossible. Come now, Ben," she smiled suddenly, "You can see as well as I what a waste it would be—taking all the corners which have the best view in the whole building," she spread her arms to embrace the rough-scarped dome of College Hill etched against an ineffable sky—"and using them for bathrooms!"

The plans were changed, the fixtures removed, the carefully laid masonry torn out. The corner rooms of the new students' hostel were changed into sleeping porches. Expensive and unnecessary? Mr. Rottschaefer the builder and Mr. Dann the architect thought so, but not Ida. A cheap enough price to pay for giving her beloved students the glory of ten thousand sunrises!

Slowly the college of her dreams took shape, became a long graceful quadrangle of stone buildings rimmed by arched verandahs; became twin white domes, Indian as the Taj, facing each other across a sunken garden with a round lily pool; became sleeping quarters, lounges, classrooms, laboratories, dining room, assembly hall, equipped with all the beauty and utility which the art of one civilization and the science of another had to offer.

The skill of an expert horticulturist plus her own artistry created patterns of beauty which could become fully apparent only to future generations. The two mahogany trees planted on either side of the chapel would become twin replicas of its dome. The sunken garden was to be a symphony in blue and white: big white zinnias, borders of sweet alyssum, white cosmos, Queen Anne's lace, Duranta, frangipani; blue salvia, anchusa, torenia; the pillars alternating white Antigonon and bluebells. There would be always color, always fragrance.

When the buildings were nearly finished, Ida moved her household from the hospital compound to the principal's bungalow at College Hill, taking her two servants, Kanakaroyan and David, almost as much a part of her family as Ida B. and Gertrude. With her also went Lady Grenfell, her beautiful and beloved Labrador retriever.

Ida was not the only one to rejoice over the changes. Dell Houghton, since 1909 superintendent of the nursing school, and her assistant, Vera Pitman, could now move their forty-five nursing students from their crowded quarters in the peanut godown into Rachel Fillebrown, the beautiful nursing home built on the town hospital compound as a bride's wedding present. Jealous for her beloved charges and intensely proud of them, Dell had smarted for years—and justifiably—at the preferential treatment accorded Ida's precious medical students. Now, at last, her nursing school could come into its own.

Lord Willingdon, now viceroy, had promised to open the new buildings on his anticipated trip south in August, 1932, but to Ida's intense disappointment the trip was canceled. There were other disappointments. Due to the world-wide depression, friends could not come from the United States, including the William Bancroft Hills, donors of the lovely Weyerhauser Chapel. But the bitterest disappointment of all came when the American Council wrote saying it would be impossible to finance the Bachelor of Medicine course this year, and for the present they must continue as a Licensed Medical Practitioner

261

school. The raising of the medical school to college standard with university affiliation, which permitted the granting of degrees instead of merely certificates, must again be postponed.

In July the student body of 105 poured into the spacious rooms of the new hostel at the south end of the long stone quadrangle bearing its plaque in loving memory of Laura Spelman Rockefeller. In August the new chapel in the heart of the quadrangle was dedicated before being put to daily use.

It was a perfect Sunday evening. As the guests filed through the sunken garden with its green ferns and flashing fountain, into the lovely octagonal building of gray stone, they were struck silent with its beauty.

"As we entered," wrote one of them, "the cool spaciousness of the grained marble floor, unmarred by benches or chairs, the simple platform with its swinging brass-pierced Indian lamp, the dignity of the rough stone pillars and walls, and the windows framing the blue hills outside, gave an instant impression of reverent beauty and peace.

"The guests seated themselves in the low balconies against the wall, and presently the students entered in perfect silence, each wearing a snowy sari, and seated themselves on small mats, completely filling the central space save for a cross-shaped aisle. Suddenly from without came strains of music, growing louder and more triumphant until in a burst of gladness the white-robed choir entered, singing 'Worship the Lord in the Beauty of Holiness.' "

There would be more jubilant moments later: the formal opening of the college buildings on December 2, 1932, by Governor George Stanley and Lady Beatrix, the turning of the silver key, the planting of blue and white lilies in the pool, the joining of old and new students in joyous singing of "The Silver and the Blue," the triumphant burst of fireworks. But for Ida they would all be anticlimax. *This* was her high moment, perhaps the highest in all her life, as she sat here in the center of her dream's fulfillment, listening to the story of Solomon and his temple, and watched the high openings beneath the dome change from sunset crimson to purple, to mauve, to pale violet like the surrounding hills, to a deep blue-black studded with stars.

262

Sir George made one mistake when he delivered the address at the opening. He referred to the new achievement at College Hill as the "final buildings." How wrong he was!

Gertrude Dodd, even more thrifty and systematic than she was wealthy, ran both bursar's office and principal's bungalow with a soft-gloved but iron hand. "Oh, we could be so much more efficient," someone was always heard sighing, "if Miss Dodd didn't make us cut down! She says it isn't in the budget!"

As rigid with her own expenditures as with those of the college, she seldom threw anything away. She was generous only where the needs of others were concerned. "Even the abdominal sponges," marveled Ebbie, looking back over the years, "were Miss Dodd's gifts!"

But occasionally she forgot her frugality. Sometimes she indulged in a veritable purge of possessions. On one such occasion, when she had filled a number of wastebaskets with half the things she owned, she returned an hour later to find Ida and her niece Ida B. down on their knees picking things over and salvaging. "Get out of there!" she ordered gruffly.

When she went home with Ida on furlough in 1934, she gave away almost all her dresses. When the travelers got ready to leave, all the staff was lined up to say good-by, every one of them, regardless of size, wearing one of Miss Dodd's dresses.

As usual, the two women spent the vacation part of their furlough in travel: Arabia, Palestine, Europe. At Bahrein, while visiting a Scudder cousin, Beth, Ida was persuaded to perform several operations on wealthy Mohammedan women. Delighted with the idea of making a couple of thousand dollars for her hospital and college, she stayed on for three weeks, operating every day. Again, while visiting a hospital in Tiberias on the Sea of Galilee, she was drafted to operate on a girl with a bad intestinal obstruction—and kept on operating. On a trip to the headwaters of the Jordan, she found a woman suffering from the worst case of vaginal fistula she had ever seen. Horrified, she brought the patient back to Tiberias and spent four hours repairing a V.V.F. before going on to Nazareth and Mount Carmel.

It was for this operation—repairing vesicovaginal fistula—that Ida had for years been acquiring fame. A common condition among her woman patients, victims of barbers' wives' obstetrics, it had challenged all her medical skill and imagination. An article written on the subject for a leading medical journal had brought her patients from all over India and the Eastern Hemisphere. One Catholic nun had come to her from Europe. In a report made this same year of 1934 to the American College of Surgeons she claimed to have performed over a thousand of these operations. It was her infinite care and patience, not brilliance as a surgeon, that gave her such skill in this most delicate piece of surgery. The underlined words in a few paragraphs written in a notebook, briefly outlining the procedure for her students, gave the secret of her success.

"... locate *most carefully* the fistula. Large ones are most easy. Outline it *most carefully* with a sharp knife. Remove the scar tissue *most gently*. Locate *very carefully* the bladder tissue. Make a *most careful* dissection between the bladder mucous membrane and do not injure the m.m. ..."

Most carefully ... very carefully ... most gently.... The words were a dozen times repeated, and always underlined.

She used a tiny needle about half an inch long, closed the incision with fine stitches as neat as embroidery. While performing the operation she often endured for hours the most uncomfortable positions, leaning over to peer up into the cavity and almost standing on her head.

"Ouch, my neck hurts!" she exclaimed on one such occasion, righting herself with a painful grunt. "Awful position to be in, but I'd rather do it than sew a fine seam!"

The test of the operation's success was made by pouring milk into the cavity to discover if there was any leak. Great was Ida's rejoicing when the tissues stood the test, and the whole hospital must rejoice with her. If there was a leak, it merely meant more hours of careful work. She refused to give up until success was achieved. For her the operation began long before the patient reached the table, ended only when she was completely healed. So intense was her interest in her patients as people, so terrific her determination that they get well, that she was able to elicit their fullest cooperation.

"They would hold their breath all day if she told them to," one of her colleagues remarked.

But the trip was not all work. Traveling to Petra by car and horse, they found oleanders in bloom and a skeleton in a cave, from which Ida extracted a humerus as a souvenir. At Jericho they spent the night in the Winter Palace Hotel, in company with thirty-eight cats. Journeying on a cattle boat, they visited Tripoli, Tarsus, Cyprus, Salamis, Piraeus, where Ida, worrying about the sheep and goats packed tightly in the hold, was glad to leave the boat before the cargo was unloaded. She loved Greece, but especially Epidaurus, where Aesculapius, god of healing, was born and lived, marveled at the modern-looking instruments he had used, the huge ruin of a hotel with 600 rooms where he had housed patients. At Parnassus it was the lovely blue and purple thistles that impressed her, and she tried to get some seed to send to her gardener at Hill Top.

In Italy they feasted again on the glories of Venice; were delighted with the good roads, the mountains hung with bluebells, forget-me-nots, and gentians, ablaze with fireweed; but Ida regretted being so overweight that she was ashamed to appear in a bathing suit for swimming. She also dreaded exposing her shabby clothes to the customs officer on the Swiss border.

In Oberammergau she lived sixteen days in the home of the Christus, a delightful household containing in addition to its remarkable family two dogs, two cats, and a thirty-year-old turtle. She saw the Passion Play twice and performed an operation, receiving in payment a carved thorn-crowned head of Christ. She spent hours writing in longhand an inspired account of the play to send back to her students.

She sat in Cologne cathedral and thought of the vision someone must have had to build it. It's human character, she thought, not stones and stained glass that we are trying to build at Vellore. From that moment her absorption in the journey was over. Her face was set with impatience toward the coming campaign in the United States.

At first it seemed much like others, that campaign of 1934 and 1935. There were the same excited preparations, buying clothes, studying itineraries, becoming familiar with the new slogans. "YOU HAVE BUILT, WILL YOU MAINTAIN?" .... "India's Women are Looking Westward for Aid in their Cause of Education".... "We do not appeal for buildings, which American women have provided. These schools, which are training leadership for the women of India, must have endowment and maintenance."

True, she should have been warned by Lucy Peabody's manner of dogged desperation, the strained tightness of Hilda Olson's lips; warned too by the worried faces in the streets, the talk of the recent bank holiday, of bread lines, of increasing unemployment, of small businesses failing.

"Lucy and Hilda are imagining difficulties," she told herself, thinking without the slightest egotism. "Things will happen when I get on the road. They always have."

Weeks flew by with the usual flurry of activity. After New Year's Day there was a luncheon at Collegiate Church with the Norman Vincent Peales in attendance; a tea with Mrs. Roosevelt at the White House. She made a six-week tour of Florida, speaking sixty times in forty-one days.

"A perfectly wonderful Sabbath," she wrote in her diary on February 10. "I spoke to a church packed with the rich!"

She addressed the same large audiences as always: 1,500 in Chicago on the World Day of Prayer, 1,800 in Milwaukee, not quite so many in Detroit, Battle Creek, Grand Rapids. Then Washington, Philadelphia, Boston, Providence, New Haven.

They opened the campaign with the goal of a million dollars for endowment, $600,000 of it for Vellore, the remainder for the other women's colleges of Asia. There were now in America seven cooperating denominational women's mission groups— and Congregational, American Baptist, Methodist Episcopal, Reformed Church of America, Canadian Baptist, United Lutheran Church in America, the Augustana Synod Lutheran)—so the appeal of the project was of wide general interest.

To Ida's delight, word came from the Council in India that, if the other two governing councils, one in America and one in Britain, agreed and it became financially possible, the Missionary Medical School for Women should go on at once for the M.B., B.S. (Bachelor of Medicine, Bachelor of Surgery) degree, necessitating ten more professors; so the campaign committee decided to aim in addition for the endowment of ten professors' chairs at $25,000 each. They succeeded in getting only two.

Mrs. Peabody, worn out and half ill, threw herself into the work with indefatigable zeal. Hilda Olson worked often until two in the morning. For Ida there were the same night-and-day exertion, the same crowds, the same enthusiasm as in previous campaigns, but not the same results. She found the doors of corporations and foundations closed, with their funds allocated far ahead. Donations came by the hundreds instead of the thousands, pennies from where dollars had once poured. She was faced with the problem, not of making possible the raising of the school to college standard—that would be out of the question now for years to come—but of finding funds to keep it going. At last Ida knew the meaning of the word depression.

There were high moments of personal satisfaction. In June she was made a member of the American College of Surgeons, an honor she particularly coveted because of the prestige it would add to her position among the medical officials in India. In the same month she received a Doctor of Science degree from Rutgers, being the twenty-third member of her family to receive recognition at the commencement exercises of that institution. But even honors were flavored with the bitter taste of failure.

Failure! It was scarcely twelve months since she had given such glib advice on the subject to her failing seniors. "I attribute what success I have had in reaching the goal of my earlier ambitions to my failures. Yes. I mean just that. We learn very little in this life from success. Success feeds ego, failure chastens it. Success makes you look up and the sun dazzles your eyes; failure forces you to look down, and you mind your step. Those who can fail and learn, who can try and fall and get up and go on, who can make a new start and be defeated and *still go on* are the ones who succeed in the end."

She set sail with Gertrude Dodd from New York to Naples on midday of June 15, 1935, continuing her campaign by writing 112 letters, longhand, on shipboard. A month later they arrived in India. Harry and Margaret had made Hill Top ready for their coming, Ida had a few days of blessed relaxation, of renewal for both body and spirit.

She needed them. For at sixty-five years of age she was about to enter the most crucial and strenuous ten years of her career.

22

It was worth returning to the July heat of Vellore to waken again to the squeak of an irrigation wheel, the shouting of peasants at the plodding bullock, their chanting song as the goatskin sacks were drawn up dripping and sloshed into the ditches; worth leaving the quiet of College Hill for a night emergency to see the blazing loveliness of Scorpio or, best of all, the hospital shimmering in full moonlight, lovely as the Taj, all its stains and scars rubbed out ... yes, even though your first glimpse of it must be coincident with the richly augmented fumes of the open drain just outside the gate!

That drain! Sometimes Ida thought it was the supreme ambition of her life to get it covered. More even than a symbol, it was the actual embodiment of the disease, the ugliness, the ignorance, the apathy, the indifference, which she had dedicated her life to combat. And, except for verbal protests to the municipality—and she made them frequently—she could do nothing about it.

In the rush of work she could almost forget her disappointment over the campaign, the impossibility of raising the medical school to college status, her deep uneasiness about the future. It might have been any normal year.

"August 13, 1935. A busy morning operating until twelve.

268

Bible class in P.M. and then hurried to Medical Association, then to the Ladies' Recreation Club, delightful dinner, about 60 there.

"August 14. Went to Gudiyattam. It's so wonderful having the little hospital there, with one of our own doctors in residence. Long and intensely interesting day. 478 patients with 77 lepers.

"August 20. Council meeting. We need so much if we are ever to go on to M.B., B.S. buildings. Decided to build a new building for the X ray.

"Sept. 1. Infection in leg from infected bite. Painful, but kept operating.

"Oct. 20. Did terrible fistula on a little dwarf, half idiot. She had been sold to a man for 200 rupees.

"Nov. 23. Morning in hospital very busy, not through until 1:30. Started at 3:00 for Ponnai Bridge laying. Very grand affair. Late for giving out prizes at No. Arcot Athletic Association. Company for dinner.

"Nov. 26. Did very terrible V.V.F. that had been sent away from two hospitals as inoperable.

"Jan. 25. Cable saying radium ordered. We can hardly wait for it. Two other cancer cases were sent away today.

"March 5. Had long executive meeting. Budget deficit *59,000 rupees.*"

Busy or not, she had to face it. It was not just any normal year. It was 1936, with the world just beginning to recover from one of the greatest depressions in history, and in India significant political changes taking place. A British Government of India Act in 1935 had given India a new constitution designed to palliate some of the nationalist unrest. While dominion status was not mentioned and the central government under the viceroy was to be given greater rather than less power in many areas, provincial legislatures were to be directly elected and given more autonomy. Though the new reforms fell far short of their major aim of independence, nationalists decided to support the scheme by entering candidates and campaigning in the forthcoming local elections. As a result, a new nationalist government would soon be coming into power in Madras Presidency which might bring about vast social and political changes affecting both schools and hospitals.

The deficit of the college and hospital was staggering, and there were no funds in prospect to meet it. In America Lucy Peabody was making a gigantic effort, with a hard trip west to help Dr. Carol Jameson, home on furlough, to organize a big campaign in California, and with the sending out of 15,000 letters for the promotion of Dollar Day in May. Still tireless and unyielding, she refused to lower her sights or to admit defeat. "Mr. R. has indicated that he might give us a 'handsome contribution,' " she wrote Ida, adding with grim levity, "Nothing less than $25,000 would seem 'handsome' to me." In the months following, however, she had to acknowledge defeat. Dollar Day was not a success. Milwaukee, Chicago, Rochester, Pittsburgh ... in her campaign back across the country from California she left a trail of failures.

But there were triumphs also. The new X-ray Block was already being built on the hospital compound in the center of the town. The precious radium, long anticipated, arrived, made possible by one of treasurer Hilda Olson's happy exchanges of bonds, netting, in spite of the depression, a return of $5,000. Exercising with single-minded zeal her remarkable faculty for playing the stock market, Miss Olson was inclined to frown on less profitable recreations.

"The idea," she wrote Ida, "of your playing tennis with all you have to do, and at your age!"

Ida read the words with an unholy pleasure. She wished Hilda Olson had been present in Vellore on a certain day not too long before.

Scheduled for a tennis tournament in the Ladies' Recreation Club, Ida had drawn as opponent in the singles the teen-age champion, the daughter of an Indian doctor.

"I've pulled a grannie!" wailed the girl to her mother, who laughingly repeated the remark. Ida, hearing it, did not share her friend's amusement.

"I'll teach her to 'grannie' me!" she exclaimed indignantly.

She did, wiping the court with her teen-age opponent, who won not a single game in the two sets of the match.

It was the worst financial crisis the hospital had ever faced. Salaries were cut 10 per cent, tried workers discharged. A branch hospital and dispensary had to be closed, part of one Roadside discontinued. Even the food budget had to be cut from 660 rupees a month to 330 (about $220 to $110). In the hospital kitchen the confusion was worse than ever.

Mrs. Devasagayam, the hospital matron, had had troubles enough before supplying all the foods to fill the various diet requirements: wheat conjee, rice and ragi conjee, boiled rice, twice-boiled rice, curries, some prepared in ghee, some in gingelly oil, some in coconut oil for the Malayalim, some with chillies, some without, some with Indian vegetables, some with English vegetables, vegetable soup, liver soup, bread, curds, chapatties, sprouted dhal, to say nothing of all the liquid diets. And she had no waterman or gardener to go to market as they had in the nurses' home and the medical school.

"Lower price you say you must have?" The bazaar salesmen all smiled and shrugged. "You only are asking for such a low price. Just now I gave this same for Big Bungalow Lazarus for such and such a price. This is American hospital, is not? We all know that America is rich, so American hospital must too be rich."

There was only one solution, Ida decided. The patients themselves must pay a greater share of the expense. The hospital management tried charging additional fees. All except the very poor were asked to pay four annas (about seven cents) a day for their beds, as well as to feed themselves. The news spread through the countryside like wildfire, and the hospital practically emptied itself overnight. Not even on feast days or in times of plague had there been so few patients.

"There's ingratitude for you!" said Ida to herself grimly.

But on Hospital Day in February, when hosts of former patients voluntarily showed their gratitude, it was another story. Now in its third year, this institution received the enthusiastic support of all friends. A committee of Hindu men and women had been formed to forward plans. Many Vellore citizens loaned their cars for canvassing. Wards and corridors were freshly painted and decorated with flowers, buckets placed under tables for the reception of gifts.

Before sunrise people started to come. Bullock bandies drove up, loaded with bags of rice, ragi, and sugar. Guests poured into the entrance hall beneath the clock tower of the administration building, through the silver gate of the dispensary, arms laden with coffee, brown sugar, dahl, tamarinds, fruits, chickens, ducks, turkeys, pigeons, eggs, soap, cloth for bandages, frocks for babies, matches, pins, towels, toys, bottles, money. Soon the buckets were brim-full, and others were brought. One mother of ten hugged a big white turkey gobbler under one arm and held a toddler's hand with the other, two of her children following with a basket of six ducks, the other six bringing up the rear with fresh vegetables and eggs, the family donations representing more than a half-month's wages. A sack of rice worth seven rupees came from the hospital peons, cooks, watermen, sweepers, and cleaners, none of whom received more than eleven rupees a month.

One little old woman, very poor, wan, and hungry, came and placed three *pies* (about a sixth of a cent), all she had, in Ida's hand. An old man brought to her his gift of two annas, saying, "I am a coolie and have no garden, nor have I any grain to give, but may I give this for those in greater need than I?"

At ten A.M. groups of white-robed purdah women came in droves, in their midst a North Indian Mohammedan woman in black burka, each bringing her gift and dropping it in the box. At three in the afternoon ceremonies began in earnest. Hundreds came from the highest officials of the town to the humblest villagers, some of whom had walked many painful miles to show their gratitude. Adults and children of all castes and creeds gazed in wide-eyed amazement at operating rooms, wards, ice house, and kitchen; listened to health lectures under the huge spreading pipal tree; were entertained with drama and music on the tennis court.

The lack of money for running the hospital was a serious but not insurmountable difficulty. Dedicated missionary personnel were willing to work with a minimum of salary; their Indian associates were used to a sub-subsistence wage. Scarcity of food was the rule in that part of the world rather than the exception. While efficiency was impaired and expansion curtailed, the work of both hospital and college continued without interruption. Then, suddenly, a blow fell which threatened the college's very existence.

It was October, 1937. Ida was returning to Vellore with three of her fellow workers from a brief vacation in Kodai, all doubts swept away by the winds from far horizons, courage resurrected by the miracle of white Easter lilies growing wild on all the mountain slopes.

They stopped in Trichinopoly to repair a punctured tire, buy rice and curry at the station restaurant. While waiting, Ida glanced over the latest edition of the *Madras Mail*. Suddenly her heart seemed to stop beating.

"Oh—*no!*" she exclaimed.

It was only a small paragraph, a terse announcement by the new Indian minister of public health that no new applicants should be considered after July, 1938, by D.M.S. schools in Madras Presidency giving, as Vellore had been required to do since 1933, a diploma in medicine and surgery for a five-year course. Henceforth all entering students in medical schools throughout the presidency must be candidates for a college degree in an institution affiliated with the University of Madras. No applicants for a diploma course would be recognized. It was a commendable action, proof that the new Congress government was contenting itself with only the highest of standards. Ida would be the first to commend it for its courage. Yet, coming at this time, with the raising of the school to college standard financially impossible perhaps for years to come, it sounded a death knell for her beloved medical school.

She had been warned that this crisis was coming, yet somehow she hadn't really believed it. "Something will happen," she had told herself comfortably. "Someone will give us a big donation." Or— "Surely they'll let us keep on the way we've been going— for a while, at least." Now at last she had to face the truth. Either the medical school must be raised immediately to college standard, qualified for university affiliation, or it must close its doors.

Now for the first time Ida knew the paralyzing sensation of fear. During the following days it slowed her step, took the sparkle from her eye, and, though she tried to hide her concern, it loomed over the whole school and hospital like a black cloud.

The fear was still with her on October 25 when Lord Erskine, the Governor of Madras, came to Vellore with his wife to open the new X-ray Block. It was the fulfillment of many years' desire and planning, this new department for the deep X-ray and radium treatment so desperately needed, and for efficient diagnostic radiology. To do justice to the occasion all the government secretaries wore their high hats with red pompoms and their coats resplendent with gold braid.

"Two hundred twenty-nine graduate doctors have received their Licensed Medical Practitioners' diplomas," Ida announced in her outline of the work through the years.

She watched Lady Marjorie break ground for a blue creeper and thought, *It's really a grave she's digging. For my dead dream of a medical college.*

On November 1 the surgeon general arrived to look over the situation, and soon after came the chief minister of health, Dr. Rajan. All Ida's fears were justified. The buildings were good, but the staff inadequate. None of the doctors on the staff, not even Ida herself, possessed a medical degree coupled with sufficient experience of teaching in M.D.-grade colleges to satisfy government requirements. There must be at least twelve new professors, each with a degree higher than the M.B., B.S. for which she would be training students. The hospital must be better equipped, with new pathological, physiological, and bacteriological laboratories. Its 268 teaching beds must be increased to at least 500. The school could not possibly expect to receive M.B., B.S. status in time to admit a new class in 1938 ... or ever, unless a miracle took place.

"We need double our income," Ida wrote bleakly to Hilda Olson. "Even a million in endowment would not be enough."

Ironical that the blow should come on the very eve of the school's twentieth anniversary, with Lucy Peabody already on her way to India to participate in the celebration.

It was on a morning when her courage had sunk to its lowest ebb that one of her students came to her. "Doctor," she said hesitantly, "I—I had the strangest dream. Would—would you mind if I told you?"

274

"Of course not, Annamma, my dear." Ida smiled warmly, for the girl was one of her favorite pupils. "Just don't expect me to interpret it. I'm no Daniel."

The dark eyes in the thin earnest face were deeply troubled. "I dreamed," said Annamma, "that I was in a beautiful garden filled with lovely flowers, and in this garden was a well. There was a wall around the well, with steps leading down into it. On the steps were many beautiful jars, some large, some small. In my dream I went to the well to get some water, and as I descended the steps I—I paused to choose a water jar. The first one I picked up was a large one, but after lifting it to my head I decided it was too heavy, so—so I put it down and picked up a smaller one."

Ida's attention wandered, and her gaze, though still fixed on the girl's face, changed from concern to amused indulgence. It was a very natural dream. Indian women were always going to wells to draw water.

"I filled my jar," continued the young voice earnestly, "and as I came up the steps I noticed that the flowers were all dying, and I started to water them. Finally I came to one flower, the most beautiful one of all, and it was almost dead. Then—then I found my jar was empty! 'Too late, too late!' cried the flower. Then I too cried out." There was agony in the girl's dark eyes. "'Oh!' I cried. 'If I had only chosen the larger jar!' It—it was a strange dream, wasn't it?"

Ida's attention was not wandering now. "Yes," she said.

"What do you suppose it meant?"

"It meant," said Ida gently, taking the anxious little face between her hands, "that you have a more sensitive spirit than most of us and will never be satisfied with giving anything except your very best. Thank you, my dear. Thank you very much for telling me."

After the girl had gone, Ida went to her room. She took the small black notebook which was her constant companion and, snapping in a fresh leaf to make a new front page, began to write. The words were bold and black.

"First ponder, then dare. Know your facts. Count the cost. Money is not the most important thing. What you are building is not a medical school. It is the Kingdom of God. Don't err on the side of being too small. If this is the will of God that we should find some way to keep the college open, *it has to be done.*" From that moment she was no longer afraid.

Crisis or no crisis, things were right again in the hospital. Even the patients on Roadside noticed the difference, and their somber eyes brightened. Their Doctor *Ammal* was herself again. Students were inspired anew by the serenity of her face as she led them in chapel and in Tuesday afternoon Bible study. Patients listened for the sound of her quick steps along the hospital corridors. Nurses, following her up and down stairs and along the wards, tried in vain to keep up with her. And young doctors, both students and graduates, learned, merely from being in her presence, a deeper wisdom than could be found in books.

Dr. Bernardine Siebers, fresh from America by way of the hill station language school, looked up late one Wednesday to see Dr. Ida returning from her day on Roadside. Dead-tired from her own day of unaccustomed and baffling problems, the young woman gazed at the older with mingled wonder and sympathy. If the day had been difficult in a well-equipped and efficient hospital, what must it have been treating five hundred patients in the Roadside dust!

"Patient for you, Bernie," announced Dr. Ida cheerfully. A dark frightened face peered around the curve of her shoulder.

"Clean or septic?" asked Dr. Siebers, hoping the answer would indicate a ward on the ground floor of the hospital.

It didn't. "Come with me," she said, taking the shrinking little figure by the arm. Ida walked with them to the long flight of stairs, the woman clinging tightly to her hand. "I'll take her up," said the young doctor.

"No," replied Ida. She patted the clinging hand. "She's just gotten used to me. I'll go along too. We'll put her to bed together."

That night the young American doctor learned a lesson she was never to forget, watching this woman prolong a desperately wearying day by gently removing the rags from the dirty body of an outcaste villager and quieting her fears with a mother's patient, understanding tenderness.

276

But courage and serenity did little to solve the problem of a medical school in jeopardy. Under the calm exterior was a seething conflict of questions, impossible plans, wishful thinking, indecision.

And then suddenly in November, a month after the news of the government's action had broken, Ida caught the first glimpse of a possible solution. Dr. F. H. Hume, a British church leader representing several denominations, was making a three-month tour of India, one of his objectives being preliminary studies and recommendations for the building of an All-India Christian Medical College for men. On November 16 he came to Vellore. His decision was prompt and enthusiastic.

"This is the place," he declared. "With a coeducational college here, what couldn't we accomplish in training doctors in a Christian environment!"

The proposal was not wholly new. Dr. John R. Mott, eminent American churchman, had made the same recommendation on his visit to India some months ago, and Ida, enthusiastic, had reported the proposal to Mrs. Peabody and others on the American Council, but they had seemed shocked at the suggestion. Once Ida also would have been violently opposed. The very purpose in founding the school had been to minister to the needs of women. But India was changing. Her women were seeking equality, not segregation. The initial necessity, perhaps even the greatest usefulness, of separate medical education for women was past. Now Ida saw in the proposition a gleam of hope. With groups of all denominations, men as well as women, united in one great effort to build a coeducational medical college here at Vellore, surely her project could be saved! But she could not be sure her approval did not spring from emotion rather than reason. Was she willing to compromise principle merely for the sake of saving her college? She could hardly wait to discuss the possible solution with Lucy Peabody.

Yet when Mrs. Peabody arrived in December, Ida for some reason postponed mentioning the proposition. Apprised of the crisis by cable, Mrs. Peabody apparently did not sense the full gravity of the situation. She hinted mysteriously of "plans" and was sure something could be worked out. Meeting her in

Bombay, Ida took her by train to North India to see the Taj, then showed her the Lady Hardinge Medical College in Delhi, and arranged for her an interview with the vicereine, Lady Linlithgow.

On their arival in Vellore the nurses had planned to line the road and welcome them, but it was late at night and raining. "All too symbolic," thought Ida, "of the problems we both have to face."

She put off the broaching of her solution until Mrs. Peabody had enjoyed her first thrilling tour of the buildings she had helped create. They had climbed to the lower ledges of College Hill, the same spot where, a quarter-century before almost to a day, they had looked out over green rice fields and barren grazing lands.

"Well," said Lucy Peabody, "there it is. Your site has certainly turned into a sight, hasn't it? A sight worth traveling halfway around the world to see. And worth saving," she continued firmly, "for the cause for which a million women sacrificed to build it—education and healing for Indian women."

Was there more than necessary emphasis on the last three words? Ida knew the time had come. She plunged into her news. "You remember I wrote you about Dr. Mott's visit and how enthusiastic he was about—" She stopped, warned by the tightening of the other woman's lips.

"About making *our women's college* coeducational." This time there was no mistaking the emphasis. "Yes. You wrote about it."

"As you know, Dr. Hume was here in November," continued Ida hurriedly, "trying to locate the best place for an All-India Medical College to be built and supported with the help of the National Christian Council of India. He stayed five days. He was tremendously impressed with Vellore."

"No wonder!" interposed Lucy Peabody bluntly. "A million-dollar set of buildings ready-made for the *men* to take over! I suppose he has a half-million dollars or so all ready to finance the project?"

"Well—no, there aren't any funds as yet," admitted Ida. "But he feels that by making the college coeducational we would have a much wider appeal in raising funds. It—it might even make

278

the difference between saving the college or having to close it!"

"By compromising the very principles on which it was built?" The visitor's tone was hot, her eyes cold. "Don't forget, my dear Dr. Ida, it was you who awakened us to the special needs of Indian women—the little wives dying because no man doctor could attend them, the girls who could never become doctors because it meant attending classes with men in government medical schools."

"I know." Ida met the cold gaze with steady eyes. "But—India is changing," she said. "She has been making marvelous progress. I—I'm not sure that coeducation might not be one of the best things that could happen for this generation of our young people."

Lucy Peabody's face was flushed from more than the exertion of the climb. "That's not Ida Scudder talking," she retorted heatedly. "It's John R. Mott and Dr. Hume and Dr. Frimodt-Möller of your National Christian Council. All of them men, and all thoroughly convinced that Vellore is the one spot in India where there should be an All-India Medical College. Not Allahabad, not Miraj, where there's already a men's medical school! But Vellore, where there's a million dollars' worth of fine buildings all ready-made for them!"

Ida's troubled gaze lowered to embrace the impressive quadrangle of stone buildings. "But—suppose they're right," she murmured.

"My dear!" Lucy Peabody melted into sudden warmth. With a rare outburst of affection she slipped her arm through Ida's and stood with her, shoulder to shoulder, just as, figuratively, they had faced four long and hard campaigns together, conquered seemingly insuperable obstacles. "I understand. You're frightened for fear of losing it. You'd do almost anything to save it. But we're not beaten yet, and you're not going to compromise. We'll win this battle as we've won others. A million dollars you say we'll need for endowment to meet the crisis. We'll raise it. And—*we don't need any men to help us!*"

Never had the procession of students, white-clad and bearing long chains of jasmine blossoms, looked lovelier than on that February day in 1938 when they celebrated the school's twentieth anniversary. One hundred of the 240 graduates of the medical school and 122 graduate nurses and 75 trained compounders and technicians were present.

For Ida the long white chains stretched farther than around the lily pool, across the sunken garden, down the aisles of the Assembly Hall. On and on they kept winding through India, into Ceylon, Burma, Africa, Arabia, carrying fragrance and beauty to all the cities and villages where her graduates were working. Of the 240 who had earned L.M.P. diplomas, 87 were in mission work, 114 in government service, 30 in private practice. Nine of them had died. Almost without exception those in missions and villages had refused posts with much higher salaries.

Mrs. Peabody, delegate of the American section of the governing board of the medical school, sat on the platform with Dr. Frimodt-Möller, head of the Madanapalle tuberculosis sanatorium and master of ceremonies. She looked none too happy.

"He's been talking to her about coeducation," thought Ida uneasily.

For the first time at such a gathering she noticed the preponderance of Indians among the eminent guests including her own special friend, the distinguished Dr. Hilda Lazarus. Startled, she realized that it was so also in the hospital. At Schell in the beginning there had been three foreign doctors and an Indian assistant. Now there were nine Western doctors, eleven Indian doctors, fourteen Indian staff nurses, and eleven Indian postgraduate nurses.

"This is a turning point," she thought with mingled sadness and satisfaction. "It is as it should be. From now on they must increase, we must decrease. This is their work, not ours."

Looking at Hilda Lazarus, keen, vitally alert, thoroughly Indian yet sensitive to the best values in Western culture, Ida became suddenly conscious that she herself was nearly sixty-eight years old. The awareness sharpened slowly into a gleam of purpose. Dr. Lazarus must be her successor!

Later in the darkened chapel Ida and Lucy Peabody held lighted candles from which hundreds of small flames were kindled, streaming out to illuminate the shadowed campus. But not for long! As Ida watched her own candle flicker, panic

280

seized her. Was this to be the end? Twenty years—such a bright burning flame—then nothing but darkness?

Mrs. Peabody had bold plans for meeting the crisis: a new American campaign the following year, with Ida participating; a book which she had asked Dr. Pauline Jeffery to write, telling Ida's dramatic story; an immediate appeal to wealthy Indians to contribute. The results of her efforts in the India area were bitterly disappointing. India too was suffering from the world-wide recession. The maharajahs and their ilk had never been much concerned with public welfare. Patriotic Indians were looking more and more askance at philanthropies which had their roots in Western colonialism. At another time the Tatas, India's great industrialist Parsees of Bombay, founders of her largest steel firm and her leading airline, might have been a likely source of contribution; for, through the Tata Trusts, 85 per cent of the family industrial profits were devoted to such philanthropies as health services for Tata employes, famine and flood relief, a child guidance clinic, various institutes of scientific research. But the foundation displayed no interest in the Vellore project, having just embarked on the building of a cancer research hospital. Mrs. Peabody went home tired and discouraged, but with two consolations: Pauline's manuscript, and the belief that she had saved Vellore from the clutches of designing males.

Ida had acquiesced in this decision only by her silence. She was not at all sure yet what was the right thing to do. As spring approached, however, her worries were buried temporarily beneath flurries of activity, social as well as professional. The wedding of one of her staff members was no sooner out of the way than she began making plans for a gala birthday celebration to honor Gertrude Dodd.

Gertrude had never been willing to tell her age. Trying to keep up with Ida for twenty years had kept her young. So keen was her mind that she could give the address, offhand, of almost any alumna of the medical school. And the neat roll of hair above her temples was still so raven-black that students of the last dozen classes had wondered if she wore a wig.

But on Gertrude's eightieth birthday Ida insisted on divulging the truth. The day was August 15, later to become a momentous date in the Indian calendar, marking the winning of independence. The modest wrenlike figure was deposited in a huge birthday chair and half buried in garlands. There was tea in the women's lounge and sunken garden, and afterward a public meeting in the school assembly hall. People came from far and near. There was a great birthday cake with eighty candles, and as each was blown out one of the guests paid personal tribute to her generosity. The Christian community of Vellore presented a printed "Address of Congratulation" to the "Revered and Beloved Madam" whose life had been blessed "with expanding breadth and fullness, of beneficence and service."

The extent of her philanthropies was amazing. She had largely supported the children's home, the tuberculosis sanatorium at Madanapalle, the mission hospital at Gudiyattam. The clock at the hospital and a good part of the public contribution for the tower were her gifts. She had endowed a number of hospital beds and a professorship in the medical school, supported two missionaries, rescued the mission in crisis after crisis. And at least eight students, including Pauline Jeffery, were in debt to her for the complete cost of their advanced education.

All her life Gertrude had worn no ornaments, even measuring her busy days by a cheap little Ingersoll watch. Now the jewels she had refused to wear were spread at her feet in the shining gratitude of all the lives she had enriched. She was touched by the gratitude but unimpressed, being always inclined to regard the most unusual developments in life with a droll humor.

One day, coming into the laboratory after Ida had finished operating, she noticed a specimen in the kidney tray. "What's this?" She pointed at it gingerly.

"An appendix sent in to be analyzed," she was told by the technician.

She regarded the object with a layman's appraising curiosity. "Looks to me like a perfectly normal appendix," she commented drily.

Ida's worries refused to stay buried. The necessity of starting the new school year in July, 1938, with no entering class had caused a hurt which even the heaven of Hill Top in September could not heal. For a few brief days she almost managed to forget her problems. Roses were blooming in profusion. Much rain had fallen, and the hundreds of little rice fields seven thousand feet below looked like shining panes of glass. Ida and Gertrude and Dell Houghton took the forty-mile drive out among the mountains, reveling in the thousands of white lilies, some bearing seven blossoms on a stalk. They returned with huge bunches.

On the way home they stopped at a village called Dharapuram, where Mary Varkkey, a graduate of 1925, was in private practice. After working in a mission hospital for a year and then for some time in government service, Mary had decided to devote her life to village work. Now, in addition to her small dispensary, she had built out of her own earnings a nine-bed ward and operating room, and had asked Ida and Gertrude to stop and dedicate this "Dr. Ida S. Scudder Nursing Home."

Seeing this lovely young woman and hearing the many tributes of affection for her, Ida's heart was filled with joy. She actually wept for happiness. Here was her life's purpose in action. With her joy was mingled a sudden sense of awe and exaltation. This was not *her* work. She was only the hands, the voice, the feet, not the Will which had inspired the act. If the thing she had helped create was indeed an expression of the divine Purpose for human beings, surely some way would be found to save it. For the first time since being confronted with the crisis almost a year ago, she knew inward serenity and peace.

Returning home, as if in confirmation of her renewed faith, she found a letter from a missionary in that mountain section of South India known as the Nilgiris, asking if she might start a world-wide Prayer Fellowship, to be known as the Friends of Vellore. In her reply Ida wrote back, "I feel that the great burden which was upon me has been lifted!"

23

The visitor from the United States rode with Dr. Ida from the hospital to the college bungalow at College Hill. He was a strong man in his prime, but it had been a strenuous day of sightseeing, and he was worn to the bone. He marveled to see this woman of nearly seventy still gay and smiling.

Coming into the dining room to a late breakfast after oversleeping, the guest learned that an emergency call had taken his hostess to the hospital at 2 A.M. to perform an operation on a patient who had been carried seventy miles over unimproved roads. Yet here she sat at the head of the table, apparently unwearied, pouring the coffee, radiant because the operation had been a success.

"Her secret," thought Dr. Daniel Poling, popular and spiritually dynamic leader of the World Christian Endeavor movement, "lies in her Cause. The passion of her life has been kindred to the passion of the Great Physician himself."

Many other guests beside Dr. Poling came to Vellore from the great world conference of churches held in Tambaram, near Madras, in 1938, among them Dr. and Mrs. Douglas Horton of the United States, Dr. Wu and Dr. Koo of China, Dr. Kagawa of Japan. They began coming in November and kept coming through the following weeks and months, a full hundred of them.

Ida was an active participant in the conference. Always anxious to have Vellore in the forefront of activity (as well as in the public eye), she arranged to have it represented by two other delegates, Vera Pitman, one of her most capable teachers in the school of nursing, and Dr. Jessie Findlay. She gave them definite instructions.

"Here's one thing you *must* do." The warmth of her excitement imbued them with her own enthusiasm. "Persuade Dr. Hilda Lazarus to come to Vellore and join our staff."

During this conference she tried to determine the course she should pursue. At a meeting of the International Missionary Council in Madras, with representatives from England, America, and India, she became convinced of two things: Without the admission of men her medical school at Vellore could not be saved, and without the saving of her school there would be no All-India Christian Medical College.

The requirements for raising the school to college level were staggering. New buildings would be necessary, involving an expenditure of at least $800,000. The hospital must be opened to men patients in order to satisfy university standards, its number of beds nearly doubled. A minimum of four new departments must be introduced. Not only must many of the present staff pursue further study in order to qualify for teaching clinical subjects, but twelve new professors must be added to the staff. Without the cooperation of all mission boards the necessary funds could not possibly be raised. And many of the denominations were unwilling to cooperate in promoting merely a women's college.

Equally staggering were the difficulties involved in creating an All-India Medical College for men. The Christian Medical Association of India had no funds for building, and even if they were able to raise them, the duplication of facilities would jeopardize the possibility of securing further funds for both a men's and a women's college to attain university affiliation. With a joint effort there was a bare possibility of success. Without it there was almost certain failure.

Ida was confident that, once these facts were made clear, Lucy Peabody, Hilda Olson, and others on the governing board in America would understand. On December 14, 1938 she wrote to the board, expressing herself in favor of cooperation.

"I feel," she said, "it would be very selfish of us in Vellore to close our doors to men if it is going to be impossible to build a new expensive medical center in some place like Allahabad."

The result was shattering. Hilda Olson's comments were bitterly unbelieving. "Vellore is as you say God's work, but I would like to add God's work *for women*. Every dollar would have to be given back to the givers."

But it was Lucy Peabody's letter to Casey Wierenga, secretary of the India Council, which cut Ida to the quick. She read it with shocked incredulity, reading into it even more denunciation than was intended.

"Dr. Ida knows perfectly well the stand our board has taken. They will be deeply grieved that she has not been loyal to their plans which she instigated, and which they, with my help, have fostered all these years."

They were accusing her of being disloyal to her own dream!

In the following days and weeks Ida plumbed the depths of bitterness and despair. She took no part in the interchange of argument between the council in India and the boards in America and Britain. In February she went to Hill Top and tried to blow her spirit clean of hurt and rancor. But it was no use. A letter from the United States followed her there, and finally on February 22 she yielded to compulsion and wrote what was in her heart.

"Your letter was received yesterday. I hardly know how to answer it. I have not misrepresented you. I have not been disloyal, as you claim I have been. I have stated again and again that without your full sanction of a coordinated college, we simply could not go into it. Your distrust after so many years of cooperation in this great work has hurt me so deeply and cruelly that I have no heart to carry on. Good-by. Ida S. Scudder."

The reply came back from Lucy Peabody immediately—contrite, loving, conciliatory. Ida had not understood. Her friends in America had thought they were the ones being criticized, *their* feelings had been hurt. But now that they all understood each other, let the misunderstanding be forgotten. They would go on working together for the *women* of India as they always had. And they would win. Nothing should stop them.

Ida was torn as she had never been since that night long ago when the three men had come to her door and she had decided she must become a doctor. She must keep her medical school open. She had given her life to bringing it into being. She was desperately afraid she could not do so without yielding to the almost unanimous demand of the council in India for cooperation. Yet she was sailing in six months for a campaign both in England and in America. She could not, dared not, face such a campaign without the loyal support of Lucy Peabody. It was like choosing between the life of your child and that of your best friend.

It was April before she decided. The brain-fever birds were wearying the ears with their forebodings of hot weather. The paradise flycatchers, orange and black and white, were streaking northward in their long migration. As she watched them, Ida felt suddenly old and tired. In another year she would be seventy, much too old to embark on a new pilgrimage with new and untried partners.

On April 12 she wrote Lucy Peabody that she would work only for a women's college. Their misunderstanding would be forgotten. They would face the crisis together.

She would have had more courage if she could have attended the huge International Dinner at the Hotel Roosevelt in New York on May 11, which brought together five nations, with officers of the six denominational boards represented on the Vellore Board of Governors. After the international meal, the campaign was instigated to meet the challenge of the crisis. Among the distinguished sponsors either speaking or sending messages were Dr. Daniel Poling, Sir Wilfred Grenfell, Mrs. Douglas Horton, Mrs. Prem Nath Das and Mrs. Rajah Manikam of India, Dr. Sam Higginbotham, and P. W. Wilson, editor of the new biography of Dr. Ida.

But she would have been disappointed also. For they were setting as their goal only a million dollars, not the two million she had requested.

It was September 1, 1939. The bungalow garden at College

Hill was crowded with guests, come to wish Ida and Gertrude Godspeed on their coming trip to Britain and America. They were sailing from Bombay on September 9. Ida faced the journey with great hope, for she already had engagements to speak thirty-three times in England and Scotland. It was to be a voyage of triumph also, for she had been awarded the gold bar to her Kaisar-i-Hind medal of honor and was to receive her decoration in London from the King.

As usual, an elaborate printed document had been prepared for their farewell. "We your devoted and loving friends and admirers," ran the long discourse, "beg leave to approach you on the eve of your departure to America . . . trying to give expression . . . deep sense of gratitude and affection . . . womanhood and childhood of our land. . . ."

As the reader launched into a detailed history of the preceding thirty-seven years, Ida's attention wandered along the borders of pink and green crotons, the bell-like yellow blossoms of the allamanda; climbed the luxuriant white waterfall of the horsetail creeper to the green spears of palmyras and the blue heavens high above. Impossible that in a sky of such loveliness clouds of war should be gathering! She strained her ears again to catch the muted blare of the radio in the room off the upstairs verandah. Occasionally someone would come and relay the latest war news from the balcony. Someone was coming now. She waited impatiently for the speech to be finished so she could find out what the news might be.

"In closing we wish you and Miss Dodd a happy voyage, a pleasant stay at home, all success in the mission. . ."

Suddenly she saw a servant weaving his way among the guests, an envelope in his hand. She felt a hollow emptiness. She knew it was bad news before she tore it open.

The cable read: CANCEL PLANS FOR ENGLAND STOP GOVERNMENT REQUESTS ALL AMERICANS IN EUROPE LEAVE FOR HOME IMMEDIATELY ADVISE POSTPONING TRIP.

During the following months, while war was overspreading Europe and Ida was marking time in India, it was maddening for her to know how much depended on the campaign now being waged by friends of Vellore in America, and yet not be there

288

to help; disheartening to sense their misunderstanding of the situation, yet have no means of communication except letters and cablegrams! Hilda Olson wrote that they were trying to build up endowment funds instead of providing the buildings necessary to raise the school to M.B., B.S. status. But—what use endowments if there was to be no college to endow? How make them understand that haste was the prime necessity, that unless application could be made immediately for university affiliation, the opportunity might be forever lost? Already there were only three classes remaining in the school, permitted to finish the five-year course started before the new law went into effect. If the school was allowed to close, the chances were that it would never reopen.

"At present," explained an eminent Indian Christian at a meeting of the Board of Governors, American Section, held in January, 1940, "the university commission is made up of men of friendly disposition toward missions. But there are indications that changes are imminent."

Mrs. Peabody was advocating delay. "Please, please," Ida wrote in a frenzy of concern, "can't you all understand that we must *hurry?*"

Juldi, juldi! If she could only do the hurrying for all of them!

There were rays of sunshine through the ominous clouds. Ida received her decoration from Lord Erskine in the presence of the staff and students of the medical school. Ida B., her niece, returned by way of the Pacific from her years of intensive training in both the United States and England to take over her new duties as head of the department of radiology. The new X-ray Block with its desperately needed radium was by now overcrowded with patients like all the others, and she was soon working all hours of the day and night. For years Treva Marshall had been working in X ray with a tiny machine that could give shocks to any unwary person. Now she became Ida B.'s invaluable assistant in diagnostic and therapy, and for years her only one.

Since arriving in India in 1931 the younger Dr. Ida had served in a variety of capacities. When Pauline Jeffery, after specializing in ophthalmics, had been obliged to leave Vellore for treatment in a tuberculosis sanatorium, she had substituted for her in running ophthalmology. For a year Ida B. had been in charge of medicine while Dr. Flora Innes, long a valued member of the staff, was on leave, and for two more years she had helped Dr. Carol Jameson in obstetrics, then during her leave acted as head of the department. So the long hours and frustrating activity were no new experience.

"What a pity!" thought Ida, on her Wednesday trip to Gudiyattam with the blossoming sugar cane fretting the blue sky and green palms with spun silver. "Poor Ida B. cooped up all day every day of the week in those dark little X-ray rooms! I must do something about it."

She did. Her beloved niece was soon getting out of doors and into the country for a whole day each week . . . on Roadside.

Fortunately this younger Scudder was cut of the same fabric as her tireless and enthusiastic relative. It seemed to be Ida B.'s idea of a weekly holiday also—working for twelve hours at a stretch treating five hundred to a thousand patients!

This was not the only occasion when Ida used Roadside as a therapy.

These first years of the war were troubled ones in India. The day war was declared Great Britain had taken the country into the conflict by proclamation and without consultation. In spite of Gandhi's and other leaders' sympathy for England in this crisis, and their distaste for Hitlerism, Indian nationalists viewed this action with a resentment not unmixed with opportunism. India would gladly join with other free nations in mutual defense, said the Congress Party, but only by her own choice and as a free nation. Britain, headed by the conservative Churchill, had no intention of purchasing India's cooperation with freedom, independence, dominion status, or any other new concession. Kindled by these fires of resentment, nationalism was at white heat throughout the country, eclipsing for the moment the normal good will of individual Indians for individual Britishers. Feelings were easily hurt. Even old friends and associates on the Vellore staff became involved in misunderstandings.

One morning Ida mounted the private bus which transported students and staff several times each day from college to hospital and back. Instantly she sensed an atmosphere of strain among the members of the staff. Soon one of the Indian doctors made a disparaging remark about one of her British colleagues riding in the bus, questioning her loyalty to the best interests of India. Ida said nothing, but she was sorely troubled. Though the two doctors had never had occasion for intimate association, their relations had presumably been friendly. Arriving at the hospital, she walked along with the young Englishwoman, pulled her down on the low wall of the verandah.

"What can we do to help that person?" she asked with deep concern.

That very day she arranged to have the Indian doctor go out with this English member of the staff on Roadside. In the evening the Indian woman came to her British colleague, all mistrust and dislike gone from her face.

"I'm sorry," she said sincerely. "I disliked you when you came because you were English. I can see I was wrong. I didn't know you. I ask you to forgive me."

What a pity, thought Ida fervently, that the leaders of all the great nations of the earth could not spend a day together on Roadside!

A year passed, and still conditions were too uncertain to warrant her leaving for America. In one way she was glad, for she could direct all her energies toward safeguarding the school in the interim. Her idea was to upgrade it sufficiently to pass the university standard for the first two premedical years of the college course. While this would by no means insure college status or final university affiliation, it would at least make it possible to admit a class of new students for a two-year course and keep the school open while further attempts at upgrading were being made. Ida waited in an agony of suspense for the government inspection which would determine the school's immediate fate.

It came in January, 1941. It was not an auspicious time, for many of the staff members were out of the country earning their advanced degrees, which would enable them to conform to the new requirements, and the staff was sadly depleted. Already there was a rumor abroad that the college could not pass this preliminary test. There were important Indians on the visiting

291

commission—Brahmins, other high-caste Hindus, an Indian Jew—some of them ardent nationalists. With them came Sri Lakshmanaswamy Mudaliar, vice-chancellor of Madras University.

They came at 10:30 in the morning and could stay only until three.

Ida met them at the door, gracious, charming, but inwardly quaking. As a touch of informality she pinned the name of each one of them on his lapel as he entered. She saw at once that this had been a mistake. Some of the members of the commission considered it an indignity. It was the group on trial that should have been presented to *them!* But during the delicious luncheon they began to thaw. Afterward they sat down with the staff for a round-table conference. The visitors were obviously skeptical.

"Surely," exclaimed one of them, "you can't keep your staff for these petty salaries you are paying!"

"Ask them," said Ida.

The commissioner did so, beginning with the first staff member in the circle. "Will you stay here at this low salary you are getting when you could receive so much more in a government college or hospital?"

Ida held her breath. She scarcely dared hope, for some of the staff were Hindus, from whom a Christian institution could hardly expect sacrificial loyalty.

"Yes," replied every one of them.

After this the visitors were cordial. They went through the hospital with minute care, asking many questions, some of them staying after the others had to leave.

Ida had high hopes when they went away. If they only presented a favorable report, so the university syndicate could take the matter up in February, there would be ample time to prepare for a first premedical class to enter in July. But February passed into March, and she heard nothing.

On March 5, the beginning of the hot season, Ida started on a tour south with Dr. Liza Chacko, professor of anatomy, and Casey Wierenga, secretary of the India Council, meeting with various groups who had been trying to form "Friends of Vellore." Though the heat was intense, during the following weeks in 1941 they held meetings constantly.

At the famous Syrian Church convention, held in a huge thatched temporary shelter on a dry river bed, Ida spoke for an hour to 30,000 people. They visited the Maharajah of Travancore and his rani, tried unsuccessfully to see the royalty of the neighboring state of Cochin. The head of the Syrian Church received them graciously but said a man in his high position should be expected to give much; therefore he felt he could give nothing. But he would bless the medical school, even though he considered its theology bad, very bad.

In Trivandrum, principal city of Travancore, Vellore graduates had prepared for them a nineteen-course dinner. The team visited medical associations and ladies' clubs. In Nagercoil they called on the dewan in his palace. He was courteous and expressed his great interest in Vellore, which he was eager to visit; not eager to contribute money to, however, only his hopes and best wishes. There were triumphs and discouragements. Many persons gave generously. One tea planter promised to send 200 pounds of tea. But for the most part the results of the trip were disappointing.

Unfortunately the report of the inspection commission failed to reach the university syndicate until the middle of March. No hope of hearing news of their possible affiliation with the University of Madras until May, too late to reopen the school in July. A whole year to wait, and the situation daily growing more crucial! For, if granted, the affiliation would be only temporary even for the two years of the premedical course, and provisional upon their securing adequate staff and buildings within the next two years. After that there would still remain the task of upgrading the school to the full college standard.

Raising sufficient funds to meet this crisis seemed impossible. The three councils, or governing boards, of the Missionary Medical School for Women, one in India, one in England, one in the United States, were by no means agreed on the proper procedure of attempting to solve the problem. Though Ida herself had agreed to work only for a women's college, the issue of coeducation was still paramount. In India the council had voted in August, 1940, favoring coeducation, which would mean uniting with the Christian Medical Association of India in an attempt to raise funds for an All-India Christian Medical College for both men and women; but they had not dared to make the vote public for fear of alienating the American governing board. In the United States, though Lucy Peabody held the majority of the board firmly in opposition to coeducation, several denominational representatives were refusing to support a united appeal except for one coeducational college. It was a hopeless impasse, and Ida felt that her presence was sorely needed in America.

Acting in the hope that the American board would give her leave to come, she feverishly began making inquiries. Passages for America were hard to get, but she found one cabin on a boat leaving Bombay at the end of June. Still she was uncertain as to the wisdom of making the trip. Half the world was at war. Letters from home urged her not to come. Even her dear friends, the William Bancroft Hills, advised her to give up her goal of a medical college and content herself with training nurses.

The needs of the hospital as well as of the school demanded expansion. One day the children's specialist came to her in great excitement. "Dr. Ida! Please come with me to the children's ward."

They entered together, and Ida looked about her. Every bed was full and sixteen children were on the floor!

"What shall I do?" The doctor was almost in tears. "That one has pneumonia, this one isolated in the corner has dysentery. Oh, what *can* I do!"

Ida made no reply. There was none to make. Though the hospital was supposed to have a capacity of 268 beds, there were 332 patients on the beds, under them, along the corridors. If they could meet the university requirements, there would be 500 beds!

It was at Hill Top, looking out over the broad vistas, that she suddenly saw the problem clearly. *What was she doing here— a general twelve thousand miles from the line of battle! Since when had she waited for others to give her leave to do a job needing to be done?*

Returning to Vellore, as if in answer to her decision, she found waiting the long-delayed report from the university syndicate. The government inspection committee had reported favorably. Her school had been granted temporary affiliation with

294

the University of Madras and was permitted to enroll students in a two-year premedical course. Though it was too late to admit a class this year, the school had received the green light to go ahead. All that remained now was to raise the necessary million dollars.

On May 21, 1941 Ida sent a cable to the American governing board via its treasurer Hilda Olson: UNIVERSITY AFFILIATION GRANTED. MANY CONDITIONS PREVENT OPENING UNTIL '42. MONEY, ADDITIONAL EQUIPMENT NECESSARY. COMING AMERICA IMMEDIATELY VIA CALIFORNIA. CAN CAMPAIGN BE ORGANIZED. IDA S.

She wept when the train carrying her and Gertrude pulled out of Katpadi Station. For she was then over seventy, and Gertrude was eighty-two, and she was afraid it was the last time they would be leaving India together.

"See you next year!" she called bravely to Ida B. and Treva Marshall.

Fortunately she could not know that it would be four long years before she would be returning to India—alone.

24

"MISSIONARY SEEKS ANGEL WITH MIL-
LION." ... "JAPANESE BOMB PEARL
HARBOR!" ... "DR. SCUDDER, 44 YEARS
A MISSIONARY, IN CITY." ... "SINGAPORE FALLS!" ... "DR.
IDA SCUDDER CAMPAIGNING TO RAISE MILLION DOLLARS FOR
HOSPITAL AND COLLEGE." ... "JAPANESE CAPTURE RAN-
GOON, BURMA!" ... "WOMAN DOCTOR, 72, TELLS INDIA'S
NEEDS"

Day after day, week after week, the modest newspaper headlines marking her trail were crowded into back pages by the
more urgent headlines of global disaster. After her arrival in
America in late 1941, Ida traveled constantly, speaking almost
every day and often three or four times, to churches, high
schools, colleges, service groups, women's clubs, universities,
YWCAs, over radio stations, to country clubs, chambers of
commerce, schools of nursing, to any group, small or large, that
was willing to listen. For almost four years she traveled, zeal
never wavering, fighting a life-and-death battle to save her
life's great purpose.

The black headlines were formidable competitors, but Ida
too was news. As one newspaper commented, "A woman wanting a million dollars is no rarity, but one working for her third

million is something else again." Add to this the facts that the crusader was an intensely dynamic and attractive woman in her seventies, that forty-two members of her family through four generations had given a total of over a thousand years in missionary service, that she had one of the most dramatic stories in the world to tell, and even a war-harried press was obliged to sit up occasionally and take notice.

"This extraordinary white-haired woman," wrote Jerome Beatty in the *Reader's Digest,* "has, at 72, a spring in her step, a sparkle in her eye and the skilled, strong hands of a surgeon of 45. For 18 years she has been head of the medical association in a district with a population of 2,000,000. Doctors all over India send her their most difficult gynecological cases. Women and children come just to touch her, so exalted is her reputation for healing."

In the United States, however, the possible future annihilation and the urgent present needs of a medical school half a world away paled in importance for women whose brothers and sons and husbands were risking present annihilation in Bataan, Guadalcanal, Okinawa. Hands busy rolling bandages for servicemen were not easily diverted to providing them for Roadside lepers. Ida's appeal, dramatic though it was, ran constant competition with dozens of war charities, from Red Cross and local canteens to British, French, and Russian relief. The wonder was not that she failed to win sweeping victory for her cause, but that she succeeded in arousing as much publicity, audience loyalty, and financial support as she did.

Competition was not her only hardship. It was a time when travel was difficult. Trains were crowded, compartments often unavailable. There were no porters to carry baggage. Besides personal luggage there was always a heavy suitcase weighted with printed materials, which Gertrude insisted on carrying, following with the same loyalty as she had shown along the edges of sheer slopes in Kashmir. Though remaining ever in the background, Gertrude was the major-domo of every expedition, making appointments for luncheons and teas, arranging interviews, purchasing railroad tickets, conducting the voluminous business correspondence.

But Ida's battle was not all fought on platforms and across

luncheon tables and office desks. The fiercest struggle of all was within herself.

"You must tell us where you stand," wrote Lucy Peabody early in the campaign, "before we can go out for more appeals. Some people say you favor this cooperation with the men. If you and the majority of the board wish this coeducational work and desire to turn *our* plant and endowment over to men who have not done one single thing to help us, of course the charter can be legally changed, and the board can give up and move out and let the men take charge!"

From India the demands for a decision were even more insistent as the school and hospital faced the crisis. The council in India had declared itself firmly in favor of coordination. James C. McGilvray—"Mac"—bursar and secretary of the council, who was attempting to steer the institution through these critical days, and others of the handicapped and depleted staff were outspoken in their urgent letters.

"Aunt Ida," wrote Ida B. with desperate earnestness, "we must not put off any longer. Vellore must say 'yes' to this development, because if we try to go on as a women's college only, we'll never do it. That is, we might just struggle along, but we want Vellore to be the most wonderful college, with a great and unique contribution. If we hold out, they'll decide on Miraj as the place. Miraj will jump at the chance. So!!"

"If men use our buildings," wrote Hilda Olson, "we'll lose two of our biggest promised gifts, one of $25,000 and one of $100,000."

"I trust," wrote Lucy Peabody, without whose brilliant leadership College Hill would still be grazing lands and unbroken stones, "you will stand firm on the principle for which Vellore was instituted and pledged *and be loyal* to the 'three calls in the night' which led you into this work *for women*."

Ida could no longer postpone taking a stand.

She was traveling east through the Rocky Mountains with Gertrude. Towering on either side of the train rose massive cliffs, beautiful but overpowering. Now and then they passed a ravine which gave a brief vista into some far country, then plunged again into a green tunnel. Ida felt stifled. She was

298

glad when night came and she could close her eyes, but it was only to dream that she was rushing headlong into narrowing darkness. In the morning she raised the shade to find bright sunlight and broad plains stretching to the far horizons.

And suddenly all the long uncertainty was swept away. A new day had come. Why was she trying to live in yesterday? Was she getting old, that she must keep to the narrow familiar paths, instead of venturing into new and unexplored country? The structure she had built was big enough for the India of yesterday; perhaps even for the India of today, still groping her way through the narrow gorges. But not for the India of tomorrow! How stupid she had been, waiting for divine guidance to show her the way! What could be any plainer than to have one wide door opened before you and all others slammed behind?

That very day she wrote the American governing board, approving the plan of cooperation that would make Vellore an interdenominational Christian medical college for both men and women, sending at the same time a confirming cable to India.

The results were what she had expected: joy in India and unanimous endorsement of cooperation by the council; bitterness from the two women who had been her most loyal friends and supporters in America. The letters she received from them hurt her cruelly.

In December of 1942 the secretary of the American Governing Board reported that all the difficulties in the way of cooperation had been cleared away. On Thursday afternoon, January 28, the board met to make its decision. Every denomination was represented. Two members had come down from Canada. Lucy Peabody, who had made a special trip from her home in Florida, announced that even if her vote should be the only one against cooperation she would stand alone. It was Mrs. Doane, another stanch opponent of coeducation, who saved the day, working on the wording of the resolution in her quiet way until she was sure that the principle of medical education for women would be permanently safeguarded. The vote for cooperation was finally unanimous.

Ida could scarcely believe it when she received a wire telling of the board's decision.

Back and forth across the country she went, with Gertrude, and the big suitcase of brochures. She met Scudders everywhere she went—nieces, nephews, cousins—and for the first time in her seventy years she had time to get acquainted with them. She reveled in it. One niece was having a baby, and she was all anticipatory thrills. One nephew was building a house; she must have a part in its decoration. When the flyer son of another niece was missing over Germany, she was all compassion until word was received that he was safe in a German prison; then later all excitement over his wedding. She visited her brother Harry in New Brunswick, New Jersey, where he had taken a church on retirement. She visited the Scudder cottage on Shelter Island and went swimming again every day.

But always the campaign went on: the crowded railroad stations, the marching headlines, the eager tireless voice.

Philadelphia, Columbus. . . . "India has awakened. Women are being emancipated. The new India deserves only the best."

Detroit, Minneapolis, Cleveland . . . San Francisco, Fort Myers, Los Angeles. . . . "This war is setting us an example, for no sooner is a ship bombed than help is sent. Vellore has been hit by a bomb. She will sink unless we send help."

V. for Victory. Victory for Vellore.

Toronto. "His Honor the Lieutenant Governor and Mrs. Albert Matthews gave a reception Saturday in their Queen's Park suite in honor of Dr. Ida Scudder."

Holland, Muskegon, Grand Rapids, Kalamazoo . . . "We would like to make it the greatest school in India, and it could be done. Only one million people giving a dollar apiece!"

There were not a million people. By February, 1943, they had raised only $28,000, by December only $60,000. The big gifts were not forthcoming. After attempting for nearly three years to interview the widow of a great automobile magnate, Ida was finally asked if she would care to return to Detroit for the privilege of a telephone conversation.

"No!" she replied with vigor. "I guess the Lord doesn't want her money."

Obstacles seemed insurmountable. In India the land for the new hospital buildings was proving expensive, hard to get and building materials impossible to secure. Mr. McGilvray was still negotiating for new staff members with the required degrees, trying to raise salaries 100 per cent, pleading with Dr. Hilda Lazarus to come to the college as principal. But, keenly interested though she was in the Vellore project, the distinguished Indian Christian doctor, strongly pressed by reason of the war emergency to assume a responsible government position in New Delhi with the Women's Medical Service for India, was as yet unable to commit herself.

And in America dissension continued. The opponents of coeducation were still making trouble, insisting that the vote of the Governing board had meant "cooperation," not "coeducation," and that even the hospital for men must not adjoin that for women. Offers of the two largest gifts were withdrawn. And Hilda Olson, still performing wonders with the endowment fund, was insisting to the board that it should be built up still further by the proceeds of this campaign.

"Can't you understand," Ida wrote in November, 1943, "that it's buildings we must have now, not endowment? If we don't get them assured by October of 1944, our work will be closed! We *must* have them—pathology, dispensary, medical, surgery, maternity, library. I can't go on asking for endowment, but I'll give my last ounce of strength to save Vellore."

However, there was some good news. Word came from India that the extension to the Anatomy Block was completed, plans prepared for extending the nurses' home to the third story, a few capable new staff members secured. Dr. Miriam Manuel, one of Ida's finest graduates, refused a position paying five hundred rupees a month in order to stay at Vellore. A church in Morrison, Illinois, had taken an Easter offering of $1,510. The Methodist Church was placing the work at Vellore high on its great "Crusade for Christ" campaign goals. And, now that the decision had been made for cooperation, the resources of interest and financial aid had become infinitely wider. In America both men and women of at least twenty denominations were now committed to the building of an All-India Christian Medical College at Vellore. In Great Britain seven missionary societies of five denominations were involved in the united campaign. And there were also active groups of supporters in Denmark and Australia.

Yet in spite of this assurance Ida could not have borne the pressure of anxiety without the loyal support of her stanch intimate friends. It was almost a death blow to her courage when suddenly she found herself facing the loss of the most loyal friend of all.

It was December 17, 1943, and Ida sat in a room in St. Petersburg, Florida. From her window she could look out on a scene lovely as India: palms and creepers, roofs painted a brilliant green, masses of glorious poinsettias. Yet these were among the darkest hours of her life. For the room was in a hospital. And Gertrude Dodd lay beside her, dying.

They had returned from a long Western trip early in December, and were enjoying a brief rest before the big three-month Florida campaign. Ida's brother Harry and his wife Margaret were coming soon to join them. Though Gertrude had seemed tired, she had assured everyone that she was perfectly well. But she had slept a great deal and had stopped writing letters.

"I must write," she had said, when Ida had insisted on attending to her business correspondence. "You mustn't baby me."

Then had come the sudden acute illness, the unsuccessful operation, and now the long hours of waiting.

"9:00 A.M.," wrote Ida with a doctor's neat precision of detail. "Gertrude is slipping away but she has been so dear. Keeps saying, 'Oh Idee, you have been so good to me . . . Idee, are you there? Don't leave me.'

"10:15. 'Idee, don't keep me any longer, just let me go, because you will get so tired, you are all working so hard. Oh, Idee, I simply can't leave you alone.' Intravenous glucose being given, pulse very irregular.

"10:30. 'Idee, my dearest, you will never know what you have been in my life. But you must rest. If I go, you won't have to work so hard.' "

But days passed, and she did not go.

On January 6 Ida was still writing, this time to Ida B. and Treva. "I am sitting alone at the bedside of our beloved Gertrude. As yet I don't know how I can face life alone, without her absolute faith in me, her loyal love. She always saw the best in me and inspired me to do my best."

302

On Sunday, January 9 she wrote: "The saddest day of my life. Gertrude died ten to one, and my heart broke."

On Tuesday she started for New York. "Glad to have a long quiet day to think. We are taking our last ride together."

It was not a sad funeral. "A beautiful, beautiful day of sunshine," wrote Ida afterward to her friends and Gertrude's, "and Collegiate Church was glorious with flowers. Pale yellow roses, violets and pansies, a beautiful spray of orchids covered her with an exquisite blanket. Dr. Sizoo read the Scriptures— "I was an hungred and ye fed me." Dr. Peale made a most touching tribute. Dr. Romig's prayer lifted us from earth to heaven. But, oh, the road ahead looks sad and lonely!"

There was no time for grieving, little enough for reading and answering the four hundred letters of sympathy and tribute which came from all over the world, though she answered all of them, sending 203 letters in one day.

Except that the lines of her still-beautiful but aging face were etched a little deeper, her resonant voice became a bit gentler, and her unfading blue eyes revealed a deeper sensitivity, if possible, to the sufferings of the war-torn world through which she moved, Ida went on with her campaign as if nothing had happened, starting the Florida Chain of Missionary Assemblies on January 26.

Months passed while she waited for the war to end or for permission to return to India. Between rigorous speaking tours she swam at Shelter Island, gardened at Harry's in New Brunswick, played tennis at the summer conference center in Northfield. There was scarcely an entry in her diary that failed to start with some phrase which showed her zest for living. "A happy day.... A beautiful day.... A perfect day.... A busy day.... A perfectly glorious day...."

In spite of the fact that the new Joint Committee on Promotion for Vellore had hired a professional fund-raising company to run the new inclusive campaign, and she herself had contributed $5,000 to its cost, she still insisted on campaigning. During the early months of 1945 she had Mr. McGilvray— "Mac"—home on furlough, to help her. She found his assistance invaluable, in minor as well as major issues of the campaign. Once she even took him along with her to help choose a hat.

"That's it!" exclaimed Mac enthusiastically.

She removed the small toque of iridescent feathers and looked at the price tag. "But—"

"It's made for you! With that on, you'll knock your audiences cold!"

Ida bought the hat, though the thought of the price still shocked her. It was in a good cause, and if Vellore was going coeducational, she must dress to please men as well as women!

The triumph of V-E Day in May, 1945, was dimmed by her sadness over the meeting of the governing board held during the same month in New York, when both Hilda Olson and Lucy Peabody resigned.

But the prospects for Vellore's survival looked more hopeful. In India Dr. Robert Cochrane, famous leprosy specialist loaned by the Church of Scotland, had become first principal of the new medical college, with the gigantic task of assembling a staff to fulfill university requirements by October, 1945. The building program was proceeding slowly but steadily. And Friends of Vellore, the prayer fellowship formed in India during the first months of crisis, was spreading to all parts of the world. There were speeches in America, in England, where Dr. Leslie Weatherhead had become its ardent supporter, in Canada, Scotland, Denmark, and Australia. It looked like V Day indeed: victory not only for a world tired of war, but for Vellore as well. The next hurdle to be jumped was the passing of inspection by the university syndicate in October, and Ida set her heart on being in India in time for the commission's visit.

The world was rocking to the echoes of Hiroshima and Nagasaki when her visa finally came through, but when she set sail from New York on the Gripsholm at 6:30 on August 28, the frightening mushroom clouds were slowly yielding to the dawn of V-J Day. She was glad to be heading East on a new mission from America to the millions of Asia—one of healing instead of annihilation.

Because she was in such a hurry, she went from Cairo to Bombay by plane, and loved it. For the first time in her life she was moving fast enough to suit her!

304

25

India again! Ida could hardly bear the joy of it. Her senses reveled in all the sights and sounds and smells: the rickshas, the bullock carts, the surging masses of color; the beat of drums, clang of temple gongs, clatter of hoofs, chanting of hucksters, clucking of mule drivers; in the bazaars the fragrance of cloves, cinnamon, turmeric, chillies, sheen of sunlight on brass, tang of cow-dung smoke; yes, even the miserably sick and under-fed bodies, for they made her fingers itch to get at them!

Ida was greeted at Arkonum, the railroad junction close to Vellore, by Ida B. and another doctor, Kamala Vythilingam, who had been a pupil in her second medical-school class and now, possessor of an advanced degree, was one of the hospital's medical specialists.

It was night when they drove through the gates at College Hill. Ida caught her breath in amazement. Then her eyes misted. Lined up on each side of the drive as far as she could see were students and staff members, with college peons holding blazing torches, rags wrapped around long sticks and soaked in kerosene. As the car passed through the avenue of light, hands reached out and decked her with garlands, burying her so deep that all but her eyes were covered. Voices began chanting in rhythm, the sound swelling into a deafening chorus.

"Doc-tor I-da Scud-der-ji! Doc-tor I-da Scud-der-ji!"

Her long journey was over. She had come home.

But not to the India she had known. The four war years had brought changes more profound than the country had often seen in the course of centuries. Churchill's refusal to "preside at the liquidation of the British empire" in granting even a semblance of independence to a people demanding the right to defend itself as a free nation against invasion, had resulted in a storm of rebellion. Following the instigation by Gandhi of a new civil disobedience movement in August of 1942, scores of top-ranking Congress leaders, including Gandhi and Nehru, had been jailed. Their absence had opened the sluice gates of a flood of violence: firing of buildings, sabotage of railroads and telegraph lines, assault of British officials. Gandhi, blamed unjustly for this turbulence, had undertaken a three-week fast which almost killed him.

Now, however, in 1945, with the advent of a new Labor government in Britain, independence seemed a coming realization. Lord Wavell, the viceroy, had promised not only the restoration of provincial rule by Indians but also an assembly to draft a federal constitution. All that prevented agreement on the details of Indian independence was the insistence of the Moslem League upon partition. Certain political leaders of the Moslem minority, chief among them Mohammed Ali Jinnah, were fearful that independence would bring Hindu control of chief government posts and economic advantages, and were determined to have a nation of their own. The country seethed with hopes and fears, nationalist emotions and religious tensions.

But Vellore also bore the marks of the troublous war years. Ida was quick to inform herself of developments during her absence. Listening to the reports some of her colleagues, including Ida B., were now ready to give, she was able to relive with them experiences which had not only taxed their strength and powers of endurance but threatened the very existence of the hospital and college buildings.

In early 1942 the war was drawing closer and closer to South

India. Emotions were at the boiling point. Famine, worst in a hundred years, was sweeping from Bengal through the whole subcontinent. Servants on the college compound, teachers in the villages, were often reduced to one meal a day.

In April Colombo was bombed by the Japanese, and soon after, on a night following a huge rain and flood, there was a bombing of Madras. Word came that the Japanese fleet was steaming northward, and invasion of the city seemed imminent. The whole area was swept with panic, and the city began evacuating. As Vellore lay in a direct path between Madras and Bangalore, the hospital was ordered to reduce patients to a minimum and prepare for casualties. First-year nursing students were sent home, plans made for the quick evacuation of other nurses to the country home of Dr. Gurupatham, the eye specialist. Any of the staff who wished were permitted to leave, but most remained quietly at work. Fortunately most of the students, the last of the Licensed Medical Practitioner group and 135 girls from St. Christopher's, a mission school in Madras whose buildings had been requisitioned as air-raid headquarters for the "duration," were home on vacation. The presence of her cousin Helen, Uncle Harry's daughter, who was a St. Christopher teacher, made these hectic days more livable for Ida B.

On a Tuesday the college buildings were requisitioned to accommodate the evacuating C.I.D. (Crime Investigation Department) from Madras. In a frenzy of haste and amid broiling temperatures, Mr. McGilvray, Ida B., who was acting medical superintendent, and others of the staff, transferred all the furniture from the students' hostel into other buildings. The servants were horrified to see them filling the chapel to the very doors, until they understood the reason. It was like a nightmare. That night, too exhausted to sleep, Ida B. lay in her room overlooking the courtyard and tried to memorize the peace and beauty of the place against the future. She awoke to the sound of the advance police guards dousing themselves under the tap in the courtyard.

She was in the big bungalow resting after more frenzied activity when the head of the C.I.D. arrived and summoned members of the staff. They went with grim foreboding. Every extra corner of the campus was already filled with evacuees, the hospital overflowing. What more could they be asked to do?

The officer frowned at them. "I tell you, we're not moving into these buildings!" he exploded indignantly. "I won't have it. These buildings are too beautiful to use for government offices. I advise you to go to Madras at once and have them requisitioned by the University for educational purposes only."

For a moment none of the staff could speak. It was too incredibly good to be true. Then—"Right!" said Mac heartily, and started posthaste for Madras. His request was granted, and, thanks to one man's sensitivity to beauty, the buildings were saved, unsullied, for their intended purpose.

In spite of difficulties plans went forward for the reception of the first M.B., B.S. class of twenty-five girls in the summer of 1942. There were a few weeks of worried uncertainty when, in spite of the permission granted by the university syndicate to offer the first two years of premedical work, the American governing board decided that it was not the time to launch the new enterprise. But when the board cabled the council to postpone opening, Mac registered violent protest. "It's now or never!" he warned urgently by cable. Mrs. Rossman, the board secretary, finally cabled back: AUTHORIZE OPENING JULY.

Other developments in Vellore during those war years were equally constructive. The new men's outpatient department, built out of the old peanut godown, was opened "to the glory of God and with good will toward men"; it was opened appropriately, in Ida's absence, by another woman doctor, secretary of the Christian Medical Association of India, Dr. Choné Oliver, without whose tireless efforts cooperation might never have been achieved. And, most significant of all, the tottering wall separating the building from the imposing two-storied hospital for women was razed to the ground. Nothing could have been more symbolic of the vast changes taking place in India.

By 1944 the first men doctors had already arrived: Dr. M. Asirvatham, pathologist, who started the men's outpatient work in a small way; Dr. Norman MacPherson, who left his work in North India to come as surgeon; Dr. Theodore Gault, an Australian, coming to develop the pathology department. The first unit for men inpatients was formed out of one entire block of the women's hospital. There was opposition to this even in India.

"Are we being loyal to Dr. Ida and her work for women?" people asked.

"But women can no longer be saved through isolation," came the reply in words Ida herself might have used. "They don't want to be isolated. They are sensitive to this stigma of inferiority. From now on they want to be saved as part of the family."

By July, 1944, the new men's ward was already overcrowded. And the building schedule was way behind. The institution could not possibly stand inspection by the university commission in October! Fortunately the university syndicate agreed to postpone inspection for one year. Third-year students would be allowed to take their clinical work for a few months at Madras Medical College while the necessary hospital units were being completed.

Ida listened with interest to all these reports, observed all the new developments in both hospital and college, and was able to greet the commission of inspection when it came in October, 1945, with her usual command of facts and contagious enthusiasm. The commission reported favorably, recommending to the university syndicate that the college be permitted to teach the clinical subjects. There was great rejoicing when word was received at the college that the long-coveted university affiliation had been granted. It was only a temporary and provisional affiliation, however. Another commission would come in 1947, when more staff had been secured and more buildings completed, to make a final inspection. If the goals were not reached, all the progress so painfully achieved could still be forfeited.

Already there were so many changes in the hospital buildings that Ida marveled anew each time she drove into the compound. There were a new Pathology and Research Block, a gynecology building, new maternity and antenatal quarters, additional stories added to the Administration Building, the children's ward, Cole Dispensary, and the Weyerhauser Surgical Block. There were new wings and stories for the nurses' home, new dispensaries, laboratories, staff bungalows, servants' quarters.

Still, however, there were only 371 beds compared with the 600 which must be made available by the time of the next inspection. Still clinical space must be provided for the ten men students who were to be admitted in 1947. And further development was urgently needed in a variety of departments, such as urology, orthopedics, tuberculosis, leprosy, skin diseases, thoracic surgery. But the changes already effected in the attempt to meet the crisis were nothing short of miraculous.

And there were new staff members to get acquainted with as well as new buildings. Among the newcomers were men as well as women, and the group represented a variety of cultures. Several were from Australia; a woman teacher of anatomy from Ireland; some from England, Canada, the United States; a number of gifted Indians who had left important posts to help Vellore meet its staff requirements. Ida found new doctors supervising eight departments. And many of these departments themselves were new, one of the most recent being the psychiatric section, so much needed in a country where, as in Scriptural days, people still wandered about aimlessly, "possessed of devils."

It was a young Canadian woman, Dr. Florence Nichols, first woman psychiatrist in India, who soon arrived to head this department. Dr. Nichols was introduced to Ida in the spirit even before she met her in the flesh. She arrived in Madras with a great mass of luggage just as the train was leaving for Vellore. Despairing of getting her trunks on the train in time, she went to the station master.

"Where are you going?" he asked with no great concern.

"Vellore," she replied. "The Vellore Christian Medical College."

His expression changed. "The train will not go," he assured her, "until all your baggage is on."

"But—it might hold it up for ten minutes!"

"I said—the train will not go until all your baggage is on."

He himself conducted her to her compartment, saw that the baggage was all in, closed the door, and then spoke to her through the window.

"Now do you know why I have done this for you?" he asked.

"Dr. Ida Scudder once saved my life." Quickly he told how he had fallen from a horse and she had operated on him. "There is nothing I would not do for her or her hospital."

On December 9, 1945, a few months after her return, Ida was seventy-five years old. Though she was ten years beyond the usual retirement age for missionaries and while in America, at her own request, had been made principal emerita, she had never been officially retired from the college and hospital staff. Now, to her great delight, when Dr. Cochrane, principal and director of the new Christian Medical College and Hospital, went on business to England in December, Ida was asked by the council to become acting principal. On her fiftieth birthday she had expressed the wish that she might celebrate her diamond jubilee in heaven. But surely Vellore, struggling through its first six months of temporary affiliation with Madras University, was the next thing to it!

She slipped into the old grooves as easily as if she had never left them. Again students experienced the charm and inspiration of her radiant spirit—her Tuesday Bible classes, her reading of the "love" chapter each Monday morning, the quiet conferences on Sundays.

The fever of building was in her blood. She loved all the bustle and confusion. Now that wartime restrictions were over, the construction was proceeding at—for India—a dizzying rate. Each morning when she went to the hospital, no matter how early, there were the long lines of bullock carts, the processions of coolies, women in bright saris, men in white, marching along the roads of the hospital compound, climbing ladders, heads piled high with stone blocks, bricks, jars of water, baskets of sand and mortar. All day, whether at hospital or college, the sounds of building set a rhythm for her swift motions: pounding of hammers as each block of granite was cut by hand with chisels heated in charcoal fires, wheezing of bellows, chanting of water carriers, rhythmic concerted yellings as the great teakwood girders were rolled and strained and hoisted up long bamboo trunks to the new upper stories.

That year also Ida saw another of her hopes fulfilled, when

the school of nursing received its first B.Sc. students. As yet there was no school granting university degrees to nurses in all India.

"This course can be given only in a medical college," Dr. Mudaliar had told the council. "I want it in Vellore."

There had been opposition from the staff. Even Dr. Cochrane and Vera Pitman, who had followed Dell Houghton as nursing superintendent, had been staggered by the proposition. But Ida was behind it all the way. Never had she felt greater satisfaction than on the evening of the first nurses' graduation after her return, standing in the darkened chapel holding the little silver lamp shaped like a teapot, a replica of Florence Nightingale's, and watched it kindle into flame.

She spent long mornings in the hospital, long afternoons immersed in the college budget, emerging to her dismay with a two-lakhs ($40,000) deficit. She conducted sessions of the senatus and attended the annual council meeting, entertaining the visitors afterward—forty-seven of them—for lunch. She went out on Roadside and took part in leprosy clinics, sometimes helping to treat as many as three hundred patients. Tired out from three days of medical meetings in Nagpur, she spent her usual busy morning performing operations, an afternoon and evening going over new student applications, managing to catch a few minutes for tennis in between. She sat by the bedside of her beloved first nurse, Salomi, who became suddenly, desperately ill, watched helplessly as she slipped away, grieved over her death as if she had been a sister. She welcomed students, led chapel services, taught classes, entertained, worked, played. . . .

But the activity could not last forever. With the return of Dr. Cochrane and her relinquishment of the acting principalship, Ida knew that the time had come for definite retirement. And she refused to be a mother who kept her child tied to her apron strings. Not only for her own sake but for others', she knew the break must be swift and clean. Only one thing she insisted upon. She would not, like most other missionaries on retirement, go home to the land of her citizenship. Not America, but India, her birthplace, her residence for over fifty of her seventy-five years, was her home. She would go to Hill Top, as she had long planned, and finish her life as close to heaven as it was possible in this world to be.

Her official retirement in August, 1946, was not a sad occasion. She would not let it be. After all, she had been virtually retired for years, ever since she had been made principal emerita. And at Hill Top, she reminded her sorrowing friends gaily, she would be only a day's journey from Vellore by car. Far closer than she had been in America. She had to be gay to keep from weeping.

There were, of course, many parties in her honor. The students made a love chair, a bower of flowers, beautiful as a palanquin for a god, and set her in it, the "goddess of love." They performed a dance of love about her, white jasmine flowers in their hair, lighted lamps in their hands, decking her with chains and garlands of jasmine and roses and at the end prostrating themselves before her chair. In the evening there was a huge reception, with a big crowd of Vellore citizens attending and much speaking.

"Had delightful farewell," Ida wrote simply in her diary.

The following notation was almost as brief: "August 19, 1946. *Left Vellore*. Oh, it was so hard to say good-by!"

Was it to comfort her in her loneliness that at Hill Top the *kurinji*—strobilanthus—was in bloom? The hills were covered with the tiny flowers, like little bluebells only a paler blue or mauve, and blooming only once in twelve years!

"Thank you, God," she said. "Thank you for letting it be now."

She had time now, *time to contemplate the vast, centuries-long things*.

But she had always done that. She had spent her life in contemplating—wide plains, mountains, in the act of crossing, climbing them; flowers and trees, in the act of nurturing; human life, in the act of saving. She could do no differently now. She contemplated, as always, by activity. She did all the things she had wanted all her life to do—and had managed to find time for. Only she did more of them.

She wrote letters, hundreds, to old students, "Friends of Vellore" around the world. She extended the garden terraces

313

farther and farther down the hill. She had Chinneken the gardener trim all the high eucalyptus trees—higher than usual, and top all the lower ones—lower than usual, so that the view from the verandahs would be unbroken by foliage. (There must always be a view, her friends accused her, even though the gardener might have to break his neck to get it for her!) She took gifts of flowers to her friends in the missionary colony at Kodai. She made boutonnieres for the student ushers at High Clerc, the American school for missionary children conducted the year round at Kodai, and on Sunday mornings the ushers vied with each other to escort her to her seat in the front of the chapel. She invited them to Hill Top, where Sebastian, her gifted cook, fed them one of his wonderful rice-and-curry dinners.

She played tennis. In March, when the new court was opened, she was asked to serve the first ball.

"Oh, dear!" she thought. "What if it should be a dud, Ida? Your brothers would never forgive you!"

But she need not have worried. Her serve was perfect.

She took her dogs walking . . . once too often.

It was a day in October, with the mimosas in golden-yellow bloom. Grannie was scampering ahead and behind and all about, Punch trotting sedately at her side, begging for a stone to chase. She found a stone and threw it. No sooner had Punch leaped than a neighbor's dog rushed out of the bushes and attacked him. Both were large dogs, and the fight was furious. Screams, commands were of no avail. Finally Ida, without a thought for her own safety, sailed into the fray and pulled the dogs apart. In the process she was knocked down, her body bruised, her left hand bitten. The hand continued to be painful, and when she went down to Madura early in November, X rays showed fractures of the hand and wrist.

"At least it's not the right, my operating hand!" she consoled herself, adding grimly, "I should say now, my *digging* hand."

She planted trees. Not that one ever just "planted a tree" at Hill Top. There was too much of St. Francis in Ida for that. A tree was a created being, a personality, like the rose bush she had named "Mab" because one of her pet dogs was buried under it.

"Come, Chinneken," she said gaily to the gardener as they carefully planted a tender green eucalyptus, "Sing! Sing with me:

"Grow, grow, grow,
Unto the God who made you!"

And the gardener, knowing not a word of English but belonging to a race which did not think it strange to sing at work, obediently burst into melody.

She achieved a long-latent ambition. Hill Top, she had long ago decided, must have a waterfall, a difficult engineering feat for the top of a mountain where there was no water! But somehow she and Chinneken accomplished it. They built a pool at the top of the terraces to catch drainage from the roofs, then two more pools farther down. Between were smooth sheer rocks for the water to descend. She would gather her guests at a vantage point, then undam the pool and let the water flow down in one brief but grand *whoosh*.

For of course there were guests. During twelve months of the year now instead of two, Hill Top became an asylum for weary bodies, tired nerves. An Australian doctor and his wife came in September, exclaiming in delight because the wattles and gums reminded them of their home. Her old friend Lavina Honegger, long-widowed but as blithely gay as on the day they had shed their red flannel petticoats, was a frequent guest. And there was a constant coming and going of doctors, nurses, students, travelers.

Not that it was any rest to visit Hill Top! After breakfast each guest was given a handful of seeds and a trowel; after lunch, armed with scissors, he would spend a half hour cutting off dead heads or rooting up *pulachis,* the stubborn weeds which were Ida's worst enemy. She couldn't pass one by even if she was wearing evening dress and had no weapon sharper than her fingernails.

Each guest received the full treatment. On the morning when one, a young nurse, was returning to Vellore, Ida suddenly stared at her in consternation. "Oh, dear, what have we been thinking of! You can't go without a picnic!"

She planned one immediately. Taking their fruit and eggs, they journeyed to Moir Point, cooked outdoors, and had breakfast and prayers close to the world's ceiling. The nurse never forgot it.

Guests were expected to play host also, especially during the vacation season when visitors, often forty or fifty in one day, came to look at the gardens.

"Please," Ida B. had been pleading for years, "put up a sign, Aunt Ida! 'Visitors on such and such days!'" But Ida wouldn't hear of it. If anybody wanted to see her gardens, he was welcome at any time of day or night. She would get up the minute she had lain down to rest if a visitor came. And all the household must get up with her!

Retirement only sharpened her zest for entertaining. No dignitary was safe from her designs if he came within a hundred miles of Hill Top. When, some years later, she heard that her friend Sri Prakasa, one of the first Indian governors of Madras, was to be in the vicinity of Kodai on an official visit, she invited him for lunch. Learning that the governor's party included two sons, one daughter-in-law, one daughter with two children, a private secretary, an aide-de-camp, and the Collector of Madura, she gracefully deferred to his suggestion that the lunch be changed to tea. But what a tea! Sebastian outdid himself with a six layer cake, frosted pink and green, with a model of Government House on top. There were sweets of the same colors, and paper-thin sandwiches, also a spicy mixture of ten varieties. Sebastian, tall and dignified in his long white coat and neatly bound turban, looked fully as impressive as the aide-de-camp.

The affair progressed with proper formality until the arrival of Colonel, the gray Sydney Silkie that had followed Grannie. Though always missing during prayers and at bedtime, Colonel was always in evidence at mealtime. Obviously sharing his mistress' partiality for dignitaries, he made straight for the governor's chair, and graciously His Excellency extended a generous portion of Sebastian's rich resplendent cake.

"Oh, no, Colonel!" protested Ida vigorously. "You mustn't eat that. You'll have indigestion!"

Her friends gasped in shocked amazement, but not the Governor. "What about me?" he retorted with a chuckle.

It was these vacation months that made the others bearable.

She could almost deceive herself into thinking she herself was only on vacation. Her days were full again. Her calendar for one of these summer months recorded twelve luncheons, seven teas, an indefinite number of entertainments, fairs, tennis tournaments. Not that there was a dearth of excitement the rest of the year, however! On even the dullest days at Kodai something exciting had always been likely to happen. Take, for example, the deer.

Her servant Nateson came one morning, babbling about it excitedly. It had been killed by a tiger during the night, and it was on the Doctor *Ammal's* own land. Immediately Ida set forth to see it. After exhausting the full possibilities of sympathy for the creature, she noticed the remarkable beauty of the head with its spreading antlers. "Bring me a carving knife," she ordered briskly.

Nateson obeyed, eyes wide. She severed the head neatly, employing her best surgeon's skill as with any other amputation and despatched it to a good taxidermist in Madura, whence it returned, beautifully mounted, to occupy a place of honor in the living room.

Soon some forest officers came to call. With great enthusiasm and even more naïveté Ida showed them the deer head and told them all about the incident.

One of the visitors cleared his throat. "Madam," he said solemnly, "that is why we have come. Do you know that you have broken the law?"

Meekly Ida paid her fine of fifty rupees.

26

August 15, 1947. The day of independence came, bittersweet as most births, for the dream of a united country had been betrayed. To Gandhi and many others, it was a day not of triumph, but of mourning.

The partition of India had been a late development. For decades Hindu and Moslem leaders had worked side by side in the struggle for independence; for centuries their humbler followers had lived side by side in cities, towns, and villages in comparative harmony. They possessed the same languages, the same racial backgrounds, for 95 per cent of India's Moslems were descendants of Hindus converted to the new religion either by force or by choice during the late Moslem invasions. They had the same needs and the same basic problems—poverty, disease, illiteracy, absentee landlordism, low living standards —which they hoped independence would help solve.

Even as late as August, 1946, unity had seemed the only possible outcome of the growing disagreement between the Congress Party and the Moslem League. A British Cabinet Mission arriving in March had recommended a united India with a limited federal government, which would protect religious minorities, and provincial governments with wide powers. Partition had come largely because of the political aspirations of one man, Mohammed Ali Jinnah, leader of the Moslem League yet not a strong Moslem by conviction. When Nehru had been authorized by the British to form a cabinet on August 12, 1946, Jinnah had declared August 16 to be Direct Action Day. Reason had been forged into a political tool of passion. A fire of Hindu-Moslem antagonism had been whipped into flame. Riots started in Calcutta had swept through other parts of India.

Facing Jinnah's threat of civil war, a reluctant Britain, represented by Lord Mountbatten, and an even more dismayed Indian leadership, including an anguished Gandhi, had accepted a partition which seemed contrary to both wisdom and reason. It cut arbitrary lines in provinces, creating as large Hindu minorities as there had been Moslem before, and vice versa. It separated utilities from skilled workers, factories from raw materials. It attempted to construct a unified nation out of segments removed from each other by a thousand miles of alien territory. The folly of the decision was soon demonstrated in one of the most tragic transmigrations in history, engulfing ten million refugees in destitution, floods, and massacre.

Yet mingled with the pain of travail on that August 15 were all of fulfillment's triumph and ecstasy. The students at Vellore —Christians, Hindus, Moslems—awoke that day with a new sense of their unity and human dignity. Even colors seemed sharper, shot through the clear spectrum of freedom. The sunken garden at College Hill blazed with golds and yellows, purples and blues and crimsons.

At six in the morning students gathered in the chapel for thanksgiving, then marched to the front of the college buildings to see the flag of a new nation hoisted into sunlight.

"*Jai Hind! Jai Hind!* Victory to India!" rose the triumphant shout as the brave tricolor floated at last in the dawn of a free country.

The women students had a right to feel proud, because Vellore for a half-century had been helping to make India's womanhood more nearly ready for this day. It was because of such institutions that the minority of educated women in the country were now able to assume positions of leadership unprecedented not only in a new democratic country but in any country; that

319

a Christian woman, Rajkumari Amrit Kaur, brilliant follower of Gandhi, was to be named Minister of Health in the federal government; that a woman poet, Sarojini Naidu, was to become governor of West Bengal; that Mrs. Pandit, Indira Gandhi, Santha Rama Rau, and others were in coming years to be in the forefront of not only national but also world activities.

Vellore Christian Medical College had not only kept pace but had actually led in the emancipation of Indian womanhood. It had mitigated the evils of child marriage and widowhood long before the Sarda Act. It had united Brahmins and untouchables years before Gandhi denounced caste and championed the cause of his *Harijans*.

And today it was in step with the quickened pace of a new nation attempting to solve its colossal problems through democratic processes based on equality of sex, race, and religion. For when the students gathered about the flagpole, mingled among the raptly upturned faces of India's daughters were eleven of her sons'. And that year of 1947, in response to an appeal from Government to aid in the emergency caused by communal riots, the medical college offered to open its doors to Hindu and Sikh refugee medical students from Pakistan.

There was another innovation even more significant. It was not Dr. Cochrane, an Englishman, who led the students in their march to the flag-hoisting ceremony. It was not Dr. Ida, an American. It was a tiny, dark-skinned, sari-clad woman, mature in years but remarkably youthful in appearance with her springing step, shining dark hair, and earnest brilliant eyes. For at last Dr. Hilda Lazarus, released from her responsible army post as chief medical officer of the women's branch of the Indian Medical Service, with the rank of lieutenant colonel, was able to fulfill the long desire of both staff and Council. She brought to her new office of Principal and Director of Vellore Christian Medical College and Hospital the intense dedication of a Christian whose two Brahmin grandfathers had suffered persecution and ostracism from their families because of conversion to the new faith; a long and invaluable experience in education; a keen talent for organization; seven distinguished medical degrees earned in India, Ireland, Canada, and the United States, plus such honors as the King Edward Thanksgiving Medal, the King

George Coronation Medal, the Kaisar-i-Hind Gold Medal, and the Companion of the British Empire; a spirit selflessly dedicated to the service of her people; a quick wit and lively sense of humor.

The two latter were brought into full play when a patient objected to being operated upon on a certain day because the stars would not be propitious.

"I quite understand," said Dr. Lazarus with swift sympathy, "for I too believe in the stars. I work under the greatest of them all, the star of Bethlehem. Have no fear. I shall operate on you tomorrow morning."

She was not only an instrument and product of the new free India. She was its living embodiment. Her experience in government made her ideal for the task of piloting Vellore through this period of crisis. Having been a member of the Bhore Commission which surveyed India's postwar medical needs, she was able to view the many-sided claims for advancement in clear perspective. And she was not afraid of building the future on the past.

"Dr. Ida retired at Hill Top!" she exclaimed in consternation. "No! We need her here. She must come back." And she insisted on setting aside a room for Ida's constant use in the principal's bungalow at College Hill.

But Ida returned to Vellore infrequently and only as an interested guest and spectator. She attended council meetings— and kept her mouth shut. She observed operations performed by new doctors in new ways—and never commented on how she would have done them.

"Have you seen Dr. So-and-So do such-and-such an operation?" she would ask enthusiastically. "He's very good!" Or— "How wonderful are these new ways of doing things!"

She who had been all her life a leader—some had called it dictator—now found it possible to be a follower. She had but one regret—that she could not do as much for people as before.

"If I could only do something to help!" she moaned when a terrible motor accident involved members of the staff. Impossible to convince her that a handclasp, a carefully plucked flower, an understanding word could be as therapeutic as an antiseptic drug or scalpel.

"My friend," she said gently to the Russian doctor from Kashmir who had come to Vellore to have his fears of cancer verified, "I have just heard a piece of good news, that you're likely to get to heaven before I do. Not long before, but maybe a little. Isn't it wonderful that you'll be there to welcome me!"

In January of 1948 she rushed down from Hill Top to help Dr. Lazarus receive important guests: the Honorable Rajkumari Amrit Kaur, federal minister of health, Lady Nye, wife of the Governor of Madras, and Lady Mountbatten, Countess of Burma and wife of the Governor General who had so ably ushered in independence.

"I should be going to see you," the countess greeted her humbly, "not you to see me."

"You can't do that!" bristled a pompous official to the Swiss couple innocently taking a snapshot of Government House in Madras with the Indian flag flying.

The couple apologized. They had meant no harm. They were merely tourists who had been working in a Christian hospital in Vellore, and—

"Oh!" the official interrupted, beaming. "Dr. Scudder's hospital? Then that's perfectly all right. Go ahead and take your picture."

"I'm going to Vellore," said a touring member of the Scudder clan to the lovely young Indian girl in the travel agency in Delhi. "I have an aunt there—"

"Vellore!" The girl's face brightened. "Oh, Dr. Ida? I know her well. She saved my little brother's life."

Her mother, it seemed, one of the two wives of the Maharajah of Nabi who had been exiled in Kodai, fearful of the consequences if she did not bear a son, had come to Dr. Ida for help, giving her full credit when the son was born. Later, when he had become dangerously ill, Dr. Ida had saved his life.

What's in a name? Magic, if you live in South India and the name happens to be Scudder.

A Brahmin from Polur, a town thirty miles from Vellore, whose wife Ida had delivered of a healthy boy, once sent a messenger posthaste when another member of his family was about to deliver, it was hoped, an heir.

"A Scudder! Must have a Scudder!" insisted the messenger excitedly.

Ida's niece, Dr. Ida B., was summoned. Though she was no longer working in the obstetrics department, she *was* a Scudder. Taking the nurse through whom the appeal had come, she started out. It was 3 A.M. and cold. The two women had taken no sweaters and took turns riding in the drafty back seat of the car among the bags. Arriving in Polur at five, in ample time, they slept two hours, scrubbed, and prepared their instruments. When all were properly cleaned and sterile, they found themselves suddenly deluged with a drenching shower. "Holy water," it was explained, "to purify them."

They had barely time to repeat the cleansing process before the baby arrived.

"An prillai! Boy baby!" rose the glad cry.

After another hour they were fed a huge chicken dinner, with *puris*. The family had waited for the baby's arrival before killing the chicken. Had it been a girl, they would have served only coffee. But it was a boy! The magic name Scudder had remained unsullied.

Aunt Ida, as she was now often called by both staff and students, found each visit to Vellore a new and thrilling adventure. Changes she had never dreamed of were taking place. The hospital staff was constantly increasing, pioneering in new areas, and she wanted to have an eye on, if not a finger in it all. Invited to see firsthand a new technique which Dr. Rambo, the missionary eye specialist, had evolved for reducing the appalling prevalence of eye disease, she was ready for the trip and in her car long before the hour specified.

Not for months—years—had she been so excited. She was pioneering all over again. It was like starting on her first trip to Gudiyattam in the little one-cylinder Peugeot. Strange that on this trip she should be traveling the same road!

She sounded a brisk blast on the horn, and her driver came running. *"Ammal?"*

"Where are they all, Kannaya? Miss Marshall? Dr. Lazarus?"

"Ayoh, but it is not yet time, *ammal.* Seven o'clock you said."

In her desire for promptness Ida always leaned over backward, by at least fifteen minutes. The one to four clocks in her room were all kept five minutes ahead of time. She possessed her soul now in impatience until the rest of her party arrived, exactly on the stroke of seven.

"*Nai-a? Pai-a?* Your dog? Your purse?" checked Kannaya meticulously.

As they drove over the familiar route to Gudiyattam, Ida's excitement rose. It was all she could do to keep from stopping at the old stations along the way. But she was even more anxious to reach the destination.

"Tell me again this wonderful new thing Dr. Rambo is doing," she demanded of Dr. Lazarus. "What is it he's going to call it?"

It was an "eye camp," explained the Indian woman with equal enthusiasm. Dr. Rambo, head of the Schell Eye Hospital, had conceived the idea of taking a team of doctors, nurses, and technicians into centers within a radius of perhaps fifty miles of Vellore, examining any who wished to come from surrounding villages, and performing needed operations, leaving a few members of the team in charge, and returning after intervals to change dressings, remove stitches, even provide necessary glasses. The first experimental trip was being made today to Gudiyattam. A "teller of good news" had been sent ahead some days ago to tour the surrounding villages and tell all those suffering from eye diseases that if they came to the branch hospital this morning they would be given free examinations. If people came and there were many needing operations, the team would remain and operate through the day.

If people came! The tiny hospital compound looked like a village *shandy*. Ida and her companions had to leave their car at the gate and inch their way through the crowd. At least three hundred there must be—men, women, children, babes in arms, Hindus, Mohammedans, townsmen, villagers.

Dr. Rambo and his team were already at work. Tables had been set up, the patients arranged in long queues, each awaiting his turn to kneel at one of the tables for examination. If he needed an operation a tag was sewn to his garments indicating the type of operation and the eye or eyes needing attention. If there was no hope, he was sent away as gently as possible.

324

Ida was soon in the thick of the excitement, helping with the examinations, passing on the necessary information to the writer.

"Govind, age 14, blind from birth with congenital cataract."

"Ganesan, blind from his sixth year; his sister Thiama, blind from her seventh year."

Ida looked down at the patient little face framed by the bright blue scarf, the clasped hands and thin brown wrists jangling copper-colored glass bangles. Would an operation really make her see again? So many in this country, even tiny babies, were blinded by cataracts, a curse, it seemed, which went hand in hand with hunger and malnutrition!

One after another they came, kneeling, as once blind Bartimaeus had come. An old saffron-robed holy man, who lived alone in a hut on a faraway hill. A Hindu with head shaven except for a white tuft on the crown. A Brahmin with the trident of Vishnu scored in saffron on his forehead. A ragged woman with a tiny baby, its eyes terribly inflamed. An old man in a red muffler, patiently squatting, holding out his chit. A young man fiercely eager to see but with one eye hopelessly mutilated by a Mohammedan coucher, the self-styled physician who traveled about the country "curing" cataracts by thrusting an unsanitary needle deep into the affected eye and pushing aside the clouded lens. For a while relief and vision might seem to follow the crude and painful operation, until the dire infection set in which usually caused total blindness. Mercifully only one of the young man's eyes revealed the displaced lens far inside the eye; in the other the core of clouded whiteness had not been touched.

As the hours passed, the figures kneeling before Ida ceased to wear garments, faces; became a succession of eyes. Eyes blind from birth. Children's eyes, obscured by malnutrition and vitamin deficiency. Eyes of working men, injured by a leaf, a bit of straw, a flying tool. Eyes hardened into sightlessness by leucoma. Eyes inflamed because they would not close. But all uplifted, pleading, hoping.

What wilt thou of me?

Lord, that I may receive my sight!

There were fifty-seven cataract cases needing operations. The facilities of the tiny hospital were swamped. But a nearby mill owner came forward and offered the loan of his warehouse. At one end of it two makeshift operating tables were set up, a canvas spread above them to give protection. Dr. Rambo's team, carefully coached, moved into action. One group prepared the patients, shaving brows, administering anesthetic. Another sterilized the instruments. Another operated. A fourth bandaged, set in motion the delicate postoperative care.

It was a marathon. With all groups functioning, it was possible to perform, barring complications, only six operations an hour. Noon came, and they had barely begun. Sunset, and there was still a long row of patiently waiting figures. Using flashlights and kerosene-pressure lanterns, Dr. Rambo and his assistants, two other doctors, two medical students, and three nurses, kept on working. When they had finished and the fifty-seven patients lay in rows along the warehouse floor on long strips of matting, a cook left to provide their food and a physician-nurse to continue the precise and delicate postoperative supervision which would be necessary until the return of the team a week later, night had long since fallen.

Ida stayed until the end. Riding home through the long avenues of tamarinds and banyans, she could scarcely contain her delight. "I've never seen anything like it," she exulted. "And to think they're going to do it twice a month!"

"If they can get the money," reminded one of her companions pointedly. "It will have to be done, remember, by special voluntary gifts."

Money! Even in the darkness Ida's blue eyes blazed. Did anybody think lack of money could stop an idea like this? Didn't they understand that it was a question of *restoring sight to the blind?* Today over fifty people had been given new eyes. Before the month was over there would be a hundred, in a year a thousand, in ten years. . . .

As the car sped through the green tunnels, past moonlit rice fields, she could feel the swift currents of change stirring the night. No more beggars lifting empty eyes and wailing, *"Kan teriathu*—I'm blind!" Instead, ten thousand people crying, "Whereas I was blind, now I see!" Only ten years was such a long time! She didn't want to wait.

"Kannaya." She called the driver's name, intending to tell

him to go faster. "Kannaya!" she repeated sharply, for the car had slowed to a mere crawl. *"Yenna sungathi?* What's the matter?"

There was no need of a reply. Ahead of them the road had narrowed to a thin ribbon, curving along the high rim of a dike separating two ponds, and upon it, as far as the eye could see, were plodding bullock carts, piled high with sugar cane, one close behind the other. The caravan moved at a snail's pace, tiny bobbing lanterns forming a thin crescent in the dark, each driver except the ones at front and rear sprawled across his load, sleeping. There could be no passing along the dike. There was nothing to do but move at a snail's pace after them.

Ida closed her eyes, the night air heavy and motionless against her face. She had suddenly remembered that at the last report and at conservative estimate there were half a million people blind with cataract in India.

True, the medical problems still facing the new nation were staggering, but what changes she had seen taking place in the country in her fifty years of service! What changes had taken place in the science of medicine itself!

For years on end she had used open-drop chloroform as an anesthetic in the operating room, poured on an open gauze mask. In India this had been relatively safe because in the heat chloroform evaporated so rapidly. Often she had had to start the anesthesia herself, then when the patient was asleep had handed the mask and bottle to a nurse or compounder to carry on the process. Only in her last few years of surgery had she experienced the marvels of local anesthetics, the closed ether method, or spinal anesthesia.

In her early days there had been no effective treatment of sepsis, bacillary dysentery, gonorrhea, syphilis, yaws. Now there were the sulphonamides and penicillin.

She had treated amebic dysentery through all the successive remedies from ipecac to emetine to tetracycline.

She had seen cholera, the invincible, yield to hypertonic saline infusions; filariasis to Hertrazan; tuberculosis to streptomycin; the fly-borne diseases to DDT and Gamexene insecticides; formerly incurable cancer to radium therapy.

Now, even in India, the conquest of smallpox by compulsory

vaccination, malaria and plague by the widespread use of DDT, was only a matter of time.

But perhaps the greatest developments of all were in the treatment of leprosy.

It was in 1937 that the discovery of a new sulphone substance was first published, but not until 1942 that some of its nontoxic derivatives had been found effective as medicine. Not proving successful in the treatment of tuberculosis, the new drug had been tried on leprosy, with amazing results. But the new sulphone drugs, given by mouth—Promin, Diasone, and Sulphetrone—had proved very expensive. In 1946 the Christian Medical College, in cooperation with other Indian agencies, had embarked on a long and intensive research to discover a cheaper sulphone drug which could be made available to the host of leprosy victims in India and other countries. Already the experiment was meeting with striking success.

But there were soon to be other developments equally dramatic. A few months after the first "eye camp" Ida stood with a group of doctors and nurses, intently watching an earnest young doctor remove a plaster cast from a patient's hand. She scarcely breathed. For she was just possibly watching medical history being made. If the series of operations preceding the removal of this cast proved successful, it would mean revolution in the treatment of some of leprosy's worst mutilations and distortions.

The young doctor was an Englishman, Paul Brand, orthopedic surgeon born in India and come recently to Vellore from the Children's Hospital in London. The patient was a young Hindu of twenty-four, with hands so paralyzed by leprosy that he could not pick up his rice with his fingers.

"Do what you wish with them," the young man had said stoically when asked if he would permit the operations. "They are no good to me." No good, he might have added, except for begging. For the "claw hand," curse of a large percentage of leprosy sufferers in India, had been a symbol not only of shame and disgrace, but also of beggary. With twisted, misshapen, fingers stiffly clenched into the palm, it was thrust out everywhere in mute pleading.

After exhaustive study and experiment young Dr. Brand had

discovered that one set of arm muscles would never be affected by paralysis. He was now attempting to transplant the good muscles and tendons into the disabled hand to do the work of the paralyzed ones. Preceding operations on this same hand had led him to proceed with renewed confidence. But today would tell the story.

Above the raw grating of sawteeth against webbed plaster Ida could hear the pounding of her heart. She was far less calm than either of the two principal actors: the young doctor with his sure slim fingers and intent eyes, particularly slow and careful that he might not cause injury to the tissues that had no feeling; the patient with his grimly stoic features. The cast fell away, the bandages were slowly unwound. Still gravely intent, the young doctor examined his handiwork, stroking the tender flesh, spreading the fingers apart, flexing the new muscles, like a sculptor adding the finishing touches to his creation.

"Now," he said simply, relinquishing his hold and smiling warmly at the young Hindu, "let's see you use it."

Slowly, features still inscrutable, the youth raised his new hand and looked at it; stared at it with wondering, incredulous eyes. He lifted his other hand and compared the curled misshapen fingers with the long straight ones. Gingerly he activated the new muscles, releasing joints which for years had been locked tight, curved a long-stiffened thumb inward above the palm, and slowly brought the tips of his fingers to meet it. Then he reached over the table where bits of the plaster were still lying and, while the whole room held its breath, managed finally after some fumbling *to pick one of them up and hold it in his hand*. Then only did light break over his dark sober features. He smiled at the young doctor.

"This new hand you give me," he said, "it is not mine. It belongs to your God, who made possible this miracle."

Miracle, yes. Ida closed her eyes as if the brightness were too great to bear. Even her wildest dreams had not been big enough to include this. It was more than healing. It was creation. For what greater wonder had life ever achieved than the transforming of a claw into a human hand?

27

The little yellow plaster Tamil church in Vellore was more full of memories than usual that Sunday morning. Sitting in her usual seat in the front row of the left transept, in imagination Ida saw black dresses and frock coats mingling with the bright saris and white shirts of the congregation, pinafores and knee breeches scattered among the long full skirts and neat shorts of the flower-decked children squatted on jute mats in front of the congregation. Solemn and bearded, preachers of past generations entered the old double doors at each side of the platform and occupied the pulpit: Uncle Henry, who had been the church's first minister back in 1855; Uncle Ezekiel Carman; Uncle William; her father, Dr. John. For this was no ordinary Sunday. It was January 1, 1950, just a half century since, with a vision and an M.D., she had arrived in India. Her golden jubilee!

Since college was not in session on this first day of the year, celebration of the event was postponed until January 7. His Excellency, the Maharajah of Bhavnagar, Governor of Madras, with Her Highness the Maharani, arrived the night before in order to be at the hospital compound in the city at nine in the morning. The Maharani cut the ribbons before the door of

330

the new Nurses' Block and Hostel. Prouder and more beautiful than ever now was Rachel Fillebrown Nurses' Home in her new bricks and mortar, rising four stories high on three sides of a broad rectangle. Later, on the college campus four miles away, the Governor opened the new Laboratory of Physiology and Biochemistry, white in the blazing sunshine.

Seated on the platform of the assembly hall, looking out over the faces of friends come from near and far, and listening to the glowing tributes of the Governor, of Dr. Hilda Lazarus, of her beloved early pupil Dr. Kamala Vythilingam, Ida wandered in memory through the fifty years. Yes, she and her vision had come a long way. From one woman doctor to 43 now on the college staff, 44 on the hospital. At first a little corner ten-by-twelve room—now a 484-bed hospital, with 60 more beds in Schell Eye Hospital. One patient—now an annual attendance in hospitals and mobile clinics of 200,000. One untrained nurse, Salomi—now 108 staff nurses and 174 nursing students. Not one medical student—now 200, with 275 graduates having received the Licensed Medical Practitioner's certificate, 31 the degree of Bachelor of Medicine, Bachelor of Surgery. Ida's eyes swam as, out of the blur of faces down below, there sprang into focus the dark, solidly dependable features of her first compounder, Mrs. Gnanammal.

"You are one of those rare spirits," said His Excellency the Governor, "that is sent to the earth once in a generation."

Ida scarcely heard the words. She was reliving the last torturous ten years. By what miracle had they achieved the impossible? Twelve new professors and six associates, specialists in their fields from all over the world! Seven new bungalows for staff, five new wards, vast additions to the nurses' home, third and fourth stories on many of the old hospital buildings, new laboratories and classrooms! Departments of biochemistry, radiology, thoracic surgery, psychiatry, neurosurgery! Only now at long last, with the arrival of young Dr. Moody from Australia to head dental surgery, had the challenge of the crisis almost been met; almost, for not yet had Vellore received its final accreditation from Madras University. The examining committee had come in October, but the syndicate would not meet to pass on its report until late January. There had been no word of assurance. And to Ida's disappointment her loyal friend the vice-chancellor, Sir Lakshmanaswamy Mudaliar, was not here today. Could his absence indicate an unfavorable report? There could be no real jubilee for Ida until she was certain.

And then suddenly her pulses began to pound. Dr. Hilda Lazarus was reading greetings from the vice-chancellor. Sir Lakshmanaswamy had not waited for the syndicate to meet. He had sent a special messenger all over Madras State with a closed box in which each member could put his secret ballot. And he was now happy to announce that permanent affiliation with Madras University had been granted to Vellore Christian Medical College.

For Ida this was the climax of her jubilee celebration. Neither the tremendous ovation as she rose to speak nor the hundreds of letters received from friends all over the world, not even the gifts of money to Vellore amounting to a lakh of rupees ($20,000), could add to the fulfillment of this moment. The continuation of her life's purpose was at last assured, its future linked irrevocably with that of the young free nation which was this very month becoming a republic.

This was only the beginning of her year of jubilee. In March the citizens of Vellore raised funds to erect a bronze statue of her in the middle of the town.

"Mercy, no!" exclaimed Ida in horror. "Please use the funds for something useful for the hospital. Or"—her blue eyes gleamed with purposeful vigor—"if you really want to please me, then *cover up that drain!*"

Instead they decided to build a new road opposite the hospital leading toward Arcot, and call it the "Dr. Ida Scudder Road."

In March also she stood marveling in the operating room, while Dr. Reeve H. Betts, skilled surgeon who had given up his lucrative practice in Boston to head the new department of thoracic surgery, performed an operation never before seen in India. The patient, a three-and-a-half-year-old child, under-developed for his age, was suffering from a heart condition known as "patent ductus arteriosus," a communication between the two large arteries leaving the heart which usually closes of itself at birth but had remained open in this child. Marveling, Ida saw the skilled fingers lay bare the large vessels at the base of the heart and, after the diagnosis had been confirmed, securely close the abnormal communication.

"Wonderful!" she exclaimed, emerging starry-eyed from her mask. "Only think of being alive to see it!"

More wonderful still was the letter received a few weeks later by Mr. Savarirayan, the capable general superintendent of the hospital.

"Dear Sir,
We the boys of Standard III have collected this money for any sick boy who cannot afford to pay for himself. The amount of money is Rs. 12.

Yours faithfully,

The letter was signed by the young patient and nineteen of his schoolmates.

The hands at whose skill Ida marveled in these days were more often dark than white, for more and more of the responsible posts at Vellore were being filled by gifted and highly trained Indians. There were Dr. Kutumbiah, at the head of medicine; Dr. Bhakthaviziam in dermatology; Dr. Jacob Chandy, brilliant head of neurosurgery; Dr. Miriam Manuel in obstetrics and Dr. Kamala Vythilingam in cardiology; Drs. Cornelius, Asirvatham, and Devadatta in hygiene, pathology, and physiology. This very year Annamma Jacob had returned from two years of study at McGill to take Vera Pitman's place as nursing superintendent. Ida exulted in them all.

So exciting was life in Vellore that she hated to spend even the hot months at Hill Top. The problem of housing the men students was becoming more and more desperate, yet this year the college had been deluged with applications from 223 women and 581 men. At Hill Top in June Ida shared to the full in the heartbreaking task of selection, and awaited in suspense the letter from her niece, Dr. Ida B., telling that 15 men and 30 women had been selected. And still there was only one doctor in India to every 6,000 of the population.

"Our most desperate need," wrote Dr. Lazarus to Ida that June, "is for the men's student hostel. But—how? It should cost at least $150,000!"

In 1948 a temporary hostel had been built, crowded and noisy, with the kitchen in the center. By this June of 1950 the 62 men were overflowing into the adjoining servants' quarters and five other tiny houses. Somebody saw a mud and thatch building in the Vellore Fort area and suggested, "Why don't we have one at the college?" The project was started immediately. Using palmyra trees for pillars, Dr. Lazarus and her committee put up a makeshift dining hall of bush and thatch in a fortnight's time. When the men arrived in July they gleefully dubbed the new building the "banqueting hall."

Ida could not stay away. Too much was happening. Arriving in Vellore in August, she inspected the new thatched building, peered into the well which had been dug near the site of the proposed men's hostel at the south end of the campus, and exulted that good water had been found at only twenty-five feet. A triumph indeed in a section where there had been no good rains for the last three years! But when she saw the plans for the new hostel, the materials—bricks, crushed stone, iron —all piled up ready and waiting, her eyes struck fire.

"This is no way to treat the men," she accused Dr. Edward Gault, the men's dean. "Why don't you build them a decent hostel?"

"We want to, Aunt Ida," he explained patiently. "As you see, we have the plans drawn, even some materials ready. We're just waiting for the money to come."

Her blue eyes seared him. "Huh!" she replied disdainfully. "If I'd waited for the money to come, we wouldn't have anything. Come on, let's get going!"

She did so. What better use for her jubilee money than at least to start a men's hostel? True, a lakh (20,000) would not go far toward an eight-lakh building, but there was another half lakh she had intended leaving to Vellore in her will. She made the decision in the morning and turned the sod for the new building that afternoon.

The council, while grateful, was still cautious. "After the

one-and-a-half lakhs are gone," it warned, "you must stop."
Ida only smiled.

There were other exciting things happening that summer of her jubilee year. In August she helped open Vellore's new rural health center at Kavanur sixteen miles away, chosen as an experimental area in the treatment and prevention of leprosy because it was the center of a group of villages where the incidence of the disease was highest in the whole British Commonwealth. Nearby villages had agreed to cooperate in the experiment. One of them, about a mile from the center, with over seventy-six known leprosy cases, was being used in an experiment of night segregation, the cases under treatment coming to the center for their evening meal and spending the night there. In another village a half mile away patients being treated with the new drug were permitted to remain at home. This experiment was designed to test the efficacy both of home treatment and of night segregation as a means of preventing spread of the disease. Since it was most contagious to children and was spread chiefly by close contacts under overcrowded conditions, night segregation offered a promising technique of treatment.

Kavanur itself, with a population of 2,700—1,500 Hindus, 200 Moslems, and 1,000 Harijans—had been selected for generalized public health work with special emphasis on maternity and child hygiene, sanitation, and improved methods of agriculture, as well as experimental treatment of leprosy. The center was already being used as a practice field for third-year nursing students. Living here for a month, planning their own menus, treating inpatients and making trips into the villages each day, the students both learned and taught. They gave health talks to mothers, introduced new types of latrines and soakage pits and smokeless *chulhas,* improved models of the simple clay stoves used in village homes. Under the direction of the resident trained midwife, they taught the village *dais,* midwives, to use clean methods.

"We are not trying to change local customs," explained the competent midwife to Ida, "except where they need to be changed." For example, they would not interfere with family and friends when, during delivery, they burned fire in a pot and danced around it to keep off evil spirits, but they would expect that no baby should be branded with a hot iron to keep away gastrointestinal disease.

Ida was thrilled. Here was one of her fondest desires at last being accomplished: prevention of disease instead of the often frustrating attempts to cure it. In the next ten years she was to reenact this dedication scene in four such centers, extending the work of social uplift into forty villages; see the movement spearheaded by a rural health center and hospital on the college site, which, working in close cooperation with the government Social Welfare Board, was to face with realistic courage the colossal task of bringing new life through public health education into an area twelve miles long and four miles wide, containing thirty to forty thousand ill-fed and unschooled villagers."

Ida's jubilee year saw also dramatic progress in the field of leprosy rehabilitation. After his first remarkable operation on the hands of a patient suffering from the deformities of the neural form of leprosy, Dr. Paul Brand and his colleagues had performed many others, not only to restore crippled hands to usefulness but also to relieve foot distortion and correct the disfigurement of facial contours through skilled plastic surgery. One day not long after his first successful series of operations, however, the young doctor found himself staring at one of his former patients in amazement.

"Harmed you?" Dumfounded, he repeated the man's strange accusation. "You say I have *harmed* you by giving you new hands?"

"*Amma*, yes, Doctor Sahib," replied the patient. "I have new hands, yes, but what can I do with them? When I go to find work, like other men, people see the signs of leprosy and will not employ me. And if I hold out my hands to beg, no one has pity. Dr. Brand, it is bad hands you have given me, not good—bad begging hands. You see?"

"Yes," said the young doctor slowly. "I see."

So clear had been his vision and so strong his purpose that now, near the end of her jubilee year, Ida stood in a remote corner of two-hundred-acre College Hill, marveling at the visible results.

"*Neva Jeeve Nilyam*," she repeated, eyes shining. "Place of New Life."

What she saw was a little village of thatched, whitewashed huts where leprosy patients with reconstructed hands and feet could live together for short periods and learn to become useful, self-sufficient citizens. In the large central shed was a carpenter's table with tools specially constructed and arranged: pliers and scissors with springs to facilitate firm handling, nails hanging by their heads in convenient grooves, compartments from which protruding tool handles could be easily grasped. New skills were being developed in carpentry, masonry, painting, toymaking, fitting together plastic boxes. She exclaimed delightedly over jigsaw puzzles, chinese checker boards, wooden animals, walking birds. The Leprosy Rehabilitation Center, with accommodations for twenty-four men, would not only teach each member a trade but would also provide a medium through which his products, safely disinfected, could be marketed. The men would help grow their own food, take turns at doing the menial tasks of cleaning, drawing water, cultivating.

"Wonderful!" exclaimed Ida, envying the English missionary, "Mother" Eaton, 84-year-old sufferer from incurable rheumatoid arthritis, whose sacrificial gift of £500 had made the little community possible.

"You've thought of everything!" she marveled to young Dr. Brand, eyes misting at sight of the wooden rings and reed baskets designed to protect hands which had no feeling from dangerous contact with hot metal cups and plates.

The young doctor, just honored by election to the Royal College of Surgeons in London, shook his head. "We've barely begun," he said. Then his dark eyes kindled. "But—if only we had enough workers and enough money for a world-wide rehabilitation program, how many millions of the partially or totally crippled we could restore to complete independence!"

Ida sighed. *If only*—! If only it were her thirtieth, not eightieth birthday which was just around the corner!

"It's a girl, Fida!" Dr. John Scudder had announced just eighty years ago, bending over the woman who had previously given birth to his five sons.

"I don't believe it!" she had retorted spiritedly.

Now, on December 9, 1950, Ida neither looked nor felt her eighty years. Her figure, always generously proportioned, was still youthfully vigorous, her shoulders straight, her step swift and springing. The lines in her broad forehead and fair pink cheeks, though abundant, seemed the emblems of deep interests and concerns rather than of age.

There was no need of crows or coppersmiths to stir the compound into wakefulness. Dawn found both students and servants hard at work gathering flowers for the birthday chair, making the chapel beautiful with blue and white blossoms, preparing lacy *opams* to be served with coconut milk for breakfast.

First to bring greetings was Mr. Rajamanickam, Ida's faithful driver for many years, now supervisor of the campus, proudly presenting a cake resplendent with greetings and a sand tray bearing eighty lighted candles. But he was only the beginning. Ida loved it all—the chapel service, the birthday chairs at both college and hospital, the lavish luncheon, the long and ornate speeches, tributes of students, nurses, colleagues, servants, townspeople, former patients—and hated it. She felt like a corpse brought back to life to enjoy its funeral eulogies. She was glad when the embarrassing barrage ceased long enough to give her a few moments of relaxation on the tennis court. Though she wasn't able to run so fast these days, if a ball came near her she seldom let it go past.

"An exciting game!" her young partner commented. "I hope it wasn't too tiring."

"I hope not," she retorted tartly. "You do look a bit fagged."

At six o'clock she was tapping her foot to the music of the police college band, a few moments later marching down the aisle on the arm of Sir Samuel Ranganathan, council chairman, tall and imposing in his well-cut English clothes. The nurses' badminton court in the hospital compound, scene of the big public meeting in her honor, was massed tightly with turbans, white Congress caps, and flowered coiffures. In front of the

338

platform was a huge eight-tiered imitation birthday cake, adorned with eighty colored lights, its base nearly as broad as the platform, its top tier on a level with her eyes when she sat down.

There were more speeches, in Hindi, English, and Urdu, greetings from friends all over the world presented in a silver-bound folder. Twenty-two children of the staff, each in the costume of a different country, presented to her twenty-two golden purses, gifts of as many organizations, Indian states, and foreign countries. The donations amounted to half a lakh of rupees ($10,000). She could hardly wait for the meeting to be over so she could get the money converted into stones and bricks and mortar for the men's hostel!

Her enthusiasm was contagious. In the following weeks somebody made a model of the proposed hostel, and somebody else took a picture of it. Stamps imprinted with the photo were put on sale at the value of each stone which would make up the building. Students sold them, raising 1,400 rupees through these alone. Inspired by Dr. Gault, dean of the college men, the Madras Chamber of Commerce raised half a lakh at one of its meetings. The Rank Trust, a philanthropic organization in Dr. Gault's native Australia, contributed generously.

In February of the following year Ida laid the foundation stone, and in two more years she saw the first men students move into the beautiful three-storied stone building built on five sides of a hexagon. On the sixth side, of course, there was a garden.

Ever since male students had been admitted to her school, "Aunt Ida" had belonged to them. Impervious to barriers of sex as to those of race or color, she gave them exactly the same affection and concern as she did her girls. They attended her Bible classes, gathered about her on the floor of the big bungalow, brought her their problems, vied with one another to help her out of the car when she came to their hostel for Sunday dinner. Their affection embraced more than admiration, more than gallantry. It was like the love of sons for their mother.

Yet if the harvest of Ida's long nurturing seemed increasingly abundant in those first years following her jubilee, it was not so with other harvests in the land. One after another the monsoon seasons came and went, bringing with them dry winds, unclouded skies, and famine.

Rain! Would it never come? Three years... four... five. As she drove along the dusty roads between Hill Top and Vellore, Ida saw as in an evil dream an endless procession of lean kine, older than Genesis, as old as human hunger. And people. Having nothing to do, no fields to till, they sat mutely beside the roads, sparse flesh wrapped in the dust of their dry rice fields, eyes and cheeks as hollow as their empty wells.

This is where I came in, she thought, *over three-quarters of a century ago. And we have done little in all that time to change it.*

It was comfort as well as agony to go out with Dr. Ida B. on Friday Roadside. For while officials in America were pondering whether to share their huge surpluses with a people whose pride in their new independence made them reluctant to take gifts with strings attached, there were CARE and Church World Service and UNICEF.

"Dr. *Ammal,* oh, *ammal,* please see my baby. She is like a rag. She does not play or laugh. Oh, *ammal,* see her, please. She is my only baby."

"Yes, *ammal,* we will see. But first let us ask our Father God to help us."

"See, Dr. *Ammal,* this Sreenivasen? Three years old he is, but he can scarcely stand, his little legs and arms are like sticks, his stomach too big, and all the time he cries."

"Yes, *ammal,* I see. What does he eat?"

"What we do. A little *kulu, kambu,* when we can get it. Some rice water."

"But he is a baby. He must have good cow's milk every day, and one egg, and vegetables, and orange or tomato juice. You must get it for him."

"Dr. *Ammal,* I cannot. I have no money. I could buy one orange each market day, maybe an egg. But I cannot buy milk. What shall I do?"

"Your husband, Nagamma, can he not help you get food for your children?"

"My husband, *ammal?* He has gone away. I do not know where he is."

"Why did he go?"

"*Ammal,* he could get no work. He is a coolie. But there is no work because there is no rain. He said he would find work and bring us help, but he has been gone four months. Oh, Dr. *Ammal,* we are hungry. See my little Panchalai. She was a pretty baby, now she will not walk or even stand. Shanmugan here is a good little boy, but he is tired all the time too. Can you help?"

"Yes, *ammal,* yes. Thank God we can help."

Of the 575 patients seen in a single day on Roadside, 106 children needing dried milk and vitamins! They line up beside the table, each showing a Christmas card all bright and gay, and are given the precious rations. As the weeks pass, they begin to look more alive, their skins become soft and normal, sore tongues are better, and swelling of the feet lessens.

But still along every road she traveled there were the lean kine, the thin bodies, the sunken cheeks. The round empty zeroes of her childhood all over again!

28

Whether she was at Kodai or at Vellore, Ida's days were full. She rose at 5:30, had chota hazri at six. When she was in Vellore, she usually went to the hospital in time for morning prayers with staff and nurses in the hospital chapel at seven, then traveled through the wards visiting patients. She accompanied timid ones to the operating room and was at their bedsides when the anesthetic wore off. When they left the hospital, she was there to give them her farewell blessing.

On one typical day she went at 6:30 to open a rural center for one of Mrs. Venketachari's village projects, then came back to open the exhibition for the All-India Conference of Surgeons being held at the college. She was hostess at the big luncheon for five hundred people in the women's hostel at noon, attended all the conference meetings in the afternoon, later presided at another large dinner.

Then suddenly, for almost the first time, she was receiving instead of giving, on the operating table instead of beside it. It was a novel experience which she enjoyed immensely. The operation was not serious, a hernia, and, given a local anesthetic, she followed the whole proceeding with the greatest interest. In her private room she and her little dog Colonel reigned supreme. She was surrounded constantly by flowers, wore a pretty bed jacket, had her hair curled every day, and entertained like royalty. Nurses came to her for advice, doctors dropped in for consultation. Not even her most recent honor, receiving of the New York Infirmary's Blackwell Citation for distinguished service in the field of medicine, had accorded her so much of satisfaction. It was one of her few passive but happy interludes.

Only an interlude, however. At eighty-three she was still serving a wicked tennis ball. At eighty-four she was showing guests over the three floors and multitudinous wings of the hospital, making pauses only for them to regain their breath. At eighty-five she was taking her first ride on an elephant.

They took the trip into Mysore on their way home from the hill station of Coonoor after settling Cousin Dixie's estate —Ida B., Aunt Ida, her driver Jared, and Lizzie, her genial and capable companion-ayah. At one point on the road they saw signs of great excitement.

"What is it?" demanded Aunt Ida, immediately agog.

Jared went to inquire. "The point-to-point races," he reported.

"Oh!" she exclaimed. "Let's go!"

Turning off, they drove among the hills over a bumpy road. The starting point, on top of a high hill, was as festive as a carnival, with bright tents, prancing horses, riders in scarlet caps and shirts, officials in uniform, and screaming vendors. They bought their tickets, which entitled them to seats.

Flags were planted on surrounding hills. Each rider was required to go around each stake in order; otherwise he could pick his own course, leaping chasms, climbing or descending sheer slopes by whatever route he chose. From the sound of the first starting gun, Aunt Ida was enthralled. She refused to sit still, and Ida B. was constantly following her about with her chair. It was hard to get her away. But the races were interminable, and they had a rendezvous with an elephant.

"It worries me," complained Aunt Ida when they were on their way again. "Everybody seems to know me, and I don't know them."

They drove about twenty miles down the Gudular Ghat

along a beautiful but dizzy mountain-edge and stayed at the Gudular guest house overnight. Arrangements had been made ahead for an elephant ride into the jungle to look for animals.

Rising at three, they breakfasted and went off into inky blackness. Arriving at the designated place, they flashed their electric torches among shadowy figures.

"The *yarnai*—elephant?" someone asked doubtfully.

"Oh, yes, he's here," came the reply.

A dark mountainous shape loomed in front of them. Flashing their torches, they finally distinguished a pair of legs, a little flight of steps disappearing into upper darkness. Jared and Lizzie mounted first to find the most comfortable place on the elephant for Aunt Ida to sit.

"My!" quavered the latter in dismay. "Can I ever get up there?"

The game warden helped to boost her. The last step was the worst. It took pushing and determination to complete the ascent, more determination than pushing. She sat near the head, not too good a choice. The others took their seats, more or less securely, on the lumpy cushions behind her. The front half of the mountain began to quake and, while they clung to the shaky iron bars for dear life, rise up in a huge volcanic heave, leaving them teetering precariously until the rear half arose to meet it. Then the elephant lumbered off with a slow stride.

After ten minutes of rolling and pitching, Aunt Ida quaked, "Oh, Ida B., this is dreadful!"

"Want to go back, Aunt Ida?"

"Oh, mercy, no!"

They rode for four hours through the slowly waning darkness. When an animal came in view, the mahout would say nothing, merely nudge them. As faint light came sifting through the slender bamboos, they saw a spotted deer leap across their path. What looked like a huge tree trunk developed the great curving horns of a wild bison. But unfortunately they saw no tigers.

The difficulty of ascent, it seemed, had been the lesser of two problems. How to get her down? It was the mahout who solved it.

"*Va, ammal,* come!" he invited, holding out his arms, and with all the faith she could muster, Ida finally slid into them. Her muscles were so stiff that she could scarcely move for a week.

The day after her eighty-sixth birthday she took a plane trip far up the east coast of India, to see Dr. Hilda Lazarus, who had regretfully resigned from her position at Vellore to become Director of Postgraduate Studies in Obstetrics and Gynecology at Andhra University Medical College in Vizapattinam. Though her place at Vellore had been capably filled by Dr. John Carman, a Baptist missionary, as director, and by Dr. David, former Indian surgeon general of Madras, as principal, Ida felt the absence of her friend Dr. Lazarus keenly, and anticipated the reunion with as much excitement as the plane ride. Her one trip by air over ten years ago now seemed far in the past.

"My, how my heart's going pitter-patter!" she deplored as they waited for the plane to take off. But once in the air she loved it.

"I'm envious!" she exclaimed to Dr. Lazarus in admiration of the fine hospital and college overlooking the blue Indian Ocean.

"Get her away!" urged her niece Ida B. in mock horror. "Next thing Aunt Ida will want us to dig a pond for the sea at Vellore!"

Ida's unquenchable thirst for adventure was not an unmixed blessing. At least once it induced near tragedy.

It was less than a month after her eighty-sixth birthday. She was helping to dedicate a large new bus, the gift of a Methodist church and pastor in Bluffton, Indiana. Flower-garlanded and filled with students, it was standing in front of the college administration building, about to make its maiden trip to the hospital. Ida mounted the steps and started to take her place.

"Try the driver's seat, Aunt Ida," somebody suggested gaily. "See if it feels like the old Peugeot."

The driver moved over and let her take the wheel. Curiously she began fingering the gadgets. Suddenly the bus leaped forward, heading straight for a tree. Somehow the driver managed to seize control of the wheel just in time to avert tragedy.

It was torture to be growing old in a nation which had re-gained its vigorous youth. Ida observed the growing pains of the new republic with absorbed interest. She was especially interested in the goals and achievements of the two Five-Year Plans in areas of public health.

She noted the increase in India's medical colleges between 1950 and 1956 from 30 to 42; of qualified doctors from 70,000 to 82,500; of trained nurses from 17,000 to 22,000. But of the latter there was still only one for every 16,000 of the population.

She learned with fascination that by the end of the Second Five-Year Plan the government hoped to have the whole coun-try covered by its malaria-control program. Already in areas served by the 162 units established under the first plan, where there was an estimated incidence of about 60 million cases, there had been a reduction of about 20 million cases in only the first year of the plan's operation.

In the years just preceding 1950 the infant mortality rate had dropped from 143 per 1000 births to 122 (compared with 25 in the United States). The average life expectancy had risen to over thirty years.

But she was most fascinated by the Community Develop-ment programs of the two Five-Year Plans, which boldly at-tempted to raise the living standards of over 500,000 villages. By 1956 a total of 700 Community Development blocks had been established, covering some 70,000 villages. She approved of the principle by which the plan was implemented, stimulating villagers to improve their own conditions in such areas as agriculture, housing, basic education, family planning, sanita-tion, irrigation, public health. She wanted to be alive to see what was happening in 1961, when the Plan envisioned more than 1,800 Community Development blocks reaching 40 per cent of India's rural population. And she wanted to see the one man who, above all others except Gandhi, was responsible for his country's new awakening.

She had her chance. When Prime Minister Nehru came to Madras to celebrate the centenary of Madras University, Ida had a seat in the front row. After laying the foundation stone of a new building, the official guests returned to the auditorium in an impressive procession, headed by the Prime Minister and the university vice-chancellor. Obedient to request, the members of the audience remained seated—all but one.

"Sit down, Aunt Ida," begged Ida B.

"But I can't see," objected Ida calmly.

She remained standing. Her friend the vice-chancellor spied her, and his face beamed. He halted the formal procession and presented her to the Prime Minister, wherepon the moment instantly divested itself of any embarrassment and became clothed with peculiar dignity and drama. For it was a meeting which seemed destined to take place, that of Dr. Ida Scudder and this sensitive, impassioned leader of the people both had devoted their lives to serving. It was no mere coincidence that one wore a spray of roses on her blue lace dress and the other a neat rosebud in the third buttonhole of his high-collared *achkan*. The harmony of detail, for each habitual, was symbolic of an even more fundamental unity of attitude and purpose.

"I am honored, Doctor." The sincerity of the simple words was to be emphasized even more strongly when a few years later Jawaharlal Nehru proclaimed to the world that the most exciting and hopeful thing happening in India was not industrialization, nor advancement in science, nor rural development, but the *education of women*. "This release of the feminine thought," he said later to a distinguished American journalist, "is changing the social fabric of India."

Ida had given voice to the same opinion over fifty years before.

The work at Vellore was keeping pace with the nation in its own Community Devolopment program. Scarcely a month passed without something new to be dedicated, for the institution was constantly rerooting and spreading like a banyan tree.

A new ward was opened for the Department of Neurology on Hospital Day in 1953, with the Honorable Rajkumari Amrit Kaur, federal Minister of Health, in attendance. New quarters for physiotherapy were finished in 1954, with short-wave rooms, a splint room, an office, and a hydrotherapy pool. Not wanting to sever the ribbon, Ida asked that a bow be tied instead, and, drawing upon its strings, she opened the door to new opportunity for polio and palsy patients.

In June, 1955, she saw the opening of the great new Leprosy Research Sanatorium at Karigeri, a cooperative project with the British Mission to Lepers. Here in a beautiful two-winged hospital with a colonnaded porch between, experimentation treatment could be given, operations performed on distorted hands and feet and faces. Dr. Brand's experimental surgery had given rise to other techniques and devices: sandals molded in the shape of ulcerated feet to prevent other ulcers from recurring; an operation on eyelids that refused to close because the nerve had died. In this latter operation the eyelid was connected by surgery to a chewing muscle, so that the patient could clench his teeth and close his eyes while sleeping. This was an invaluable aid in preventing blindness, which was especially unfortunate for persons who had no feeling in their fingers or feet. The cooperative project aimed to develop both a sanatorium for children suffering from leprosy and a leprosy research sanatorium for adults.

And in 1957, Ida's eighty-seventh year, as if her own suddenly dissipating energy were expending itself in bursts of creative activity, there came the greatest progress of all.

February saw the opening of the rural hospital health center, on the grounds at College Hill, furnishing new facilities for training students in rural problems and for bringing medical care and education closer to surrounding villages. The hospital was to be kept simple, using only such equipment as would be available in villages. Patients would be encouraged to bring members of their families to nurse them, and while there would participate in an educational program, learning through practice and visual aids better ways of village living.

Working with the government Social Welfare Board, specializing in social education, the rural health center would send out nurses, public health workers, and practicing students, into four subsidiary centers around Vellore, ministering to about forty villages. Their work would include nutrition surveys, medical examinations, training of local midwives, promotion of sanitary latrines and smokeless *chulhas*, educational and social clubs for women, crafts, and a hundred other activities designed to improve village health and well-being.

This was a project close to Ida's heart. Eagerly one day she watched a group of students preparing to start out with their Indian director, Dr. Benjamin, and the American Public Health teacher, Pauline King, for an afternoon practice session in their year-and-a-half of preclinical internship.

"Wonderful!" she exclaimed. "How I envy you young people! Getting into the villages day after day and watching these marvelous changes take place!"

One of the students shrugged. "Seems sort of a waste of time," he commented, "when we'll probably never see another village after we get through here."

"Changes?" echoed another skeptically. "Villages are pretty hopeless, Aunt Ida. You must have found that out. Work with them for two years and they'll go back to the same old ways the minute your back is turned. Villages don't change!"

"Oh, yes, they do!" countered a third, eyes kindling. "Look what Aunt Ida has done in the last fifty years. Look what we've accomplished already under our five-year plans. It's up to us whether they change or not. If some of us care enough to go into the villages and live and *show* the people—!"

Ida watched them climb into the bus, men in white, girls in neat whites and blues, with their compact kits of medical supplies, their literacy charts, their health exhibits, their shining tools for turning the furrows of a new and better world. How well she understood! She had felt exactly like the first two of them until that night of her call nearly seventy years ago. She waved them off. Not a bad harvest, surely, if one out of three seeds you planted came to flower.

She saw other developments in that year of great fulfillment: the opening of a new radiation therapy ward; completion of a hospital duplex extension, with six new duplex apartments, twelve new ward rooms; ground broken on the hospital compound for a new outpatient dispensary.

On her first tour of inspection of this new building, a year later, she would feel like weeping with joy at sight of it all: the cool long corridors and verandahs; the unique plan of the departments, with their individual doctor-patient cubicles and teaching rooms, their separate student section; the convenient arrangements for laboratory work and medication; especially the bright clean children's section, with its alluring colors, its airy waiting room, and, loveliest of all, its beautiful painting of the Christ in his flowing Oriental dress, looking as much at home against the background of the stark Vellore hills as in his stony Palestine, with a host of little Indian children running joyously toward him.

There was so much happening these days that Ida had hard work keeping up with it all. One Friday afternoon, visiting little old Schell, now the eye hospital, she watched the preparations for an eye camp. In the new eye ambulance, dedicated the preceding month, were crowded Dr. Roy Ebenezer, head of the eye hospital, two other Indian doctors, nurses, a cook, his helper, an evangelist, and other assistants. Behind them was a trailer piled high with grass mats and pillows, food, dressings, gospels, musical instruments, lanterns, oil, and medical supplies. The team waved to her gaily.

"How far this time?" Ida asked Dr. Ebenezer with keen interest.

"About seventy miles," he said, smiling. "We should have started earlier, but this is an extra, you know. It has to be done after hours, and I had twenty-eight cataracts to do first. We're using a cattle shed this time."

"And how many camps have you held since you started ten years ago?"   •

"A hundred and sixty-five, Aunt Ida," replied the Indian physician. "We've done nearly 10,000 operations, treated about 25,000 other cases."

"*San thosham*, happiness!" exclaimed Ida, blue eyes glinting. "How I wish I could help!"

She was thrilled each time she visited the edge of the college campus, where once there had been wasteland and an old brick kiln, to see the five new white buildings of the mental health center fast nearing completion.

Since her arrival in 1946 Dr. Florence Nichols, head of the psychiatric department, had carried on her pioneer work with a minimum of help and equipment, often acting not only as psychiatrist but as nurse and therapist as well. With no adequate

350

accommodation for patients, she had sometimes cared for them in her own room twenty-four hours a day for months on end.

Though Dr. Nichols had found psychiatry a neglected field in India, as in most areas of the world, she had found also a surprising interest in the new science. India had been the first country to ask United Nations assistance for mental health work. There were already two fine centers training psychiatrists in Bangalore and Bombay. She had even found an Indian psychiatric nurse in the United States and had persuaded him to join her staff.

The buildings were already in use, with ten general and eight private beds together with an outpatient department. Designed as an active treatment center and a pilot project which other institutions might copy, the hospital was purposely kept small, its atmosphere relaxed and informal. There were no locked doors. When the chief psychiatric nurse complained that villagers were using the grounds as a short cut, Dr. Nichols refused to build a fence. She was glad that the villagers were not afraid of the project; glad too that when movies and other entertainments were presented, there were as many outsiders in the audience as patients.

She had found the incidence of mental disease practically the same in India as in the West, exhibiting the same symptoms and causes, responding to the same treatments. However, effort was being made to coordinate treatment with Indian customs and traditions. Relatives were encouraged to accompany the patients to the hospital, remain with them, join in their treatment programs. The family understanding this created was a means of therapy in itself, since mental illness was often the result of unhealthy relationships in the home.

Ida exulted in the new white buildings, with their green lawns and gardens, their atmosphere of peace and beauty which must bring healing to disturbed minds. The 200-acre tract of wasteland had produced miracles of which she had never dreamed. And there was still room for more. A children's hospital, perhaps. She could hear the hammers already pounding for it, crushing the rocks of the valley to bits.

June of that same year, 1957, brought to India a seven-man production team from the National Broadcasting Company in

New York, filming a program for the annual "March of Medicine," to be titled *M.D. International* and viewed by an estimated twenty million people. Its theme was to show Western doctors around the world as ambassadors of good will.

Vellore was their only stop in India, and they stayed for seventeen days, with the temperature a humid 100 degrees, taking more footage than could be used in the entire fifty-five minutes of the program. They filmed Dr. Paul Brand and his now world-famous orthopedic surgery and leprosy rehabilitation; Dr. Reeve H. Betts and his thoracic surgery trainees; Dr. Ida B. on Roadside; Dr. Rambo in his mobile eye clinic. For the eye clinic they had to travel 73 miles, staying overnight in a Traveler's Bungalow, with Mrs. Reeve Betts, the publicity director, taking along mattresses, linen, mosquito nets, a cook, helper, food, dishes, lanterns—everything but blankets! And of course they filmed Dr. Ida in the sunken garden.

But it was not the Ida of swift feet and ringing voice and unbending shoulders. The years had at last taken their toll.

When, nearly two years later, one of the last and most significant honors of her life was paid her, she was physically unable to fulfill its usual requirement of accepting it in person. But her alma mater was pleased to set aside its long traditions in honoring this first woman graduate on which it had conferred a medical degree just sixty years before. The presentation of the award in Vellore on her eighty-eighth birthday was recorded on tape and film, and her fellow alumni, meeting in New York in April, 1959, heard the citation read, saw her receive the honor, heard her express her gratitude—12,000 miles away.

THE ALUMNI ASSOCIATION
OF CORNELL UNIVERSITY
MEDICAL COLLEGE
TAKES PRIDE IN PRESENTING THE
1959
AWARD OF DISTINCTION
to
IDA SOPHIA SCUDDER, M.D.
Class of 1899

*In recognition of her notable contributions to Medical
Education, Public Health, and international understanding
Her life of devoted service to mankind is an inspiration to all
and has brought honor and acclaim to the Medical College*

29

She awoke knowing that she had a tryst to keep. Where? With whom? She wasn't sure exactly. There were so many things she wasn't sure of these days. She knew only that she must be ready for it when it came.

The horsetail creeper descended in a waterfall of snow beside her sleeping porch. Outside the screen a small palli hung motionless, tail curved like a silver sickle. Already the little sunbirds were flitting restlessly from blossom to blossom in the cassia trees. And the sky behind College Hill was the bright sharp blue of a roller bird's wing.

But, much as she loved it, Ida knew the tryst was not with beauty.

Passing the gate of the old mission compound on her daily trip to the hospital, she suddenly felt an urge to see the little room where her work had started. Perhaps that was the trysting place where these strange stirrings of expectation within her would be satisfied.

They swung along the curving road beyond the gate. There were the ancient tamarind trees, the well where the bullock had gone round and round. She entered the little ten-by-twelve room. Somebody threw back the shutters of the familiar window, and she stood in it again, remembering how over fifty years ago she had handed out medicines to one after another in the long waiting queues. But there were no patients here today, only the green lawn and a bush of bright red poinsettias and a laughing boy with a monkey on his shoulder.

And she knew that her tryst was not with the past.

They went on to the hospital, and, once inside the wrought-iron gate, she became absorbed in human need. She talked to mothers about their children, anxious husbands about their wives. She found a frightened village woman waiting to have a fearful abscess treated. "Don't be afraid, *ammal*. I'll be right beside you."

But when the morning was gone and she left the little woman lying quietly, a smile on her face, she knew that the tryst this time was not with human need.

On the high horizon Fort Hill was blazing in noonday sun. Was there a figure standing on its crest? And, if so, was Grandfather John, dreamer of long over a century ago, satisfied with what he saw? Suddenly she wanted to show it to him, the fulfillment of his dream, which they had wrought together. She could hardly wait for her brief siesta to be over. Feeling his presence beside her, again she got into her car and rode and rode, showing him the beautiful stone quadrangle of the college, the rural and mental health Centers, the "Place of New Life." She took him to Schell and all about the main hospital, even into the new dispensary, blinding white in the afternoon sun, at the end of one of its long corridors the picture of Christ with Indian children. If only Salomi and Gnanammal could have known the joy of this! "See!" It was to them she marveled silently as well as to Grandfather John. "See how far we have come from the little room and the crowded verandah at Schell? Oh, God has been very good to us!"

Yet when she emerged finally from the hospital, the high radiance of triumph had faded. The sun's rays were slanting, and she was very tired. The dream's fulfillment seemed no longer big and shining, but pitifully small. Though hammers pounded from dawn to dark, they never seemed to keep pace with the agonized beating of human hearts. In spite of new stories, new wings, new buildings, there were still the waiting crowds, crouching patiently on floors and benches. Patients were being turned away. There was never enough time or room, never enough hands or equipment or money. As willing hands helped her into the car, she was no longer conscious of an unseen presence.

"Home," she told her driver wearily.

Then suddenly as they rolled through the gate of the hospital compound she came sharply erect. "Stop!" she cried. "Let me out, *juldi*, quick!"

She could hardly believe her eyes. At first she thought the sun was playing tricks. She rubbed them and looked again. There was no mistake. The figures were real, stooping, digging, pounding, laying boards, pouring a thick layer of cement. *They were covering up the drain!*

Ida laughed aloud. She lifted her eyes to Fort Hill, crest blazoned red in the sunlight, black ancient stones casting long shadows. Surely one of them was a tall straight figure.... She was no longer tired. She felt strong enough to climb the long flights of rough-hewn steps, mount to the very top. But, however strong her will, her limbs remained earth-bound, and one did not climb mountains with a cane.

"Wait for me!" she cried silently. "We haven't seen anything yet!"

But as she climbed painfully back into the car, she knew the tryst was not with Grandfather John and the dream they had shared together.

Suddenly she remembered that it was Friday. Ida B.'s Roadside. She had almost forgotten it. She gave a brisk command to her driver.

It was dusk when they reached Odugathur, the last Roadside stop. Under the tree where the ambulance was parked long queues of patients were still waiting.

Ida B. smiled a weary welcome. "Over a thousand patients today, Aunt Ida."

They were wasting no words or motions, Ida B. and her team—the two young Indian doctors, the students, the nurses, the compounders, Mary Taber Sebastian with her rations of dried milk, the evangelist with his violin, Dr. Ponniah the leprosy specialist, with his table a little apart from the others.

356

Even Judy, Ida B.'s cocker spaniel, was efficiently diverting some of the small whimpering sufferers.

Ida took her place with them. She kept firm hold of the hand of a terrified woman, quieting her screams while the younger Dr. Ida cut through the horny flesh of her heel to release a deep infection. She helped Dr. Ponniah dispense the new wonder drugs for leprosy. She comforted an old woman who found there was no hope for her young grandson's blindness. She sat on a folding stool close to the tree trunk and held a scrap of a baby while its mother lay on the ground behind a curtain of saris for a lengthy examination.

Darkness had fallen, and both faces and figures blended in a blur of dust and lantern light. The crowd possessed neither form nor shape. Ida seemed vaguely conscious of a figure in white moving among them—one of the young Indian doctors?—but she couldn't see it plainly. She was so tired that, once she had succeeded in quieting the baby, she leaned her head against the tree and closed her eyes.

Perhaps she opened them again, perhaps she dozed and dreamed, to see the figure in white detach itself from the blur and come to stand by her side. It was not one of the Indian doctors, after all, though the face was familiar. She had seen it often on Roadside, by hospital bed or operating table, when she was so tired, like this, that it seemed she couldn't keep on any longer. Earlier today she had seen it, painted in glowing colors, lighted with joy and compassion to welcome little children.

Now, as always, consciousness of the divine Presence gave her a faint sense of guilt. She should be kneeling in love and gratitude, contemplating, as Burchfield Milliken had urged her long ago, not sitting like this or keeping on with her work. But always there seemed something to prevent, like this child to be kept quiet in her arms.

She raised her face with sudden awareness, as if listening. "But—I don't understand," she murmured, half aloud. "I know you, Master, yes. I've known you all my life, wanted to know you better. But—I've done so little for you—always been so busy. Why should you be thanking me?"

Nobody else heard the reply if there was one. And those

who would have understood were all too occupied. But the scrap of a baby reached up suddenly and touched the white fluff of her hair.

Inasmuch as you have done it unto one of the least of these my brethren, you have done it unto me.

The day was nearly over. She had kept the tryst.

Lecturing, traveling, and helping her minister husband in the supervision of over ninety churches that fall within his jurisdiction as Superintendent of the Bangor District of the Methodist Church, Dorothy Clarke Wilson leads a rich and busy life. Yet she has found or created the time and energy to write six novels, five of them with Biblical backgrounds, over sixty religious plays, a journal of her extensive travels in India, and innumerable articles and stories published in a wide variety of religious periodicals.

Writing was early Mrs. Wilson's chief ambition. Her first poem, written when she was ten, appeared in the children's section of a local newspaper. At fourteen, she wrote her first Biblical story and that too was promptly published, in a religious paper. As an undergraduate at Bates College in Lewiston, Maine, she majored in English and, together with Gladys Hasty Carroll and Erwin Canham, two classmates of hers who are now themselves distinguished writers, was active in the college's literary society. She graduated with high honors, Phi Beta Kappa, and the following year was married and began her professional career by writing a series of religious plays to fill a need in her husband's church program.

In 1949 the Board of Missions of the Methodist Church sent Mrs. Wilson to India to gather material for a novel on missions, and her knowledge of and interest in that country that grew out of that trip prompted her to undertake a biography of Dr. Ida Scudder. For this project she returned to India in 1957, established herself at Vellore, the home of Dr. Scudder's medical center, and from there traveled widely through the south of India gathering first-hand material for her book.

Mrs. Wilson is a native of Maine, where she and her husband now live. She is the mother of two grown children, Joan and Harold.